International Conference WWW/Internet (CIAWI 2020)

Held online due to COVID-19

Lisbon, Portugal
18 – 20 November 2020

ISBN: 978-1-7138-2227-1

Printed from e-media with permission by:

Curran Associates, Inc.
57 Morehouse Lane
Red Hook, NY 12571

Some format issues inherent in the e-media version may also appear in this print version.

Printed with permission by Curran Associates, Inc. (2021)

For permission requests, please contact International Association for Development of the Information Society (IADIS) at the address below.

International Association for Development of the Information Society (IADIS)
Rua Sao Sebastiao Da Pedreira
No. 100, 30, 1050-209
Lisbon, Portugal

Phone: 351 21 3151373
Fax: 351 21 3151244

secretariat@iadis.org

Additional copies of this publication are available from:

Curran Associates, Inc.
57 Morehouse Lane
Red Hook, NY 12571 USA
Phone: 845-758-0400
Fax: 845-758-2633
Email: curran@proceedings.com
Web: www.proceedings.com

TABLE OF CONTENTS

A BOT-ENABLED APPROACH FOR WEB SERVICE DISCOVERY

Bahareh Zarei, Mahda Noura and Martin Gaedke
Technische Universität Chemnitz, Chemnitz, Germany

ABSTRACT

With the wide adoption of service-oriented architectures, many service-based systems (SBSs) and mashups composed of Web services have been developed. Meanwhile, web service discovery, as a crucial component to guarantee the quality of Web service composition in SBS, gained increasing attention. Web service discovery aims to select the set of best service candidates according to the service requester's requirements. Existing syntactic and semantic-based approaches are proven to have low recall and precision or expecting high level of expertise from the service requesters. In this paper, we propose an approach for Web service discovery based on chatbots which obtains the best suited set of services to address the goals of service requesters. Chatbot-based interfaces are the emerging trend to provide a more natural human-device interaction. Compared to the existing web service discovery techniques, our approach alleviates the need for service requesters to have prior knowledge about the service location or its structure and enables them to identify services by leveraging natural language. We evaluated the approach through the collection of 56 queries from the test subject group on our repository of existing web service descriptions and report on quality metrics. The results shows high precision and recall.

KEYWORDS

Web Service Discovery, Service-Based Systems, Conversational interfaces, Natural Language Processing, Chat-Bot

1. INTRODUCTION

The web service paradigm has brought several advantages to software development and SOA-based applications. Providing simplicity by promoting reusability, agility and loose coupling are among the reasons for their widespread adoption in both academia and industry. The web services from major providers such as Google, Amazon and Facebook are published through public registries enabling developers to build loosely coupled applications (Zhang *et al.*, 2018). The number of registered web services in ProgrammableWeb[1] (PW) as of 2017 was reported more than 17,600 and this number has increased to almost 23,000 web services in just three years. Such services can be used to create service-based systems (SBS) or web compositions and mashups to offer value-added services (Zhang *et al.*, 2018). One of the main challenges in SBSs is providing scalable and automated methods for selecting the relevant web services according to the service requester's requirements (Klusch, 2018). Web service discovery is a central component of service-based applications that can highly impact the effectiveness of web service compositions (Bhardwaj, 2015). Over the last decade a number of solutions have been proposed to address this challenge with respect to factors such as service description language or intended use of selected services (Klusch, 2018). The widely used techniques in the literature for Web service discovery are *syntactic* and *semantic-based* solutions. However, the existing solutions suffer in terms of low precision and recall (Zhang *et al.*, 2018).

On the other hand, *conversational interfaces* as found in personal assistants such as Siri, Google Assistant, and Amazon Alexa represent a popular medium for users to interact with different smart devices and web services. Such interfaces provide a more natural method of interaction and a high level of usability for users (David Yoffie *et al.*, 2018). Conversational agents and natural language interfaces, a.k.a. chatbots mimic human intelligence in conversations by reacting to the user's input through a realistic response.

[1] www.programmableweb.com

According to Fuckner et al. (2013) enabling users to perform a task via natural language interaction can save up to 30% in time and 60% in the required effort. Using chatbots has proven to increase the retrieval accuracy (Abdul-Kader and Woods, 2015) and they can influence the user's behavior towards more informative interactions and thus more precise result.

The proposed solution by Fuckner et al. (2013) leveraged the idea of using chatbots to invoke desired web services. In this solution, a keyword-based matching is used. Despite the provided simplicity, keyword-based solutions are insufficient to discover all the relevant web services because users are assumed to not use the best keywords (in here best means the keywords already used in the web service description) to formulate the queries. To address this limitation several query expansion approaches have been proposed (Zhang *et al.*, 2018, Ma *et al.*, 2013). The goal of query expansion is to enhance the original query with the relevant concepts to increase the recall. Nevertheless, the proposed solutions either solely depend on the external knowledge bases such as ontologies or do not engage users for further communication.

To address the gaps of existing systems, we aim to design a chatbot able to understand the goal of service requesters (i.e., SBS and Web composition designers): The discovery chatbot receives textual utterances from service requesters as input, analyzes them using the query expansion technique to identify the domain and intended operations, generates reasonable responses according to our defined conversational flowchart and finally invoke the suitable web services. The contributions of this work are outlined as follows:

1. We proposed a method for creating a domain specific chatbot interface for web service discovery which is the first of its kind. The proposed approach is not reliant on the semantic descriptions of services and the requesters are not required to have prior knowledge about the service structure. Moreover, the approach integrates well-known query expansion techniques to extract the essential parameters from the requester's query and generate suitable follow up conversations.
2. We implement a prototype of the solution and conduct two sets of experiments to demonstrate its effectiveness for Web service discovery and query expansion.

The rest of the paper is organized as follows. In Section 2, our solution concept is discussed as well as an overview of the proposed architecture. To clarify the chatbot function a use case scenario is presented in Section 3 and Section 4 provides the study evaluation. The related work is reviewed in Section 5 and finally, Section 6 concludes the paper and provides future insights.

2. DISCOVERY CHATBOT APPROACH

In this section, we elaborate on the concept of our chatbot solution for web service discovery. The key requirements, design principles and overall architecture are discussed here.

2.1 Concept

Our solution is based on the bi-directional natural language communication between the service requester and the discovery chatbot. The envisioned chatbot is responsible for identifying the best web service candidates according to the requester's input. In the conventional input-intent-action-response conversation model (Baez and Daniel, 2019), the user expresses his intention as an input (e.g. "*add a new appointment on July 4th, 5 p.m. to my calendar*"). Then the chatbot extracts the user's intents using a Natural Language Understanding (NLU) unit (e.g. "*add a new entry in the calendar*") and maps it to an action that results in meeting the user's request ("*addToCalander*"). The execution of the action generates an output which will be used to produce a suitable response to the user (e.g." *you have a meeting at the same time, do you want to reschedule?*").

However, in our solution we use a customized version of the input-intent-action-response model to match web service discovery field. The customization is performed by refining the *intent* and *action* phases. The intent extraction involves identifying the key parameters of the desired web service (*domain* and *operations* (Zhang *et al.*, 2018)) and the action refers to the matchmaking part to find the most relevant web services. Our solution is built on the following design principles:

- Discovery chatbot is a domain-specific chatbot that only handles the conversations regarding web services, therefore we use textual web service-related articles such as research papers as our dataset. All the steps of preprocessing were performed on the corpus which later transformed into numeric vectors.

- Most of service descriptions are either XML-based (e.g. WSDL) or textual-based. In this work we use the textual description since it is more widely used specially in the case of APIs and RESTful web services.

2.2 Architecture

Figure 1 gives an overview of the discovery chatbot with its two main modules: The Natural Language Unit and Dialogue Manager. The service requesters can type in a description of the desired web service in the form of natural language text. This text will be analyzed by NLU to extract parameters such as target domain, operations, and entities. Such parameters are used to instantiate the Request Template. We define a Request Template as a generic objective description, in XML syntax, that is instantiated during run time. To address the problem of incomplete queries the chatbot includes the service requester in a conversation loop to provide the missing information such as domain and operations. The conversation flow and response generation are managed by the Dialogue Manager.

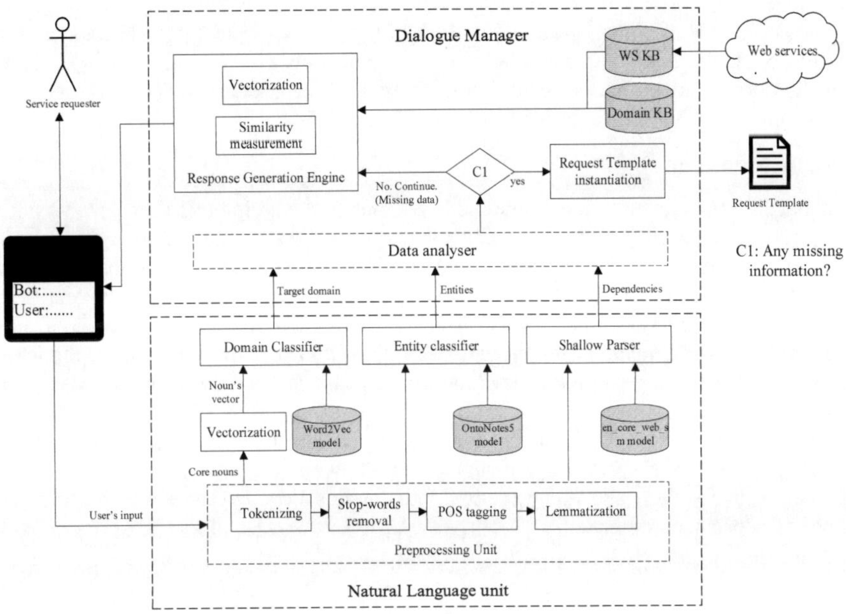

Figure 1. Overview of proposed approach

2.2.1 Natural Language Unit

The NLU consists of three main components: the *Preprocessing Unit (PU)*, *Classifiers* and *Shallow Parser*. The PU pipeline is responsible for annotating the requester's query with tokens, removing stop-words, tagging each word with part-of-speech tags e.g. Nouns, Verbs, etc. and Lemmatization (Zarei and Gaedke, 2018). The output of PU is used as an input for classifiers. As defined in Abdul-Kader et al. 2015, classifiers are crucial components of chatbots responsible for normalizing the user's query and segmenting it into logical parts.

Domain Classifier determines the user's target domain. This way we efficiently reduce the search scope to potentially relevant services in that domain. As the first step we identified a set of words as representatives of each domain then upon every query the similarity among domain's representative words and the query's core nouns is calculated by the help of trained Word2vec model. The reason behind using query's core nouns is the greater importance of the core nouns in determining the domain. For example the two queries: "buy flight tickets" and "buy a house" refer to the different domains reflecting by core nouns "flight" and "house"

(Zhang *et al.*, 2018). To avoid missing some relevant services in the case of overlaps among two domains we consider both as target domains.

Entity classifier labels the entities with identifiers from the knowledge base. Entities are real-world objects such as locations, persons, countries, etc. For instance, the entities in the following sentence are labeled with respective identifiers: "find a Mark Twain (PERSON) book costs \$30(MONEY)". Such entities will be used as web service parameters. The entity classifier uses spaCy[2] library written in Python and a model trained on the OntoNotes5 corpus.

The next step is finding the requester's desired functionalities via Shallow parser. Each web service offers number of functionalities in the form of operations. To efficiently enhance the web service discovery, we have to take these operations into account. We defined the web service operation as $sf\ =< AV, AN, \{P_i, P_o\} >$ where AV denotes the action verb describing an operation and the AN as action noun that the operation effects on. The P_i and P_o are optional parameters for input and output. For instance, the query "Locate hotels in a given location" formulates as $sf\ =< locate, hotels, \{GPS\ coordinates, -\} >$. The – here stands for an empty output. To extract operations from a given query we need to extract grammatical dependencies between pairs of words in the query. To obtain this, we used the spaCy dependency parser.

Not all the dependencies convey meaning with respect to service operations. Therefore, in this work, we use four main dependencies namely nsubj (nominal subject), dobj (direct object), iobj (indirect object) and prep (preposition) to extract the service operations. These dependencies are the core arguments in the English language according to Universal Dependencies[3].

2.2.2 Dialogue Manager

Dialogue Manager is the chatbot's core component. Similar to the architecture presented by Raghuvanshi et al. 2018, it assesses the processed queries, applies the conversation's logic, and generates the best response. The parameters extracted from the query by NLU such as domain and operations are assessed by Data Analyzer for completeness and soundness. Based on the analysis result, the Data Analyzer triggers the Response Generation Engine to either ask the user for more detailed description or confirm the extracted parameters. The Request Template is only instantiated once both Data Analyzer and the requester confirm the parameters. By asking for the requester's confirmation we guarantee that the exact intended web services will be retrieved.

An important module of the Dialogue Manager is the Response Generation Engine (refer to Figure 1). The responses are generated according to the conversation flowchart in Figure 2. This flowchart describes the logic behind the conversations and orchestrates the dialogue's flow by predicting the user's behavior and generating the response accordingly.

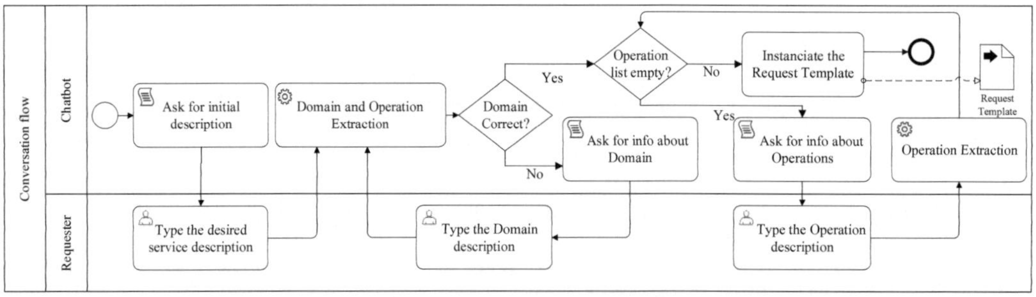

Figure 2. BPMN diagram for conversation flowchart

To further assist the requesters, the discovery chatbot is trained to respond to general queries about web services such as "What are the RESTful verbs?". The response's quality is highly dependent on the knowledge base used to train the chatbot. Developers can either write a database from scratch or make the chatbot learn from a textual corpus (Abdul-Kader and Woods, 2015). As already explained in the design

---

[2] https://spacy.io/

[3] https://universaldependencies.org/

principles in Section 2, we developed a domain-specific training set as the chatbot knowledge base. To generate the best response, the TF-IDF (Term Frequency-Inverse Document Frequency) formula is used to calculate the similarity between the query Q in document D and the sentences in the training set:

$$S(Q, D) = \sum_{w} tf_{wq} \cdot \frac{tf_{wD}}{tf_{wD} + \frac{k|D|}{avg|D|}} . log \frac{|C|}{df_w}$$

The tf_{wq} is the term frequency of word w in Q. The summation indicates that the term's frequency has a direct impact on its importance. While the second part of the formula shows that the repetition is less important in the case of a short document.

The IDF component, in the end, gives higher weight to rare words compare to common words where $|C|$ is the total number of documents and df_w is the number of documents containing word w. This formula helps us to retrieve sentences as the potential response to the user's questions.

3. AN EXAMPLE SCENARIO

In this section, we walk through a use case scenario to demonstrate our approach in detail and highlight it's technical and architectural significance. A possible usage scenario for applying web services is in the context of Order Management Systems (OMS). Depending on the products, organizations use OMS to receive and process orders. Web services such as marketing, credit verification, billing, and financial services as well as shipment tracking are integrated to develop OMS. To further extend an existing OMS, the service requester plans to integrate the online tax calculation service. Such an API enables organizations to trade globally.

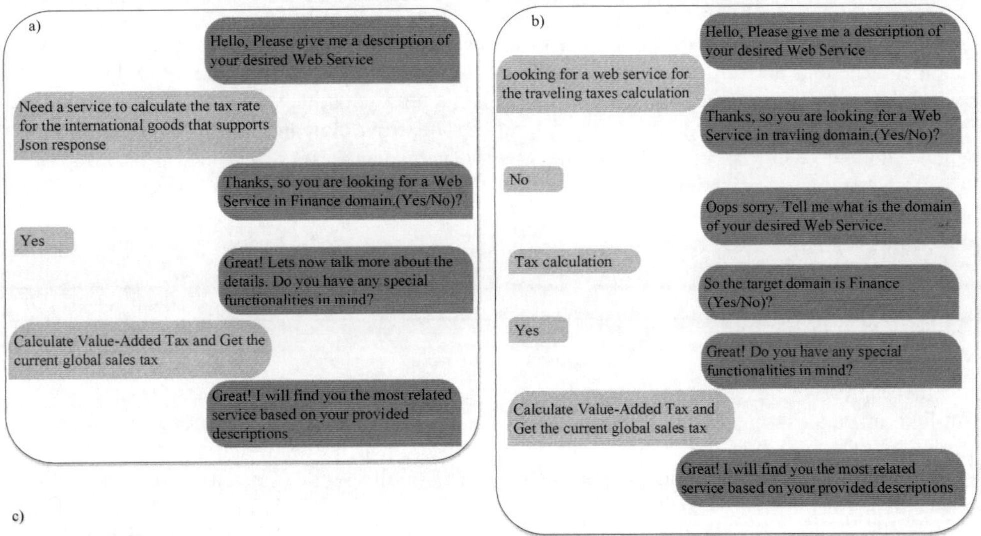

c)

```
<RequestTemplate>
  <domain>Finance</domain>
  <operation>(calculate, tax rate)</operation>
  <operation>(calculate, Value-Added tax)</operation>
  <operation>(get, sales tax)</operation>
  <operation>(support, json response)</operation>
</RequestTemplate>
```

Figure 3. Example of various paths driven by chatbot. c) snippet of the Request template in XML syntax

Rounds of conversation among the service requester (gray boxes) and discovery chatbot (blue boxes) is presented in Figure 3. These examples are the two possible paths that conversation can be led to (based on the conversation flowchart in Figure 2). The chatbot is responsible for leading the user towards an informative response. The straightest forward path is when the user's initial description is informative enough (the domain and key operations are extractable. e.g. Figure 3 a). In the case of missing or wrongly extracted domain the chatbot keeps asking for more information until the requester confirms the domain and chatbot moves on to the operation extraction step (e.g. Figure 3 b). The key operations are extracted from the initial description as well as follow up inputs. Extracted parameters are used to generate the Request Template as shown in Figure 3 c.

4. EVALUATION

We conducted two series of experiments to evaluate the NLU in terms of extracted domains and operations and calculate the precision and recall for retrieved web services. For this aim, we collected descriptive data of 1000 web services including tags and textual descriptions from the public PW registry. The web services are divided into 5 domains: *Transportation*, *Mapping*, *Weather*, *Mobile*, and *Social*. According to PW these categories are the most popular categories for web services and APIs. Popularity was measured as the ratio of the APIs have been used by mashups to all the existing APIs in that particular domain. We recruited eight subject requesters (including four developers, two postgraduate and two undergraduate students) to perform the two following tasks: 1) proposing ten words as domain representatives for each of the five target domains; and 2) constructing experimental queries to request web services in those domains. The final sets of representative words are built manually by selecting reasonable ones. Collectively 56 queries were constructed by our subject requesters. There was no limitation on the query length, and they range from short queries such as "extract GPS" to relatively long ones such as the queries in the use case scenario (Section 4).

4.1 Evaluation Result

For the first experiment the NLU output is evaluated. For each query the requesters verify the identified domain and the relevance of extracted operations. As already explained, we calculated the cosine similarity between the query's core nouns and each of the domain's representative vector, then the domain with highest similarity is chosen as the target domain. 98% of the identified domains for 56 queries matched with the intended domain. On the other hand, the operation relevance is determined based on a 0-3 scale ("0"- irrelevant, "1"-poorly relevant, "2"- relevant, "3"-highly relevant) and the evaluation result is shown in Table 1.

Table 1. NLU evaluation result

Irrelevant	Poorly relevant	Relevant	Highly relevant
9%	10%	20%	61%

A thorough review determined that the irrelevant and poorly relevant operations (around 19% of the total identified operations) are mainly derived from the general phrases in the query in the case of long descriptions. On the other hand, more relevant operations will be derived if we consider other types of dependencies such as propositions dependencies. This will be one of our directions for the future enhancement.

To evaluate the quality of discovery process, for each query we calculated the two parameters: precision and recall as follows:

$$\text{Precision} = \frac{|WS_{rt} \cap WS_{rl}|}{WS_{rt}} \text{ and Recall} = \frac{|WS_{rt} \cap WS_{rl}|}{WS_{rl}}$$

where precision indicates the preciseness of the approach in discovering the intended web services and recall refers to the probability of a relevant document retrieval. The WS_{rt} and WS_{rl} in above formula denote the retrieved and relevant web services. The calculated precision and recall for our approach are respectively 0.78 and 0.80. This result represents the good performance of our approach in discovering meaningful and relevant web services.

4.2 Threats to Validity

In this section, we discuss the threats to our evaluation's internal and external validity. The *internal validity* concerns with the experiment's result repeatability. In our experiments, we relied on our subjects with different backgrounds to manually build the domain's representative set, construct the experiment queries, and evaluate the relativeness of the retrieved web service. A threat to internal validity can occur due to the subject's lack of familiarity with the selected domains and process. To resolve this threat, we used domain-related web pages to familiarize the subjects with the domains and described them the process step by step.

The *external validity* concerns about generalizing the study result to situations outside the context of this study. One external validity threat in this work concerns the APIs used for our experiments. We extracted the APIs from five popular domains in the public PW repository. Since this repository relies on the input APIs from API providers, the popularity and domain scales will change over time. Therefore, this will introduce a threat to domain selection validity. To overcome this threat, we plan to evaluate our work on multiple registries other than PW.

5. RELATED WORK

Our work aims at providing a novel solution for web service discovery issue by leveraging chatbot technology. The number of works associated with chatbots is increasing every day and they cover different areas ranges from chatbot strategy design and response improvement to the variety of applications which they contribute to. This technology has a high evolving potential from one contribution to the next by adding new features (Abdul-Kader and Woods, 2015). To be able to justify the novelty of our work we review number of practices in the web service discovery field.

Existing discovery approaches can be categorized based on various metrics such as web service's functional and non-functional requirements or Quality of Service (QoS). From matchmaking point of view, the two dominant research directions are syntactic-based and semantic-based approaches (Mohebbi et al., 2010). The syntactic-based solutions like keyword matching and some of the recent enhancements such as clustering algorithms and WSDL structural matching are relatively easy nevertheless they mainly failed to fulfill the user's requirements in the terms of precision and recall (Bhardwaj, 2015, Zhang et al., 2018). The semantic-based approaches managed to overcome these drawbacks to some extent by proposing solutions in mainly two subcategories of logic and non-logic based (Zhang et al., 2018). In the logic-based solutions, a reasoning algorithm based on the domain ontology and semantic Web service description language (SAWSDL) is designed (Klusch, 2008). The discovery solutions can benefit from ontological knowledge with more precise results since the comparison is based on the semantic matching at the abstraction level. The good performance of such approaches has been proved, although the effort required for managing ontologies and service annotation is high (Bhardwaj, 2015, Mohebbi et al., 2010). The ontology heterogeneity is another issue, meaning the service provider and requester are not using a unique ontology. In such cases, coordination among ontologies should be done by ontology mapping algorithms (Mohebbi et al., 2010).

In one relevant study, Fuckner et al. 2013 proposed a dialogue-based multi-agent platform using the WSDL file as the only source of information. The key concepts from the user's request will be extracted and used to select and execute the exact web services. The concept matching is mainly keyword-based which the limitations were discussed earlier. On the other hand, as a non-logic-based solution, Zhang et al. 2018 proposed an approach that focuses on improving the user's query quality by presenting a novel goal-oriented query expansion based on the service goals. Authors utilized the Stanford parser to extract the linguistic structure of the sentences used in web service description to categorize services. Compared to this work, we propose a novel approach that leveraged the chatbot technology to retrieve the best set of web service candidates based on the user's query. We use the query expansion technique to extract the domain and operations. This way the approach performance in the terms of precision and recall will be increased.

6. CONCLUSION AND FUTURE WORK

This paper proposed a novel web service discovery method by leveraging chatbot technology. The discovery process is performed based on conversations among the requester and the chatbot. Such conversations are built upon a conversation flowchart that leads users into more informative responses. With the help of NLP and query expansion techniques, the crucial parameters are extracted from the requester's responses that enable us to generate a Request Template as the representation of the desired web service. By integrating the chatbot with the web service discovery process, we improve the retrieval rate in the terms of precision and recall and provide a natural language interface for the requesters to retrieve the desired services.

During the last decade number of researches have been conducted on applying chatbots and conversational interfaces in different fields (e.g. healthcare, educational systems, and disability care). However, the idea of integrating chatbots into the service discovery process opens up new research directions in the area of SBSs, SaaS, and mashup. The chatbot technology can cover the wide range of applications in these areas such as bot-enabled mashups and web compositions for enhancing the end-user development or requirement extraction chatbot for SaaS applications. These examples could be topics for future research.

ACKNOWLEDGEMENT

This work has been supported by the ESF and the Free State of Saxony with grant number 1000235478.

REFERENCES

Abdul-Kader, S. A. and Woods, J. (2015) 'Survey on Chatbot Design Techniques in Speech Conversation Systems', *(IJACSA) International Journal of Advanced Computer Science and Applications*, 6(7), pp. 72–80. Available at: www.ijacsa.thesai.org (Accessed: 30 December 2019).

Baez, M. and Daniel, F. (2019) 'Conversational Web Interaction: Proposal of a Dialog-Based Natural Language Interaction Paradigm for the Web', (October).

Bhardwaj, K. C. (2015) 'Machine Learning in Efficient And Effective Web Service Discovery', 14(3), pp. 196–214.

David Yoffie, P. B. *et al.* (2018) *Voice War: Hey Google vs. Alexa vs. Siri*. Available at: www.hbsp.harvard.edu. (Accessed: 6 January 2020).

Klusch, M. (2008) 'Semantic Web Service Description', *CASCOM: Intelligent Service Coordination in the Semantic Web*, pp. 31–57. doi: 10.1007/978-3-7643-8575-0_3.

Klusch, M. (2018) 'Service Discovery', in Alhajj, R. and Rokne, J. (eds) *Encyclopedia of Social Network Analysis and Mining*. New York, NY: Springer New York, pp. 2474–2484. doi: 10.1007/978-1-4939-7131-2_121.

Ma, S. P. *et al.* (2013) 'Web service discovery using lexical and semantic query expansion', *Proceedings - 2013 IEEE 10th International Conference on e-Business Engineering, ICEBE 2013*. IEEE, pp. 423–428. doi: 10.1109/ICEBE.2013.65.

Mohebbi, K. *et al.* (2010) 'A comparative evaluation of Semantic Web service discovery approaches', in *iiWAS2010 - 12th International Conference on Information Integration and Web-Based Applications and Services*. Paris, France, pp. 33–39. doi: 10.1145/1967486.1967496.

Raghuvanshi, A., Carroll, L. and Raghunathan, K. (2018) 'Developing Production-Level Conversational Interfaces with Shallow Semantic Parsing', in *Proceedings of the 2018 Conference on Empirical Methods in Natural Language Processing: System Demonstrations*. Brussels, pp. 157–162.

Zarei, B. and Gaedke, M. (2018) 'GOWDA: Goal-oriented Web Documents Querying tool', in *DocEng '18 Proceedings of the ACM Symposium on Document Engineering* . Halifax: ACM New York, NY, USA, p. No.47. doi: 10.1145/3209280.3229099.

Zhang, N. *et al.* (2018) 'The Journal of Systems and Software Web service discovery based on goal-oriented query expansion', *The Journal of Systems & Software*. Elsevier Inc., 142, pp. 73–91. doi: 10.1016/j.jss.2018.04.046.

THE APPLICATION OF BLOCKCHAIN TECHNOLOGY IN LOYALTY PROGRAMS

Valerio Stallone[1,2], Anja Collenberg[1], Andreas Rüedlinger[1], Martin Wetzels[2] and Michael Klaas[1]
[1]ZHAW School of Management and Law, Center for Digital Marketing, Theaterstrasse 17, CH-8401 Winterthur, Switzerland
[2]Maastricht University, School of Business and Economics, Tongerstraat 53, NL-6211 Maastricht, The Netherlands

ABSTRACT

This study investigated a digital app (loyalz), which enables users in Switzerland to collect, redeem, and share loyalty points offered by multiple merchants. The question of particular interest in this context was whether a new service (Swiss Loyalty Scheme), which will also enable the peer-to-peer (P2P) exchange of loyalty points between users, should be based on Blockchain technology (BCT), and whether this technology meets both the app users' and the merchants' requirements. A comparison of the different implementation possibilities of a BCT-based SLS solution with the qualitative survey results and the conditions the surveyed merchants have for the SLS that can be derived from these results shows that there is limited room for maneuver in the implementation or that due to this even the advantages of BCT disappear.

KEYWORDS

Blockchain, Loyalty Programs, Acceptance

1. INTRODUCTION

Between January 2019 and September 2019, the number of marketing technology companies based on the Blockchain increased worldwide from 80 to 250 (Epstein, 2019). Advocacy, loyalty, and referral applications promise to revolutionize approaches to increasing transparency and efficiency in operational customer relationship management (Epstein, 2019), especially in terms of cost efficiency, accuracy of accounting, and resulting data-driven decisions. Existing solutions do not meet companies' requirements, however, mainly owing to a lack of transparency (Wang, Luo, & Xue, 2018). It has been suggested, therefore, that companies that already have a loyalty program should consider implementing a program based on crypto currencies (Shelper, Lowe, & Kanhere, 2018).

For data protection reasons, the company with which the study was conducted is only mentioned anonymously as "loyalz". The loyalz App provides a digitalized version of the traditional stamp card offered by many stores, enabling customers to collect and redeem the loyalty points not only of one but all affiliated merchants. The company wants to develop a loyalty platform that also enables the P2P exchange of multi-brand loyalty points between users in real time: User A, who lives close to Merchant X, could thus collect loyalty points and, when visiting a district where Merchant Y is located, exchange these loyalty points with another user in order to redeem rewards there. loyalz would like to develop a solution it calls Swiss Loyalty Scheme (SLS). To make the new platform scalable, transparent, trustworthy, and audit-proof, the loyalz considers basing it on Blockchain technology (BCT).

We studied the possible acceptance and the feasibility of the SLS. In two different surveys, the views of stakeholders - the affiliated merchants and the users of the loyalz App - were collected to determine the conditions under which they would welcome the development of the SLS. This paper presents our findings and makes recommendations for the technical implementation of such a solution.

2. LOYALTY PROGRAMS & BLOCKCHAIN

In distributed ledger (DL) accounting, the use of BCT ensures that future transactions in a distributed system build on past transactions. Consistency and correctness are achieved by ensuring that a future transaction is only valid if it proves knowledge of all previous transactions and thus recognizes them as correct. A traditional accounting system, on the other hand, is managed by a single central office in which all stakeholders have confidence, not by several independent network participants, which only requires the confidence of the majority of participants. With the additional effort of multiple storage of the account book in the network and the cryptographic proof of correctness, a certain degree of independence and thus transparency, auditability, and scalability are achieved.

Loyalty programs (LPs) are incentive programs offered by merchants to reward customers for previous purchases and to motivate them to buy again. From retail outlets to specialty stores, most companies already have such a system in place. In B2B markets, loyal customers are traditionally treated better than those that buy *in the marketplace* (Lacey & Morgan, 2009). Detailed program planning and incentive schemes must be put in place to retain selected target groups across the selected programs (Braun, Reinecke, & Tomczak, 2017). According to representative studies, however, most memberships are inactive, and members rarely redeem their rewards (Kowalewski, McLaughlin, & Hill, 2017; Heiniger, 2018). Wang, Luo, and Xue (2008) analyzed companies in the field of advocacy, loyalty, and referrals, such as Appsolutel, Bitrewards, Coupon Chain, Gatcoin, Incent, Loyalcoin, Loyyal, Qiibee, Sandblock, The Rouge Project and Tokenomy and also reviewed the literature on the topic. They identified three main entities of BCT-based LP design: the issuer, who owns the platform and distributes the loyalty points, the company (merchant), where the rewards are redeemed, and the customer (user), who redeems the rewards.

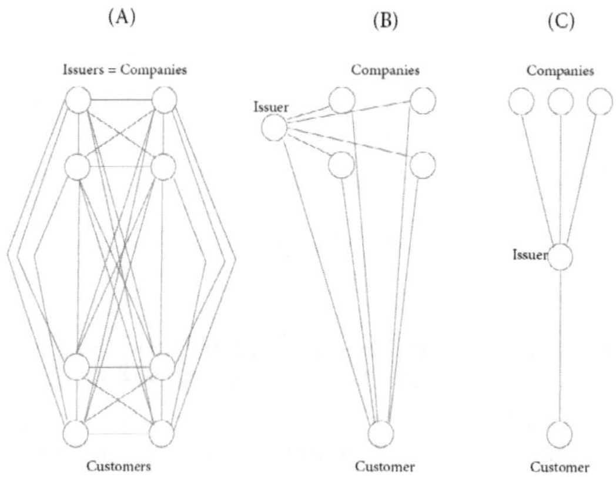

Figure 1. Entities in Blockchain-based loyalty programs

Figure 1 shows the three different LP designs for BCT. (A) represents a typical BCT adoption in loyalty programs that is trustworthy, P2P, and multi-brand: The absence of a central issuer is one of the main requirements emphasized in the literature (Shelper, Lowe, & Kanhere, 2018; Wang, Luo, & Xue, 2018). (B) is the version of an LP platform that still requires the issuer. In such cases, the issuer is represented either by a manufacturer or by a credit card payment provider (Bulbul and Ince, 2018; Choi, 2018; Napoli, 2018). (C) represents the existing LPs beyond the BCT world (Udegbe, 2017; Agrawal et al., 2018).

From a consumer's point of view, the use of BCT can lead to increased interaction with a brand because loyalty points can be redeemed more easily, which can lead to greater customer satisfaction: Customers store all their loyalty points in a single wallet and are awarded for their loyalty in real time (Kowalewski, McLaughlin , & Hill, 2017; Burnett, 2018). A feature allowing users to trade points with other users will be an added benefit.

3. EMPIRICAL RESEARCH

The aim of the empirical study was to conduct an acceptance analysis with regard to a multi-brand approach and the associated use of BCT. In the course of this analysis, merchants already in the loyalz portfolio as well as users of the loyalz App were interviewed regarding their acceptance of the proposed changes. In addition to the factors for the acceptance of a multi-brand approach, companies and users were asked about further characteristics in connection with the SLS, such as P2P.

3.1 Methodology

A two-stage procedure was chosen for the empirical examination of the research question. In a first step, a qualitative survey was carried out followed by a quantitative survey. To determine the relevant factors that can influence the acceptance of the SLS and of the P2P solution, qualitative interviews were first conducted with a small sample of subjects. For this purpose, five merchants were recruited from the loyalz portfolio. The 30-minute interviews were designed as guideline-based telephone interviews.

Following the qualitative interviews, particularly relevant topics were taken up and, based on a quantitative data collection with a larger sample consisting of merchants from the loyalz portfolio, a systematized and standardized online survey was conducted. In total, 71 data sets were available by the end of the survey period. Parallel to the survey of the merchants, users of the loyalz App were also interviewed about their perception of the concept of the SLS, again by means of a quantitative online survey. This survey focused on the acceptance of possible implementation variants. After completion of the data collection, a total of 128 data sets were available.

3.2 Qualitative Data Collection

The results from the qualitative interviews show that opinions regarding the introduction of the SLS are mixed. All the retailers who were surveyed agreed that the most important factors in the introduction of the SLS are transparency and traceability of billing. Other factors that were mentioned included the respectability of the dealers within the network and how easy the potential system would be to use. The P2P approach was seen as a customer advantage and less as an added value for merchants. The insights gained from the qualitative interviews were further investigated in the quantitative survey.

3.3 Quantitative Data Collection

As described above, the qualitative data collection consisted of a survey of affiliated merchants and a survey of app users. In the following, a descriptive overview of those samples is given. The majority of the surveyed businesses, about 63%, have between 1-9 employees, about 20% have about 10-49 employees, and only about 14% have more than 50 employees. Approximately half of the merchants surveyed serve fewer than 30 customers per day, about 30% serve between 30 and 100 customers, and 23% have more than 100 customers. The average revenue per sales transaction is below CHF 50 for about half of the companies. The percentage of customers using the loyalz App is less than 10% for more than 60% of the companies. It should be noted that most of the surveyed merchants are either active in the service segment or in the catering industry. About 12% of the merchants came from the retail or wellness sectors. A closer look at the sample of loyalz users shows that about 20% of the users belong to one of two age groups, 16-25 years or 26-35 years. The largest part, 34% of the surveyed users, is between 36-45 years old and about 20% are older than 46 years. In terms of income, 19% of the surveyed users earn less than CHF 4,000 per month, 38% have a monthly income of between CHF 4,000 and 8,000, and about 40% earn more than CHF 8,000. As shown in Figure 3 below, the vast majority of the surveyed users use the loyalz App several times a month. Finally, the users were asked in how many stores they use the loyalz App. About 30% use it in 1-2 stores, 48% use it in 3-5 stores, and about 20% in more than 6 stores.

4. RESULTS

In the following sections, the results of the analysis of the acceptance of the SLS and of P2P by merchants and users are discussed. In addition, it is shown how the technical aspects of the solution described in the survey could play an essential role in the acceptance itself.

4.1 Attractiveness of SLS

Based on a short scenario described in a few sentences, the subjects were asked to rate the attractiveness of the SLS on a scale of 1 (very unattractive) to 6 (very attractive). With regard to this evaluation of the attractiveness, significant differences (t(93)=-8,849, p=,000) were found between merchants and users. While the users had a very positive attitude towards the SLS (MW=5.26, SD=1.12, n=125), the merchants were more critical (MW=3.20, SD=1.70, n=65). With an effect strength of r= 0.67, this corresponds to a strong effect according to Cohen (1998). The histogram in Figure 2 illustrates these differences graphically.

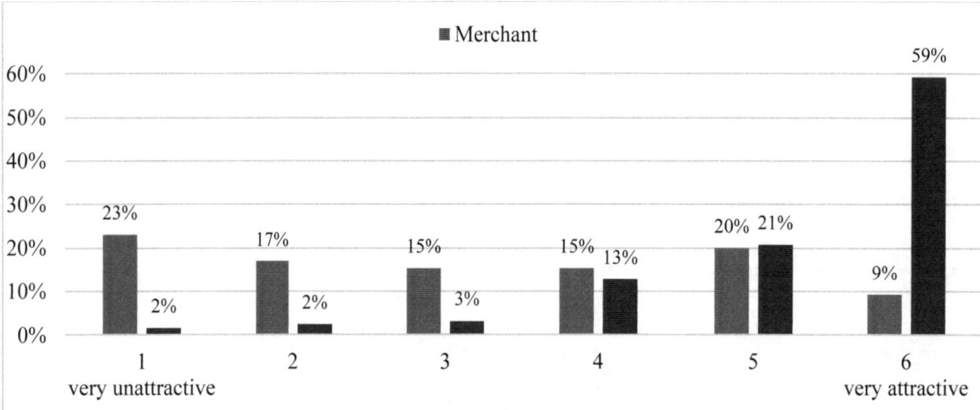

Figure 2. Attractiveness SLS (n= 190)

Advantages of the proposed SLS as mentioned by the merchants included the possibility of winning new customers, the fulfillment of a customer need, as well as the possibility to profit from the loyalz network. The merchants saw the implementation of such a system as too complicated and, therefore, as a disadvantage. There were also concerns that the customers no longer would redeem the loyalty points from the merchant offering them. The surveyed users liked the flexibility of the system in terms of redeeming points and the fact that they would be able to try out new products or services.

4.2 Attractiveness of P2P

Both the affiliated merchants and the users of the loyalz App were asked how attractive they considered a P2P approach on a scale from 1 (very unattractive) to 6 (very attractive). The attractiveness of a P2P solution was rated significantly higher (t(184)=-6,665, p=,000) by users (MW=4.86, SD=1.37, n=123) than by merchants (MW=3.21, SD=1.99, n=62).

4.3 Technical Aspects of SLS and P2P

In addition to answering questions concerning the acceptability of the SLS as well as of additional features, the merchants were also asked about aspects concerning the technical implementation of the SLS. Regarding the trust they would place in the loyalz as the operator of the SLS, the opinions of the merchants were divided. 21% of the merchants stated that they trusted the company completely, while 23% wanted to check the correctness of the data themselves. About one-quarter of the merchants stated that they trusted the loyalz as long as an independent authority was involved in controlling the system. However, a large proportion of merchants would not be willing to accept an increase in fees to pay for an independent control authority.

When asked how familiar they were with the term "BCT", 44% of the merchants stated that the term was unfamiliar to them. About one-third of the merchants stated that the term was somewhat familiar to them from the media, and about one-quarter thought that they understood the principles of BCT. Of those merchants who reported that they understood the technology in its basic principles, nine stated that they saw certain advantages in using BCT for a service such as the SLS. These advantages included the security of having a control authority that is cost-effective and supports abuse prevention.

Another point that was addressed in terms of the technical implementation of the SLS was the mapping of transactions. The merchants were asked to rate on a scale from 1 (not at all agree) to 6 (fully agree) whether they would be willing to purchase loyalty points from the loyalz in advance and then distribute them to their customers. As shown in Figure 3, this was not an option for these merchants (MW=2.19, SD=1.42, n=63). In addition, merchants were asked what effort they would be willing to invest to ensure the security of a transaction within the SLS. Here, too, the collected data show clear results. 64% of the merchants stated that the process of purchasing points must not become more complicated and that the existing system must be sufficient.

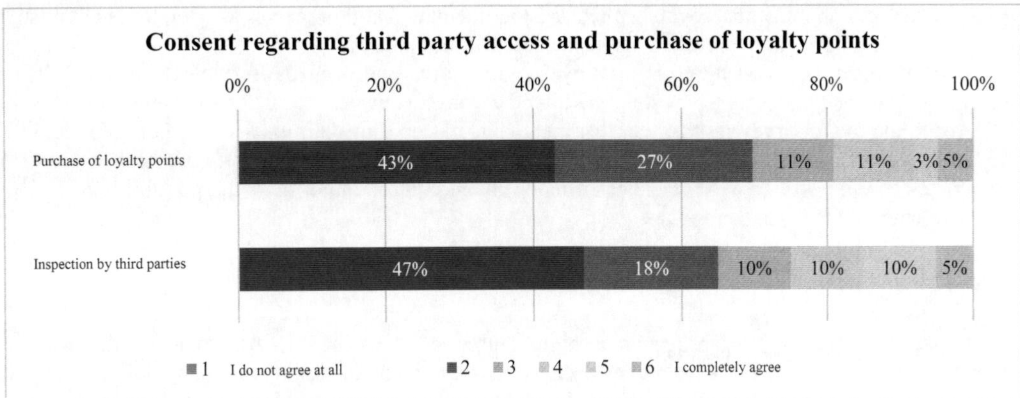

Figure 3. Consent regarding third-party access and the purchase of loyalty points (60<n<63)

Merchants were also asked whether they would agree to allowing customers or third parties to see how many loyalty points a merchant was selling. Responses were again measured on a scale from 1 (I do not agree at all) to 6 (I completely agree). As shown in Figure 3, more than half of the merchants would not agree to such an option (MW=2.33, SD=1.61, n=60). Regarding the question of whether an SLS must offer the possibility to evaluate a transaction in a detailed manner, 61% of the merchants were of the opinion that evaluations should be possible, but that the privacy of the user has a high priority.

5. DISCUSSION

As the collected data shows, a multi-brand approach would be particularly attractive from the users' point of view because it gives them more flexibility in redeeming loyalty points as well as the opportunity to try out new products or services. The merchants surveyed, on the other hand, are rather critical of such an approach and see major problems in its practical implementation. Possible reasons for the merchants' critical attitude could be that they use loyalz primarily for gaining new customers and increasing customer loyalty. In their eyes, the introduction of such a multi-brand approach would minimize the benefits of customer retention. In addition, many of the merchants expressed concerns about transparent billing.

The results of the data analysis show that from a user's perspective, the introduction of a P2P program would be an attractive option. However, this option was rated as significantly less attractive by the merchants surveyed. Possible reasons for user approval are the greater flexibility that would result from the exchange of loyalty points among users. This is, however, where merchants see the danger: Recalling the example made earlier on, Merchant Y does not benefit if it allows a customer to redeem a reward earned with points from another merchant. In addition, merchants were found to be unwilling to "buy" loyalty points in advance. Finally, merchants are concerned about the cost of developing the new system: The potential introduction of a multi-brand approach would have to be as cost effective as possible. Only very few merchants would be willing to pay more to be affiliated with the SLS.

5.1 Trustworthiness

The most important advantage of implementing the SLS as a decentralized solution is that there is no need to trust the service operator loyalz, only the network operators. The trust issue encompasses the following types of trust, in particular (Shelper, Lowe, & Kanhere, 2018):

- Manipulations: The trust of merchants that loyalz will not manipulate transactions out of self-interest (e.g., that no loyalty points are generated or deleted without justification).
- IT security: The trust that loyalz will operate the SLS in such a way that neither internal nor external attackers can manipulate the service in the long term. (For example, the service should be adequately secured against hacker attacks so that manipulations can be prevented or at least detected and reversed afterwards.)
- Privacy: The trust that loyalz will ensure that the data that it processes as operator is not misused and that it is adequately protected against access by third parties.
- Fair play: The trust by users that loyalz will continue to offer the service at fair conditions in the future and that customers will not be forced to make an expensive switch to another loyalty scheme.

According to the survey results, the trust merchants place in loyalz is extensive. Many of them fully trust loyalz as an intermediary and service provider. However, after the SLS is introduced, a large part of the merchants would also like to have either an independent control authority or the possibility to easily check the correctness of the data themselves.

5.2 Transparency

BCT-based services offer participants a high degree of transparency. All data for the validation of transactions and blocks are available to every network participant at any time. In many cases, the participants in the network are not anonymous, but pseudonymized at best (e.g., Bitcoin). While this mostly protects the system from manipulations, it also entails risks (Wang, Luo, & Xue, 2018). For instance, third parties who gain knowledge of the pseudonyms can use big data analysis to obtain a whole range of information about the behavior and business activities of individual persons and companies. This can result in gross interference with the privacy of individuals or the business secrets of companies, which are no longer under the control of the service provider due to the public nature of the data. Complex techniques for concealing such information are used in some DL solutions. However, on the one hand, the traceability of the system suffers from this and, on the other hand, the smallest errors in these experimental protocols can lead to irrevocable, retroactive de-anonymization (Shelper, Lowe, & Kanhere, 2018).

According to the survey, merchants agree that data concerning their business activities with the SLS must not be visible to others and would, therefore, have to be concealed in a DL. However, the merchants would like to have full transparency regarding the origin of "foreign" loyalty points that are redeemed and comprehensive evaluations of the transaction data. In order to address this dilemma, the concealment or pseudonymization of the data would have to be even more complex, so that both the anonymity of the stakeholders and the possibility of evaluation and verifiability are guaranteed. This technical balancing act involves security risks and can create additional dependencies. A cloud service with a database that is not publicly accessible can be protected more easily from unauthorized third parties. Anonymized or non-anonymized extracts of the data can be produced as required. In addition, parts of the data history that are no longer relevant can be moved to offline systems (for auditing purposes), so that they do not fall into the hands of attackers even if the active service systems are breached.

5.3 Audit Safety

Another advantage of a DL is the auditing security of the transactions. It could be argued that the cryptographic security mechanisms required for consensus in the network automatically provide this security.

Therefore, a player with unlawful intentions cannot falsify past transactions or import new invalid transactions into the network. For the variant "real-time transactions", however, further cryptographic security mechanisms are necessary to ensure the authenticity and integrity of the real-time transactions in the DL. For such signatures and calculations, private key material is needed, which must be managed and protected with extreme care. In case such key material is compromised, an attacker can perform any action on behalf of the compromised user. In contrast to a traditional cloud solution, these actions cannot be undone in the DL (Wang, Luo, & Xue, 2018). Furthermore, implementation errors in the cryptographic security mechanisms would have fatal consequences of a similar magnitude: Manipulations could probably not be undone or would not even be detected.

5.4 Scalability

The scalability of both a DL application and a cloud solution for the framework of the proposed SLS is no problem with today's technology and in both cases can be achieved cost-effectively (Wang, Luo, & Xue, 2018). In connection with scalability, however, the expandability of a system must also be considered. Especially considering that most merchants are skeptical about a cross-company LS, the following questions arise:

- Is it possible to start with a small proof-of-concept (PoC) system?
- Can additional players be easily added to the SLS at a later date as interest grows?
- Is it possible to dynamically define within the SLS subgroups what "peer-to-peer" transactions are allowed?

Additional merchants can be added without any problems and no adjustments to the running system are required. However, the restriction of certain loyalty points to subgroups of merchants is not possible in this case without introducing a "separate currency" for each subgroup (Wang, Luo, & Xue, 2018).

In the implementation with real-time transactions, an extension of the accepted merchants requires an adjustment to the software (adding the permitted signature keys). Support for dynamic subgroups would also be conceivable in this scenario, but again requires significantly more complex developments and security checks than in a traditional cloud solution of a service such as the SLS.

6. RECOMMENDATIONS

A comparison of the different implementation possibilities of a BCT-based SLS solution with the qualitative survey results and the conditions the surveyed merchants have for the SLS that can be derived from these results shows that there is limited room for maneuver in the implementation or that due to this even the advantages of BCT disappear.

Starting from a traditional cloud service – such as the existing platform of the loyalz App - measures can be taken to increase the required transparency and authenticity, and thus ensure users' trust in the service. With a manageable effort, the SLS can be set up in a way that meets the identified requirements. To ensure the integrity of user interactions (e.g., generating and redeeming rewards), these can be provided with customer signatures in the database. Since only the respective customer is in possession of the private key, the service operator or external attackers cannot manipulate or forge user interactions. The service operator loyalz regularly signs and publishes the data stocks in an irrevocable manner. This publication of the data prevents subsequent manipulation of transactions and offers sufficient transparency for checks of the data by customers or third parties. The combination of both measures offers almost the same security as a BCT-based solution and can be used in both multi-brand and P2P versions.

7. CONCLUSION

Loyalz wants to develop a loyalty platform (the SLS) that enables the exchange of loyalty points between different users in real time and, if possible, should be based on BCT to be scalable, transparent, trustworthy, and audit-proof. Our acceptance analysis revealed that certain aspects of the project are highly desirable from a user's perspective: The multi-brand approach and the points exchange feature should be pursued further. From a merchant's point of view, however, there is a need for more clarity. Whether the use of BCT will provide sufficient clarity was critically examined within the scope of a feasibility analysis. Several arguments were found that speak against the use of BCT and in favor of developing a solution with cloud service technology, which loyalz considers trustworthy. While the use of BCT was found to have potential, loyalz currently will not have the need to implement this technology to achieve their goals concerning the realization of their SLS.

REFERENCES

Agrawal, D. *et al.* (2018) 'Loyalty Points on the Blockchain', *Business and Management Studies*, 4(3). doi: 10.2139/ssrn.3246395.

Braun, L., Reinecke, S. and Tomczak, T. (2017) *Kundenbindung durch Loyalitätsprogramme*. Available at: https://www.alexandria.unisg.ch/250550/1/BraunReineckeTomczak_Loyalitätsprogramme.pdf (Accessed: 4 April 2019).

Bulbul, S. and Ince, G. (2018) 'Blockchain-based Framework for Customer Loyalty Program', in *2018 3rd International Conference on Computer Science and Engineering (UBMK)*. IEEE, pp. 342–346. doi: 10.1109/UBMK.2018.8566642.

Burnett, S. (2018) *Council Post: Can Blockchain Reinvigorate Loyalty Programs?*, *forbes.com*. Available at: https://www.forbes.com/sites/forbesagencycouncil/2018/12/11/can-blockchain-reinvigorate-loyalty-programs/ (Accessed: 4 April 2019).

Choi, J. (2018) 'Modeling the Integrated Customer Loyalty Program on Blockchain Technology by Using Credit Card', *International Journal on Future Revolution in Computer Science & Communication Engineering*, 4(2), pp. 388–391. Available at: http://www.ijfrcsce.org (Accessed: 23 June 2019).

Epstein, J. (2019) *Blockchain Marketing Technology Landscape*. Available at: https://www.neverstopmarketing.com/download/ (Accessed: 11 October 2019).

Heiniger, B. (2018) *Cumulus & Co. Family-Card: Warum Treuepunkte liegen bleiben - Handelszeitung*, *handelszeitung.ch*. Available at: https://www.handelszeitung.ch/unternehmen/jeder-dritte-nutzt-seine-treuepunkte-nicht (Accessed: 7 July 2019).

Kowalewski, D., McLaughlin, J. and Hill, A. J. (2017) *Blockchain Will Transform Customer Loyalty Programs*, *hbr.org*. Available at: https://hbr.org/2017/03/blockchain-will-transform-customer-loyalty-programs (Accessed: 4 April 2019).

Lacey, R. and Morgan, R. M. (2009) 'Customer advocacy and the impact of B2B loyalty programs', *Journal of Business & Industrial Marketing*, 24(1). doi: 10.1108/08858620910923658.

Napoli, F. (2018) *L'impatto della tecnologia Blockchain nel marketing. Focus sui Customer Loyalty Program*. Libera Università Internazionale degli Studi Sociali. Available at: https://tesi.luiss.it/22494/1/683471_NAPOLI_FLAMINIA_TESI_FLAMINIA_NAPOLI_683471.pdf (Accessed: 9 June 2019).

Shelper, P., Lowe, A. and Kanhere, S. S. (2018) 'Experiences from the Field: Unify Rewards - A Cryptocurrency Loyalty Prorgram', in Barahmand, S., Ghandeharizadeh, S., and Krishnamachari, B. (eds) *Symposium on Foundations and Applications of Blockchain Proceedings*.

Udegbe, S. E. (2017) 'Impact Of Blockchain Technology In Enhancing Customer Loyalty Programs In Airline Business', *International Journal of Innovative Research and Advanced Studies (IJIRAS)*, 4(6). Available at: www.ijiras.com (Accessed: 4 December 2018).

Wang, L., Luo, X. and Xue, B. (2018) 'Too Good to Be True? Understanding How Blockchain Revolutionizes Loyalty Programs', in *24th Americas Conference on Information Systems, AMCIS 2018*. Available at: https://aisel.aisnet.org/cgi/viewcontent.cgi?article=1298&context=amcis2018 (Accessed: 4 December 2018).

THE MAIN ROLE OF VIDEO ADS' STRUCTURE ON SOCIAL MEDIA ENGAGEMENT

Sónia de Almeida Ferreira[1], Sara Santos[2] and Pedro Espírito Santo[3]
[1]*Center for Studies in Education and Innovation, School of Education, Polytechnic of Viseu, Portugal*
[2]*School of Education, Polytechnic of Viseu, Portugal*
[3]*School of Technology and Management of Oliveira do Hospital, Polytechnic of Coimbra, Portugal*

ABSTRACT

Social networks play an important role in the life of today's societies. Brands create and share advertising video ads on social media networks and, in the context of the COVID-19 pandemic, social networks have allowed brands to communicate with their consumers, and creativity and narrative structures were important to consumers. Brands are producing video ads that show consumers' day context in order to obtain greater social media engagement. Considering that, this paper aims to study whether that goal is being achieved. The empirical research, from which we obtained 427 responses and which was tested using structural equations using the AMOS software, allows to conclude that creativity, the structure of the narrative and the consumer's congruence with the brand are determinants of engagement in social media. Further, presents practical and theoretical recommendations.

KEYWORDS

Video Ads, Narrative Structure, Creativity, Brand Congruence, Social Media Engagement

1. INTRODUCTION

The human capacity to create narratives as a way of communicating is one of the oldest tools we know. Disciplines such as marketing and advertising easily recognize the power of storytelling and the importance of implementing approaches that provoke individuals' attitudes and behavior.

With the new media, brands have access to new ways to disseminate information and enhance collaboration, community, conversation and sharing between consumers and among them and brands (Hennig-Thurau et al., 2010). Thus, social media platforms have been adopted in a large part of marketing strategies to enhance consumer engagement (Harrigan, Evers, Miles, & Daly, 2017) through stories (Brechman & Purvis 2015).

We agree that the receptivity to advertising messages differs from individual to individual, considering their contexts and demographic, social, educational characteristics, among others, but, according to Brechman and Purvis (2015), they are increasingly willing to be transported to the advertising narrative, which further enhances this area of expertise.

On the other side, as consumers prefer products congruent with their self-concept, self-congruence could trigger emotional, attitudinal and behavioural reactions to the brand (Grohmann, 2009). So, engage consumers special through social media platforms is essential to create an effective strategic role in branding and advertising.

Considering the framework, this study aims to analyze whether the advertising videos produced by the brands that show, more and more, the daily lives of the public are being effective in engaging in social media. Specifically, study the effects of creativity and the structure of narratives on social media engagement. Additionally, we studied the mediating effects of brand congruence. A questionnaire survey was applied and the data obtained were tested using structural equations in the AMOS software.

2. LITERATURE REVIEW

2.1 Video Ad's Narrative Structure and Creativity

It is important to clarify the concept of transportation for the advertising narrative, initially proposed by Green, in 1996. According to the author, it defines the process of transporting the individual to a fictional reality created from a narrative, creating evident effects on their beliefs, attitudes and behaviors (Green & Clark, 2012), losing access to the real and experiencing the emotions evoked by history (Green & Block, 2000).

In terms of the structure narrative creation, Escadas (2007) states that the ads are not openly persuasive. They present an affective component that unconsciously directs the consumer. Structurally, the narratives are based on a plot with incidents and surprises, on characters to whom conflicts and events happen and at a climax moment where the resolution of the story is presented (Snowden, 1999; van Laer et al., 2014) and the major conflict finally resolved.

According to Bruner (Brechman & Purvis, 2015), the traditional definitions propose that the narratives present a chronology, organizing the events with a temporal dimension, finding a beginning, middle and end. In addition, they seek to achieve causality, that is, the structuring of the elements of history in an organized manner that allows for causal inference. In addition to including emotional appeals, narratives are endowed with structural elements that "provide context, usually establishing an environment that has physical, social and temporal components, and the story is further enhanced with the use of images to guide consumers' imaginations, involvement or immersion in the story (Brechman & Purvis, 2015). Along with information and entertainment, creativity is also understood as a constructor of consumer attitudes and associations towards ads (Gao & Koufaris, 2006; Taylor, Lewin, & Strutton, 2011) According to Lee and Hong (2016), both informativeness and creativity, often emphasized in public literature, prove to be the main drivers of behavior favorable to advertisements on social networking services, promoting purchase intentions.

In addition, according to Dessart (2018), the commercial strategy must also involve balancing the elements of the narrative with facts. Using facts, figures and arguments only tends to alienate the individual and promote a distant attitude (Gottschal, 2012), but the symbiosis between the structure of the narrative and the elements of the story creates a powerful tool for transmitting information (Brechman & Purvis 2015) and, when created efficiently, allows for more favorable cognitive responses, warm feelings and positive attitudes of the narrative advertisement, when compared to the advertising of arguments (Chang, 2009). Thus, we tested the following hypothesis:

H1: Creativity has a positive impact on narrative structure.

2.2 Brand Congruence

Consumers use brands that give meaning to their self-concept to themselves and to others (Aaker, 1999). The brand congruence theory evidences that people are satisfied with brands or products that are congruent with their actual or desired self-concept (Sirgy & Su, 2000). So, brands represent social or cultural meaning congruent with consumer's own self-concept (Sirgy, 1982).

For Sirgy (1982) self-image congruity is a process whereby consumers purchase products/brands congruent with symbolic attributes similar to their images of themselves. This congruence has impacts on purchase behaviour, because consumers use products according with their self-image (Pedersen, Nysveen, & Thorbjørnsen, 2003).

The consumer's mental representation of the self-concept consists in two essential aspects (e.g. Sirgy, 1982): the 'actual self' (one's self-image as it currently is) and the 'ideal self' (the image of oneself as one would like to be) that are linked to relevant motives that impact brand congruence: self-consistency and self-esteem (Sirgy, 1982).

Because "the consumer tends to purchase brands which have a similar image to his/her self-image" (Engel, 2001, p. 399). Some authors argue that self-brand congruence match with consumers self on dimensions on cultural values (Torelli et al., 2012), gender identity (Grohmann, 2009) and brand personality (Mulyanegara et al., 2007). Addictionally, narrative ads, and their creativity have an important role positive attitudes as a brand congruence (Gottschal, 2012). Therefore, we proposed the following hypotheses:

H2: Creativity has positive effects on brand congruence

H3: Narrative Ads Structure has positive effects on brand congruence

2.3 Social Media Engagement

Consumer engagement has been defined in a number of ways in the literary, from emotional attachment to a brand (Calvert et al., 2014), to more cognitive, behavioral or emotional perspectives (Gambetti & Graffigna, 2010). Hollebeek et al. (2014) define consumer brand engagement in social media as the ability to create a psychological state in the consumer's mind as they interact with the brand. This interaction in social media varies according to different levels of engagement from "following" (lower level) to "commenting" (higher level) (Pentina et al., 2018).

Tsai and Men (2013) based on consumers' brand related activities on online media (COBRA's) model of Muntinga, Moorman, and Smit's (2011) evidence two levels of engagement: passive consumption (e.g., viewing videos and pictures, reading product reviews) and active content contributing (e.g., responding to comments and other SNS posts, posting one's own product reviews, uploading user-created videos and pictures).

As a result, engagement in social media allows creating relationships between brands and multiple actors, engaging consumers (Westberg, Stavros, Smith, Munro, & Argus, 2018), playing a strategic role in branding (Hajli, Shanmugam, Papagiannidis, Zahay, & Richard, 2017). As consequence it also increases loyalty (Schivinski and Dabrowski, 2015), brand awareness/associations, perceived quality (Schivinski and Dabrowski, 2015) as well as purchases (Brodie et al., 2013).

Creative video ads increase motivation to process the ad and improve the attitude toward the ad (Lee & Hong, 2016). Therefore, we proposed the following hypotheses:

H4: Creativity video ads is positive related with social media engagement.

H5: Narrative Ads Structure has positive effects on social media engagement.

Positive brand attitudes/evaluations (Graeff, 1997) and social media engagement appears as a consequence of self-brand congruence, because consumers express brand preference, loyalty and emotional attachment (Malär et al., 2011). Thus, we proposed the following hypothesis:

H6: Self Brand congruence is positively related with social media engagement.

3. METHODOLOGY

The research was conducted in a telecommunications industry. Telecommunications industry is a competitive industry, with low differentiation level of products and services, where advertising and creativity play an important role in competitiveness. In this environment, brands are changing their advertising to engage more and more customers. In context of COVID-19 pandemic environment, we analysed a Vodafone advertising video produced when people are in confinement (https://www.youtube.com/watch?v=Geus4SNwVkQ).

To test the proposed hypothesis, at first stage, a video ad was presented and, at a second stage, an online survey to collect data from telecommunications customers was conducted. All the measures were adapted from prior studies and have been confirmed to be reliable and valid. Before the questionnaires were distributed, all questions were translated into Portuguese by a specialized technician. Some items were slightly modified to fit telecommunications' advertising context.

Measures

In order to measure various constructs of the research model, the questionnaire uses a five point Likert scale, ranging from "1" to "5" (1=strongly disagree, 5=strongly agree). Specifically, creativity was measured using the items adapted from Lee and Hong (2016), narrative advertising structure was measured following Dessart (2018), brand congruence was measured by the items from Hinsch, Felix, and Rauschnabel (2020) and we measured engagement from Schivinski, Christodoulides, and Dabrowski (2016).

Data collection Procedure and sample

After translation, the questionnaire was pre-tested by a sample of 15 respondents. Based on your comments and suggestions, the formats and essays have been revised to ensure reliability and clarity. Information about the proposes of the study have been provided at the beginning of the questionnaire. The data were collected through a self-completion survey. The sample has 427 valid responses and the data collection took place from April to June 2020. The demographic profiles were reported in table 1.

Table 1. Demographic profiles (N=427)

Variable	Category	Frequency	Valid %
Gender	Male	123	28.8
	Female	304	71.2
Age	< 20 years	43	10.1
	20 to 29 years	219	51.3
	30 to 39 years	55	12.9
	40 to 49 years	60	14.1
	50 to 59 years	43	10.1
	up to 60 years	7	1.6

Table 1 shows that 71,2% are female and most of the observations are originate from individuals below 40 years of age (N = 274; 74,3%) (Table 1).

4. RESULTS

The sample size of this study permits the usage of multivariate analysis techniques like Structural equation modelling (SEM) through maximum likelihood estimation, considering the rule of 5:1 (items:responses) (Hair, Black, Babin, & Anderson, 2018). SEM is a multivariate analysis technique deployed to examine the proposed relationships. This technique that takes into account the measurement error in the model and it is recommended for theory testing in case of large datasets above 200 samples.
We used AMOS v.26 software and the research through SEM was analysed in two stages. First, the we analysed the measurement model (reliability and validity) and second, we analysed the relationship between constructs and evaluate the model fit.

Preliminary data analysis

At first step, common method bias was analysed, because data were collected from the same source and there have been a problem with commom method bias. To attend to this potential bias, ex-ante and ex-post procedures was employed. Ex-ante procedures were followed by Podsakoff, MacKenzie, Lee, and Podsakoff (2003) recommendations. We pre-test the survey to avoid vague concepts and complex syntax and double barrelled questions. At the first page of the survey respondents were informed that answers are anonymous and there are no right or wrong answers to each question. Ex post, Harman's one factor test was executed and the result showed four factors and fist factor explained 32.15% of the variance.

A preliminary data analysis was conducted and we ran a series of regression models on the various constructs to calculate the Variance Inflactor Factor (VIF). The VIF value is below the threshold (VIF <5) and therefore we assume that multicollinearity is not considered problematic. We also verified the Skewness (Sk) and Kurtosis (Ku) and we concluded that the items do not diverge from normality (Sk <3; Ku <7) (Hair et al., 2018). Additionally, we calculated the Kaiser-Meyer-Olkin (KMO) as well as Bartlett's test of sphericity to measure sampling adequacy. The KMO is 0.835 (KMO>0.7) and Bartlett's test is significant at $p<0.05$. Therefore, the data are suitable for factor analysis.

Measurement model

The first step of the SEM analysis is the measurement analysis. We carried out the measurement model through confirmatory factor analysis (CFA) to assess reliability and validity. The results of model fit indices were acceptable (χ^2 = 261.884; *df* = 97; GFI = 0.929; CFI = 0.969; NFI = 0.951; IFI = 0.969; TLI = 0.961; RMSEA = 0.080).

Table 2. Results of the measurement model

Variável latente	Itens Code	λ	*t*-values	R^2	CR	AVE
CREA					**0.784**	**0.552**
	CREA1	0.794	(a)	0.63		
	CREA2	0.824	18.242	0.679		
	CREA3	0.589	12.281	0.347		
NaST					**0.840**	**0.636**
	NaST1	0.809	(a)	0.655		
	NaST2	0.834	17.014	0.696		
	NaST3	0.747	15.535	0.558		
CONG					**0.911**	**0.774**
	CONG1	0.88	(a)	0.774		
	CONG2	0.919	26.4	0.845		
	CONG3	0.839	22.804	0.705		
ENG					**0.943**	**0.735**
	ENG1	0.828	(a)	0.686		
	ENG2	0.821	29.555	0.674		
	ENG3	0.874	22.552	0.764		
	ENG4	0.875	22.592	0.765		
	ENG5	0.894	23.413	0.799		
	ENG6	0.850	21.566	0.722		

λ = standardized coefficients ; R^2 = squared multiple correlation; (a) the path is fixed at 1.0 to set the metric of the construct; AVE = Average Extracted Variance; CR = Composite reliability; MODEL FIT: χ^2 = 261.881; df = 97; Goodness of fit index (GFI) = 0.929; Comparative fit index (CFI) = 0.969; Normed Fit Index (NFI) = 0.951; Incremental fix Index (IFI) = 0.969; Tucker-Lewis Index (TLI) = 0.961 root mean square error approximation (RMSEA) = 0.080.

Convergent validity and reliability was examined through the Average Variance extracted (AVE) and Composite Reliability (CR) (Bagozzi & Yi, 1988; Fornell & Larcker, 1981). Thus, table 2 shows that AVE (ranging from 0.552 to 0.774) and CR (ranging from 0.784 to 0.943) are above the threshold values (AVE>0.5; CR>0.7). Additionally, we examine that standardized loadings (λ) are above the recommended value for each construct (λ>0.7) and their significance is considered (p<0.05) (Chin, 1998).

Discriminant validity

Moreover, discriminant validity was examined. Table 3 present a Fornell and Larcker criterion (Fornell & Larcker, 1981) to examine discriminant validity and we confirmed that all AVE values are higher than squared inter-construct correlation estimates.

Table 3. Discriminating Validity - criterion of Fornell and Larcker (1981)

Construct	CREA	NaST	CONG	ENG
CREA	0.552			
NaST	0.334	0.636		
CONG	0.437	0.334	0.774	
ENG	0.387	0.097	0.336	0.735

Diagonal entries are AVE values; * all correlations are significant at level 1%
CREA=Creativity; NaST=Narrative Advertising Structure; CONG=Brand Congruence; ENG=Social Networks Engagement;

The results indicate that constructs are unidimensional and show acceptable levels of reliability, convergent validity and discriminant validity.

Structural Model

The second step of the SEM analysis is the hypothesis testing through examination of the structural model and the results are shown in table 4. The result of the chi square (χ^2) test is 365.007 with *df*=98, which is statistically significant (p<0.01). Moreover, the global fit indices recommend that the model has an acceptable fit (GFI=0.901; CFI=0.901; NFI=0.932; IFI=0.949; TLI=0.938; RMSEA=0.080). The structural paths support hypotheses H1, H2, h3, H4, H5 and H6.

Table 4. Hypothesis Testing - Direct, Indirect and Total Effects

Hip	Path	β	Std Error	t-value	p-value	result
H1	CREA → NaSt	0.577	0.045	10.16	*p*<0.001	Supported
H2	CREA → CONG	0.491	0.063	8.42	*p*<0.001	Supported
H3	NaSt → CONG	0.294	0.076	5,194	*p*<0.001	Supported
H4	CREA → ENG	0.479	0.081	7.116	*p*<0.001	Supported
H5	NaSt → ENG	-0.184	0.089	-3.1	*p*<0.01	Not Supported
H6	CONG → ENG	0.376	0.071	5.935	*p*<0.001	Supported

Notes: β = Standardized Path Coefficients; R^2: NaST=0.333; CONG; 0.495; ENG=0.461
CREA=Creativity; NaST=Narrative Advertising Structure; CONG=Brand Congruence; ENG=Social Networks Engagement. *Model Global Fit*: χ^2 = 365.007; *df* = 98; Goodness of fit index (GFI) = 0.901; Comparative fit index (CFI) = 0.900; Normed Fit Index (NFI) = 0.932; Incremental fix Index (IFI) = 0.949; Tucker-Lewis Index (TLI) = 0.938; Root Mean Square Error Approximation (RMSEA) = 0.080.

5. DISCUSSION

The results evidenced the explanation of the engagement in social networks by the variables included in the model (R^2=0.461). The internet in general and social media networks specifically, generate content for users and the amount of information that they receive today is vast. This empirical study examined the creativity impacts on narrative structure. H1 is confirmed by our study ($\beta_{CREA \rightarrow NaSt}$= 0.577; $p<0.001$) as Chang (2009) states.

In order to test H2 ($\beta_{CREA \rightarrow CONG}$= 0.491; $p<0.001$) and H3 ($\beta_{NaST \rightarrow CONG}$= 0.294; $p<0.001$), our investigation support that narrative ads, and their creativity has some effects on brand congruence. These conclusions corroborate Gottschal (2012).

To support the hypothesis H4 ($\beta_{CREA \rightarrow ENG}$= 0.479; $p<0.001$), we analyse that creativity motivates the attitude toward social media engagement like Lee and Hong (2016).

Our empirical study do not support the positive relationship stated. The hypothesis H5 is not confirmed. We found some explanations for this. It is possible that the age of the respondents does not allow us to conclude about this relationship. In addition, our study has a sample with a strong percentage of women.

Finally, we state that H6 ($\beta_{CONG \rightarrow ENG}$= 0.376; $p<0.001$) is supported. This result is related with the conclusions of Malär et al. (2011).

6. CONCLUSION

Due to the centrality of social networks today, the empirical study presented here contributed to the advance of theoretical knowledge and has practical implications for management.

The study presents a model in which most of the causal relationships between the constructs were supported by our analysis. The model presented has a good fit.

This research concludes that there is a positive relationship creativity and narrative ad structure. Also demonstrates that brand congruence has effects from creativity and narrative structure. Additionally, social media engagement is explained throughout brand congruence.

Firms should reflect on these results and promote their creativity on video ad's to create mental representations on consumers' minds and, therefore, get more and mode engagement from their consumers.

Despite the important results, we considered that future researches could include other variables to help explain the model.

Thus, as further research, we suggest a model with the experience with the brand as a moderating variable.

In addition, our study only considered a sample of residents in Portugal. The analysis of users, from other countries, may be relevant for the explanation of the model presented.

ACKNOWLEDGEMENT

This work is funded by National Funds through the FCT - Foundation for Science and Technology, I.P., within the scope of the project Refª UIDB/05507/2020. Furthermore, we would like to thank the Centre for Studies in Education and Innovation (CI&DEI) and the Polytechnic of Viseu for their support.

REFERENCES

Aaker, J. L. 1999. The malleable self: The role of self-expression in persuasion. *Journal of Marketing Research,* Vol. 36, No. 1, pp. 45–57.

Bagozzi, R. P., & Yi, Y. 1988. On the evaluation of structural equation models. *Journal of the Academy of Marketing Science, 16*(1), 74-94. doi: 10.1007/BF02723327

Brechman, J. M. and Purvis, S. C., 2015. Narrative, transportation and advertising. *International Journal of Advertising*, Vol. 34, No 2, pp 366-381.

Brodie, R.J. et al, 2013. Consumer engagement in a virtual brand community: an exploratory analysis. *Journal of Business Research*, Vol. 66, No. 1, pp. 105–114.

Calvert et al., 2014. Using Implicit Methods to Develop an Objective Measure of Media Brand Engagement. *International Journal of Market Research*, Vol. 56, No. 1, pp. 15–32.

Chang, C, 2009. Being Hooked by editorial content: The implications for processing narrative advertising. *Journal of Advertising*. Vol. 38, No 1, pp 21-34.

Chin, W. 1998. The Partial Least Squares Approach to Structural Equation Modeling. *Modern Methods for Business Research, 8*.

Dessart, L. 2018. Do ads that tell a story always perform better? The role of character identification and character type in storytelling ads. *International Journal of Research in Marketing*. Vol. 35, No 2, pp. 289-304.

Engel, B. (2001). Consumer behavior. 9

Escalas, J. E. 2007. Self-referencing and persuasion: Narrative transportation versus analytical elaboration. *Journal of Consumer Research*. Vol. 33, pp 421-429.

Fornell, C., & Larcker, D. F. 1981. Evaluating Structural Equation Models with Unobservable Variables and Measurement Error. *Journal of Marketing Research, 18*(1), 39-50. doi: 10.2307/3151312

and Graffigna, G. 2010. The concept of engagement. *International Journal of Market Research*, Vol. 52, No. 6, pp. 801-826.

Gao, Y., and Koufaris, M., 2006. Perceptual antecedents of user attitude in electoniccommerce. *ACM SIGMIS*, Vol. 37, pp 43-50.

Gottschall, J. 2012. *The storytelling animal: How stories make us human*. Boston, MA: Houghton Mifflin Harcourt Publishing Company.

Graeff, T. R. 1997. Consumption situations and the effects of brand image on consumers' brand evaluations. *Psychology & Marketing*, Vol. 14, No.1, pp. 49–70.

Green, M. and Clark, J., 2012. Transportation into narrative worlds: implications for entertainment media influences on tobaco use. *Society for Study of Addiction*, Vol. 108, pp 477-484.

Green, M. C., and Brock, T. C., 2000. The role of transportation in the persuasiveness of public narratives. *Journal of Personality and Social Psychology*. Vol. 79, No.5, pp 701-721.

Grohmann, B. (2009). Gender dimensions of brand personality. *Journal of Marketing Research,* Vol. 46, No. 1, pp. 105-119.

Hair, J., Black, W., Babin, B., & Anderson, R. 2018. *Multivariate Data Analysis: Global Edition* (8th ed.). New York: Annabel Ainscow.

Hajli, N. et al, 2017. Branding co-creation with members of online brand communities. *Journal of Business Research*, Vol. 70, pp. 136–144.

Harrigan, P. et al, 2017. Customer engagement with tourism social media brands. *Tourism Management*, Vol. 59, pp. 597–609.

Hinsch, C., Felix, R., & Rauschnabel, P. A. 2020. Nostalgia beats the wow-effect: Inspiration, awe and meaningful associations in augmented reality marketing. *Journal of Retailing and Consumer Services, 53*, 101987. doi: https://doi.org/10.1016/j.jretconser.2019.101987

Hennig-Thurau, T. et al, 2010. The impact of new media on customer relationships. *Journal of Service Research,* Vol. 13, pp. 311–330.

Hollebeek, L.D. et al, 2014. Consumer brand engagement in social media: conceptualization, scale development and validation. *Journal of Interactive Marketing*, Vol. 28, No. 2, pp. 149–165.

Lee, J., and Hong, I. B., 2016. Predicting positive user responses to social media advertising: The roles of emotional appeal, informativeness, and creativity. *International Journal of Information Management,* Vol. *36*, No 3, pp 360-373.

Malar, L. et al, 2011. Emotional brand attachment and brand personality: The relative importance of the actual and ideal self. *Journal of Marketing,* Vol. 75, No. 4, pp. 35–52.

Mulyanegara, R. et al, 2007. The big five and brand personality: Investigating the impact of consumer personality on preferences towards particular brand personality. *Journal of Brand Management,* Vol. 16, No. 4, pp. 234–247.

Muntinga, D.G. et al, 2011. Introducing COBRAs: exploring motivations for brand-related social media use. *International Journal of Advertsiging,* Vol. 30, No. 1, pp. 13–46.

Pentina, I. et al, 2018. Exploring social media engagement behaviors in the context of luxury brands. *Journal of Advertising*, Vol. 47, No.1, pp. 55–69

Pedersen, P. E. et al. 2003. Identity expression in the adoption of mobile services: The case of multimedia messaging services, Working Paper, 26, pp. 1-71

Podsakoff, P., MacKenzie, S., Lee, J.-Y., & Podsakoff, N. 2003. Common Method Biases in Behavioral Research: A Critical Review of the Literature and Recommended Remedies. *The Journal of applied psychology, 88*, 879-903. doi: 10.1037/0021-9010.88.5.879

Schivinski, B., and Dabrowski, D., 2015. The impact of brand communication on brand equity through Facebook. *Journal of Research in Interactive Marketing*, Vol.9, No.1, pp. 31–53.

Schivinski, B., Christodoulides, G., & Dabrowski, D. 2016. Measuring Consumers Engagement With Brand-Related Social-Media Content. *Journal of Advertising Research, 56*(1), 64. doi: 10.2501/JAR-2016-004

Sirgy, J. M. 1982. Self-concept in consumer behaviour: A critical review. *Journal of Consumer Research,* Vol. 9, pp. 287–300.

Sirgy, J. M., and Su, C.2000. Destination image, self-congruity and travel behaviour: Toward an integrative model. *Journal of Travel Research,* Vol. 38, No.4, pp. 224–235.

Tsai, W.-H. S. and Men, L.R. 2013. Motivations and antecedents of consumer engagement with brand pages on social networking sites. *Journal of Research in Interactive Advertising*, Vol. 13, No. 2, pp. 76–87.

Torelli, C. J. et al, 2012. Brand concepts as representations of human values: Do cultural congruity and compatibility between values matter? *Journal of Marketing*, Vol. 76, No. 4, pp. 92–108.

van Laer, T., de Ruyter, K., Visconti, L. M., & Wetzels, M., 2014. The extended transportation-imagery model: A meta-analysis of the antecedents and consequences of consumers' narrative transportation. *Journal of Consumer Research*. Vol. 40, No 5, pp. 797-817.

Westberg, K. et al, 2018. An examination of how alcohol brands use sport to engage customers on social media. *Drug and Alcohol Review,* Vol. 37, No. 1, pp. 28–35

THE IMPACT OF SOCIAL MEDIA CONSUMPTION ON CULTURAL INTELLIGENCE OF USER

Petra Zecevic, Lana Miletic and Ljerka Luic
University North, Trg dr. Zarka Dolinara 1, Koprivnica, Croatia

ABSTRACT

With the digitalization and relocation of almost all human communications to the online sphere, social networks have gained great importance and room for maneuver for influence in the domain of lifelong learning. Enabling the rapid sharing of a large amount of information, ideas, but also content in general, has an impact on every user of these networks. This paper aims to show the impact of social networks, that is, the consumption of social networks, on the cultural intelligence of the individual. The subject of this paper was to determine which digital competencies, defined by information constructs Knowledge and Skills, significantly determine the level of cultural intelligence of an individual during his lifelong education, formal and informal, and the primary goal was to create a new information construct. The research was conducted online, using a survey questionnaire containing original metrics of influencing factors on the basis of which the application of quantitative statistical methods designed a conceptual model, a description that can determine the impact of each information construct (Knowledge, Skills, Experience) on digital intelligence development and its impact on degree of cultural intelligence. In this sense, this paper represents a contribution to the field of communication and educational sciences and opens initiatives for further research related to the development of an original methodology for conceptualizing digital communication in the field of non-formal education.

KEYWORDS

Digital Intelligence, Cultural Intelligence, Social Media, E-Education, Life-Long Learning

1. INTRODUCTION

Every day, thanks to global connectivity and technological advances, the individual has the opportunity to make countless contacts regardless of time and space. The networking of people leads to new situations in which it is no longer necessary to be physically present to communicate, which, consequently, leads to the possibility of communication with people from other countries, cultures, climates, and people with different life habits (Miladrovic, 2010). Increasing networking is influenced by an increasing number of social networks that allow virtual communication between two or more people, whether it is two-way or one-way communication. Social networks enable digital communication between people how to know or don't know each other, the exchange of messages between them, and their connection. And all the achieved communication, both in the real and virtual world, has an impact on the individual. Through social networks, people are allowed to present their opinions and thoughts, discuss political and social matters (Nakic, Sosic, Diklic, 2019).

For communication between people to be achievable (in the real or digital world), mutual understanding of communicators is important. It is necessary to overcome language barriers, but also different cultural situations that an individual need to be able to recognize to know how to behave in a particular situation, without creating additional problems. For an individual to be able to respond to any situation, it is important to have a pronounced cultural intelligence, whether or not cultural intelligence is meant like concept of mindfulness as a key component that links knowledge with behavioral capability (Thomas, 2006) or like a mediator between proactive personality and social adjustment (Hu, Liu, Zhang & Wang, 2020).

2. LITERATURE REVIEW

The history of the development of social networks coincides with the development of ICT and the Internet. The first prototype of social network was SixDegrees.com. It was created in 1997, and since then, social networks have become a global phenomenon (Kittinger 2012). According to its creator, A. Weinreich, the system was "ahead of its time," and therefore, unsustainable. It shut down in 2000 (Boyd and Ellison, 2007). The next wave of this global communication phenomenon begins with Ryze.com and it's social add-on Friendster (created in 2002) (Cohen, 2003). Unlike their predecessors on Friendster, users had the option to post photos in addition to their personal information (Boyd and Ellison, 2007). A large number of users and many fake profiles were crucial to Friendster because there was a software overload that engineers could no longer handle. To attract dissatisfied Friendster users, the social network MySpace was launched in 2003 and had features that other networks did not have: freedom of writing and an unlimited number of characters, the ability to customize profiles to user requirements, add music, etc. (Boyd and Ellison, 2007).

Facebook was initially developed and intended for university students (Kittinger, 2012), but quickly became available to anyone over the age of 13 who has their email address (Stern and Taylor, 2007). In 2005, it was the most visited website (Schwartz, 2012). Unlike hitherto popular networks, Facebook has developed new features so that users can better customize their profile (Cheung, Chill, Lee, 2011, according to Hill, 2014). Over the next two years, Facebook's numbers grew steadily, so it's no surprise that in 2007, it surpassed its competitor MySpace (Boyd and Ellison, 2007). Today, Facebook has 2.6 billion active users per month (Clement, 2020), making it the number one social network in the world.

Beside Facebook, Twitter and Instagram are social networks that are most often mentioned in both literature and the media world. The social network Twitter was launched in 2006 and today has 326 million users (Clement, 2020). It belongs to the so-called microblogging and, as such, allows easy sharing of messages (status) either publicly or within a social network. Unlike other social networks (Facebook, MySpace, etc.) on Twitter, a user's tracking does not necessarily have to be reciprocated (Huberman et al., 2019). In October 2010, Instagram was launched - a mobile application that allows users to turn their photos into visually appealing ones, which they then share with other users online (Soloman, 2013). Of course, Instagram's capabilities and features have changed in many ways since 2010, and today, this social network is the sixth in the number of users (1.1 billion) (Clement, 2020). It allows posting multiple photos in one post, saving pictures and videos, exchanging messages, various filters, and animations, and perhaps the most used feature so-called. "Instagram stories" - posting photos and / or videos in a row. Historically, Facebook, Twitter, and Instagram are the most famous social networks. But today, we can also talk about many others that gather more and more users every day. Facebook is still the most dominant social network; however, it is followed by Youtube (2 billion users), WhatsApp (2 billion users), Facebook Messenger (1.3 billion), and WeChat (1.2 billion). Twitter, once the most popular, now has only 326 million users (Clement, 2020).

Human is a social being who, from the beginning of his existence, seeks interaction with other people, with a tendency to create a community in which he will be able (with the direct or indirect support of all members) to realize his potential for the benefit of himself and his environment. Providing social support is one of the essential functions of social relations. Thus, the term social network refers to a system of social relations within which individuals may or may not provide social support and serve those functions that are not related to providing support (Ferlander, 2007). This notion of the human as a social being can be transferred to the digital world. If we talk and observe social networks from an IT perspective, the literature provides several definitions, but they all talk about social networks as tools for communicating with each other. Perhaps the most commonly used definition of social networks that appears in the literature is that given by Kaplan and Haenlein (2010), in which social networks are described as "group of Internet-based applications that build on the ideological and technological foundations of Web 2.0, and that allow the creation and exchange of User Generated Content. ".A more precise definition is given by Carr and Hayes (2015), according to which social networks are internet-based mass communication channels that enable interaction between users, gaining value primarily from user content. The same authors explain the given definition, stating that users can self-present through social networks, either in real-time or asynchronously (without defined time intervals), regardless of whether they present themselves and exchange information with a wider or narrow audience.

2.1 Cultural Intelligence

Thanks to digitalization and communication in the online sphere, people's connection is the greatest in history. Given the trends, everyday innovations, and the expansion of the online sphere, we can only expect even greater connectivity between people, increasing online sharing of information, content, ideas, and influence. All of this sharing and interactions among people from different backgrounds, whether sharing in physical presence or not, affect human nature inseparable from culture (Cervone and Pervin, 2013).

This inseparability of culture from human nature is contained in cultural intelligence. There is no single definition, especially when one considers that there is no consensus among scientists and authors on what intelligence is and what intelligence types exist. Each of the communicators enters the communication from a particular starting point. When we consider that the communicators come from different cultures, then the cultural starting point is different among them. To understand the other side, to understand communication in its original, intended form, communicators need to have specific skills and competencies. When it comes to culture, strong cultural intelligence is required to understand others. As there is no single accepted definition of cultural intelligence, different authors have presented their cultural intelligence views. Thus, according to Thomas (2015), cultural intelligence is defined as an ability that enables effectiveness in intercultural interactions. Earley and Mosakowski (2004) describe cultural intelligence as the seemingly innate ability of each person to interpret the unknown and ambiguous gestures of members of another culture in the same way that people who are members of that culture would do so. Earley and Ang (Ang et al., 2007) are on the trail of this: cultural intelligence is the ability to adapt to new cultural contexts. But according to them, the concept of cultural intelligence is contained through four aspects: cognitive, metacognitive, motivational, and behavioral. The cognitive aspect is the specific knowledge that people acquire about a new culture while metacognitively making superior judgments that they make in their thought processes. A tendency to act on the cognitive aspect and the persistence in acquiring knowledge constitute the motivational aspect. In contrast, the behavioral aspect is the ability to carry out the desired or intended action.

Each of these authors confirms with his definition of cultural intelligence the theory of multiple intelligences, of which cultural is only one of the few that together build a person's intelligence. Also, the authors define cultural intelligence as an ability, and ability is measurable. Early and Mosakowski (2004) decided to measure the (under) development and (in) presence of cultural intelligence through the profiles of cultural intelligence they created. In their paper, they made a presentation on how to make a cultural intelligence profile and how to measure it. According to them, to arrive at a cultural intelligence profile, it is necessary to present to the respondent several statements from three different domains: cognitive, physical, and emotional/motivational.Each of these domains contains four predetermined statements to which the respondent gives grades from 1 to 5, where 1 indicates complete disagreement, and 5 fully agrees with what has been said/written. Within each domain, the scores next to statements are added up and divided by four. The obtained figure is an indicator of the level of that part of cultural intelligence. The results of all three domains summed and divided by three give the final outcome of cultural intelligence. According to Earley and Mosakowski, a score of less than 3 shows a lack of cultural intelligence and the need to work on it (since cultural intelligence is defined as an ability, it is possible to reduce and increase it), while scores of more than 4.5 are satisfactory and show the presence of strong cultural intelligence.

2.2 The Connection between Cultural Intelligence and Social Networks

Following social-cognitive theories of personality, which is "based on the importance of learning by observation, and on the thought processes on which individual differences are based" (Penava Brekalo, 2010), social networks and cultural intelligence can be linked. Daily use, high exposure to different content, which includes various cultural situations that an individual witnesses through viewing content on social networks, and possibly a participant, if involved in a discussion or conversation with another party or sites that are different cultures, influencing the individual. Whether an individual uses social networks to inform, gain friends, or to stay in touch with existing friends and family, he is exposed to content that he is not primarily interested in, or is not yet aware that he is interested, but which captures his attention and, consequently, affect it. Social networks enable virtual reality or another life (Milardovic, 2010), a life in which everyone presents themselves in a certain way that may or may not correspond to the real situation in the actual reality. According to Milardovic (2010), social networks enable the disclosure of specific data due to a large amount of personal information that can be misused. The data found on social networks is the property of the social networks on which they are located, not the individual ones that relate. Due to that, a clear line of demarcation between the private and public is lost, and there is a possibility of manipulating this data.

Bilic (2020) stand out that social media users bring different values and features, including their cultural ones, into social media environment which makes it dynamic and similar to the physical environment and relations. That is the reason why social media connect social actors with connections of varying intensity.

Furthermore, according to Milardovic (2010), virtual friends are an oxymoron because friends are those, in reality, people to whom the individual is close, and in the possibility of making face-to-face contact. That is why the virtual social community, to which an individual can tend to or be a part of it, makes a paradox because it lacks real social connection. This leads to the fact that virtual friends in the real world are strangers: "The phenomenon of a stranger in society is as old as human society. This phenomenon in the social sense is the subject of phenomenological sociology. In modern society, strangers are members of other cultures who came to a society to stay. Today, in the age of globalization, more and more parties in societies are attractive as a society of accepting and founding a new life. In these societies, strangers are the "others" we encounter, tolerate, or avoid in our daily lives. By constructing artificial or virtual reality, we face a new phenomenon of a cyber stranger. Cyber or IC technology creates a new kind of virtual strangers. Techniques and technology in the anthropological sense do not only have the function of relief. They produce mutations, transformations, and new alienations. Cyberspace is a space of alienation. In cyberspace, man is a stranger to man. It is actually a space of strangers." (Milardovic, 2010). Guided by the fact that everyone is a stranger to social networks (if we take a smaller number of acquaintances and real friends with whom he intentionally communicates via a social network), it is essential to find out what impact they have on social networks, especially in terms of cultural intelligence. In this way, the cyberspace in which the users of social networks find themselves is seen as real situations, situations face to ear, in which there are people of different cultures. In cyberspace, it is an encounter without face-to-face communication, but it is still an encounter of different cultures and should be observed in this way.

3. RESEARCH METHODOLOGY

Based on the reviewed methodological literature, we conclude that the questionnaire, especially in the social sciences, is the essential measuring instrument for data collection. The questionnaire is used to survey public opinion and collect demographic, socioeconomic, and other informations of respondents (Mejovsek, M, 2013). Since this work was mostly aimed at social network users, it is natural to use an online questionnaire in which closed-ended questions were asked (respondents were offered an answer in advance), thus facilitating the statistical processing of the obtained data and their interpretation.

The questionnaire created for this paper is based on two previously used questionnaires in similar surveys. The first part examines the ways and frequency of social network consumption. This part was adapted from the questionnaire posted on research.net (NSE, 2020). The second part is based on Christopher Earley and Elaine Mosakowski's questionnaire (2004) to determine the cultural intelligence level. The questionnaire was distributed online, more specifically via Google Form posted on all current social networks and email addresses of respondents. In order to obtain the most diverse and wide range of the structure of the respondents, the sample was simple random. The research was nationally based: all respondents are from Croatia. The entire statistical analysis was made in the SPSS program.

For the purposes of the paper, the objectives of the research are defined:

- show the impact of social networks on the cultural intelligence of the individual
- determine which digital competencies determine the level of cultural intelligence of an individual
- create a new information construct

Accordingly, the paper hypothesizes are:

H1: There is a positive correlation between social media consumption and cultural intelligence.

H1.1: There is a positive correlation between the greater use of social networks and cultural intelligence

H1.2: There is a positive correlation between the length of use of social networks and cultural intelligence

4. RESULTS AND DISCUSSIONS

According to the obtained results, it can be concluded that all respondents use social networks, regardless of age and gender, and the largest number of respondents is aged 26 to 39 years. Equally, 137 female and 78 male respondents participated in the study. Comparing the age variable with the variable number of social networks that respondents use and the time they spend on them, we find that there is a significant negative correlation in both analyzes. In other words, the younger the respondents are active on more social networks, and the time they spend on social networks is longer compared to older age groups (Tables 1 and 2). According to the research results, it can be concluded that younger respondents have a higher degree of cultural intelligence; however, the correlation between these two variables is not significant (Table 3).

Table 1. Correlation between age and number of networks used by respondents

		Number	Age
Number of soc. netw.	Pearson Correlation	1	-,316**
	Sig. (2-tailed)		,000
	N	215	215
Age	Pearson Correlation	-,316**	1
	Sig. (2-tailed)	,000	
	N	215	215

Table 2. Correlation between age and time that respondents spend on network

		Age	Time
Age	Pearson Correlation	1	-,260**
	Sig. (2-tailed)		,000
	N	215	215
Time spent on soc.netw	Pearson Correlation	-,260**	1
	Sig. (2-tailed)	,000	
	N	215	215

Table 3. Correlation between age and and cultural intelligence

		Age	CQ
Age	Pearson Correlation	1	-,021
	Sig. (2-tailed)		,755
	N	215	215
CQ	Pearson Correlation	-,021	1
	Sig. (2-tailed)	,755	
	N	215	215

When comparing the gender variable with the number of social networks used by the respondents and the time, they spend on them, the research results show that there is a positive correlation. Still, it is not significant (Tables 4 and 5). The situation is similar if we compare the gender variable with the cultural intelligence level variable (Table 6).

Table 4. Correlation between gender and and number of networks used by respondents

		Gender	Number
Gender	Pearson Correlation	1	,068
	Sig. (2-tailed)		,323
	N	215	215
Number of soc. netw.	Pearson Correlation	,068	1
	Sig. (2-tailed)	,323	
	N	215	215

Table 5. Correlation between gender and and time that respondents spend on network

		Gender	Time
Gender	Pearson Correlation	1	,085
	Sig. (2-tailed)		,214
	N	215	215
Time spent on soc. netw.	Pearson Correlation	,085	1
	Sig. (2-tailed)	,214	
	N	215	215

Table 6. Correlation between gender and cultural intelligence

		CQ	Gender
CQ	Pearson Correlation	1	CQ
	Sig. (2-tailed)		
	N	215	
Gender	Pearson Correlation	-,019	Gender
	Sig. (2-tailed)	,783	
	N	215	

In the analysis of given hypotheses and sub-hypotheses, we do not come to significant results. According to the obtained results, it is evident that there is a tiny positive correlation between the consumption of social networks (whether it is the number of social networks or the time spent on them) (0.128 and 0.059). In other words, we can conclude that the given hypothesis is confirmed in this paper, but not significantly. The results are shown in Tables 7 and 8.

Table 7. Correlation between cultural intelligence and and number of networks used by respondents

		CQ	Number
CQ	Pearson Correlation	1	,128
	Sig. (2-tailed)		,062
	N	215	215
Number of soc. netw.	Pearson Correlation	,128	1
	Sig. (2-tailed)	,062	
	N	215	215

Table 8. Correlation between cultural intelligence and time that respondents spend on network

		CQ	Time
CQ	Pearson Correlation	1	,059
	Sig. (2-tailed)		,390
	N	215	215
Time spent on soc. netw.	Pearson Correlation	,059	1
	Sig. (2-tailed)	,390	
	N	215	215

The reason for such results can be found in the following three facts; first of all, the research was conducted on a small sample, and it is to be assumed that a larger sample of respondents would give more significant results. Likewise, although the survey was anonymous, it is about questioning the respondents' attitudes towards other cultures members. Such questions are always sociologically sensitive, and it may happen that respondents do not give honest answers, but answers that they think are socially acceptable and desirable. The third reason can be related to ignorance or misunderstanding of the concept of cultural intelligence.

5. CONCLUSION

Although this research results are not statistically significant, this paper shows us that with the increase in the number of social networks used by the respondent and with the longer time spent on them, the level of cultural intelligence increases. This conclusion is not too surprising if we consider that the largest percentage of respondents belong to the so-called Generation Y age group.

Although they are not digital natives (as their followers, generation Z), they have been very familiar with the Internet and social networks since their teenage years, which have greatly influenced their attitudes towards society. Furthermore, this generation has grown up in an age of significant social change and is much more tolerant and socially vulnerable. This research only scratches the surface of the problems of today's global phenomenon of social networks and their impact on the behavior of the individual in different cultural communities than the one in which he lives.

For a deeper and more adequate analysis, it would be desirable to do research that would enter the online world and look at those respondents who do not use social networks. In this way, a more detailed comparison of the users and non-user behavior of social networks in the context of their cultural intelligence could be made. Furthermore, this research is only a presentation of "theoretical answers" that may not be consistent with the behavior that would occur if a person were indeed in a multicultural situation/environment. Therefore, it is necessary to research focus groups (after a questionnaire examines the respondents) and see how similar our ideas are about how tolerant we are and what level of cultural intelligence we possess with the real situation in real-time.

ACKNOWLEDGEMENT

Publication of this paper was supported by mentors and PhD students grant from the University North to which the authors of this article are grateful for the big support.

REFERENCES

Ang, S. ... [et al]. 2007. Cultural Intelligence: Its Measurement and Effects on Cultural Judgment and Decision Making, Cultural Adaptation and Task Performance. *Management and Organization Review*, 3(3), 335-371. doi:10.1111/j.1740-8784.2007.00082.x

Bilic, P. 2020. *Sociology of media: routines, technology and power*. Zagreb: Naklada Jesenski i Turk

Boyd, D. M., & Ellison, N. B. 2007. Social network sites: Definition, history, and scholarship. *Journal of computer-mediated communication, 13*(1), 210-230. URL: https://onlinelibrary.wiley.com/doi/pdf/10.1111/j.1083-6101.2007.00393.x (accessed: 15.9.2020)

Celment, J. 2020. Global social networks ranked by number of users 2020. Statista. August 21, URL; https://www.statista.com/statistics/272014/global-social-networks-ranked-by-number-of-users/ (accessed: 23.9.2020)

Cervone D., Pervin L.A. 2013. Personality: *Theory and Research* (12. edition). SAD: Wiley

Cohen, R. 2003. Livewire: Web Sites Try to Make Internet Dating Less Creepy, July 5, URL: http://www.zephoria.org/thoughts/archives/2003/07/05/livewire_web_sites_try_to_make_internet_dating_less_creepy.html (accessed: 27.9.2020)

Diklic, J., Nakic, M., Sosic, D. 2019. Educational role of social networks in child media education, *Communication Management Review*, 04(01), str. 178-195. https://doi.org/10.22522/cmr20190146

Earley, P. C., Mosakowski, E. 2004. Cultural Intelligence, *Harvard Business Review*, https://hbr.org/2004/10/cultural-intelligence (accessed: 1.9.2020)

Ferlander, S. 2007. The Importance of Different Forms of Social Capital for Health. *Acta Sociologica, 50*(2), 115-128. Retrieved September 28, 2020, from http://www.jstor.org/stable/20459987 (accessed: 27.9.2020)

Goltnik Urnaut, A. 2014. 'Education for successful intercultural communication and cultural intelligence', *Journal of economic and social developmen*, 1(1), str. 63-73. URL: https://hrcak.srce.hr/128529 (accessed: 1.9.2020)

Hayes, R. A. 2015. Social Media: Defining, Developing, and Divining Caleb T. Carr, Ph. D. School of Communication Illinois State University 456 Fell Hall, Campus Box 4480, Illinois State University, N ormal, IL 61790-4880 USA. *Atlantic Journal of Communication*, *23*, 1. URL: https://my.ilstu.edu/~ctcarr/research/CarrHayes_2015.pdf (accessed: 27. 9.2020)

Hill, C.L. 2014. An investigation of the connections between use of Facebook and the self-esteem/ well-being of students with disabilities in the University of Iowa Reach Program. PhD (Doctor of Philosophy) thesis, University of Iowa, URL: https://doi.org/10.17077/etd.5fxjx7dz (accessed: 15.9.2020)

Hu, S., Gu, J., & Zhang, S. 2017. Social media usage, self-efficacy and cultural intelligence: A longitudinal empirical research in China. In *Wuhan International Conference on e-Business*. Association for Information Systems.

Hu, S., Liu, H., Zhang, S., & Wang, G. (2020). Proactive personality and cross-cultural adjustment: Roles of social media usage and cultural intelligence. *International Journal of Intercultural Relations*, *74*, 42-57.

Huberman, B. A., Romero, D. M., & Wu, F. (2008). Social networks that matter: Twitter under the microscope. *arXiv preprint arXiv:0812.1045*. URL: https://www.researchgate.net/publication/23573983_Social_Networks_that_Matter_Twitter_Under_the_Microscope (accessed: 15.9.2020)

Kaplan, A. M., & Haenlein, M. 2010. Users of the world, unite! The challenges and opportunities of Social Media. *Business horizons*, *53*(1), 59-68. URL: https://www.researchgate.net/publication/222403703_Users_of_the_World_Unite_The_Challenges_and_Opportunities_of_Social_Media (accessed: 27.9.2020)

Kittinger, R., Correia, C. J., & Irons, J. G. 2012. Relationship between Facebook use and problematic Internet use among college students. *Cyberpsychology, Behavior, and Social Networking*, *15*(6), 324-327.URL: https://www.researchgate.net/publication/227162158_Relationship_Between_Facebook_Use_and_Problematic_Internet_Use_Among_College_Students (accessed: 15.9.2020)

Liao Y., Thomas D.C. 2020. Conceptualizing Cultural Intelligence. In: *Cultural Intelligence in the World of Work. Springer Series in Emerging Cultural Perspectives in Work, Organizational, and Personnel Studies.* Springer, Cham

Mejovsek, M. 2013. *Scientific research methods in social sciences*. Jastrebarsko: Naklada Slap

Milardovic, A. 2010. *Global Village*. Zagreb: Center for Political Science Research.

Nakic, M., Sosic, D., Diklic, J. (2019). 'INFLUENCE OF SOCIAL NETWORKS ON CIVIC ACTIVISM AND DEVELOPMENT OF CIVIC SOCIETY', *South Eastern European Journal of Communication*, I(1), str. 105-105. https://hrcak.srce.hr/233063 (Accessed: 26.10.2020)

NSE. 2020. 'Media Consumption Behavior'. https://www.research.net/r/interestmedia (Accessed: 26.6.2020)

Paska, I. (2019). 'Digital Media Environments and their Implications: Instagram', *In medias res*, 8(15), str. 2347-2364. https://hrcak.srce.hr/225457 (Accessed: 26.10.2020)

Penava Brekalo, Z. 2010. The Social Cognitive Theory of Personality in the Context of Personal Marketing. *Ekonomski vjesnik/ Econviews: Review of Contemporary Entrepreneurship, Business, and Economic Issues*, *23*(1), 240-246.

Salomon, D. 2013. Moving on from Facebook: Using Instagram to connect with undergraduates and engage in teaching and learning. *College & Research Libraries News*, *74*(8), 408-412. URL: https://www.researchgate.net/publication/275043870_Moving_on_from_Facebook_Using_Instagram_to_Connect_with_Undergraduates_and_Engage_in_Teaching_and_Learning (accessed: 21.9.2020)

Schwartz, S. 2012. Does Facebook Influence Well-Being and Self-Esteem Among Early Adolescents?. URL: https://sophia.stkate.edu/cgi/viewcontent.cgi?article=1091&context=msw_papers (accessed: 22.9.2020)

Stern, L. A., & Taylor, K. 2007. Social networking on Facebook. *Journal of the Communication, Speech & Theatre Association of North Dakota*, *20*(2007), 9-20.

Thomas, D. C. (2006) 'Domain and Development of Cultural Intelligence: The Importance of Mindfulness', *Group & Organization Management*, 31(1), pp. 78–99. doi: 10.1177/1059601105275266.

Zlof, K., Herljevic, Z., & Hadzic, S. (2014). Journalists' perception of the importance of social networks in the production of media contents', *Media, culture and public relations*, 5(1), 17-29. https://hrcak.srce.hr/122433 (Accessed: 26.10.2020)

COMBINING DISTRIBUTED AND CENTRALISED APPROACHES TO DEVELOP A HYBRID METHODOLOGY FOR DATA MANAGEMENT IN HEALTHCARE

Christos Kontzinos[1], Panagiotis Kapsalis, Spiros Mouzakitis, Michael Kontoulis, Ourania Markaki, Dimitris Askounis, Haralampos Karanikas[2,3], Alexandros Christodoulakis[3] and Panagiotis Dimitrakopoulos[3]

[1]*Decision Support Systems Lab, National Technical University of Athens, Athens, Greece*

[2]*Department of Computer Science and Biomedical Informatics, University of Thessaly, Athens, Greece*

[3]*Datamed SA, Athens, Greece*

ABSTRACT

In the 21st century, the combination of rapid technological developments as well as the adoption of emerging technologies has impacted almost every area of everyday life. These developments have even affected domains that traditionally operate without the help of Information and Communication technologies (ICT) but now see an increase in digitization of their processes. Healthcare is one of those domains that is being revolutionized via the emergence of the e-health and m-health paradigms as well as the automation of medical processes, robotics, and Internet of Things (IoT) medical devices and sensors. These developments, apart from modernizing healthcare and providing quality-of-life solutions to both healthcare practitioners and patients, have also led to an increase in the availability of digital medical data, which are nowadays being structured in Electronic Health Records (EHRs). EHRs contain various health data about a patient and are the basis for the development and implementation of various innovative solutions in healthcare. Such solutions mainly aim to address some of the current shortcomings of EHRs such as the centralized storage, which makes them vulnerable to mass hacker attacks as well as the lack of interoperability among various medical standards that are used to structure EHRs, which makes it hard to manage and share them across different healthcare providers. The scope of this publication is to introduce blockchain technology as a potential solution to the aforementioned challenges and present a novel methodology and architecture that have been developed to be implemented in a healthcare application. The methodology presented in this paper leverages both blockchain and centralized databases, making it a hybrid approach but aims to set the basis for developing blockchain-powered healthcare solutions for data management. Under that context and the need to combine blockchain with centralized databases, the security parameters of the system are also tailored to work specifically with that kind of approach. The end-goal of the methodology and architecture presented in this publication is to give patients ownership of their data, help them manage and share them as they see fit, while at the same time keeping in mind that large healthcare providers must have access to the same information in a secure manner for the well-being of their patients. It is considered that this hybrid approach offers a well-tailored solution for both stakeholders.

KEYWORDS

Blockchain, Healthcare, Electronic Health Record, Key Management, Consensus, Hash

1. INTRODUCTION

In the fast evolving 21st century, the rapid development of innovative Information and Communication Technologies (ICT) has revolutionized almost every aspect and task of everyday life. In addition, automation and the introduction of the Internet of Things have introduced and generated in a similar way a wealth of digital data. The aforementioned, combined with the rapid increase in database capacity as well as innovative storage and processing technologies, create opportunities for digitization in various sectors through the development of ICT-powered applications. Especially in health, automation of medical examinations, robotics and self-diagnosis have already led to improved population care, better patient experience and the production of large amounts of medical data. Medical or health data are defined as any data relating to health conditions, the effects of the reproductive process, the causes of death and the general quality of life for an individual or a population group (Segen 2006). Such data are collected when individuals interact with healthcare applications or hospital administration systems and usually include a record of the services offered, the conditions under which they were provided and the clinical outcomes or other information related to those medical services (Tzourakis 1996). Medical data are nowadays increasingly organized and structured through Electronic Health Records (EHRs), which emerged as a direct result of the aforementioned developments and aim to leverage the opportunities afforded by the increasing digitization in the health sector. EHRs are the systematic collection of patient health information in electronic form (Gunter and Terry 2005) and include data such as demographics, medical history, allergies and medication, laboratory test results, vital signs and personal statistics among others (Top Mobile Trends 2014). EHRs can in theory be shared among digital applications of different healthcare organizations (hospitals, insurance companies, etc.) and individuals (doctors, patients, etc.) and are considered to be a critical factor in improving the intelligence and quality of medical procedures (Yue et al. 2016), as well as reducing healthcare costs (Kemkarl and Dahikar 2012). In fact, the exchange of medical data between different EHR systems can provide a better understanding of public health standards and trends (Ge et al. 2013), which can in turn offer better quality of care (Jothi et al. 2015), personalized referrals for patients (Zhang et al. 2017) and increased efficiency in health care provision both at a national and global level. The structuring of medical data for EHR systems is achieved through medical standards, some of the most popular ones being Health Level 7 or HL7 (HL7 International 1989), Fast Healthcare Interoperability Resources or FHIR (HL7 International 2018), and openEHR (openEHR Foundation 2018).

Currently, the biggest challenge for the widespread adoption of EHR systems is finding ways to collect, store and analyze sensitive health data without raising concerns about the patients' privacy (Clifton et al. 2013). According to a report produced by the ONA General Council (ONA General Council 2016), the lack of adequate measures to safeguard patient privacy has led to many breaches of EHR systems, which leave patients exposed to profiling and exploitation by malicious users. Such violations, in addition to impacting patient care, usually have financial and legal consequences for health care providers as well (Peterson et al. 2016). In fact, securing EHRs, while also keeping them shareable among different applications is hard to achieve with traditional approaches and the consequences of breaches in such systems are a strong disincentive to the exchange of data between different providers (Barrows and Clayton 1996). Another major obstacle to the exchange of medical data is the lack of agreement regarding technical requirements and specifications on the infrastructure that will be used. In addition, most healthcare systems require either a centralized data source or bulk data transmission from one system to another. However, centralized data storages increases the risk of massive eavesdropping and malicious attacks, while bulk sending medical data requires organizations to authorize the use and processing of data to other healthcare providers, which may breach their terms of services with the patients depending on the data usage and processing activities by the third party.

In conclusion, although EHRs offer many possibilities, due to the aforementioned challenges, they have not been widely applied in the healthcare domain. One technology that can provide solutions and reduce or even eliminate the disadvantages of existing systems and applications is blockchain. Blockchain is based on distributed data storage, which can reduce the cost of implementing new systems, while the security it offers is greater than that provided by existing solutions. In this context, the purpose of this study is to explore existing applications of blockchain in healthcare and most importantly present a hybrid methodology that combines blockchain and traditional databases for the effective and secure management, sharing and processing of sensitive medical data. This methodology is designed as part of the Impilo research project, which aims to develop an innovative solution for the healthcare domain, building on blockchain and social media practices. The platform will consist of a blockchain ledger, which will act as a healthcare data repository for the construction and retrieval of EHRs, as well as the Impilo application, which will offer added-value services on top of the blockchain ledger and manage the interactions and data transactions among doctors and patients.

Section 1 introduces the scope of this paper by presenting the current situation and challenges arising from the lack of suitable technical solutions in the healthcare domain. Section 2 includes a short state-of-the-art analysis regarding current blockchain approaches in healthcare. Section 3 presents in detail, Impilo's methodology for healthcare data management that is based on blockchain. Finally, Section 4 concludes the document and details steps for future work.

2. RELATED WORK

The main scope of this section is to present blockchain-based research approaches that have been designed and developed to provide efficient and secure exchange of medical information between patients, physicians and other organizations. Peterson et al. (2016) designed a hybrid approach to developing a healthcare blockchain that makes use of the rising FHIR standard for structuring medical information. In this system, the network nodes represent patient data transactions and describe the addition of a resource (i.e., a specific medical information) to the official patient file. Transactions, however, do not include the actual medical information record document. Instead, they point to where the FHIR resources are stored via URL pointers, and that is where the system hybridizes between the blockchain and the central databases. The way the system is structured allows healthcare providers to maintain functional control of their data as it maintains sensitive patient data outside of the blockchain. Yue et al. (2016) developed a blockchain-based architecture that allows the patients to own, control, and share their medical data with ease and security. The system collects the patients' medical data from a variety of systems (medical records information systems, data analysis algorithms, etc.) and allows them to manage them in a unified manner via a personalized data portal. The data is stored in a private blockchain cloud, which ensures, through various cryptographic techniques that they cannot be accessed or altered by anyone, including physicians and patients, that have no authorization on a given patient's medical record. MedRec (Ekblaw et al. 2016) is a decentralized blockchain-based electronic health record system that provides patients with a complete and immutable medical diary that allows them to have easy access to their medical information regardless of their healthcare provider(s). By utilizing the inherent features of blockchain, MedRec offers accessibility, confidentiality and secure data exchange, which are critical issues when managing sensitive medical data. Users of the system can view and validate themselves the authenticity and history of their data and manage access rights to it, while the system has a variety of APIs that allow it to integrate with existing databases of various health care providers. In general, it can be observed in the respective research literature that the general case of blockchain use in healthcare is within the framework of the techniques already presented. In fact, in a relevant publication by Gordon and Catalini (2018), all the ways and methodologies for patient-driven healthcare interoperability were studied and presented, based on existing and emerging technologies, aiming to improve the management of medical information in healthcare. For blockchain-based systems, the general case is the one that has been presented in the current section. It is therefore concluded that in the field of health the use of blockchain is mainly intended to add a layer of security to patients' sensitive data, allow them to manage access rights on them, and facilitate communication between different organizations that provide medical services to patients. In the general case, the actual patient data is stored either in centralized databases of various healthcare organization or in distributed data wallets. However, the blockchain in these systems helps patients verify the authenticity of their information and view their medical history through a trusted digital trail.

3. BLOCKCHAIN-BASED METHODOLOGY FOR DATA MANAGEMENT IN HEALTHCARE

This section presents Impilo's blockchain-based methodology for data management in healthcare and describes not only structural (block structure, system architecture) but also security parameters (hash function, key management, consensus) of the projected system. The main differentiation between Impilo and the approaches presented in the previous section lie in the fact that Impilo will develop the blockchain ledger based on the new Hyperledger Iroha platform (Hyperledger 2019) that is specifically tailored for development of non-cryptocurrency data management solutions and has built-in algorithms that deal with various shortcomings and bottlenecks of other platforms.

3.1 Hybrid Methodology for Data Management

3.1.1 Block Structure

This section, taking into account the respective literature and the requirements of the projected Impilo platform, presents the structure of any given block of the Impilo blockchain as well as the information that will be contained within (see Figure 1). In general, the structure of the Impilo blockchain is based on Merkle trees. In computer science, a Merkle tree or hash tree is a tree that labels leaf nodes with the cryptographic hash of a block of data and non-leaf nodes with the cryptographic hash of its child nodes. Merkle trees allow for the efficient and secure verification of the contents of large data structures (Becker 2008). In the Impilo system, the nodes of the Merkle tree represent patient data transactions and describe the addition of a resource (i.e., specific medical information) to the official patient record. The hashes of all transactions in a block contribute to the hash of the Merkle root, or block header, which contains the following metadata used to validate each new block: the hash of the block, the hash of the previous block (for validation purposes), the subscriber signatures of each node that contributed to the block (to ensure that the block will remain valid after being assembled by the respective miner) and the miner elections (in which each node that contributed to the block is required to provide a random number encrypted with the node's private key to prepare for the next miner election).

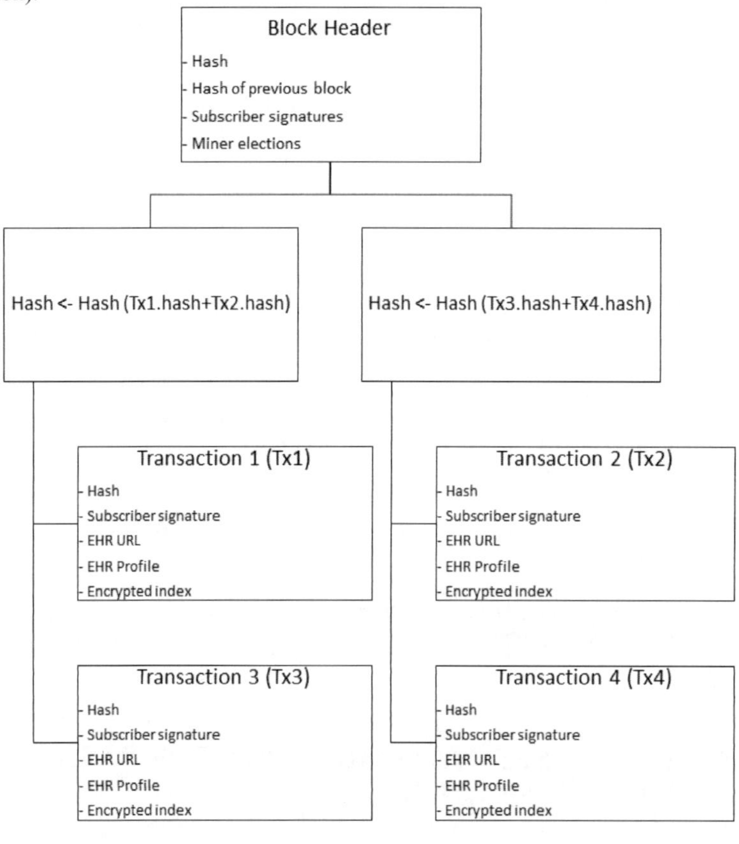

Figure 1. Block structure

In this approach, a medical transaction stored in a blockchain includes the following information (see Figure 1): the transaction hash (although the resource is not inserted into the blockchain, its contents can be verified using the transaction hash during retrieval), the signature of origin (digital signature of the source node), the URL of the EHR (link to the actual location of the EHR resource where the data is located), the profile of the EHR (URI of the EHR profile to which this resource corresponds) and, finally, an encrypted index that allows data to be discovered without leaking file information. Although the block itself does not contain the actual data, it must provide search and tracking capabilities, as well as a data access mechanism once the appropriate transactions have been found. External entities, with the appropriate permissions, can query the blockchain, using keywords in the encrypted index field of the transaction. These keywords can be searched despite the fact that they are encrypted to avoid data leakage (Ioannidis 2005).

3.1.2 System Architecture

In Impilo patient data will be stored in an external database, as previously mentioned, while blockchain will be used to validate and store transactions. This sub-section presents the high-level architecture of the projected system (see Figure 2). The Impilo high-end architecture consists of three individual elements. Firstly, the client is the Impilo application through which users will have access to the various functions that will be developed, the blockchain database and the central database. Following that, the blockchain repository will be used to validate and store transactions related to a patient's health data. A sufficient number of computer nodes will be employed for storing the Impilo blockchain in a distributed manner so that users' personal (portable and non-portable) devices are not burdened with storing the entire chain, but at the same time maintain access to it. This also increases the likelihood of some malicious action being detected. Finally, the central database is where the actual medical information will be stored. To enhance system security, the data will be encrypted to preserve their integrity and prevent their processing by third-party malicious users.

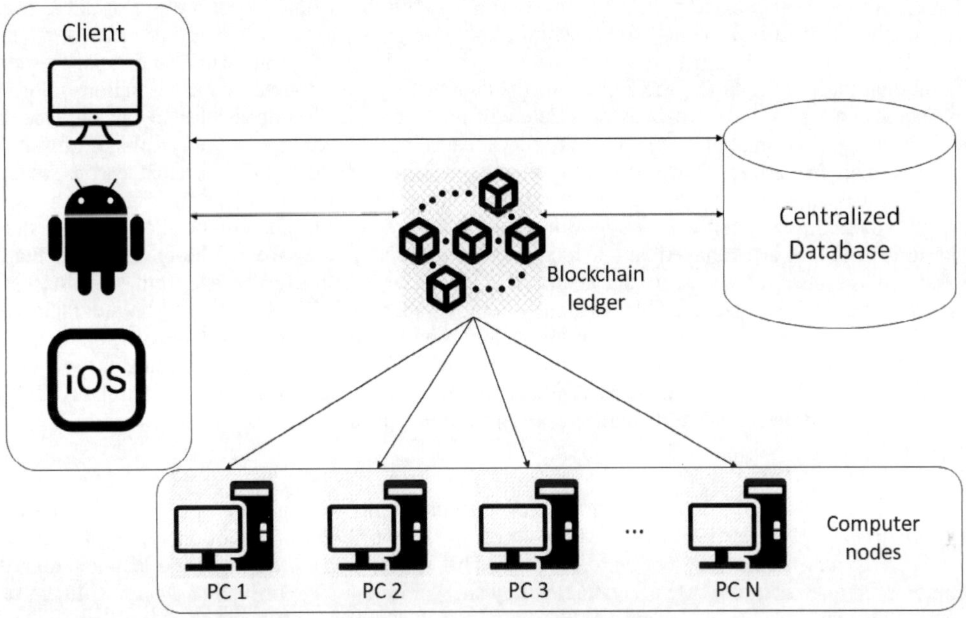

Figure 2. System architecture

The operation of the system can be made clear through the following example. Suppose an Impilo user wants to save his blood tests in his medical file. He logs in to the Impilo application with his credentials and performs the actions required to store new information in his medical file. The Impilo client communicates with the central database and stores the information in the patient's file. The blockchain ledger communicates with both the client and the database to generate the hash that will be needed to store the transaction details in a block. After storing the new information, the client and the database communicate with the blockchain, verify that the hash is the same in both of them and if it is, the transaction details are stored in a blockchain block. It is worth noting that to increase overall security, patient data in the central database will be hashed and the decryption key will be the users' password with which they access the Impilo application. This means that only users can decrypt their data when accessing the application and in case of a malicious attack on the system, the attacking party will have to know the passwords of the patients in order to receive the correct information.

3.2 Hash Function, Key Management and Consensus Approach

In general, blockchain systems use encryption techniques to ensure the integrity of their content and to detect breaches. For increased data protection, Merkle trees are used to build blocks. In this case, any change in the system state leads to a new hash value of the root node. This way, all nodes in the system are notified of the change in a block and can approve or reject the change. If a system state change is accepted by its nodes, it is attached to the network in the form of a new immutable block (Mohanta et al. 2019). In the following sub-sections, Impilo's following security parameters will be presented: selected hash function, key management system and consensus algorithm. It should be noted that the Impilo application will be built on the Hyperledger Iroha platform that works with specific options for hash functions, key management systems and consensus algorithms. As such and given the platform requirements, an assessment of various blockchain platforms was performed to identify the one that best suits the needs of the projected application. Hyperledger Iroha was selected because it is mainly used for digital data management, has a robust permission system, gives users the ability to manage access rights to their data based on predefined commands and is the easiest one to set up in a real-life scenario. As such, the security parameters described in the following sub-section follow the general guidelines of Hyperledger Iroha, tailored though for a healthcare blockchain system.

3.2.1 Hash Chains

A hash chain is the sequential application of a cryptographic hash function to a piece of data. In computer security, a hash chain is a method for generating multiple keys from a single key or password. These keys can be used once each to gain access to the data concerned. A hash function can also be applied sequentially to additional pieces of data to keep records of the data history. Cryptographic hash functions allow the hash to be calculated easily. However, it is considered difficult - practically impossible - to calculate the data from which it emerged. Hash chains are similar to blockchains, as in both cases cryptographic hash functions are used to connect two nodes. However, a blockchain generally aims to support distributed consensus across a network and incorporates a set of rules for encapsulating data and related permissions for accessing and managing them. In blockchain, hash algorithms are used to determine the unique state of the system at any given time. The blocks are linked data ledgers, while, as mentioned above, the block header includes a hash pointing to the previous block of the chain. The blocks are connected to each other via hashes, which represent data within the previous blocks along with their addresses. The best-known cryptographic functions are MD5, SHA-1, SHA-2 and SHA-3 that are widely used in various projects. However, under the scope of the Impilo project, the BLAKE2 hash function is employed. BLAKE2 is a cryptographic hash function that is faster than MD5, SHA-1, SHA-2 and SHA-3, and as secure as the latest SHA-3 standard. BLAKE2 has been adopted by many projects due to its high speed, safety and simplicity.

3.2.2 Key Management

Blockchain employs public key cryptography or asymmetric cryptography, which was invented in the late 1970s (Diffie and Hellman 1976) and provides a completely different model of encryption key management from earlier symmetric key encryption methods. The basic idea is that the sender and recipient do not share a common secret key as in the case of symmetric key encryption but have different keys for different functions. Specifically, each user has two encryption keys: one is called a private key and the other a public key. These two keys (private and public) are mathematically related to each other. If one is used to encrypt a message, then the other is used to decrypt it. The success of this type of cryptographic algorithm is based on the fact that knowledge of the public encryption key does not in any way allow the calculation of the private encryption key. The public key can be disclosed to third parties, and is used to encrypt data, while the private key is used to decrypt it (Stallings 1998). The blockchain security model assumes the existence of public key encryption. Identities, including user identities and transactions, are derived from public key certificates. Therefore, secure key management is essential for every blockchain project. As already mentioned, the Impilo project will specifically use Hyperledger Iroha, which is a platform for developing blockchain applications. Therefore, the management of public and private keys will follow the instructions of this platform's documentation.

3.2.3 Consensus Algorithm

The role of consensus in blockchain systems is to ensure that all non-faulty network users perform the same system status updates in the order in which the events that changed the status occurred. Achieving consensus on decentralized systems, such as the Impilo blockchain, which receive asynchronous events and are subject to "Byzantine Fault Tolerance" is a common challenge in many applications. The YAC (Yet Another Consensus) algorithm (Muratov et al. 2018) will be used to reach consensus on the Impilo system. YAC is a practical decentralized consensus algorithm, which attempts to solve traditional problems in Byzantine Fault Tolerance, such as inefficient message transmission and the fact that the system is dependent on "powerful leaders". Powerful leaders in a blockchain system (i.e., users who occupy many of its nodes) make sense in a cryptocurrency blockchain. However, a medical blockchain must ensure independence of users from the "leaders" of the system. YAC is actually used to provide Byzantine consent to the Hyperledger Iroha Blockchain project and empirical results show that this solution achieves low system inertia, which leads to high transaction efficiency.

YAC operates in the following way. Initially, typical YAC participants include the client, peer and ordering service. Every client is essentially a user who has a public key registered in the blockchain. The client's role lies in generating transactions and sending them to the ordering service. The client is also able to develop smart contracts that are used to define the rights of other users on his/her data as well as to query the other peers. A peer is one of the network participants who are responsible for validating and reaching an agreement regarding the transactions that have transpired and their storage in the system's blocks. Peers maintain a complete digital trail of transactions in the system and validate new block proposals. Finally, the ordering service is a unit that receives a set of transactions and generates new block proposals. A block proposal contains a list of transactions, which must be accepted by the peers.

For the application of YAC in the Impilo system, the following set of rules will be followed to better explain the consensus algorithm. Firstly, the client will be known to the peers and each client can interact with a specific list of peers. In addition, Impilo users will be incentivized to store their keys on a device, such as their mobile phone. Finally, the client will have the rights to execute a specific subset of orders/smart contracts, such as creation of a transaction. The high-level operating system flow can be described by the following steps. Initially, a client creates a transaction through orders that he/she has the right to execute and signs it with his/her private key. The client then sends the transaction to a peer, who receives it, validates it to ensure it is in the correct form (as this is defined by the system) and transfers it to the ordering service. Finally, the ordering service forms a block proposal, which contains a list of transactions that will potentially be added to the blockchain. The block proposal can only be formed if the ordering service has collected a certain number of transactions or after a specific time period and is then sent to all system peers. Following that, the peers exchange votes through the system and finally decide on the new block. In essence, at this stage, each peer must calculate whether the block proposal (set of transactions) sent by the ordering service is valid. The block is created by the peer and contains a suggested hash, the transactions of the block proposal and the data required for the cryptographic validation of the blockchain. The suggested hash defines a unique proposition for each transaction round as it represents the peer's intention to store a set of transactions in the chain. These hashes are an integral part, as it is possible that different peers calculate different blocks from a proposal. Next, peers must send in their vote via a message that contains the aforementioned hashes as well as a signature that verifies the peer. The order in which peers will vote for a block hash is determined via a permutation function. During the voting process, the message is sent to the first peer of the list and then to the next one either after the first sends a vote, or after a certain period of time. The process continues until the network receives a valid message accepting or rejecting the changes. Network consensus requires at least 2/3 of the network. When a peer receives the majority of the network it transmits an acceptance message to the others. Finally, the peer to whom the transaction was originally sent saves the block in its local copy.

4. CONCLUSION

The purpose of this publication was the analysis of the research field regarding the use of blockchain in healthcare, as well as the presentation of a novel methodology and architecture that have been developed to facilitate data management in the domain. Initially, the relevant literature studied supports the application of blockchain technology in conjunction with popular medical standards and traditional approaches for structuring medical information. In the technical part of the publication, research approaches on the construction of medical data via blockchain were presented and then the methodology and architecture that Impilo will follow for the construction of medical information were described. The network on the one hand benefits from the blockchain properties for security and stability and on the other hand is flexible in the requirements of the users by leveraging central databases that can facilitate faster data transactions. The last section of the publication describes the techniques that will be used to secure health data and, more specifically, the hash functions, key management and network consensus. Overall, it can be said that the application of blockchain technology in areas other than cryptocurrencies is of particular value. This is evident from the ever-increasing research interest in blockchain, in areas where it has traditionally not been implemented. Especially in the health sector, where Impilo operates, blockchain may create more reliable and resilient networks, while facilitating seamless communication between the various stakeholders (doctors, patients, hospitals, etc.). The next steps of the Impilo research project include the development of the system and its pilot application to specific healthcare providers and a sample of patients.

ACKNOWLEDGEMENT

The IMPILO project is funded by the Greek operational program "Competitiveness, Entrepreneurship, Innovation" - EPANEK (2014–2020), in the national action: "RESEARCH - CREATE - INNOVATE", with project code T1EDK-01382.

REFERENCES

Barrows R.C. Jr and Clayton P.D., 1996, Privacy, confidentiality, and electronic medical records. *Journal of the American Medical Informatics Association*. No 3, pp 139–148.

Becker G., 2008, *Merkle signature schemes, merkle trees and their cryptanalysis*. Ruhr-University Bochum, Tech. Rep.

Clifton C. et al, 2004, Privacy-preserving data integration and sharing. *Proceedings of the 9th ACM SIGMOD Workshop on Research Issues in Data Mining and Knowledge Discovery*. Paris, pp 19–26.

Diffie W. and Hellman M.E., 1976, Multiuser cryptographic techniques. *Proceedings of the June 7-10, 1976, national computer conference and exposition.*

Ekblaw A. et al, A case study for blockchain in healthcare: “MedRec” prototype for electronic health records and medical research data. *Proceedings of IEEE Open & Big Data Conference*. Washington, DC, pp 13.

Ge Y. et al, 2013, Patient-controlled sharing of medical imaging data across unaffiliated healthcare organizations. *Journal of the American Medical Informatics Association*. No 20, pp 157–163.

Gordon W.J. and Catalini C., 2018, Blockchain technology for healthcare: Facilitating the transition to patient-driven interoperability. *Computational and structural biotechnology journal*. No 16, pp 224–230.

Gunter T.D. and Terry N.P., 2005, The emergence of national electronic health record architectures in the United States and Australia: Models, costs, and questions. *Journal of medical Internet research*. No 7(1), e3.

HL7 International, 1989, *Health level 7. 1st ed. HL7*. Available at: http://www.hl7.org/implement/standards/.

HL7 International, 2018, *Fast Health Interoperability Resources (FHIR). 4th ed. HL7*. Available at: https://www.hl7.org/fhir/.

Hyperledger, 2019, *Hyperledger Iroha documentation*. Available at: https://iroha.readthedocs.io/en/latest/.

Ioannidis J., 2005, *Applied cryptography and network security*. ACNS, New York, NY.

Jothi N. et al, Data mining in healthcare – A review. *Procedia computer science*. No 72, pp 306–313.

Kemkarl O.S. and Dahikar D.P.B., Can electronic medical record systems transform health care? Potential health benefits, savings, and cost using latest advancements in ict for better interactive healthcare learning. *International Journal of Computer Science & Communication Networks*. No 2, pp 453–455.

Mohanta B.K. et al, 2019, Blockchain technology: A survey on applications and security privacy challenges. *Internet of Things*. No 8, pp 100–107.

Muratov F. et al, 2018, BFT consensus algorithm for blockchain. *arXiv preprint arXiv:1809.00554*.

Ontario Nurses’ Association General Council, 2016, *Members and patient privacy: Be aware and beware!* ONA, Toronto. Available at: https://www.ona.org/.

openEHR Foundation, 2018, *OpenEHR. 3rd ed.* Available at: https://www.openehr.org/

Peterson K. et al, 2016, A blockchain based approach to health information exchange networks. *Proceedings of NIST Workshop Blockchain Healthcare*. Gaithersburg, pp 1–10.

Segen J.C., 2006, *Concise dictionary of modern medicine*. McGraw-Hill Education, New York.

Stallings W., 1998, *Cryptography and network security: Principles and practice. 2nd ed.* Prentice-Hall Inc, Upper Saddle River, NJ.

Top Mobile Trends, 2014, *Mobile tech contributions to healthcare and patient experiences*. Available at: http://topmobiletrends.com/ mobile-technology-contributions-patient-experience-parmar/.

Tzourakis M.C., 1996, The healthcare industry and data quality. *Proceedings of the 1996 International Conference on Information Quality*. pp 87–93.

Yue X. et al, 2016. Healthcare data gateways: Found healthcare intelligence on blockchain with novel privacy risk control. *Journal of medical systems*. No 40, pp 218.

Zhang Y. et al, 2017, iDoctor: Personalized and professionalized medical recommendations based on hybrid matrix factorization. *Future Generation Computer Systems*. No 66, pp 30–35.

THE IMPACT OF CHANGING THE GRANULARITY OF PREFERENCE-INTENSITY INFORMATION ON THE ONLINE COMPENSATION ELECTION[1]

Roumen Vragov[1] and Nanda Kumar[2]
[1]*Queensborough Community College, CUNY, 22205 56th Ave, Bayside, NY 11364, USA*
[2]*Baruch College, CUNY, 1 Bernard Baruch Way, New York, NY 10036, USA*

ABSTRACT

This study investigates the effect of a change in the granularity of preference intensity information available to voters on their voting behavior in an online referendum with options to express preference intensities and receive compensation. We find that a decrease in the granularity of the real preference intensity information about others does not affect voting behavior and the referendum's compensation outcomes We discuss the implications of these results and possible future directions for research.

KEYWORDS

Information Granularity, E-Government, Digital Voting Mechanisms, Group Decision-Making, Public Goods, Semi-Field Experiment

1. INTRODUCTION

The Compensation election is a referendum-like new electronic voting mechanism that allows participants to express the intensity of their preferences and also to get compensated in case the alternative they vote for is not chosen. The intuition behind this mechanism has been expressed as early as the beginning of the 19th century by Wicksell (1896/1967) who observes that there might be a way to improve the results of referenda for every referendum participant if the voting mechanism allows some way in which the winners in the referendum can compensate the losers. Jumping to modern times, Smith (2004) provides a detailed description of procedure that can support such a referendum in practice. Here is an example of how the procedure works. Suppose that citizens A, B, and C are considering building a public stadium in their small community and they all start with the same initial endowment of 10[2]. The endowment can represent income, property and anything else of value that the individual possesses. Suppose further that the net financial effect of building the stadium to A is 2, to B is 2 and to C is -10. If the citizens vote to build a stadium using majority voting, A & B will both vote "Yes" because they gain from the proposal and C will vote "No" because s/he looses. The stadium will be built and that would result in A gaining 2 for a total final endowment of 12; B gaining 2 for a total final endowment of 12, and C loosing 10 for a total final endowment of 0. The net social gain: 2+2-10=-6 is negative and so the outcome does not increase or at least keep the social value unchanged. It could be argued also that the outcome is unjust since the citizens started on an equal financial footing but ended up with a skewed income distribution. Under the procedure proposed by Smith it is possible that A votes 1, B votes 1, and C votes -6. Since the sum of votes is negative, the stadium will not be built but C has to pay 1 to A and 1 to B because the alternative they voted for is not chosen. In this case A gains 1, B gains 1, and C gains 4. The net social gain is 6, and the final income distribution will be less skewed than under majority voting.

[1] This study was funded by a PSC-CUNY research grant and the Eugene Lang faculty research program

[2] A specific currency is not selected on purpose to keep the example more general.

A laboratory test of an electronic implementation of the above procedure is presented in Oprea et. al. (2007) and an experimental test of an online version of the mechanism is presented in Vragov & Kumar (2019). The laboratory test of the mechanism in small groups of participants with synchronous voting has shown that mechanism participants tend to reveal a fraction of their preference intensity in voting. This, combined with the compensation procedure, has resulted in improved social value and in more equitable voting outcomes among subjects in the laboratory (Oprea et. al, 2007). Vragov & Kumar (2019) find that the online version of the mechanism needs adjustment of some of the design parameters in order for the mechanism to perform satisfactorily. In this study we decide to explore one of the factors that affects the performance of any group decision-making mechanism: the amount of information that individual participants have about their decision-making environment (Blackwell, 1951, Ballou et. al., 2010, Chengalur-Smith et. al., 1999). We specifically focus on information granularity and see how changes in the level of detail of the information provided to participants in the referendum mechanism about the preference intensity of others affect individual voting behavior. We are choosing to study this issue because we think that under naturally occurring circumstances citizens will most likely have less granular information about other individuals' real preference intensities than that provided to the subjects in Oprea et. al.'s laboratory experiment and Vragov & Kumar's semi-field experiment. Thus we test the performance of a mechanism that is a little more realistic in terms of implementation than the ones tested in the two studies mentioned above. We consider this to be an important policy and design question since a long stream of previous literature on data-driven information dashboards has shown that the amount of information citizens receive has an impact on their actions (Matheus et. al, 2018, Abelson et. al., 2004, Bertot et. al., 2010). Thus our main research question is: "How would a decrease in the granularity of preference intensity information about other participants affect individual voting behavior and each individual's gains from participating in the referendum?"

To answer this question we use design science theory and a semi-field experiment. Vragov & Kumar's study acts as our baseline and our semi-field experiment represents a new treatment in which the granularity of the information each individual receives about the real preference intensities of other referendum participants is lower. We find that a decrease in the information granularity of the preference intensity information that subjects have at the beginning of the referendum does not have a significant impact on individual voting behavior. This is good news in terms of practical implications since it shows that even if participants do not possess as detailed information about the preference intensities of others as in the laboratory study, their behavior and earnings remain relatively unaffected.

2. LITERATURE REVIEW

Information granularity is one of the important dimensions of information. The term first originated in the data-mining literature to describe the level of detail contained in a database or a data warehouse. With the help of a database tool managers can drill down the data starting from the very general level (for example annual sales in a country) to a very detailed level (monthly sales in a specific region of this country) or vice versa (Baltzan, 2017). In general the ability to see information at various levels of granularity is expected to improve data analysis and the ability of a manager to make better business decisions (Peng et. al, 2007, Chengalur-Smith et. al., 1999) and also improve board oversight (Ballou, et. al., 2010).

More detailed studies on the effect of granularity on decision-making are lacking. For any decision-making task the background information provided has to be at the appropriate level of detail but it is not clear how to determine which level of detail is the most appropriate. For example Peng et, al. (2007) discuss situations when, because of search costs, decision-makers are not always able to reach the appropriate level of detail with drill down which might result in suboptimal choices.

Information granularity and information transparency have also been discussed in the electronic government literature as they relate to the implementation and usage of information dashboards for smart cities (Matheus et. al., 2018). The general consensus is that an increase in information transparency and granularity can improve citizen engagement (Abelson et. al., 2004), can help fight government corruption (Bertot et. al., 2010), and can improve government decision-making (Dawes & Helbig, 2010)

There is also a considerable stream of research in the accounting literature related to public disclosure of financial information (see Banerjee & Maier, 2016, for a review). The articles in this research stream describe situations in which groups of individuals or firms face uncertainty about the decision environment combined with uncertainty about the strategies of other individuals or firms. The situation requires some sort of coordination between these individuals or firms in order for the optimal outcome to be realized. The articles show both theoretically and experimentally that the results of such situations could be influenced both positively and negatively when more information is provided to the individuals or firms. In some cases, when individuals are given more public information, they place more importance on the public information than on their private information, which results in a coordination failure and sub-optimal outcomes. Such strategic situations are characterized by multiple equilibria, some of which are better and some of which are worse after the introduction of more information, and it is impossible to determine a priori which of these equilibria will occur (Anctil et. al, 2004). The referendum mechanism described here shares some of the general features of the situations modeled in this stream of literature because 1) there is uncertainty about individual preference intensities of others and the outcome of the referendum, 2) each individual receives private information (the individual's personal preference intensity for each alternative) and also public information (the distribution of preference intensities of other individuals before the referendum, and the results of the referendum) and 3) individuals have to implicitly coordinate their bids in order to pick the better of the two alternatives. Because of these strategic features of the mechanism studies here the outcomes when changing information granularity could go either way.

3. DESIGN SCIENCE METHODOLOGY AND SOME THEORETICAL ISSUES

There is currently no widely acceptable theoretical model that can predict the effect of change in information granularity on individual voting behavior under a referendum mechanism that involves the options of expressing preference intensities and compensation. Fortunately we have an experimental baseline provided by Vragov & Kumar (2019) so we can adopt the exploratory design science approach to investigate changes in human behavior by changing only one parameter in their design and analyzing the results. The design science theoretical approach has been discussed widely in the literature (see March & Smith, 1995; Hevner et. al., 2004; Gregor, 2006; Peffers et. al., 2007; Goes, 2013, Lang et. al, 2016). Under this approach theoretical concepts and findings from the literature are used to guide the discussion of theoretical relationships among variables of interest that structure our voting mechanism design. The discussion is used to present plausible working hypotheses, which are more akin to open research questions than theoretical predictions, to indicate that the outcome is exploratory and could very well go either way. The real utility of this approach is in the practical implications of its findings since they increase our knowledge about a mechanisms that could readily be applied in practice to solve real problems (e.g. designing a new airplane is so complex that the effect of every feature cannot be predicted theoretically, however a new model airplane can be built and tested in a wind tunnel before it is used in practice on a daily basis).

Normally one would expect that in order to formulate an optimal participation strategy the individual voter would need as much information as possible about the real preference intensities of other individuals. Having less information would probably result in an individual having a harder time finding the optimal strategy. Therefore our working hypothesis is that we expect a decrease in granularity of the information available to an individual about the distribution of real preference intensities of other individuals to have a negative effect on individual earnings.

4. EXPERIMENTAL DESIGN

In our experimental design we follow exactly the procedures described in Vragov & Kumar (2019). Subjects can log in to the voting system online from any Internet-enabled computer, read the instructions, and participate in the voting process from anywhere and anytime during the day. There are four referenda per day, and the experiment lasts 5 consecutive days. After the experiment is over subjects come to our office to collect their experimental earnings. During the time of the experiment subjects are not aware of who and how many the remaining participants in the referendum are and when they make their decisions. Subjects see the results of the voting in each referendum from the first day on the second day and so on.

We also copy the experimental environment from Vragov & Kumar (2019) as much as possible. Subjects make voting decisions, which eventually determine which alternative from two possible alternatives will be chosen. Every subject *i* is assigned a preference intensity for each of the two alternatives in these four different referenda A, B, C, D that does not change from day to day. For simplicity, subject preference intensities are normalized so that if subject *i* prefers alternative 1 in referendum R{A, B, C, D}, then *i*'s preference intensity for alternative 1 is positive and *i*'s preference intensity for alternative 2 is 0. Thus a subject always has a preference intensity of 0 for one alternative and a positive preference intensity for the other alternative. The positive preference intensities for all subjects are distributed according to a normal distribution. We use the exact same draws as in Vragov & Kumar (2019)

Every subject *i* has an assigned preference intensity of v_i^K and submits a vote of b_i^K for alternative $K\in${A1, A2, B1, B2, C1, C2, D1, D2}. Subjects are allowed to vote only on one of the two alternatives in each referendum. Let's use *-K* to represent the alternative complementary to alternative *K*. The winning alternative is determined by the sum of the votes for the two alternatives in each referendum. The alternative which has a larger sum of votes is the winning alternative. In the special case of a tie, the winning alternative is chosen at random with a flip of a coin. If individual *i* votes for alternative K and W is the winning alternative, then the earnings to subject *i* in a referendum are

$$\pi_i = \begin{cases} v_i^K - b_i^K & if \quad W = K \\ v_i^{-K} + b_i^K & if \quad W = -K \end{cases} \tag{1}$$

Subjects' earnings are summed over all referenda (four per day) and all five days of the experiment and then subjects are paid their total earnings. If a subject's total is negative, then the subject receives only the experiment participation fee of $5.00.

From equation (1) it is clear that an individual's earnings are always positive as long as the individual votes for his/her preferred alternative and his/her vote is lower than his/her preference intensity (or value). The individual risks bankruptcy if s/he decides to bid above value or bid for the 0 alternative. The bid limit is equal to $9, which is the highest possible value among the value draws. Thus if a subject is consistently voting for the alternative which s/he does not prefer, the subject could still go bankrupt but is allowed to stay in the experiment until the experiment is over. All of the described features of the voting mechanism are borrowed from Vragov & Kumar (2019)

We investigate two possible levels of granularity related to the information that the mechanism participants receive about the preferences of others.

Level 1: Describing the distribution of the sum of preference intensities for both alternatives

Level 2: Describing the distribution of the preference intensities within the population.

Oprea et. al (2007) and Vragov & Kumar (2019) use Level 2 granularity. We implement Level 1 granularity and we test for treatment effects.

The referendum participants' preference intensities are drawn from a normal distribution with different means for each referendum type. There are multiple ways in which this preference intensity information can be relayed to the referendum participants. The lowest possible level of granularity is to provide information to the referendum participants only about the expected sum of all participants' preference intensities. Next follows an example of how we specify this in the instructions:

Level 1:

"The sum of all values for alternative A1 is randomly chosen between X and Y[3] and the sum of all values for alternative A2 is randomly chosen between P and Q."

The way that information is provided in the baseline study by Vragov & Kumar (2019) has a higher level of granularity. Next follows an example of how they specify this in their instructions:

Level 2:

"On average A% of the participants prefer alternative A1 and B% of the participants prefer alternative A2.

Among those who prefer A1 values are distributed as following:

- C% are between D and E
- F% are between G and H
- I% are between J and K

---

[3] Preference intensities are drawn from a Normal distribution before the experiment starts. For simplicity In the instructions we try to provide better information about the actual draws themselves rather than the distribution from which they are drawn.

Among those who prefer alternative A2 values are distributed as following:

- L% are between M and N
- O% are between P and Q
- R% are between S and T"

As you can see the information provided in Vragov & Kumar (2019) contains much more detail. The word value is used instead of preference intensity in order to make the instruction clearer to the subjects. Also notice that neither of the instructions mentions the actual distribution from which the preference intensity is drawn again with the intention to not confuse the subjects.

We plan to record the vote of each experiment participant. Using the data we are then able to calculate the earnings for each individual. To express our working hypotheses more formally we expect:

WH1: $\bar{\pi}^{Baseline} > \bar{\pi}^{Our\ Treatment}$

where π is the average of the total earnings of each individual in the respective treatment. We are also planning on counting the number of counterbids and overbids, and the proportion of real preference intensity that is revealed in each participant's bid.

We recruit subjects from the undergraduate population at a large urban university. When they log in during the first day of the experiment, they have to read the experiment instructions and take a quiz based on the instructions to make sure that they understand them (We borrow the instructions and the quiz from Vragov & Kumar, 2019) Then, they can proceed to vote in the four referenda. If subjects miss to vote during an experimental day, they cannot go back and vote for that day during any of the following days. At the end of each day subjects can see their results from previous days. After the end of the experiment, subjects can come during our office hours and collect their earnings. There are 80 subjects in the Vragov & Kumar's study and 23 subjects in our study.

5. EXPERIMENTAL RESULTS

Our main result is that there is no statistically significant difference in individual earnings between Vragov & Kumar's baseline study and our study. This means that there is not enough evidence in support of our working hypothesis that earnings in the baseline are higher than earnings in a treatment with lower granularity of information about other people's preferences.

The result can ascertained by comparing the data from the baseline treatment and our treatment.. Vragov & Kumar (2019) report 80 independent observations and we have 23 independent observations. The sample mean in the baseline is 17.18 and the sample standard deviation is 25.83. The corresponding statistics in our study are 22.53 (the sample mean) and 20.69 (the sample standard deviation). Our initial intention has been to use one-way ANOVA but our data fails the Shapiro-Wilk test for normality, so we use the Kruskal-Wallis test for difference in medians since the two samples have similarly-shaped distributions as shown in Figure 1. The p-value under the hypothesis of no difference in medians is 0.5264. We analyze the data further at the level of individual strategies. According to Oprea et. al. (2007) strategies that individuals use to game the system (i.e. counterbidding and overbidding) are not profitable in the long run, which means that they cannot be optimal strategies. Thus, we expect that a decrease in granularity of information about the real preference intensities of other individuals is likely to cause more suboptimal votes – or more overbidding and/or counterbidding. We test for differences in each individual's proportion of counterbids, overbids, revealed preference intensity and revealed false preference intensities. The results are shown in Table 1 and the data are plotted in Figures 2,3,4 and 5. We consistently use the Kruskal-Wallis test because all data failed Shapiro-Wilk's normality test but the distribution being compared had roughly the same shape. We found no significant differences in individual behavior based on these observed variables.

We find the results related to the first hypothesis surprising. Normally one would expect that providing more preference information to individuals will help individuals make better decisions which will lead to better earnings. This is not happening in the field experiment. One explanation for this result is that both levels of granularity: the one in the baseline treatment and the one in our treatment are not at the appropriate level to make a real difference in behavior and earnings, which suggest that further experimental work will be needed to find the level of detail at which significant differences in behavior and earnings emerge. From a purely practical viewpoint, however, the results are somewhat encouraging because they indicate that individual participants might not need a lot of information in order to participate effectively in this new referendum mechanism. Gathering information about other individuals' real preference intensities is costly and so the fact that having more information has no effect on results makes participation more equitable and fair since not every individual might be able to afford getting additional information.

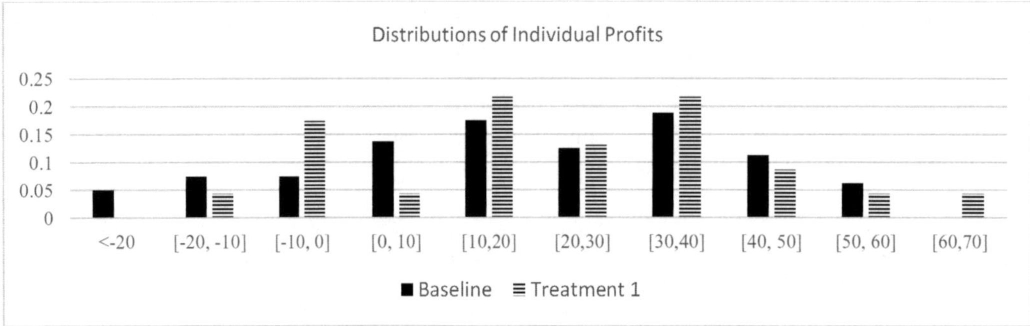

Figure 1

Table 1. Comparison of behavioral variables in the Baseline treatment with Treatment 1

	Vragov & Kumar, 2019		Current study		
Variable	Sample Mean	Sample Standard deviation	Sample Mean	Sample Standard Deviation	p-value
Proportion of Counterbids	33.64%	24.53%	33.33%	31.12%	0.7149
Proportion of Overbids	45.60%	30.96%	45.62%	33.73%	0.9526
Revealed Preference Intensity	10.7	38.08	5.34	14.29	0.2517
Revealed False Preference Intensity	8.45	23.16	6.32	18.91	0.3527

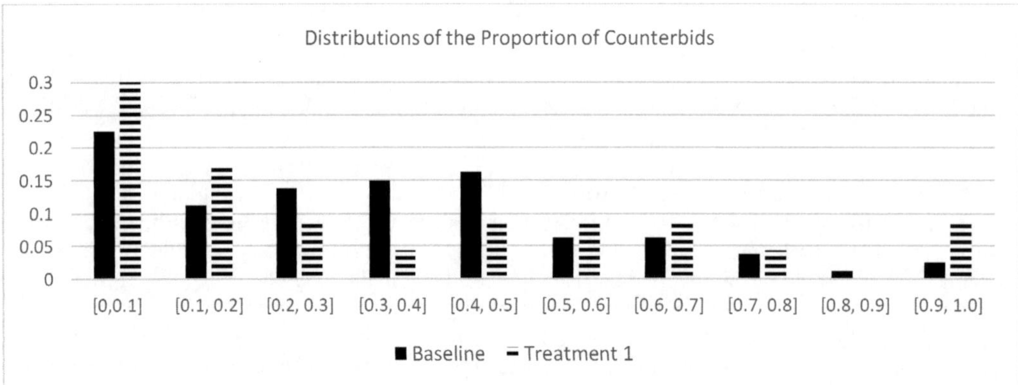

Figure 2

6. CONCLUSIONS, LIMITATIONS, AND FUTURE RESEARCH

The properties of a new electronic voting mechanism need to be explored thoroughly before such mechanism can be used in practice. Our experiment explores how a change in one feature of the mechanism, i.e. the granularity of the information individuals receive about the preference intensities of others, impacts the outcome of the mechanism. We find no significant effect on voting behavior and referendum outcomes. This arguably makes the referendum mechanism more practical since the referendum works just as well when voters have less information about the preferences of others which is a more common occurrence.

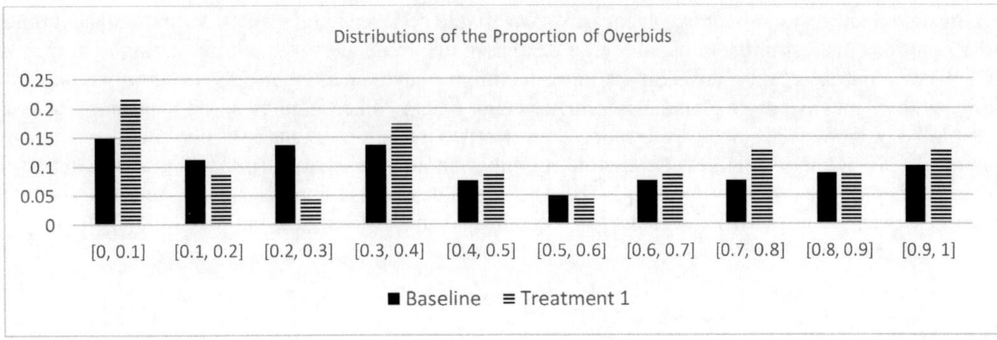

Figure 3

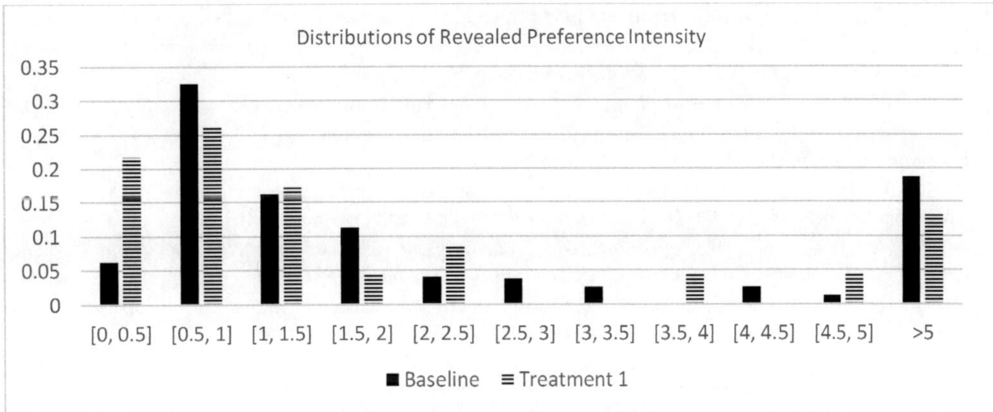

Figure 4

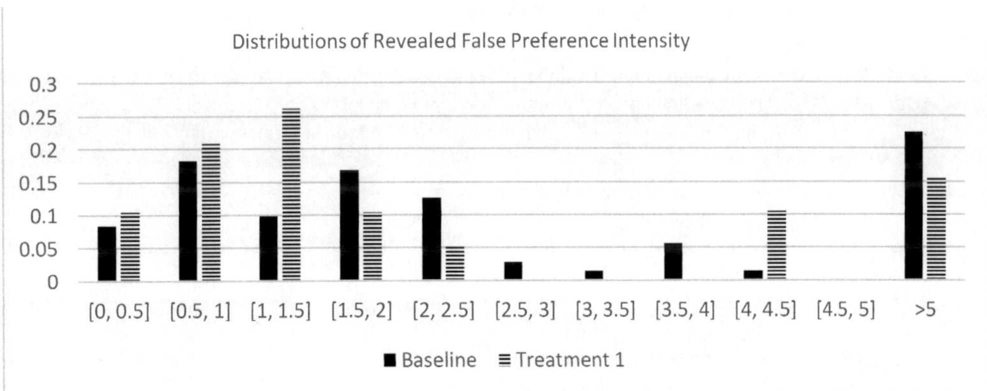

Figure 5

Our study has many limitations. Every time when one runs an experiment one has to make many operational decisions about exactly how the experiment will be conducted. In that sense it would be good to conduct experiments varying the way the information is displayed on the screen, varying the way instructions are provided to individuals, and think of ways to explore how every individual is absorbing and using the information shown on the screen. In a field experiment there are also many external variables that are not under the control of the experimenter. So even when we try our best to select similar subjects in similar environment and at a similar time. there is always a chance that an unobserved external variable has an influence over the outcome.

The next question to answer is if inequality of available preference intensity information about others can impact participants' earnings. In our study we decreased the granularity of that information uniformly among all subjects, but in reality different participants might have unequal access to information so, some participants might have more granular information than others. Other features of the mechanism also need to be explored in more detail. Some description of preference intensities might be easier to understand by voters than others. For some people Level 2 granularity might be just easier to grasp than Level 1 granularity. One might wonder whether some voters might feel excluded due to the complexity of the setting (compared to a traditional referendum). This not only violates their democratic rights but puts the legitimacy of the referendum under question.

REFERENCES

Abelson J. et al, 2004. *Transparency, Trust, and Citizen Engagement*, Ottawa, Canadian Policy Research Networks Inc.

Ballou, B. et al, 2010. Creating Effective Dashboards: How companies can improve executive decision-making and board oversight *Strategic Finance*, v91 n1, pp. 27-33

Baltzan, P.,2017. *Business Driven Technology*, 6th ed., MAcGraw Hill, New York, 2017

Banerjee, A & Maier, P., 2016. Public Information Precision and Coordination Failure: An Experiment *Journal of Accounting research*, v54 n4, September 2016, pp. 941-62

Bertot, J. et al, 2010 Using ICTSs to create a culture of transparency: E-government and social media as openness and anti-corruption tools for societies *Government Information Quarterly*, v27 n3, pp. 264-271

Blackwell, D., 1951 Comparison of Experiments In *Proceedings of the Second Berkeley Symposium in Mathematical Statistics and Probability*, University of California Press, (1951): pp. 93–102.

Chengalur-S. et al, 1999 The impact of data quality information on decision-making: An exploratory analysis *IEEE Transactions on Knowledge and Data Engineering*, v11 n6, pp. 853-864

Dawes, S. & Helbig, N., 2010 Information strategies for open government: Challenges and prospects for deriving public Value from government transparency" In *Electronic Government* pp. 50-60 Springer, 2010

Goes, P., 2013 Design science in top information systems research journals *MIS Quarterly,* v38 n1, pp. 3-8.

Gregor, S., 2006 The nature of theory in information systems. *MIS Quarterly*, v30 n3, pp. 611-642.

Hevner, A. et al,.2004 Design science in information systems research. *MIS Quarterly*, v28 n1, pp. 75-105.

Jenkins, A., 1985 Research methodologies and MIS research. *Research methods in information systems*, v*103*, pp. 117.

Lang, K et al, 2015 Consumer Co-creation of Digital Culture Products: Business Threat or New Opportunity? *Journal of the Association for Information Systems*, September 2015, v16 i9, pp. 766-798

March, S. T., & Smith, T. F., 1995 Design and natural science research on information technology. *Decision Support Systems,* v15 n4, pp. 251-266.

Matheus, R. et al, 2018 Data science empowering the public: Data-driven dashboards for transparent and accountable decision-making in smart cities *Government Information Quarterly*, in press

Oprea, R. et al, 2007 A compensation Election for Binary Social Choice *Proceedings of the National Academy of Sciences*, v104 n3, January 16, 2007, pp. 1093-1096

Peffers, K. et al, 2007 A design science research methodology for information systems research *Journal of Management Information Systems,* v24 n3, pp. 45-77

Peng, J. et al,.2007 An Experimental Study of Multidimensional Hierarchical Accounting Data: Drill-Down Paths Can Influence Economics Decisions *Journal of Information Systems,* v21 n2, Fall 2007, pp. 69-86

Smith, V. L. 2004 "Buy Me Out" *Forbes*

Vragov, R. & Kumar, N. 2019 Preparing the Laboratory-to-Field Transition of a New Electronic Voting Mechanism: Design Lessons from an Exploratory Semi-field Experiment" *International Journal Of Electronic Government Research*, v15 n4, pp. 63-89

Wicksell, K,1896 A New Principle of Just Taxation translated by J.M. Buchanan, in R.A. Musgrave and A.T.

OUTCOMES OF AN EXPERT SURVEY: ARE SINGAPORE'S MANUFACTURING SMALL AND MEDIUM ENTERPRISES READY TO EMBRACE INDUSTRY 4.0?

Gopalakrishnan Surianarayanan[1] and Thomas Menkhoff[2]
[1]*DBA Student*
[2]*Professor of Organisational Behavior and Human Resources*
Singapore Management University, Lee Kong Chian School of Business, 50 Stamford Rd. #05-01, Singapore 178899

ABSTRACT

Industry 4.0 encompasses adopting opportunities from end-to-end digitalisation with connected computers and increasingly autonomous automation systems equipped with intelligent machine learning algorithms that control the robotics without much input from humans. Smart manufacturing technologies (a part of the smart industry, an extension of Industry 4.0 initiatives and implementation) involve automating various processes. It aims to connect various units in real-time while enhancing profitability by reducing costs, increasing labour productivity, and improving overall efficiency.

The impetus for our paper is the assumption that the adoption of smart manufacturing technologies such as advanced robotics, cyber-physical systems, or the Internet of Things (IoT) continues to be a challenge for Small and Medium Enterprise (SME) manufacturing firms in Singapore. Industry 4.0 adoption issues include significant capital investment, developing technical skills, recruiting new talent, re-skilling of the workforce, training needs, top management support, etc. But the traditional manufacturing model is fast evolving. Ultimately, adopting the right enabling technologies in a phased manner with proper planning remains a critical factor for the success of Industry 4.0 initiatives.

This paper contributes to the minimal Asian management literature about Industry 4.0 matters in SMEs by interviewing eight key experts who are very knowledgeable about the subject matter. The qualitative study sheds light on the drivers and barriers to better understand current business dynamics, potential issues, focus areas, and initiatives to smoothen this implementation, to help catapult local manufacturers to the next level. A structured questionnaire was designed based on the current body of knowledge to conduct qualitative semi-structured interviews with key specialists and decision-makers across Government agencies, Institutes of Higher Learnings (IHL's), suppliers/providers of Industry 4.0 technology, business associations, and the SME sector.

The analysis of the interviews suggests that factors or drivers such as technology push by the Government with robust funding and training support, skilled labour shortages including imported labour dependence, productivity and efficiency issues, the pressure to innovate business models due to increased competition, and the impact of Covid-19 are propelling SMEs to adopt Industry 4.0. Some of the barriers include high investment costs and return on investment concerns, capability concerns, mindset issues, and lack of ecosystem concerns. The extent to which local SMEs are ready for Industry 4.0 will be further examined during the 2nd phase of the research project.

KEYWORDS

Industry 4.0, Smart Manufacturing, SME's, Qualitative, Business Model Innovation, Barriers to Adoption

1. INTRODUCTION

The First Industrial revolution commenced at the end of the 18th century and involved the mechanization through water and steam power. The Second Industrial Revolution, which originated at the start of the 20th century, involved mass production using assembly lines with electricity and division of labour. Great Britain and the United States of America were the leading proponents of the 1st and 2nd Industrial Revolution. The Third Industrial revolution commenced in the 1970s and is signified by computers and automation – it is widely prevalent even today and inter-connects associated fields like information technology, electronics, and operations technology seamlessly.

The term "Industrie 4.0," also known as I4.0 or I4, originated in Germany and was coined in the Hannover Fair during 2011. Other leading industrial nations have widely recognised it – the United States calls it the "Connected Enterprise," and the United Kingdom refers to it as the "Fourth Industrial Revolution."

Industry 4.0 adoption is expected to profoundly impact the entire spectrum of industries, especially in manufacturing. By using a confluence of automation, data, and digitalisation, Industry 4.0 aims to radically transform how organisations operate presently while increasing productivity, enhancing flexibility, reducing costs, and improving efficiency. More companies are strategically embracing so-called Industry 4.0 approaches to leverage opportunities arising from newly connected computers and increasingly autonomous automation systems (e.g., robotics), equipped with intelligent machine learning algorithms that control the robotics without much human input. In these 'smart' factories, cyber-physical systems (i.e., independently operating systems that self-optimize and communicate with each other, and ultimately optimize production) monitor the physical manufacturing processes and play an increasingly important role in terms of decision-making.

Industry 4.0 signifies three mutually interconnected factors (Zezulka et al., 2016), namely digitisation and integration of any technical-economic networks, digitisation of products and services, and new market models. At the core of this new smart manufacturing paradigm (McKeven, 2015) is the Internet of Things that drives the conversion of traditional factories into a 'smart' manufacturing environment called "Industry 4.0" (Kagermann et al., 2013), resulting in an increasingly intelligent, connected, and autonomous factory with outstanding dynamic capabilities (Teece, 2010; Eisenhardt and Martin, 2000). Smart manufacturing technologies include big data processing, machine learning, advanced robotics, cloud computing, sensors technology, additive manufacturing, and augmented reality (McKeven, 2015). By using predictive big data analytics, deep learning, or sentiment/image analysis, business leaders can identify patterns and trends in vast reams of big data. It allows them to make 'smarter' decisions (e.g., about the loss of customers or the necessary service inspection of equipment) and potentially to become more competitive in real-time.

2. RESEARCH VISION, RATIONALE AND QUESTIONS

2.1 Conceptual Framework: Industry 4.0

Characteristic features of an Industry 4.0 system (Marr, 2016; Schwab, 2016) include interoperability (machines, devices, sensors, and people that connect and communicate with one another), information transparency (the systems create a virtual copy of the physical world through sensor data to contextualize information), technical assistance (both the ability of the systems to support humans in making decisions and solving problems and the ability to assist humans with tasks that are too difficult or unsafe for humans) and decentralized decision-making (the ability of cyber-physical systems to make simple decisions on their own and become as autonomous as possible).

"The term Industry 4.0 stands for the fourth industrial revolution and is best understood as a new level of organization and control over the entire value chain of the life cycle of products, and it is geared towards increasingly individualized customer requirements" (Koch et al, 2014).

"Industry 4.0 or Smart industry refers to the technological evolution from embedded systems to cyber-physical systems. It connects embedded system production technologies and smart production processes to pave the way to a new technological age which will radically transform industry and production value chains and business models" (MacDougall, 2014).

2.2 Conceptual Framework: Sustaining Singapore's Competitiveness in Manufacturing and Technology Innovation through Industry 4.0

Industry 4.0 initiatives are also finding increased interest across South East Asian economies (ASEAN) over the last few years, with most governments taking active measures to push towards this implementation. ASEAN aspires to be the world's 4th largest economic block by 2050, and Industry 4.0 is a critical element of this growth vision across the region. Most countries, including Singapore, have created a road map with a vision for Industry 4.0. However, there is arguably limited adoption despite all the initiatives and support extended by the various Governments.

The manufacturing sector is critical for Singapore's economy as it makes up about 21% of Singapore's GDP, accounting for 14% of its workforce. Due to the lack of research data on the firms' receptiveness towards advanced Industry 4.0 technologies, it is critical to examine the impact of automation, digitization, and web-based production systems on the business models of local manufacturers in terms of successful 'production optimization', greater 'product customization,' 'predictive' maintenance and 'visionary' investments into automation solutions. According to the Singapore Business Federation, about 60% of local small and medium-sized enterprises have not made significant technological changes. Possible reasons include resistance to change, lack of technological knowledge and resources, and insufficient leadership foresight. Many local firms are still operating in 'the Industrial 2.0/3.0' era rather than embracing opportunities arising from smart 'Industry 4.0' technologies. In smart factories, cyber-physical systems (i.e., independently operating systems that self-optimize and communicate with each other) monitor the physical manufacturing processes and play an increasingly important role in decision-making. At the core of this new smart manufacturing, the paradigm is IoT, resulting in an increasingly intelligent, connected, and autonomous factory with excellent dynamic capabilities.

We expect that there is great variance amongst local manufacturing firms concerning the adoption of smart factory technologies ranging from (i) those that are entirely ignorant about the advantages of Industry 4.0 to (ii) those that are learning to implement such systems and (iii) experienced technological leaders. Many local SME's are contract manufacturers and may sense that it is not advantageous to embrace new technologies before their Principals do so. Others might have successfully implemented very comprehensive Industry 4.0 activities in addition to launching their workforce transformation programmes, e.g., to impart automation skills into the workforce.

Singapore has an adequate level of understanding with companies of the need to migrate to Industry 4.0, and the benefits of implementing this also generate much excitement. However, unlike Germany or the United States, the pace of adoption has been muted beyond a few early adopters. The Economic Development Board (EDB) in Singapore launched a Smart Industry Readiness Index (Siri) in 2017 to help firms measure their progress and to understand the gaps in implementation. Technology, Process, and Organisation were the three building blocks of Industry 4.0 identified by EDB. The Model Factory at A*Star's Advanced Remanufacturing and Technology Centre and the Operation and Technology Roadmap (OTR) launch enables firms to realise their transformation on this smart manufacturing journey. However, the take-up rate by companies seems to be still low.

Locally, efforts are underway to leverage the smart manufacturing technology potential in Singapore's manufacturing industry, representing a core sector within Singapore's economy. In 2015, the Agency for Science, Technology, and Research (A*STAR) started a Future of Manufacturing (FoM) Initiative in close consultation with the Ministry of Trade and Industry (MTI), the Economic Development Board (EDB), and SPRING Singapore under the Government's Research, Innovation & Enterprise 2020 plan. The deliberations involved extensive engagement with industry and trade associations. The initiative's goal is to sustain Singapore's competitiveness in manufacturing and technology innovation. It is a location of choice for developing, test-bedding, and deploying advanced breaking-ground technologies in the manufacturing sector. *"The three key thrusts of A*STAR's FoM Initiative are the public-private partnership platforms of Tech Access, Tech Depot, and Model Factories, that aim to drive technology innovation, knowledge transfer and adoption across the manufacturing industry (A*STAR Science and Engineering Research Council (SERC)."*

2.3 Conceptual Framework: Purpose of Research and Research Question

There are limited Singapore studies to understand the driving forces and barriers in adopting and implementing Industry 4.0. Most studies focus on the technology aspects and provide limited understanding from SME's holistic business model viewpoint. According to the Singapore Business Federation, about 60% of local SME's have not made significant adjustments to adapt to technological change. The paper attempts to address this significant knowledge gap and contribute to the minimal Asian management literature about the smart manufacturing technology research gap's impact on understanding the experts across the ecosystem. We believe that this approach will help us better understand current business dynamics, potential issues, focus areas, and developments related to the pace of adopting advanced manufacturing approaches within Singapore's manufacturing sector to help catapult Singapore's manufacturers to the next level. The core research question addressed in the paper is the following: **Are Singapore's manufacturing Small and Medium Enterprises ready to embrace Industry 4.0?**

3. RESEARCH DESIGN

3.1 Method

Our study adopted a dual-phase approach to developing a model that can clarify factors influencing the readiness of SME's for the adoption of Industry 4.0. The first phase involves expert semi-structured interviews with eight key decision-makers and heads across Government agencies, Institutes of Higher Learnings (IHLs), suppliers/providers of technology, business associations and the local SME sector. A structured questionnaire was devised based on the current body of knowledge in Industry 4.0.

The objective of the expert interviews was to allow us to dive deeper into the issues involved so as to develop a comprehensive understanding of the challenges faced by SMEs in Singapore. It also allowed us to draw on the expert insights with candour. The qualitative approach allows the interviewees to express themselves freely while providing us with the option to seek additional inputs and quality guidance. *"Qualitative research is conducted through intense and prolonged contact with a 'field' or life situation"* (Miles and Huberman, 1984).

Based on a literature review, we structured a questionnaire for the expert interviews and eventually arrived at several factors or categories (see Table 1 below) impacting Industry 4.0 adoption in SMEs after the text materials had been analysed. We conducted the eight interviews over virtual meetings application (ZOOM) and recorded the interviews with the participants' permission. The interviews were transcribed verbatim using transcription software and subsequently analysed for emerging themes using software (Nvivo).

Table 1. Factors impacting Industry 4.0 adoption in SME's

#	Factors
1	Capability and Competency
2	Collaboration – Internal and External
3	Culture of Company
4	Business Model Innovation
5	Skilled Labour Shortage and Dependencies
6	Mindset and Resistance to Change
7	Productivity and Efficiency
8	Return on Investment and Capital Costs
9	Government Subsidies, Incentives and Support
10	Talent Shortage
11	Technological Push by the Government
12	Top Management Support
13	Turnkey Solution Providers
14	Uniform Standards
15	Strategy and Implementation Roadmap

Qualitative data analysis techniques are well established in the management field, comprising three different procedures: data reduction (e.g., discarding irrelevant data in transcripts), data display (e.g., specific graphical formats derived from the data), and drawing conclusions based on field notes and emerging themes (Miles and Huberman, 2014). In line with the criteria of qualitative research, respondents' transcribed statements were clustered into common (raw data) themes and grouped into so-called first-order themes. Units with different meanings and general dimensions were established based on second-order themes (Eisenhardt and Graebner, 2007; Gioia et al., 2013). Table 1 summarizes the key outcomes of this step.

3.2 Data Collection and Analysis

Table 2 presents the profiles of the interviewed experts:

Table 2. Profile of experts interviewed

#	Designation	Industry
1	President	Industry Association
2	President – APAC	Multi-National Company – Provider of Technology
3	Executive Vice President – APAC	Multi-National Company – Provider of Technology
4	Director and Head of Industry 4.0 Labs	Institute of Higher Learning (IHL)
5	Professor and Head of Industry 4.0 Track	Institute of Higher Learning
6	Director	Government Agency for Industry 4.0
7	Deputy Director and Head (SME)	Government Agency – Industry 4.0 Technology Support and Upgrade
8	Head and Project Manager	Early Adopter of Industry 4.0 (SME) and Model company/example in Singapore

4. FINDINGS

The expert interviews helped to identify five key drivers and four main barriers with regard to the adoption and implementation of Industry 4.0 approaches as illustrated in Figure 1.

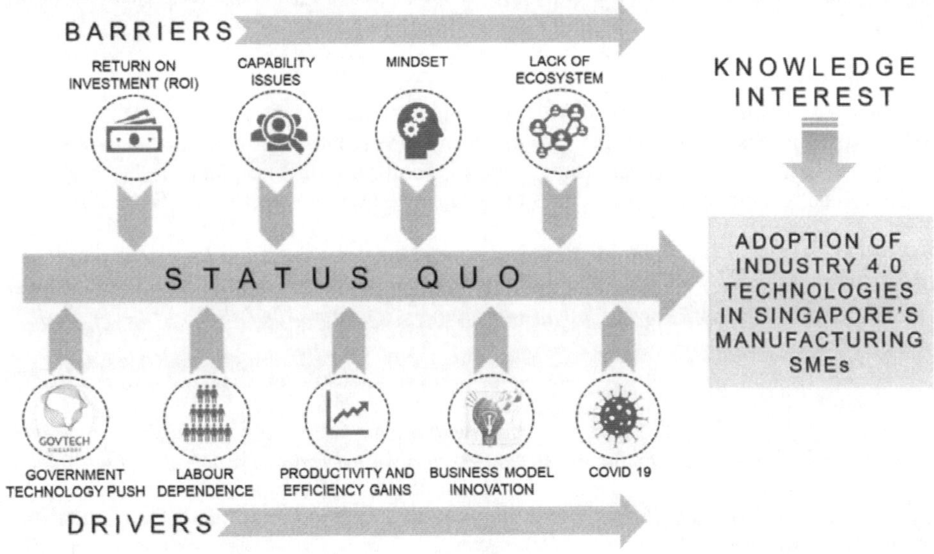

Figure 1. Drivers and barriers of Industry 4.0 adoption and implementation

Key drivers include technological push and incentives by the Government, skilled labour shortages, productivity and efficiency gains, the pressure to innovate business models due to increased competition, and the impact of Covid-19. Barriers in adoption revolve around return on investment issues, capability constraints, lack of ecosystem, and mindset factors. All experts agreed that Industry 4.0 was well recognised across the manufacturing SMEs in Singapore due to the top-down kind of initiatives embarked upon by the Government in Singapore and well supported by the agencies supporting this initiative.

"This is because Singapore has identified Industry 4.0 as an important skill and an important capability to improve productivity and to keep manufacturing content as a percentage of GDP existing in Singapore, and of course there has been a lot of downward pressure on that over the last few years."

(Interviewee 2)

The expert views were varied in terms of readiness to adopt and implement Industry 4.0 and SMEs' capabilities. They ranged between 5 to 7 on a scale of 0 to 10 (0 = very low - 10 = very high) to measure SME's readiness and capabilities to adopt and implement Industry 4.0 initiatives. The size and sector in which the SME operated played a crucial role in adopting Industry 4.0. It was unanimously felt that larger SMEs (USD 100 million and above) were very well-positioned to embrace Industry 4.0. In contrast, medium-sized SMEs (USD 10 – 100 million) were now more willing to embrace, especially on the back of Covid-19 bottlenecks and issues. Smaller SMEs below USD 10 million did not recognise Industry 4.0 benefits and were not on board due to various constraints with investment and operation scale as a hindrance. We observed that specific sectors such as hi-tech manufacturing, electronics, semiconductors, medical equipment, etc. were very well positioned to benefit from Industry 4.0 initiatives and SMEs in these sectors. One of the main drivers has been the continuous operation of these manufacturing lines in factories 24 x 7, 365 days per year, resulting in a more straightforward justification on the capital costs employed and the size of end products that were more suitable for smart manufacturing facilities. On the other hand, traditional sectors like construction, oil, and gas, amongst others, were considered to be slow adopters. The Covid-19 pandemic was viewed by most experts as a watershed moment in the adoption of Industry 4.0, even by traditional companies.

"The writing is on the wall with COVID coming in. I think Industry 4.0 will get an impetus in terms of people wanting to adopt/upgrade or maybe at least have the interest because traditional construction companies would not have changed their model."

(Interviewee 5)

"During this time, we have seen a ten-fold increase within the last six months of enterprises embarking on that journey."

(Interviewee 1)

The primary consideration here was that barring some companies who had truly embraced Industry 4.0, most SMEs were still unable to adopt Industry 4.0 despite the sound support on the Government's technical front and financial aspects. The overarching concerns' uniformly arising from all experts was the high investment, capital cost outlays, and economies of scale concerns expressed by most SMEs.

"I am not saying the small size SME cannot implement Industry 4.0, but what I am saying is if you want to reap the benefit of Industry 4.0 and you do not have that size, the cost will become very high, your returns might scare a small micro SME away. How are they going to achieve their ROI since every SME exists for the bottom line?"

(Interviewee 8)

"Our focus in the last couple of years has been more with the MNC's actually because there has been a lot of more activity, we have dedicated innovation budgets actually, for them it is a part of global roll-outs, and it comes out much more naturally. We are spending much less time discussing why this is necessary and ROI and business cases, and so honestly, not that many good examples. Most of our Industry 4.0 deployment is still with the larger players."

(Interviewee 2)

One of the critical drivers of Industry 4.0 approaches was the overarching need by SMEs to embrace business model innovation due to various factors such as a need to improve their revenue streams and cost structures and to build a robust value proposition. These needs were further exacerbated by issues like low productivity, high labour cost, increased competition due to globalisation, the impact of Covid-19, etc.

"At this timing where your equipment is not doing anything anymore, your systems are idle, especially on weekends, but if you can continue operation on the weekends, that is actually a lot of large productivity gains and gain to an additional base as well."

(Interviewee 5)

"Covid-19 presents us this opportunity to hammer down on SME's to adopt Industry 4.0 or smart manufacturing technologies in a bigger way now and also to maybe drive innovation also, where some SME's especially a large proportion in Singapore, have not kept up with as yet."

(Interviewee 2)

"We did not do this to cut the workforce. We did this project to increase productivity."

(Interviewee 8)

Good examples exist across SME's, which show very healthy ways to innovate their business models by undertaking Industry 4.0, including ways to convert from Capital Expenditure (CAPEx) to Operational Expenditure (OPEx) methods alongside services like predictive maintenance approaches. This approach allows companies to collect a premium for their end customer services over a longer time frame and a strong incentive to better service the asset. Digital technologies also facilitate collecting a considerable volume of data from production facilities, customer locations, entire supply chains, etc. which will significantly support decision-making and optimising processes.

"I think business model innovation is genuine, right. There is a huge driver where business model innovation plays a role - like this company I mentioned before, going away from pure re-selling of assets to a model where they are trying to add services on top, which is the first step. However, if you have the insight into what is happening inside the machine, there is nothing that prevents you from putting that asset on to your balance sheet. You can then run it as an operational asset and then collect a premium as you take the capital cost on your side and amortising it over a longer period while getting a premium to finance and run the asset. You also get a strong incentive to maintain the asset well, which before then, was not necessarily an incentive. You may have differently aligned incentives, and you have maybe more an incentive now to drive maintenance. So for the end customer, it is a good thing as you get the alignment of incentives, and they would be willing to take that risk and give some margin to the provider of the manufacturing equipment also."

(Interviewee 2)

A phase-wise approach to adopt Industry 4.0 was seen as the preferred way to get started according to some experts. This approach allowed the SME not to disturb their entire facility, absorb technology in stages, and amortise the capital investments over a broader horizon. The technical support and push to pursue Industry 4.0 and related automation was something that most interviewees felt was done very well by the Government. To further complement this push, the Government has been going all out to provide financial assistance, subsidies, and even offers in terms of technical consultancy to motivate SMEs to go on the path of Industry 4.0. Some interviewees felt that the high level of support from the Government had, on the contrary, made some of the SME's sit back and wait for incentives rather than drive forward and innovate to thrive and survive. SMEs' capability to engage in innovation and differentiate competitively in a global supply chain rather than local supply chain was also a limitation in some instances. Factors relating to human capital, including capability issues, skilled labour shortages, dependency on imported labour, and a dearth of top talent to meet companies' evolving needs, also formed a critical theme across all interactions.

"We are talking exactly about the capability of SMEs to innovate and transform. Moreover, human capital is missing in these SME's."

(Interviewee 2)

"What motivated us to go towards Industry 4.0 is because we faced a skilled labour shortage. We needed much-skilled labour, and we have been facing many challenges in getting skilled labour in the machining of our components."

(Interviewee 8)

A key consideration was the top management support, organisational resistance across ranks, and a culture shift focusing on managing its mindset. The vision and direction provided by the CEO and senior management was an extremely critical aspect. In the case of family-owned companies, it was felt that the younger generation's engagement to harvest the benefits of smart manufacturing was a huge determinant in their success.

"Our CEO is the one; he is the main driver who wanted to adopt the technology. So he took the opportunity to convince the board to go towards Industry 4.0 technology and grow the revenue - the top line and bottom line. Thus, the board was convinced, and therefore they gave him that support. Moreover, with that support - that is the first stage. It is the commitment and belief of the person who wants to implement it. He had to be on the top to be the main decision-maker."

(Interviewee 8)

One of the surprise benefits achieved due to Industry 4.0 adoption highlighted by an interviewee, was that the new hires were attracted to pursue their careers in these companies, which helped attract the best talent in the market among the new graduates.

"We did find that there is much resistance. It is not easy, so we have to do it systematically. Luckily we devised our in-house training roadmap. We do some in-house training to progressively and constantly talk to about people to change their mindset why we need to change, the reason, and what happens if you do not change and if you want to change what we should do. The CEO mentioned that nobody would be displaced."

(Interviewee 8)

A significant pain point for early adopters of Industry 4.0 was the lack of turnkey solution providers who would coordinate the SME's needs. In the case of SME's who lack technical resources to handle the transformation, this was an area where more support would be welcome.

5. CONCLUSIONS

The paper examines Singapore-based SME's readiness to manufacture to implement Industry 4.0 and provides initial insights. We have identified five fundamental driving forces and three main barriers based on interactions with experts. SMEs must adopt a clear strategy and define a roadmap to align their organisation and entire workforce with this Industry 4.0 adoption process's objectives. SMEs will also need to closely network with universities and educational providers to ensure that more significant industry interaction with participation like internships provided to students creates lifelong linkages with the emerging workforce. Industry 4.0 is already challenging the nature of management and leadership competencies, and the empowerment of the younger generation will be a critical factor in the times ahead. On the other hand, while transformation must be top-down, the internalization and real improvements are the people. The employees must buy-in into the SME's transformation process with clear support and guidance from top management to see this initiative succeed.

SMEs are increasingly getting convinced of the benefits of digitalisation and automation. The business case for digital transformation is getting stronger with Covid-19, which may well leave a permanent imprint on the push to adopt and transform. Digitalisation, analytics, and automation will be in significant demand, and firms providing a right work environment with a progressive mindset will reap the rewards in the times ahead. Singapore can play a critical role in ASEAN by leading Industry 4.0 initiatives like advanced manufacturing, innovation, and digital activities across the entire value chain. By leveraging trading, financial, and supply chain strengths in this ecosystem and harnessing member countries' strength in ASEAN, Singapore can lead the way ahead. Singapore can also foray into high value-added manufacturing and design by moving upstream rather than focus on mass commodity specifications. Industry 4.0 enables a great degree of customisation, which augurs well for SMEs in Singapore to move into more attractive spaces within the industry.

This study has fueled exciting insights to explore in future research. We intend to build on the expert interviews to carry out in-depth case studies with SMEs. These case studies will then allow us to examine the credibility of the findings and, in turn, also enable us to discover any new inputs that can build our theory. By examining multiple cases, we expect greater rigor, robustness, and reliability to generalize the research findings (Eisenhardt, 1991). Such an approach will also help mitigate possible adverse effects of sample bias on the study's findings (Yin, 2009).

Theoretically, the expert interviews point to several relevant theoretical concepts regarding the drivers and barriers of Industry 4.0 adoption in local SMEs, which will be further scrutinized during the 2nd phase of the research project. They include technology push (Godin, 2006) and adoption concepts such as Roger's diffusion of innovations theory (1962), the developmental state (Johnsen 1982), the resource-based view of the firm (Wernerfeld, 1984), proactive and reactive mindset concepts (Bateman and Crant, 1993), strategic leadership theory and business ecosystem concepts (Moore, 1996; Williamsen, P. and De Meyer, A., 2020) as well as business model innovation frameworks (Girotra, K. & Netyessine, S. 2014; Osterwalder et al., 2010; Taran et al., 2019).

Research Questions for Stage 2 of the Research Project

1. What are the main factors and elements of Industry 4.0 applications in the case companies?
2. How has, is, or will Industry 4.0 changed/changing/change the way the companies are doing business in terms of the nine building blocks of the business canvas (Osterwalder et al., 2010).
3. How new or intense (innovation intensity: incremental vs. breakthrough) are these changes (if any) to the nine boxes (customers, value proposition, channels, customer relationships, essential resources, activities and partners, cost structure, and revenue streams)?
4. How complex and interrelated were/are/will (be) the changes (one, several, or all building blocks)?
5. Finally, we wish to examine the reach (Taran et al., 2019) of the Industry 4.0 induced innovation(s) in terms of "new to whom" (e.g. new to the company, new to the market, new to the industry, new to the world).

REFERENCES

Bateman, T.S. and Crant, J.M. 1993. The proactive component of organizational behavior: A measure and correlates. *Journal of Organizational Behavior* 14(2), pp. 103–118. doi: 10.1002/job.4030140202.

Belton, K.B. et al. 2019. Who Will Set the Rules for Smart Factories? *Issues in Science & Technology* 35(3), pp. 70–76.

Chen, Y. et al. 2012. Origins of green innovations: the differences between proactive and reactive green innovations. *Management Decision* 50(3), pp. 368–398. doi: 10.1108/00251741211216197.

Eisenhardt, K.M. 1991. Better Stories and Better Constructs: The Case for Rigor and Comparative Logic. *Academy of Management Review* 16(3), pp. 620–627. doi: 10.5465/AMR.1991.4279496.

Eisenhardt, K.M. and Graebner, M.E. 2007. Theory Building From Cases: Opportunities And Challenges. *Academy of Management Journal* 50(1), pp. 25–32.

Fact-sheet-on-Industry-Transformation-Maps---revised-as-of-31-Mar-17.pdf. [no date]. Available at: https://www.mti.gov.sg/-/media/MTI/ITM/General/Fact-sheet-on-Industry-Transformation-Maps---revised-as-of-31-Mar-17.pdf [Accessed: 26 September 2020].

Fourth Industrial Revolution. 2020. *Wikipedia*. Available at: https://en.wikipedia.org/w/index.php?title=Fourth_Industrial_Revolution&oldid=979076316 [Accessed: 19 September 2020].

Gioia, D.A. et al. 2013. Seeking Qualitative Rigor in Inductive Research: Notes on the Gioia Methodology. *Organizational Research Methods* 16(1), pp. 15–31. doi: 10.1177/1094428112452151.

Girotra, K. and Netessine, S. 2014. Four Paths to Business Model Innovation. *Harvard Business Review* (July–August 2014) 1 July. Available at: https://hbr.org/2014/07/four-paths-to-business-model-innovation [Accessed: 29 September 2020].

Godin, B. 2006. The Linear Model of Innovation: The Historical Construction of an Analytical Framework. *Science, Technology, & Human Values* 31(6), pp. 639–667. doi: 10.1177/0162243906291865.

Godin, B. [no date]. "Innovation Studies": The Invention of a Specialty (Part II)., p. 48.

Horváth, D., and Szabó, R. Z. (2019). "Driving forces and barriers of Industry 4.0: Do multinational and small and medium-sized companies have equal opportunities?" Technological Forecasting and Social Change 146, 119-132. DOI: 10.1016/j.techfore.2019.05.021. [no date].

Industry 4.0 Gaining Momentum In ASEAN – Asia IoT Business Platform. [no date]. Available at: http://iotbusiness-platform.com/industry-4-0-gaining-momentum-in-asean/ [Accessed: 19 September 2020].

Initiatives. [no date]. Available at: https://sciath.com/initiatives/ [Accessed: 29 September 2020].

Johnson, C. 1982. *MITI and the Japanese Miracle: The Growth of Industrial Policy, 1925-1975*. Stanford: Stanford University Press. Available at: http://www.sup.org/books/title/?id=2791 [Accessed: 28 September 2020].

Julian M. Müller 2019. Assessing the barriers to Industry 4.0 implementation from a workers' perspective. *IFAC-PapersOnLine* 52(13), pp. 2189–2194. doi: doi.org/10.1016/j.ifacol.2019.11.530.

Kagermann, H.; Wahlster, W. & Helbig, J. 2013. *'Recommendations for Implementing the Strategic Initiative INDUSTRIE 4.0 -- Securing the Future of German Manufacturing Industry'* ,. acatech -- National Academy of Science and Engineering , München .

Kagermann, H., Wahlster, W. and Helbig, J. 2013. *Recommendations for implementing the Strategic Initiative Industrie 4.0 – Final Report of the Industrie 4.0 Working Group. Communication Promoters Group of the Industry-Science Research Alliance, acatech, Frankfurt am Main.* Available at: https://www.din.de /blob/76902/e8cac883f42bf28536e7e8165993f1fd/recommendations-for-implementing-industry-4-0-data.pdf.

Launch of A*STAR's Model Factory @ ARTC. [no date]. Available at: https://www.a-star.edu.sg/News-and-Events/a-star-news/news/publicity-highlights/launch-of-a-star-s-model-factory---artc [Accessed: 26 September 2020].

MacDougall, W. 2014. *Industrie 4.0: Smart Manufacturing for the Future*. Germany Trade & Invest.

Maclaurin, W. R. 1949. *Invention and Innovation in the Radio Industry, New York*. Macmillan.

Marr, B 2016. What Everyone Must Know About Industry 4.0. Available at: https://www.forbes.com/sites/bernardmarr/2016/06/20/what-everyone-must-know-about-industry-4-0/#66508a40795f [Accessed: 26 September 2020].

McKewen, E. [no date]. What is Smart Manufacturing? (Part 1A). Available at: https://www.cmtc.com/blog/what-is-smart-manufacturing-part-1a-of-6 [Accessed: 26 September 2020].

Miles, M. B., & Huberman, A. M. (1984). Drawing Valid Meaning from Qualitative Data: Toward a Shared Craft. Educational Researcher, 13(5), 20–30. https://doi.org/10.3102/0013189X013005020. [no date].

Moore, J.E. and Business, H. [no date]. The Death Of Competition: Leadership And Strategy In The Age Of Business Ecosystems., p. 29.

Olsen, T.L. and Tomlin, B. 2020. Industry 4.0: Opportunities and Challenges for Operations Management. *Manufacturing & Service Operations Management* 22(1), pp. 113–122. doi: 10.1287/msom.2019.0796.

Orzes, G. et al. 2020. Implementing Industry 4.0 in SMEs: A Focus Group Study on Organizational Requirements. n: Matt, D. T. et al. eds. *Industry 4.0 for SMEs: Challenges, Opportunities and Requirements*. Cham: Springer International Publishing, pp. 251–277. Available at: https://doi.org/10.1007/978-3-030-25425-4_9.

Osterwalder, A., Pigneur, Y., Clark, T. 2010. *Business Model Generation: A Handbook For Visionaries, Game Changers, and Challengers. Strategyzer series. Hoboken, NJ.* John Wiley & Sons.

Rogers, E. 2003. *Diffusion of Innovations*. 5th ed.

Schwab, K. 2016. The Fourth Industrial Revolution: what it means and how to respond. Available at: https://www.weforum.org/agenda/2016/01/the-fourth-industrial-revolution-what-it-means-and-how-to-respond/ [Accessed: 26 September 2020].

Singapore's companies take leap into advanced manufacturing. [no date]. Available at: https://www.edb.gov.sg/en/news-and-events/insights/manufacturing/factory-forward-advanced-manufacturing-takes-root-in-singapore.html [Accessed: 26 September 2020].

Taran, Y., Goduscheit, R.C. and Boer, H. 2019. Business Model Innovation – A Gamble or a Manageable Process? *Journal of Business Models* 7(5), pp. 90–107.

Teece, D.J. 2010. *Technological Innovation and the Theory of the Firm: The Role of Enterprise-Level Knowledge, Complementarities, and (Dynamic) Capabilities, in: Handbook of the Economics of Innovation*.

V Koch, S Kuge, R Geissbauer, S Schrauf 2014. *Industry 4.0: Opportunities and Challenges of the Industrial Internet*. PWC. Available at: https://www.pwc.nl/en/assets/documents/pwc-industrie-4-0.pdf.

van den Ende, J. & Dolfsma, W. 2005. Technology-push, demand-pull and the shaping of technological paradigms - Patterns in the development of computing technology. *Journal of Evolutionary Economics* 15, pp. 83–99. doi: doi.org/10.1007/s00191-004-0220-1.

Veile, J.W. et al. 2019. Lessons learned from Industry 4.0 implementation in the German manufacturing industry. *Journal of Manufacturing Technology Management* ahead-of-print(ahead-of-print). Available at: https://doi.org/10.1108/JMTM-08-2018-0270 [Accessed: 26 September 2020].

Wernerfelt, B. 1984. A resource-based view of the firm. *Strategic Management Journal* 5(2), pp. 171–180. doi: 10.1002/smj.4250050207.

Williamson, P. & e Meyer, A 2020. *Ecosystem Edge: Sustaining Competitiveness in the Face of Disruption*. Stanford Business Books.

Yin, R.K. 2009. Case Study Research: Design and Methods (4th Edition). *Sage, Thousand Oaks.*

Zezulka, F. et al. 2016. Industry 4.0 – An Introduction in the phenomenon. *IFAC-PapersOnLine* 49(25), pp. 8–12. doi: https://doi.org/10.1016/j.ifacol.2016.12.002

SOFTWARE CATALOGUE FOR SCIENTIFIC CONTEXT EXPLICATION

Olga Kononova[1], Dmitry Prokudin[1, 2] and Angelina Timofeeva[1]
[1]ITMO University 197101, St. Petersburg, Russia
[2]St. Petersburg State University 199034, St. Petersburg, Russia

ABSTRACT

Computerization of scientific activity has changed the interdisciplinary study mechanics and researchers' views, providing new opportunities for analysis. This paper presents a catalogue of analytical software widely used for contextual knowledge explication and scientific text mining. The catalogue focuses on the contextual knowledge types (contexts) processed with a software considered, and applies both, human-oriented and machine-oriented IS descriptions. The human-oriented description of a software catalogue is presented by a corresponding IS architecture (applications and data) on conceptualization level. The machine-oriented software description is performed with Dublin Core metadata. The Dublin Core metadata have allowed structuring the main software characteristics and provided the metadata export to other presentation formats to be place in various kinds of ISs and metadata aggregators. The machine-readable part of the catalogue performs the replenishment tasks, software effective search and its recognition in accordance with the research tasks. The practical implementation of the catalogue as an open access network platform by the OAI-PMH metadata exchange protocol provides the integration into the scientific information space as a researchers' guidance.

KEYWORDS

Human-Machine Interaction, Scientific Text Mining, Context, Software, Contextual Knowledge, IS Architecture, Architectural Description, Human-Machine Interaction, Dublin Core

1. INTRODUCTION

Modern multidisciplinary research makes extensive use of a software designed to explicate and analyze contextual knowledge. A variety of tools poses the challenge for researchers of multidisciplinary scientific fields to select a software most appropriate for their research objectives. The choice complexity lies in the lack of a software systematic description that can be used to solve a wide range of problems in scientific text mining, initially focused on business applications or solving problems in narrow subject areas (for example, linguistics). The paper describes the approach to software systematic presentation development for analysis and explication of contextual knowledge for research purposes based on identification of essential characteristics (classes of tasks to be performed, functions to be implemented and context types). Considering the existing software classifications, the main classes for contextual knowledge processing are identified and systematized. Based on the typology of contextual knowledge developed by the authors, types of contexts are distinguished as an essential software characteristics. The main functions implemented in the software are also allocated as a separate characteristics. The following is a structured description of a software to be presented in a catalogue form. Software systematization in the catalogue is performed on the enlarged classes of tasks. The catalogue is presented in two forms: human-readable and machine-readable. A human-readable catalogue representation proposes a software architecture at a conceptual level. The software architecture reflects the modules, functions, and types of contexts being processed.

The paper presents two cases to demonstrate the results obtained in the form of a structured description of T-Libla and Voyant-tools softwires. The developed systematized and structured presentation of the software replenishes the catalogue with new software, as well as ensures its effective selection for research purposes based on contextual knowledge explication and analysis.

2. SOFTWARE CLASSIFICATIONS AND TYPOLOGY OF CONTEXT SCIENTIFIC KNOWLEDGE

The target users of the developed catalogue are scientists and teachers specializing in interdisciplinary research. They usually rely on the existing approaches to software classification. Both general approaches, that single out the most general software classes, and specific ones, that focus on a more detailed description of software subclasses applied in various fields, are developed. One of the general approaches to classify Business intelligence (BI) class software is Gartner's Infrastructure and Applications Worldwide Software Market Definitions, annually updated, which reflects Gartner's general approach to estimate software market development [Woodward A. et al, 2019]. This approach is taken by International Data Corporation (IDC), one of the world's largest consulting companies, a leading provider of information and consulting services, an organizer of events in the markets of information technology, telecommunications and consumer equipment [Andsbjerg R., Vesset D., 2018]. The Computing Classification System (developed by the Association for Computing Machinery, the latest version was introduced in 2012) can also be used to classify software and information systems. The system is presented as a single source of categories and concepts that reflect the current state of computing, computer science, and information and communication technologies [Computing Classification System, 2012].

The established classifications do not allow a software designed for contextual scientific knowledge processing to be assigned to one class. Such software includes various linguistic programs. A sufficient number of catalogues of such programs is found on the Internet, for example [4 Free and Open Source ..., Text Analysis, Text Mining ..., Text Mining Software ...]. They might be used for research purposes. In these directories there are no classifiers considering the main purpose of the software, types of contexts being processed, and processing functions. Therefore, they do not fulfill the task of choosing effective tools for conducting research.

Based on the analysis of software designed for contextual knowledge processing, the following general classes of tasks for contextual knowledge processing are identified: neural network; machine learning; natural language processing; information extraction; ontology; construction and analysis of trends; creation and use of thesauri; thematic classification of texts; full-text information databases; abstract databases (only metadata). These classes of tasks in the catalogue correspond to the characteristic "category (software class)". The last two classes are characterized only by full-text and abstract information databases, which have their own mechanisms for searching, selecting, and analyzing information.

The typology of contexts developed by [] allows to determine the software necessary to solve the problems of context processing. The software analysis allowed to identify the types of contexts for each application [Kononova O.V., Prokudin D.E., 2020]. Therefore, one of the essential characteristics of the software is the "view (s) of the context being processed": corpus, fragment, paragraph, sentence, concept term, thesaurus, meta description, query collection, semantic group, publications set, thematic collections of relevant paragraphs, group of keywords, subject areas.

Software classification and context typology do not adequately reflect software capabilities. Therefore, for a more complete picture of the capabilities of the software, a list of their functions is used, which is mapped to modules, services, and contexts. Functions are represented by a separate characteristic in accordance with the scientific tasks performed. Based on this, the following functions are distinguished: clustering; forecasting; contextual analysis; intelligent search; automated exchange of data (metadata); visualization; storage.

These three main characteristics are the integral basis for the rational choice of specific software to be effective for research purposes.

3. HUMAN-READABLE AND MACHINE-READABLE CATALOGUE REPRESENTATION

3.1 Architectural Description of Information Systems

Architectural descriptions used in the catalogue are software meta-description, architectural model of applications, and taxonomy of contexts processed by software.

The software meta-description for contextual knowledge explication and processing contains the following fields: Name, URL; Vendor, country; Properties (distribution license, the latest version year, support; Software Classes (Type); Purpose; Main functions; Additional functions; List of modules, services; Types of Contexts; Links to materials on using the software).

The selection and visualization of contexts is performed in accordance with the previously developed typology of contexts [Kononova O.V., Prokudin D.E., Yelkina E.E., 2019, Kononova O.V., Prokudin D.E., 2020]. First, the contexts the information system works with are determined. Next, the contexts are compared with typology: groups and types of contexts are distinguished.

A meta-description of the application's architectural model, which determines the corresponding functions and contexts implemented in the information systems, is presented in Table 1.

Table 1. Context model of an application architecture

Modules / Services	Functions	Contexts
The list of modules or services with IS functions.	Functions implemented in IS.	The list of context types based on the typology.

The data architecture is represented in the catalogue by two artifacts: a list of entities and ERD (using Crow's Foot notation [Moss K., 2012]).

The list of entities is determined by the following criteria: types of context the system in question works with (in accordance with the typology of contexts) or other units of analysis; the results that the system provides after analysis or a form of visualization; the place for data storage. ERD describes the relations between the entities selected. This description provides information about the software for catalogue users in the most optimal variant.

3.2 Catalogue Submission in Machine-Readable Form

The information analysis of the software for contextual knowledge demonstrates that basically catalogue directories are static lists or tables in which the software is grouped by a certain attribute or presented in an unstructured form with a brief description of the features and links to relevant sites on the Internet.

Based on generally accepted approaches for software description in a catalogue, it is proposed to use the Dublin Core metadata presentation specification [Brisebois R. et al, 2017, González R. and Van Der Meer K., 2004]. Here, the main characteristics presented in the software catalogue collaterals are described by the relevant elements of the Dublin Core Metadata Element Set (DCMES) [DCMI Metadata Terms]. Therefore, a combination of element values s fully describes the software presented in the catalogue, which corresponds to the general approach of entity description with this specification [Fedotov A.M., Leonova Y.V., 2018, Noor S. et al, 2018]. Within the framework of this approach various text objects are described: articles, books, library catalogue cards, archival materials, and semantic models [SUNScholar / Metadata / By Function]. When developing a metadata presentation scheme for software description, its specification is not considered, which is important when choosing software applications (for example, types of processed contextual knowledge) [Brisebois R. et al, 2017, González R. and Van Der Meer K., 2004]. Allowing for software description specifics, the qualifiers were used to refine the characteristics values in addition to the main metadata elements. These qualifiers form the second level of metadata and refine the values of [DCMI Qualifiers] elements.

The catalogue in machine-readable form can be implemented as an information system with free Internet access. This catalogue presentation is convenient for users and for automated identification by search engines and aggregation into other information systems. To implement the catalogue, DSpace software platform (https://duraspace.org/dspace/) was chosen as the most common solution at present. In accordance with the Dublin Core specification, metadata presentation in DSpace [DSpace / dublin-core-types ...] and considering qualifier presentation, the essential software features for each catalogue element are represented by the following tags:

dc.type – categories (software classes in accordance with the developed classification)
dc.subject – keywords
dc.subject.classification – main functions (can be supplemented after the corresponding software analysis)
dc.subject.other – types of contexts processed

4. SOFTWARE CATALOGUE: CASE STUDY

The architecture is designed for the main group of system users - analysts, researchers, and scientists. For these users, it is important to obtain necessary information in proper volume and correct presentation. The architectural representation gives a user access to information about the system: the context the system works with, the modules implemented in the system, and also what results analysis can be performed using the system. Consider the architectural representation of T-libra and Voyant-tools information systems. Figure 1 demonstrates the context ontology for T-libra (a) and Voyant-tools (b) systems.

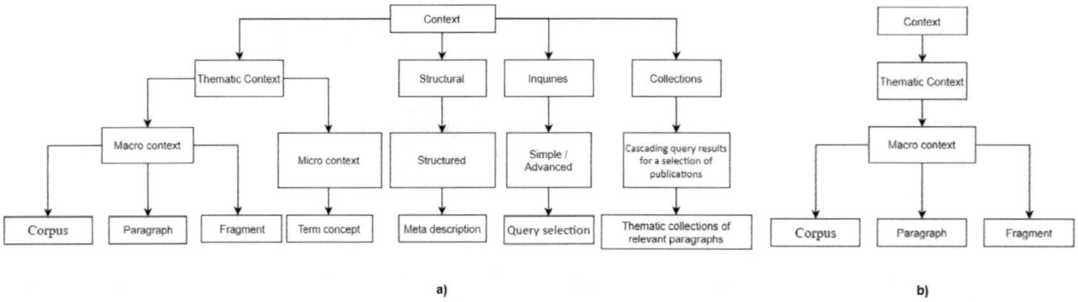

Figure 1. Context ontology. T-libra (a), Voyant-tools (b)

The ontology features the context the system works with. After defining the context, the users can learn more about the system functionality. Table 2 demonstrates T-libra and Voyant-tools functions and modules.

Table 2. Functions and modules of T-libra and Voyant-tools information systems

IS Functions	Module / Services	Contexts
	T-Libra	
Storage	Data loading and storage data (text arrays); Depositary; Catalogue	Corpus, document, query, meta description, thematic collection
Search	Implementation of several types of contextual search: absolute and relative frequency-oriented search; paragraph-oriented search (single-layer, multi-layer queries)	term concept, paragraph, fragment, query
Analysis	Explication of contexts by cascading query method; Creation of thematic collections based on query results clustering, content and expert analysis of contexts	Thematic collection of relevant paragraphs, fragment, paragraph, term-concept
Visualization	Building of terminogramma as absolute results of frequency-oriented queries; Statistics	Terminogramma (List of term)
	Voyant-tools	
Search	Absolute and relative frequency-oriented search	Absolutely oriented and frequency-oriented search
Analysis	Computer analysis to study texts on the Internet, or texts, from the user's computers; functionality addition to individual online collections, science magazines, blogs, or websites so that other users can view texts using analytic tools	Corpus, document, paragraph, fragment, compilation of publications
Visualization	Graph construction, tables, tag clouds, bubble diagrams, relationship graphs	Corpus, document, fragment, paragraph (reduced fragment), compilation of publications

The table gives catalogue users an idea of how the basic functions (storage, search, analysis, visualization) are implemented in the system. Also, the table demonstrates the types of contexts used for a particular function.

The ERDs for T-Libra and Voyant-tools are demonstrated at Figure 2. The diagram presents the entities and their relationships. This allows a user to determine the system efficiency with a particular type of context. The diagram illustrates the relationship of this context with the analysis result or data storage location.

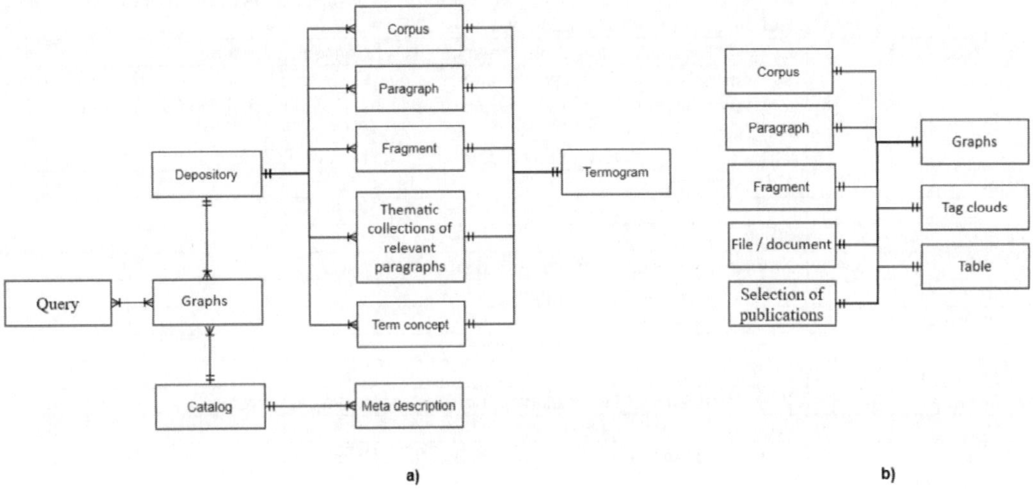

Figure 2. ERD. T-libra (a), Voyant-tools (b)

Considered is a machine-readable part of the catalogue. Tables 3 and 4 provide a machine-readable description of the T-libra and Voyant-tools information systems.

Table 3. Machine-readable description of T-Libra

dc.title	T-Libra
dc.creator	LLC "Constant", Russia
dc.subject	Collection of documents; Text Corpus; Frequency query; Contextual search; Trend; Context
dc.subject.classification	Contextual analysis; Storage; Search
dc.subject.other	Case, Document, Paragraph, Fragment, Term concept, Query, Thematic collection of relevant paragraphs (result of a search query followed by expert selection), Meta description
dc.description	information system for creating multifunctional electronic libraries with flexible thematic full-text search, multimodal expansion and metadata conversion from electronic catalogues
dc.publisher	LLC "Constant"
dc.contributor	
dc.date.issued	2017
dc.type	Full-text information databases; Natural Language Processing; Information Extraction
dc.format.mimetype	trtf; pdf
dc.identifier.uri	http://www.softconst.ru/
dc.source.uri	http://www.softconst.ru/tlibra/
dc.language	Multilanguage
dc.coverage	Web Oriented Application (Web Interface)
dc.rights	Commercial license
dc.relation. isreferencedby	Kononova O., Lyapin S. (2016) Using the Contextual Search for the Organization Scientific Research Activities. In: Chugunov A., Bolgov R., Kabanov Y., Kampis G., Wimmer M. (eds) Digital Transformation and Global Society. DTGS 2016. Communications in Computer and Information Science, vol 674, pp. 392-399. Springer, Cham. DOI: 10.1007/978-3-319-49700-6_38
dc.coverage	all

dc.rights.license	LLC "Constant"

Table 4. Machine-readable description of Voyant-tools information system.

dc.title	Voyant-tools
dc.creator	Stéfan Sinclair, McGill University; Geoffrey Rockwell, University of Alberta
dc.subject	Collection of documents; Text Corpus; Frequency query; Contextual search; Trend; Explication of contextual knowledge; Context
dc.subject.classification	Processing of individual documents; Processing by a collection of documents (corpus of texts); Classification; Clustering analysis of web pages; Frequency analysis; Contextual analysis; Building trends; Visualization of analysis results
dc.subject.other	Corpus, Document, Paragraph, Fragment, Term Concept, Thesaurus
dc.description	Voyant-tools is a web-based text reading and analysis environment to facilitate the work with a text or collection of texts in a variety of formats, including plain text, HTML, XML, PDF, RTF, and MS Word. There is a local solution in the form of an application on JETTY
dc.publisher	Voyant-tools
dc.contributor	Andrew MacDonald; Cyril Briquet; Lisa Goddard; Mark Turcato
dc.date.issued	2018
dc.type	Natural Language Processing; Information Extraction
dc.format.mimetype	txt; rtf; doc; docx; pdf; zip; html; xml
dc.identifier.uri	https://voyant-tools.org
dc.source.uri	http://voyeurtools.org/voyant-server/
dc.language	Multilanguage
dc.coverage	Web Application, Mac, Windows, JETTY server, Voyant server
dc.rights	Free Software
dc.relation. isreferencedby	Laurie J. Sampsel (2018) Voyant Tools, Music Reference Services Quarterly, 21:3, 153-157, DOI: 10.1080/10588167.2018.1496754
dc.coverage	all
dc.rights.license	Creative Commons Attribution 4.0 International (CC BY 4.0)

The table provides the information with convenient search engine. Thus, using the machine-readable part of the catalog, one can find the necessary information about the system and system specifics having analyzed the system architecture.

5. CONCLUSION

Based on the developed approach to the software systematized and structured presentation for contextual knowledge explication and processing, a software catalogue was presented in two forms — human-readable and machine-readable. The Dublin Core metadata specification was used for a structured description of the software in a machine-readable catalogue. This specification was supplemented by the DSpace software platform qualifiers. The catalogue was arranged in human readable form for further publication in a book publishing house.

The proposed approach to the software catalogue in machine-readable form is based on a Dublin Core format metadata description. Each record represents an ordered set of metadata. This provides:

– typology of contexts integrated into the catalogue developed by [Kononova O.V., Prokudin D.E., Yelkina E.E., 2019, Kononova O.V., Prokudin D.E., 2020];

–machine-readable catalogue using standard free software (for example, OJS, DSpace);

– effective search and selection of a software for research purposes in accordance with basic characteristics described in the Dublin Core tags using standard search engines;

– open access to catalogue records for both users and automated indexing;

– automated exchange using OAI-PMH protocol for aggregation of catalogue meta description to other information systems.

ACKNOWLEDGEMENT

The reported study is funded by RFBR according to the research project «The integrated approach elaboration to the analysis of the terminological base of the developing interdisciplinary research in distributed network environment» № 18-011-00923, 2018-2020.

REFERENCES

4 Free and Open Source Text Analysis Software. https://www.softwareadvice.com/resources/easiest-to-use-free-and-open-source-text-analysis-software/

Andsbjerg R., Vesset D., 2018. *IDC's Worldwide Software Taxonomy, 2018: Update*. https://www.idc.com/getdoc.jsp?containerId=US44835319

Brisebois R., Abran A., Nadembega, A., 2017. A Semantic Metadata Enrichment Software Ecosystem (SMESE) Based on a Multi-Platform Metadata Model for Digital Libraries. *In Journal of Software Engineering and Applications*. No. 10, pp. 370-405. DOI:10.4236/jsea.2017.104022

Computing Classification System. https://dl.acm.org/ccs

DCMI Qualifiers. Dublin Core Metadata Initiative. https://www.dublincore.org/specifications/dublin-core/dcmes-qualifiers

DSpace/dublin-core-types.xml at master DSpace. DSpace. GitHub. https://github.com/DSpace/DSpace/blob/master/dspace/config/registries/dublin-core-types.xml

Fedotov A.M., Leonova Y.V., 2018. Requirements for the prototype of the information resources management system in distributed information systems for the support of scientific research. *In Computational technologies*. Vol. 23, № 5, pp. 82-109. DOI:10.25743/ICT.2018.23.5.008

González R., Van Der Meer K., 2004. Standard Metadata Applied to Software Retrieval. *In Journal of Information Science*. Vol. 30(4), pp. 300–309. DOI: 10.1177/0165551504045850

Kononova O.V., Prokudin D.E., 2020. An approach to extraction, explication and presentation of contextual knowledge in the study of developing interdisciplinary research areas. *In International Journal of Open Information Technologies*. Vol 8, № 1, pp. 90-101. URL: http://injoit.org/index.php/j1/article/view/882/844

Kononova O.V., Prokudin D.E., Yelkina E.E., 2019. Contextual Knowledge Extraction: Terminological Landscape of Digital Economy. *In Sociology of Science and Technology*. Vol. 10(3), pp. 103-120. DOI:10.24411/2079-0910-2019-13006

Moss K., 2012. The Entity-Relationship model // IEEE Global Engineering Education Conference, EDUCON.

Noor S., Shah L., Adil M., Gohar N., Saman G.E., Jamil S., Qayum F., 2019. Modeling and representation of built cultural heritage data using semantic web technologies and building information model. *In Computational and Mathematical Organization Theory*, № 25, pp. 1-24. DOI: 10.1007/s10588-018-09285-y

SUNScholar/Metadata/By Function. Libopedia. https://wiki.lib.sun.ac.za/index.php/SUNScholar/ Metadata/By_Function

Text Analysis, Text Mining, and Information Retrieval Software. https://www.kdnuggets.com/software/text.html

Text Mining Software. https://www.capterra.com/text-mining-software

Text mining, text analytics & content analysis with free open source software. https://www.opensemanticsearch.org/doc/analytics/textmining

Woodward A., Anderson R., Biscotti F., Contu R., Gupta N., Hunter E., Hare J., Bhullar B., Dayley A., Roth C., Swinehart H., Dsilva V., Wurster L., Poulter J., Palanca T., Deshpande S., Pang C., Abbabatulla, B., Warrilow M., Dharmasthira Y., Kostoulas J., 2019. Market Definitions and Methodology: Software. Gartner, Stamford. https://www.gartner.com/en/documents/3906823/market-definitions-and-methodology-software

AN NVME FPGA-BASED SMART SWITCH ARCHITECTURE WITH ONLINE RECONFIGURATION

Vinicius G. Linden[1], Cassiano S. Campes[1,2], Lúcio R. Prade[1], Bruna F. Flesch[1] and Rodrigo M. de Figueiredo[1]
[1]*Polytechnic School, Unisinos University, Brazil*
[2] *College of Information and Communication Engineering, Sungkyunkwan University, South Korea*

ABSTRACT

Solid State Drives (SSDs) are replacing the traditional Hard Disk Drives (HDD) in data servers due to its very fast speeds. Furthermore, many researches have proposed improvements in different aspects of its functionality, mainly in hardware and firmware. This transition has released the previous SSDs bandwidth limitations. Cheaper and denser SSDs have facilitated their adoption to replace HDDs. With the introduction of the Non-Volatile Memory Express (NVMe), the performance enhancement revealed a new trend: the bottleneck is now at the main processor, and no longer at the storage. A PCIe switch is employed for any given computer system that uses more than one SSD at a time, but not without its limitations. NVMe commands contain essential information inside each field, which might be needed to define the destination SSD. In other words: a PCIe packet is not an NVMe command. This paper proposes an NVMe switch architecture to be applied in bridging and switching of SSD devices used in databases and web servers. With this approach, the flexible architecture is able to decide how the data is going to be stored based on specific NVMe command fields. The architecture main purpose is to provide a solution for decision criteria based on the contents of one or more NVMe fields. Therefore, an external device or even the host is able to reconfigure switching criteria at run-time. This fact increases control over SSDs. The proposed architecture is flexible and expandable in terms of functionality. Xilinx Vivado Simulator 2019 was used to design and validate the architecture in VHDL.

KEYWORDS

NVMe, SSD, Smart Switch, HDL, FPGA, Database

1. INTRODUCTION

SSD presented a major development in the past few years. Research has greatly contributed to this development, relying on hardware built by the manufacturers. An example is the NVMe base specification (NVMExpress, n. d.) that was created by the industry to allow gathering performance for the intrinsic parallelism of flash memory devices, present in SSDs. This industry reliance means that most of the implementations details are not shared, configuring parts of it as a black box. PCIe switches are used to build a multi-SSD system, yet again abstracting control away from the host. From the aforementioned, a tool that gives more control over the SSD to the host is needed.

In this study, we detail an NVMe FPGA-based Smart Switch architecture started in (Linden, 2020a) with online reconfiguration of switching criteria for NVMe SSDs, which can be expanded if required. The Smart Switch module is split between PCIe and NVMe modules in order to allow more flexibility. The switch is in datapath configuration, with the generic NVMe inside it, although it can be outsourced. Also, it contains an *arbitrator module* which classifies data and send them to the generic NVMe or the SSD. A conceptual test was performed in VHDL, whose results are discussed in section 5. The next section discuss related concepts to this work.

1.1 Background Concepts

The typical SSD architecture consists on multiple layers, built with hardware and firmware. Each of those layers has a single purpose. Communication with flash layer ICs, ECC, for implementing typical flash memory algorithms and for the host interface are addressed in specific layers. The latter depends on whether the SSD has a SATA or PCIe bus. The most advanced protocol for SSD applications is PCIe bus and it implements NVMe protocol.

The NVMe base concept steams from a simple producer consumer system, with a queue in the middle of both. This allows for multiple producers, consumers and queues in parallel. Each NVMe controller has pairs of queues, one for Submission Command (SC) and at least one for Completion Command (CC). Such pairs are known are cores.

A controller has at least two cores: one for administrative purposes and the other one for general I/O. A SC is put in a submission queue by the host and then processed by the SSD. When the memory device has processed this request, it puts the CC answer in the completion queue for the host to acknowledge the SC status. The current specification (1.4) allows for up to 65,535 queues, with each queue supporting up to 65,535 commands. In this way, parallel out-of-order completion is enabled.

Each NVMe command has multiple fields, whose presence depends on an opcode field. For example, reading, writing, flushing, among others. Furthermore, standard opcodes are listed in the base specification, with room for proprietary opcodes. Besides, a proprietary command is a manufacturer-specific command that the researcher has no access to and unlikely knows its workflow. Next subsection discusses motivation of study.

1.2 Motivation

The NVMe specification improved the SSD hardware from a simple passive device to an active one hence alleviating some CPU allocation from the host. At the same time, the host computer no longer has control over the SSDs decisions. For example, it is unable to specify where the SSD has to write specific datasets, thus generating an inconvenient situation in which the SSD cannot easily adapt to different workloads.

As previously stated, an array of SSDs is usually routed through a PCIe switch, but since PCIe packets are not the same as NVMe commands, NVMe fields are not accessible to the switch in this manner. Thus, a PCIe switch does not allow for NVMe-based command threshing. Inside each SSDs, the NVMe controllers may already separate command on a variety of criteria, such as stream IDs (Bhimani et al., 2018; Kang et al., 2014) and safety purpose, whether to use SLC or MLC (Cai et al., 2015). However, this does not allow for individual NVMe command routing. From the developed state-of-the-art, few studies address this matter. Thus, the routing criteria based on a reconfigurable aspect of the NVMe command itself is to be put-forward. These criteria are applied to separate commands based on the content of one or more of NVMe fields.

2. RELATED WORKS

This section presents studies that applied FPGAs in order to increase processing bandwidth. The work proposed in Linden (2020a) discusses how to enable fast decision criteria in NVMe SSDs with use of a switch. Commonly, such studies are formed by an FPGA with a flash memory and other processing systems developed by the CPU. Song et al. (2016) develop an open platform for SSD and flash-memory related development. Although there are several similarities between such work and the architecture detailed in this paper, they are fundamentally different. OpenSSD is a generic platform designed to implement flash memory algorithms. However, this platform lacks the bandwidth for NVMe switching and does not present SSD connectors. Cai et al. (2011) proposes an FPGA-based platform to access flash memory enabling increase of SSD. It focus on studying SSD life cycle in a short period. By targeting bad pages instead of bad blocks, they increased SSD life cycle by 51 %.

Complex algorithms are addressed in Yoshimi et al. (2016) and Jun et al. (2017). Also, a "sort-reduce" architecture for a hybrid system of CPU with FPGA accelerator is proposed by Jun et al. (2018). A Minimum spanning tree (MST) problem is studied with application of Kruscal algorithm (Li et al., 2018) in order to deal with complex systems as social media, Internet page classifications, neural networks and even virtual intentional harm attacks. Rouhani et al. (2015) defines a new prototype for matrix computing dense called SSketch. Data arrays are used densely when they have a high degree of correlation, that is, non-zero elements. SSketch uses several kernel OMPs to generate a sparse dictionary matrix and a weight matrix. A weight matrix is composed of blocks, each block being ideally independent. With the proposal for integrating programmable logic in cell phones, Coughlin et al. (2016) proposes a combination of FPGA and smartphone. For application and distribution, store of hybrid applications (software and hardware) is idealized and designed with resource restriction to prevent malicious applications from harming a smartphone.

Prior papers have used FPGA to process algorithms in-datapath configuration (Yoshimi et al, 2016; Jun et al, 2017; Rouhani et al, 2015) achieving its goals with much stricter restrictions on power and time than similar implementation in a CPU. Other researches processed information in a similar manner with an SSD as the end target (Bhimani et al, 2018; Kang et al, 2014; Cai et al, 2011). Inline deduplication for SSD storage has been developed in (Cai et al, 2011) resulting in less memory consumption and consequently extending the SSD lifetime. A novel multistream system for internally separating different commands into distinct memory locations has also been implemented (Bhimani et al, 2018). Some papers such as Song et al (2016) and Cai et al (2011) have even proposed prototyping platform specific for flash memory. However, each one of these is for NAND flash chips and not SSDs. The next section discusses the proposed system.

3. PROPOSED SYSTEM

A configuration for the arbitration is introduced via an external electronic device. The down-link may be channeled either to the SSD or to a "generic NVMe", which stands for a generic device name. The PCIe peripheral one deals with tasks related to the PCIe control portion, simulating a regular peripheral SSD, outputting the data in an intermediate bus convention. Regarding the NVMe target module, it addresses the NVMe control portion by simulating a regular SSD controller and outputting the data to an NVMe streaming convention.

The module smart switch refers to the main goal of this study and is addressed in section 3.1. Tasks related to the NVMe control portion, simulation of a regular host NVMe driver, acquisition of data as NVMe streaming convention presented in this section and outputting it to an intermediate BUS convention are developed in the NVMe host module. PCIe portion controlling, simulation of a regular PCIe root complex, receivement of data as the intermediate BUS convention and outputting it to the PCIe BUS are performed in the PCI host module. Also, general purpose clock management and global buffer line instantiation are done in the clock generation and distribution.

The external interface deals with general purpose communication with an external device, allowing for arbitration configuration to be inputted. The flow of NVMe packets occurs in a byte-to-byte basis, known as "nvme_stream". In addition, the transfer starts when both the source and sink acknowledges the first byte. Then, the rest of the bytes are automatically transferred. Length is defined according to the type of command, i.e. Submission Command (SC) or Completion Commands (CC). SC command has a burst length of 64 bytes whereas a CC has 16 bytes.

There are two additional handshake signals in the system. The "valid" one, from the source, indicates the first byte is valid. The second signal is "ready" from the sink, indicating that the sink is ready to receive a full NVMe packet. The ready signal must always be asserted when the sink is ready to receive a packet. However, when the handshake occurs, "ready" must be put unasserted. Figure 1 time diagrams describe discussed functioning of "valid" and "ready" handshake signals.

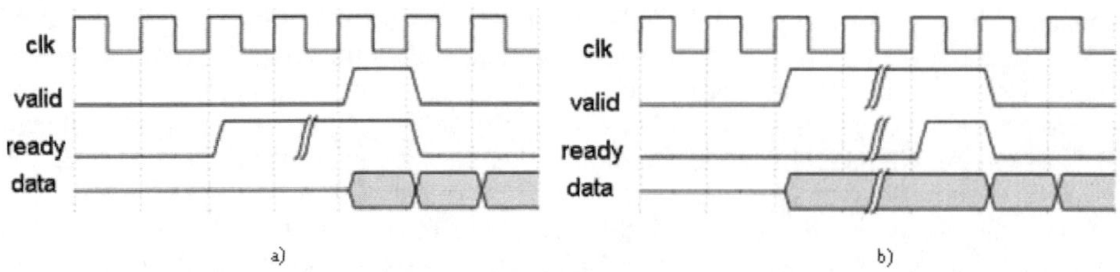

Figure 1. a) Signal *ready* asserted before valid.b) Signal *valid* assertion before ready

Figure 1 a) presents an example in which the sink is ready before a packet is available. The packet is available before sink is ready in Figure 1 b). Note that the first byte is in the bus before the handshake occurs at the next valid clock edge. With this convention established, the BUS cannot simply be split without a FIFO. Multiple sinks imply multiple ready control signals, whereas the convention can only work with one. With this convention understood, the NVMe FPGA-based proposed architecture is discussed in section 3.1.

3.1 NVMe FPGA-based Smart Switch Architecture

Figure 2 presents the proposed architecture. As shown, it establishes connection between NVMe target and NVMe host. The external interface is used to provide for the arbitrator module information of hot warn and cold data. Results presented in section 5 were obtained by implementing the Smart Switch in VHDL, whose files are available in Linden (2020b).

It is also shown that the NVMe stream passes only through the FIFO NVMe module and not through the arbitrator, which only sets the demultiplexer and unloads the FIFO. It is done based on observations of the stream.

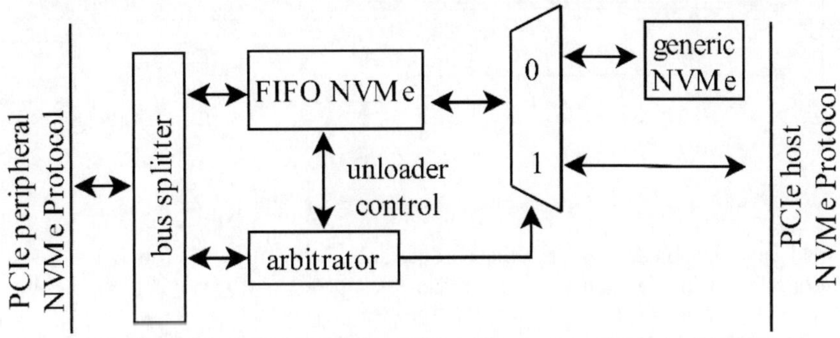

Figure 2. NVMe FPGA-based smart switch architecture block diagram

As seen in Figure 2, the proposed architecture is modular and reconfigurable. It contains a bus splitter module that splits the NVMe streaming bus into two sinks by applying combinational logic to the control ports. This fact makes with one sink blocks the other one. So, the transmission only occurs when both sinks are ready.

Part of data from the bus splitter is stores in a tailored-fit FIFO NVMe module. It acts, in the write-end, as a sink and, in the read-end, as a source. It also has control ports for unloading and giving information - e.g. for indicating if the FIFO is currently unloading. In light of this, the read-end (a source) will only assert the valid signal when there is a command stored and when the FIFO is requested to send the packet. If ready port is unasserted, it will keep valid asserted in order to unload the command. This FIFO is placed in-datapath for clock domain decoupling purposes. Having a coupled clock leaves no extra space for any possible expansion in the architecture and does not allow the arbitrator to stop the incoming flow without packet loss. The arbitrator will also have a halve in one clock domain and the other halve in the other clock domain.

The proposed system contains a demultiplexer specially assembled for the NVMe streaming convention. It is based on two regular demultiplexers and a multiplexer applied in the "nvme_stream" and handshake signals.

The generic NVMe CC module takes a command identification “cmd_id” from the arbitrator module, adds to a consulting table and filters completion commands out based on this table. This is not necessarily required, because, most of the time, there is no closed-loop control in the host driver for this completion command. It is the only module applied to the completion command inside the smart switch architecture.

3.2 Arbitrator

Arbitrator module is expanded in Figure 3. Its function is to select a packet aspect and specify its destination, whether the generic NVMe or the connected SSD. The generic NVMe stands for any device that communicates by using NVMe packet. This module implements several functions, for example, a cache memory to FS fields frequently accessed.

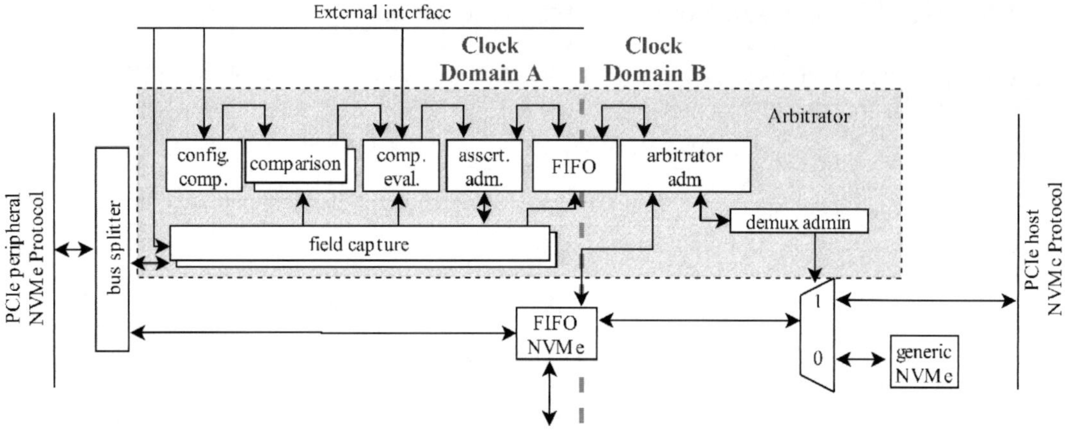

Figure 3. Architecture of arbitrator

The field capture module observes the packets and cherry-picks NVMe fields based on a particular configuration. The field selection is dependent on the opcode and configuration. Because this module is reusable, it has a clear, new data and field ports. The clear port means for the module to externalize the newly captured field, indicated its end. And the port field is the NVMe field - fixed at 64 b wide. Another two key-points are that it indicates the last "nvme_stream" byte.

Regarding comparison module, it outputs a logical '1' or '0' if comparison is true. Comparisons are reconfigurable for type of comparison and comparison values. The module takes two evaluation values and one evaluated value. Depending on the configuration, the module will compare if the evaluated value is within a certain range, defined by one or two evaluation values. Such characteristic is useful in this case, for example, in taking a Start of Logical Block (SLBA) field and seeing if this field hits a certain range inside the SSD. It also has configurations for sending a fixed output depending of the comparison. This module is reconfigurable and reusable for any number of applications. The designer may want to add mode comparison modules in parallel to check for more conditions.

The output of the comparison is evaluated in a module for two reasons. The first one is whether the configuration requires a field for which the command does not have. The second reason is when using multiple comparison modules, those outputs will have to be gated to generate a single direction. Similarly to the field capture configuration, the comparison configuration module outputs the configuration for comparison based on the configuration for arbitration.

A FIFO is employed for complete decoupling both clock domains. The new available port indicates that there is a new command to unload and the next direction port is a read enable request. The assertion FSM module is responsible for managing the field capture module, synchronizing the result with the comparison and inputting the results to the FIFO.

The demultiplexing control was planned considering more than one module asking for control and is implemented in the demux FSM module. Control can only pass to another module with consent of the current module. Therefore, an ask & lock system was implemented to address this matter. So, a module request control over the demultiplexing logic via the ask port. When the module responds with a lock, it holds on for as long as ask is asserted. Release of the control is left to the module via the ask port. Only one module is connected in the conceptual test developed in section 5. The next section presents applied methodology.

4. METHODOLOGY

This research started of by specifying target device to be used in order to identify available resources. Testing was performed with Vivado ™ Simulator 2019.1. The methodology is based on the V-model proposed in IEC 61508 (2010) for critical reliability designs, because of future works addressed in section 6.

Specification requirements, architecture and conceptual design were implemented with use of semi-formal methods applied by the same research group and presented in Flesch et al (2020). They are function block diagrams, transition state diagrams and truth tables for each subsystem that integrates the NVMe FPGA-based smart architecture.

5. RESULTS AND DISCUSSION

The proposed architecture shown in Figure 2 was implemented in VHDL. The conceptual test contains only a single comparison module. Moreover, the filter module was not added. Testing configurations are listed in Table 1. The v1 and v2 for the AC WORKLOAD configuration is respectively: 0x070605040302**00FE** and 0x070605040302**0102**.

Table 1. Tested arbitrator configurations and test packet files

Tested arbitrator configurations			**Test packet files**			
			Title	**Function**	**SLBA**	**AC WORKLOAD Result**
Configuration name	Value	Generic NVMe	Write	Write	0x07060504_030200FE	SSD
AC_IDLE	**0x00**	FALSE	Read1	Read	0x92DC3F96_11BDFCD6	SSD
AC_SEND_GENERIC	**0x01**	TRUE	Read2		0x7060504_03020100	GENERIC NVMe
AC_SEND_SSD	**0x02**	FALSE	NVMe_SQ_B	Proprietary	NA	SSD
AC_WORKLOAD	**0xFE**	$v_1 \le SLBA \le v_2$	NVMe_SQ_B		NA	SSD

Reading of these packets is activated through a bit-flip, telling the system to send the specified packet. These files are then sent to the appropriate NVMe stream channel, with valid and ready. The tested files that correlate to the NVMe packets with the relevant fields, as well as the expected result in the AC WORKLOAD configuration are also listed in Table 1. Whenever a packet does not contain a SLBA field used in AC_WORKLOAD, then the system will send it to the SSD default destination.

In the Figure 4 it is possible to analyze the whole system working. The module receives three different packets: read1, read2 and write. These packets are first loaded into the FIFO NVMe in sequence. Transmission only begins when the receiving-end asserts the ready signal. Relevant packet delivery signals are "host2ssd" and "stream" under SSD or generic for their respective nvme_stream. As expected, only the read2 packet is sent to the generic NVMe when in AC WORKLOAD configuration.

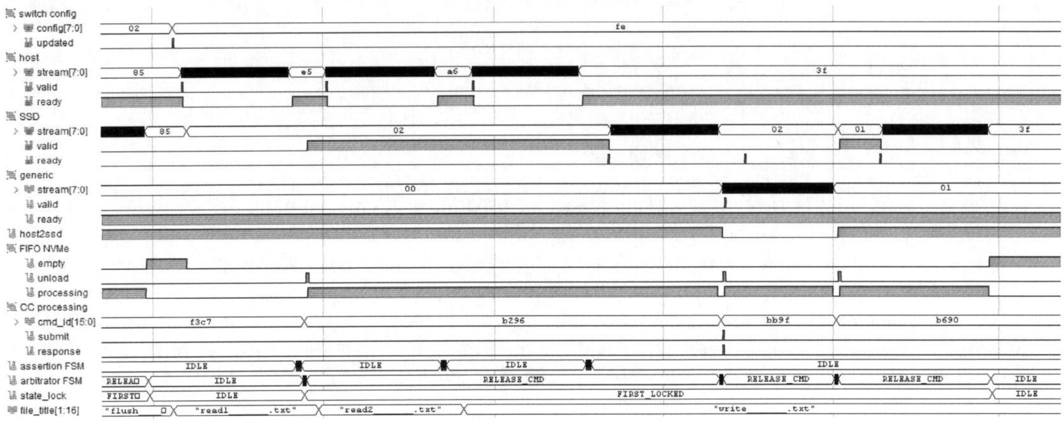

Figure 4. AC_WORKLOAD configuration results

Figure 5 presents results from a fixed direction configuration. All clock domain A logic blocks are assembled separately as the “assertion module”, excepting the field capture module. By doing this, evaluation of configurations signals is possible through testing, especially configuration ones that use range comparison.

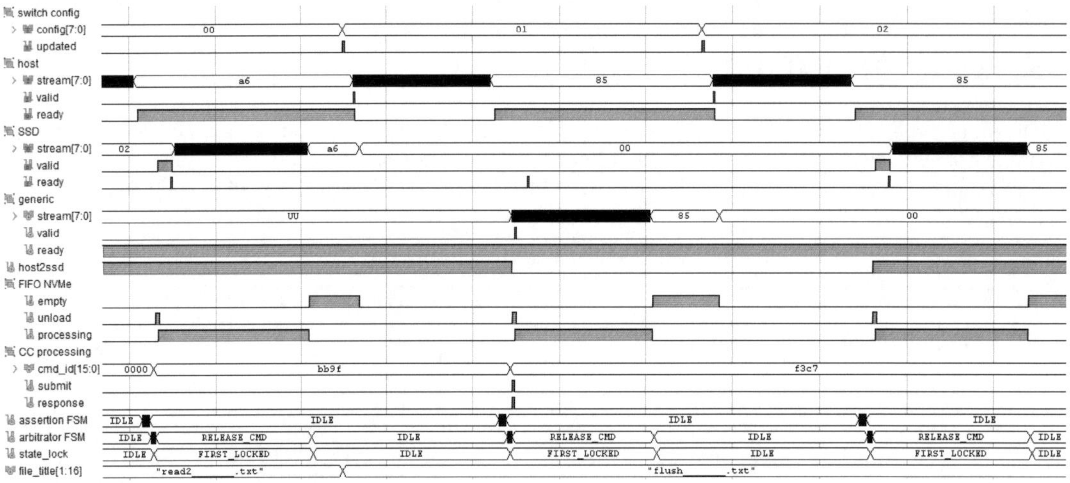

Figure 5. Fixed direction configuration results

It is not possible neither desired to use the testbench previously mentioned in the assertion module simulation. Figure 6 presents results when the proper opcode is supplied and the range is according to the specification the command goes to the generic NVMe. These results concludes the implementation analysis, demonstrating that the proposed architecture conceptual test is feasible.

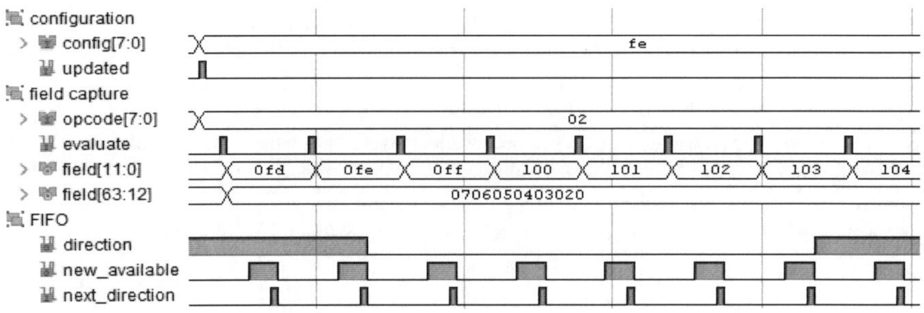

Figure 6. Range testing of assertion module

6. CONCLUSION

We have proposed an NVMe switch architecture for separating NVMe commands based on its fields, in an effort to grain increased control over the SSD. The NVMe streaming convention makes packets out of NVMe commands, thus facilitating the commands flow throughout design. This NVMe packet is the basis for the whole architecture. The conceptual test was performed by implementing a Smart Switch in VHDL.

It should be clear for the reader the scope of this paper is the main idea behind the smart architecture for switching or bridging, specification of decision criteria and implementation of a conceptual test in VHDL. Section 3.3 discusses arbitrator module which specify a packet destination based of the type of data and content of NVMe commands.

Regarding main characteristics of the smart architecture, it is flexible, reconfigurable and provides a number of possibilities in the generic NVMe. Secondly, the proposed system architecture presents a FIFO in the datapath. Packets are processed in order of arrival and there are three FSM in series, but one of them is behind a FIFO and another may be left unused. A generic NVMe CC that allows for future implementation in accordance with the generic NVMe function also forms the proposed system. Moreover, with relation to the bus splitter, it blocks the stream flow only if the FIFO NVMe is full. In this case, both parts of the generic NVMe may block the stream flow. There is a degree of parallelism for dealing with multiple commands due to the employment of FIFOs.

Results presented in section 5 prove that the proposed architecture provides a reconfigurable, flexible and expandable design that is easily modified and increased in functionality. The architecture provided a simple tool for easily implementing a number of criteria to direct NVMe commands. Future areas of study are applying functional safety to the generic NVMe module and studying how the configuration is added to the architecture by an external interface. We will also implement the PCIe and NVMe modules for translating to/from NVMe stream convention.

REFERENCES

Bhimani, J. et al, 2018. FIOS: Feature Based I/O Stream Identification for Improving Endurance of Multi-Stream SSDs. *In 2018 IEEE 11th International Conference on Cloud Computing (CLOUD).*

Cai, Y. et al, 2011. FPGA-Based Solid-State Drive Prototyping Platform. *In 2011 IEEE 19th Annual International Symposium on Field-Programmable Custom Computing Machines.*

Cai, Y. et al, 2015. Read Disturb Errors in MLC NAND Flash Memory: Characterization, Mitigation, and Recovery. *In 2015 45th Annual IEEE/IFIP International Conference on Dependable Systems and Networks.*

Coughlin, M. et al, 2016. *Apps with Hardware: Enabling Run-time Architectural Customization in Smart Phones.* [online] www.usenix.org. Available at: https://www.usenix.org/conference/atc16/technical-sessions/presentation/coughlin(Accessed: 26 July 2020).

Coughlin, M. et al, 2016. *Apps with Hardware: Enabling Run-time Architectural Customization in Smart Phones Apps with Hardware: Enabling Run-time Architectural Customization in Smart Phones.* [online] p.621. Available at: https://www.usenix.org/system/files/conference/atc16/atc16_paper-coughlin.pdf.

Flesch et al, 2020. A Functional Safety Methodology Based on IEC 61508 for Critical Reliability FPGA-Based Designs. *In 2020 International Journal of Emerging Technology and Advanced Engineering.*

Jun, S. et al, 2014. Scalable multi-access flash store for big data analytics. *In 2014 ACM/SIGDA International Symposium on Field-Programmable Gate Arrays - FPGA '14.*

Jun, S. et al, 2017. Terabyte Sort on FPGA-Accelerated Flash Storage. *In 2017 IEEE 25th Annual International Symposium on Field-Programmable Custom Computing Machines (FCCM).*

Kang, J.U. et al, 2014. *The multi-streamed solid-state drive.* [online] Available at: https://www.usenix.org/conference/hotstorage14/workshop-program/presentation/kang [Accessed 10 Nov. 2019].

Li, D. et al, 2018. CISC: Coordinating Intelligent SSD and CPU to Speedup Graph Processing. *In 2018 17th International Symposium on Parallel and Distributed Computing* (ISPDC).

Linden, V. et al, 2020a. Enabling Fast Decision Criteria in NVMe SSDs through NVMe-based Switch. IOSR Journal of Electrical and Electronics Engineering (IOSR-JEEE), [online] 15(2278–1676), pp.54–58. Available at: www.iosrjournals.org.

Linden, V. et al, 2020b. NVMe Switch [online]. Available at: https://gitlab.com/storagesystemslaboratory/nvme-switch. (Accessed: 26 July 2020).

NVMExpress, n. d.What is NVMe™? [Online]. Available at: https://nvmexpress.org/ (Accessed: 26 July 2020).

Ouyang, J. et al, 2014. SDF: *Software-Defined Flash for Web-Scale Internet Storage Systems.* [online] Available at: http://ranger.uta.edu/~sjiang/pubs/papers/ouyang14-SDF.pdf [Accessed 21 Jul. 2020].

Rouhani, B.D. et al, 2015. SSketch: An Automated Framework for Streaming Sketch-Based Analysis of Big Data on FPGA. *In 2015 IEEE 23rd Annual International Symposium on Field-Programmable Custom Computing Machines.*

Song, Y.H. (2016). *Cosmos+ OpenSSD: A NVMe-based open source SSD platform.*

Yoshimi, M. et al, 2016. Accelerating BLAST Computation on an FPGA-enhanced PC Cluster. *In 2016 Fourth International Symposium on Computing and Networking (CANDAR).*

PERSONALIZED WEB SEARCH USING KEY PHRASE-BASED USER PROFILES

Sara Abri[1], Rayan Abri[1] and Salih Cetin[2]
[1]*Department of Computer Engineering, Hacettepe University, Ankara, Turkey*
[2]*Mavinci Informatics Inc., Ankara, Turkey*

ABSTRACT

In the context of the personalized web, the structure of user profiles remains a challenge due to its effect on information retrieval efficiency. In creating a user profile, how to extract collections of metadata of documents is a significant point. Although the efficiency of the structures such as keyword-based has proven, there is not research on key phrase based user profiles in the process of personalization. Previous methods to create user profiles emphasize keyword extraction while ignoring the existence of key phrases in the documents. This article proposes the use of keyphrase-based user profiles in personalized web search. We investigate the state of the art keyphrase extraction algorithms by considering different models of supervised and unsupervised methods. This can overcome the problems of missing keyphrases in user profiles and increase the accuracy of information retrieval. Finally, we evaluate keyphrase-based user profiles using a re-ranking algorithm to complete the process of personalization using different datasets. Personalized models based on supervised keyphrase extraction approaches obtained more accuracy by 7% than unsupervised approaches.

KEYWORDS

Personalized Web Search, Keyphrase Extraction, Graph-based Methods, User Profiling

1. INTRODUCTION

In the personalization process, user profiles are created using user-specific content, user behavior, and user context. The structure of the user profile is an important issue because of its impact on ranking performance. It is clear that if the structure used in the user profile is more robust, the user profile and personalized services result in better efficiency. Therefore, the process of generating user profiles is a difficult problem, and constructing accurate and efficient user profiles is still an open challenge in personalized information retrieval.

A keyphrase consists of a set of word expressions. This set of words can be an indicator of the content or hidden topics of a document. Extracted keyphrase can be used in the fields such as information retrieval (Medelyan, O. et al, (2009)), summarization (Dredze, M. et al, (2008)), clustering (Hammouda, K.M. et al, (2005)), categorization (Hulth, A. and Megyesi, B.B. (2006)) and indexing (Gutwin, C. et al. (1999)) in the text. In this paper, several supervised and unsupervised methods have been proposed to extract keyphrases. The unsupervised methods consist of statistical approaches, topic-based clustering groups, and graphed-based methods. We evaluate several graph-based methods since those are the most commonly used. Among supervised methods, we implemented Kea and WINGNUS to compare with unsupervised methods.

We also conduct comparative research on keyphrase-based user profiles to consider keyphrase-based user profiles in the personalization process. To evaluate the method in the process of personalization, we use ranking approaches for re-ranking the result of respect to the user profiling and the submitted query by the user. The organization of the paper is as follows. Section 2 discusses the related work on keyphrase extraction and personalization. The method including creating keyphrase based user-profiles and the re-ranking process is presented in Section 3 in detail. Evaluation methodology and results are presented in Section 4. Section 5 concludes the discussion.

2. RELATED WORK

2.1 Personalization

There are different ways to create user profiles such as keyword-based or term-based (Matthijs, N. and Radlinski, F. (2011), Daoud, M. et al. (2009)), topic-based (Abri, S and Abri, R.(2020), Harvey, M. et al, (2013) and Abri, S. et al. (2020)) and ontology-based (Sieg, A. et al. (2007), Chirita, A. et al. (2005)) however the main focus to create user model is on the keyword-based in the personalized process. For example, in the personalization process Liu, F. et al. (2004), Karimi, S. and Abri, R. (2016) have created keyword-based profiles by the user's search histories to improve retrieval effectiveness in personalized web search. Weighted keyword vectors as a predominant representation of user preferences and interests as hierarchical concepts in some cases have increased (Santos, R. L. et al. (2010)). Chirita, A. et al. (2005) used a classification on ODP metadata to personalize search and Qiu, G. et al. (2007) used ODP for classifying topics and explored their relations with query ambiguity. Vicente-López, E. et al. (2014) conducted a study on different user profile representation approaches, and Amer, N. et al. (2016) investigated word embedding in the field of personalization.

To employ a keyword-based model for web personalization, it is needed to acquire keywords from documents visited by the users the same as Barla, M. and Bieliková, M. (2010). They have developed the JKeyExtractor library to extract keywords from web pages to make user models.

There are several modified versions of keyword-based user models. For example, Wei, C. et al. (2009) tried to solve a lack of semantic information of keywords and designed a user profile based on the category knowledge base. In this paper, the author attempts to improve the user model by combining the keywords and ontology concepts. Since user interests and search intentions are changing during a search session, long term and short term profiles were also discussed (Vu, T. et al. (2017) and Bennett, P. et al. (2012)). Vu, T. et al. (2017) created temporal user profiles using the user's clicked documents and the profile was used for the ranking process. In another research Vu, T. et al. (2015) also used three typical time scales for building a long-term profile, a daily profile, and a session profile, and the results were improved using click entropy and query position in a search session.

2.2 Keyphrase Extraction

Keyphrase extraction methods are divided into supervised and unsupervised. Various unsupervised methods consist of statistical approaches, topic-based clustering groups, and graphed-based methods. In unsupervised methods, it is used several graph-based methods since those are the most commonly used. From supervised methods, we implemented Kea and WINGNUS to compare with unsupervised methods. Unsupervised methods consist of corpus-dependent and corpus-independent. Most of the corpus-independent methods are graph-based.

Graph-based keyphrase extraction introduced with TextRank by Mihalcea and Tarau (2004) is applied to rank words based on their associations in the graph. Keyphrases are formed by adjacent keywords in the document. The edges may be weighted, like in SingleRank (Xiaojun, W. and Jianguo, X. (2008)), using the number of co-occurrences as weights. The nodes are scored using some node ranking metric, such as degree centrality or PageRank. Chris, M. et al. (2015) used a WordAttractionRank approach to incorporate the distance between the words.

Keywords and keyphrases can be used to enrich the presentation of search results and help users to understand the main topics of a Web page. Using keywords in creating user profiles is explored in various research however there is a little research on investigating the state of the art methods in keyphrase extraction to create keyphrase based user profiles in the process of personalization. For example, Hulth (2004) described a system along the keywords extraction process for web pages returned by Google search engine. Therefore we decided to investigate how personalization can be integrated into the state of the art keyphrase extraction models.

3. USER PROFILING PROCESS

The user modeling process is to capture, record, and manage user needs and interests, by creating a user profile. The system developed by Tang, J. et al. (2010) constructed user profiling into three sub-tasks consisting of profile extraction, integration, and interest discovery. A simple user profile is based on terms of all relevant feedback containing stemmed terms, frequency, and weight. A user profiling process can be conducted into the following subprocess, collecting information like behaviors, pre-processing of collected information, and analyzing information to create a user model. Finally, technology or application exploits the created user profile to provide personalized services.

3.1 Collecting and Pre-Processing User Data

Older systems gathered data explicitly from the users while recent research is focused on implicit methods or behavioral user profiling for collection information. There are two major matters of collecting information. The content of the data collected and techniques to collect information. The content of the data includes browsing data, bookmarking data, click-through data while methods to collect data are divided into explicit and implicit methods. In more research, implicit methods are preferred because of the access to large sources of data in contrast to explicit methods with a few data. Using an implicit dataset we can study many different users interactions while it will be infeasible with explicit data. In this paper, we use clicked pages by a user to create a user profile.

After the collection of relevant information, it might need a preprocessing process to remove duplicate and clean up the data. Besides, the extracted URL or document also needs to be cleaned. To clean, we extracted the content of clicked pages by users and then did a pre-processing on extracted documents. To do this, we did a collection of word tokenization, sentence segmentation, steaming, stop-word removing, and parsing process provided by the python Natural Language Toolkit (Nltk) for English. The candidate keyphrases are stemmed using porter steaming on words to reduce the number of mismatches.

3.2 Personalization Using Keyphrase Based Profiles

We create user profiles in the form of keyphrases extracted of clicked documents by users using keyphrase extraction methods. We use a number of models such as TF-IDF, RAKE (Stuart, R., et al. (2010)), TopicRank (Bougouin, A. et al. (2013)), TextRank (Mihalcea and Tarau (2004)), Kea(Keyphrase Extraction Algorithm) Witten, IH. et al. (1999) and WINGNUS (Thuy, D. et al. (2010)) to extract keyphrases. Current methods in unsupervised are divided into statistical models and graph-based models. Among statistical models, TF-IDF is used successfully and we intended to use it as a basic algorithm to the comparison. TF-IDF described in Equation 1. can be used for stop-words filtering in various subject fields including text summarization and classification.

$$w_{i,j} = tf_{i,j} \times log\frac{N}{df_i} \quad (1)$$

Where tf_{ij} and df_i are the number of occurrences of i in j and the number of documents containing i. N is the total number of documents. In keyphrases extraction algorithms, in the first step, keyphrase candidates are extracted from the content of the document, then candidates are ranked using a weighting mechanism or a machine learning technique as unsupervised or supervised. Finally, the top-K highest weighted candidates are selected. More on unsupervised keyphrase extraction methods, we apply efficient graph-based models such as RAKE, TopicRank, and TextRank. In graph-based models, a graph is built based on words or phrases where the edges' weights are computed using co-occurrence counts (Xiaojun, W. and Jianguo, X. (2008) and Yutaka, M., and Mitsuru, I. (2004)).

The RAKE algorithm proposed by Stuart, R., et al. (2010), is a language-independent method that extracts keywords by analyzing word frequency and its co-occurrence with other words in the text. RAKE focuses on finding multi-word phrases containing frequent words. First, RAKE splits the text into sentences using punctuation signs and generates the candidates. All words listed in the stop-word file will be treated as phrase boundaries. RAKE is based on the theory that keyphrases frequently contain multiple words but rarely contain standard punctuation or stop words or other words with minimal lexical meaning, however, it won't work in cases where the stop-word is part of the phrase.

The TextRank algorithm proposed by Mihalcea and Tarau (2004), is an algorithm based on PageRank and the same as RAKE extracts key phrases by a co-occurrence graph. In this algorithm, documents are split into the sentences, and the words with specific tags such as noun, prop, and verb. Then a graph of words is created and the weight for each node is calculated. It collects the influence of each of its connections and determines the new score for the node. In this way, TextRank considers the similarity between each sentence to all other sentences.

The TopicRank algorithm proposed by Bougouin, A. et al. (2013), is an improvement of the TextRank that extracts key phrases using a topical representation of the document. Candidate keyphrases are clustered into topics and used as vertices in a graph. A graph-based ranking model is applied to assign a score to each topic. In the TopicRank approach, ranking topics instead of words is a more straightforward way to identify the set of keyphrases that covers the main topics of a document. Also, the use of a complete graph captures the semantic relations between topics.

Given a complete graph as E=$\{(v_1,v_2)|\forall v_1,v_2 \in V\}$, $v_1 \neq v_2$ of V $\times$ V, Vertices are topics and the edge between two topics t_i and t_j is weighted according to the strength of their semantic relation. t_i and t_j have a strong semantic relation if their keyphrase candidates often appear close to each other in the document. Therefore, the weight $w_{i,j}$ of their edge is defined as defined equations by Bougouin, A. et al. (2013):

$$w_{i,j} = \sum_{c_i \in t_i} \sum_{c_j \in t_j} dist(c_i, c_j) \tag{2}$$

$$dist(c_i, c_j) = \sum_{p_i \in pos(c_i)} \sum_{p_j \in pos(c_j)} \frac{1}{|p_i - p_j|} \tag{3}$$

Where $dist(c_i, c_j)$ is the reciprocal distance between the offset positions of the candidate keyphrases c_i and c_j and $posc_i$ represents all the offset positions of the candidate keyphrase c_i. After creating a graph, the ranking model TextRank, is used to rank the topics. This ranking model considers a score to topics based on the concept of voting that high scoring topics contribute more to the score of their connected topic t_i.

$$S(t_i) = (1 - \lambda) + \lambda \times \sum_{t_j \in V_i} \frac{w_{i,j} \times S(t_j)}{\sum_{t_k \in V_j} w_{j,k}} \tag{4}$$

Where v_i are the topics voting for t_i and λ is a damping factor generally defined to 0.85. In the following to complete the benchmark, we evaluate supervised models like Kea and WINGNUS as baselines methods. Kea builds a classifier based on the Bayes Theorem using training documents, and it uses the classifier to extract keyphrases from new documents. In the training and extraction phases, KEA analyzes the input document depending on orthographic boundaries (such as punctuation marks, newlines, etc.) and exploits two features: TF-IDF and the first occurrence of the term. In WINGNUS keyphrase candidates are simplex nouns and noun phrases detected using a set of POS filtering rules. Keyphrases are then selected using a Naive Bayes classifier with a large set of features including document logical structure information. Finally extracted keyphrases are stored in the keyphrase based user profiles in the form of XML and in the next step to be applied in the ranking process.

Re-ranking documents for a new query using a keyphrase based user profile, we measure the similarity between the extracted keyphrases of each document in the query log and the keyphrase based user profile for each user by cosine similarity. The cosine similarity is useful because of measures changing between similar documents regardless of the size of the document. It can be measured using Equation 5.

$$cos(\theta) = \frac{\vec{a}.\vec{b}}{\| \vec{a} \| \| \vec{b} \|} = \frac{\Sigma a_i b_i}{\sqrt{\Sigma a_i^2}\sqrt{\Sigma b_i^2}} \tag{5}$$

Where $\vec{a}.\vec{b} = \Sigma a_i.b_i = a_1 b_1 + a_2 b_2 + \dots + a_n b_n$ is the dot product of the two vectors. For the evaluation re-ranking process using keyphrase based user profile, we tried a re-ranking algorithm on the data set and the results are presented in Chapter 4. Besides, we need to consider time in creating user profiles. To build short-term and long-term user profiles, we consider user profiles for one and three months as Vu, T. et al. (2015) and Momtazi, S., and Lindenberg, F. (2016).

4. EVALUATION

4.1 Preparing and Cleaning Data Set

In this paper, evaluation is made on two datasets to investigate the precision of methodology. In the first experiment, we used the AOL data set including the query log collected from 650k users. To clean the data, we first selected those queries which resulted in a click on a URL. In the second experiment, to achieve a more dominant result, we used the data set provided by TREC 2014 Session Track. The Session Track consists of 1021 query sessions for 60 different topics along with the clicked result and user id.

4.2 Evaluation Parameters

To evaluate the personalized model, we divided the dataset into 95% for training and the last 5% of queries for testing. The performances of personalization are evaluated in terms of success at rank k (S@k), the mean reciprocal rank (MRR), and discounted cumulative gain (DCG) up to rank 10 when a maximum of 10 key phrases are extracted (k = 10) to create user profiles. To compare with a baseline method, we use a non-personalized model as a generic ranking without personalization created based on Latent Dirichlet Allocation (LDA) topic model. Building on the same framework introduced by Harvey, M. et al, (2013) and the results presented by Abri S. et al. (2020), documents are ranked with respect to the LDA model *P(d|q)* called NonPTM (Non-Personalized Topic Model) here.

$$NonPTM(d,q) = P(d|q) \propto P(d)P(q|d) \quad (6)$$

$$= P(d)\prod_{w \in q} P(w|d) \quad (7)$$

$$= P(d)\prod_{w \in q}\sum_{z} P(w|z)P(z|d) \quad (8)$$

Where *P(d)* is the prior document probability and *z* is the topic latent variable estimated using LDA. *P(w|z)* and *P(z|d)* are obtained from the LDA topic model. The number of topics used for LDA is an important parameter. Figure 1. shows the MRR for different topic numbers ranging from 10 topics to 100 for two datasets. The results indicate that using 40 topics yields the best results in the AOL dataset and 30 topics for the TREC2014 dataset.

We compare the performance of the proposed method with the state-of-the-art algorithms using an open-source python-based keyphrase extraction toolkit, called pke. The pke toolkit is open source and available at https://github.com/boudinfl/pke. To investigate the effect of various parameters in rake, we explored these parameters depending on the text. It has shown in Figure 2. the parameters that performed best on the current dataset with at most three keywords in each phrase.

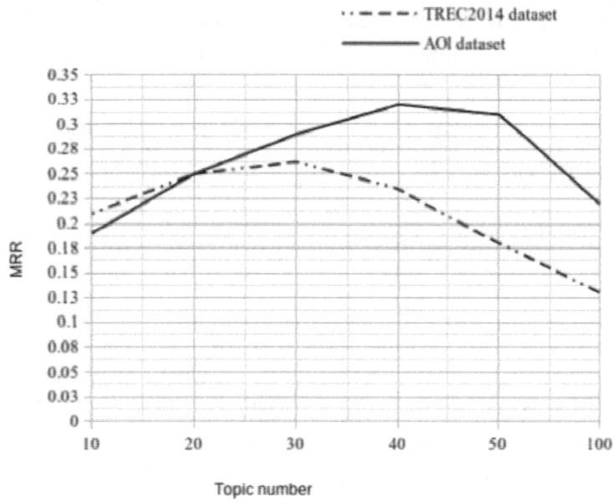

Figure 1. The Changes in MRR with different topic numbers in LDA model

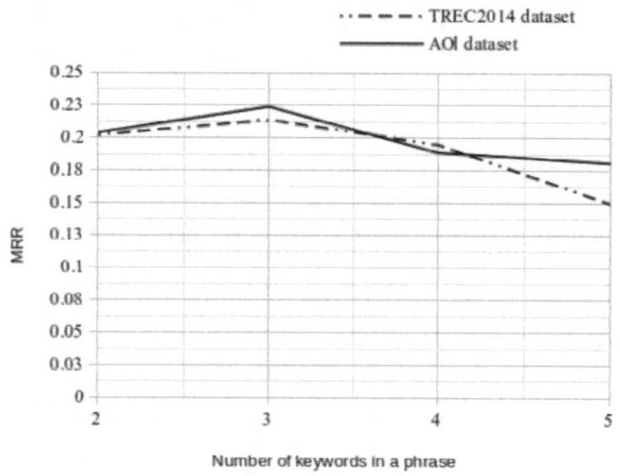

Figure 2. The MRR changes in phrase length in Rake

4.3 Experimental Result

To evaluate the proposed model we provided two experiments with different datasets. In the first experiment, we used the AOL query log data set as a big resource of explicit query log data. In both of the data sets, clicked documents are a reference in building user profiles. We will present the result of the experiments in the following. The models are called as personalized keyphrase extraction(PKM). For example, PKM-TextRank is a personalized ranking model based on TextRank keyphrase extraction. In this model, TextRank keyphrase extraction is used in creating user profiles.

Tables 1. and 2. report the MRR, S@1, S@10, and nDCG@10 scores for Non-persobnalized topic model(Non-PTM) and personalized keyphrase extraction(PKM) models in AOL and Session Track 2014 datasets. In Table 1., the columns represent the used methods including Non-PTM, TextRank, Rake, and TF-IDF. To consider the time dimension in the process of user profiling, we separated profiles as short-term and long-term user profiles. As depicted in Table 1., the best results are obtained with the Non-PTM and TextRank methods. In Personalization using the TextRank(PKM-TextRank) model, the MRR is 32% for short-term and 26% for the long-term while it needs more time to run rather than Rake and TF-IDF. It can be seen using the results that in all methods created based on the short-term profiles are more highly efficient than the long-term profiles.

Table 1. Ranking Performance of Non-PTM and personalized keyphrase based models on the AOL data set

	Non-PTM			PKM-TextRank			PKM-Rake			PKM-Tfidf		
	S@1	S@10	MRR@10	S@1	S@10	MRR@10	S@1	S@10	MRR@10	S@1	S@10	MRR@10
Long-Term	0.205	0.371	0.267	0.201	0.353	0.259	0.181	0.310	0.224	0.172	0.308	0.218
Short-Term	0.282	0.436	0.330	0.280	0.410	0.325	0.250	0.368	0.297	0.255	0.358	0.296

Table 2 represents the ranking score when using non-personalization and personalization based on keyphrase based profiles using a set of supervised and unsupervised approaches. Among supervised approaches, Kea and WINGNUS are used as basic approaches while the best results (%35 in nDCG@10)are obtained using created models using these methods. In unsupervised methods also we tried TextRank, Rake, and TopicRank as graph-based methods and TF-IDF as a feature-based unsupervised method. As shown in Table 2., PKM-TF-IDF resulted in the best performance in nDCG@10 among all approaches. To investigate the effect of the time factor in creating a user profile on the SessionTrack dataset, we compared session-based and long-term based profiles. The result is depicted in Figure 3. As the result shows supervised approaches (Kea and WINGNUS) have provided more successful results although those are needed for training data and so the bias towards the domain on which they are trained is a critical issue. The tendency in performance in session-based profiles is more than long-term profiles in all personalized models.

Table 2. Ranking Performance of Non-PTM and personalized keyphrase based models on the Session Track 2014

	S@1	S@10	MRR@10	DCG@10
Nonpersonalized topic-based model(Non-PTM)	0.216	0.340	0.262	0.291
Personalized keyphrase-based models(PKM)				
PKM-TextRank	0.197	0.318	0.238	0.263
PKM-Rake	0.175	0.303	0.214	0.249
PKM-TopicRank	0.204	0.326	0.240	0.272
PKM-Tfidf	0.213	0.335	0.257	0.280
PKM-Kea	0.257	0.390	0.304	0.348
PKM-WINGNUS	0.260	0.395	0.310	0.352

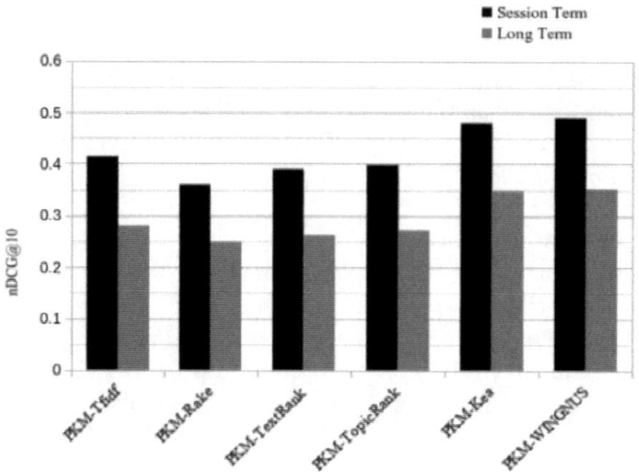

Figure 3. Ranking performance of the six models PKM-TF-IDF, Rake, TextRank, Kea ,WINGNUS and TopicRank using nDCG metric

5. CONCLUSION

In this paper, keyphrase based user profiles in the personalized web search are investigated. In this way, it is considered how integration between keyphrase extraction and personalization by state-of-the-art approaches. The personalization models are created using the state of the art keyphrase extraction approaches considering supervised and unsupervised methods. For evaluation of the model, keyphrase based user profiles using a re-ranking algorithm are applied using different datasets. The personalized models based on the supervised keyphrase extraction approaches obtained more accuracy around 7% than unsupervised approaches. In our experiments, among supervised approaches, both feature-based method and graph-based methods resulted in the same improvement average by 26% in normalized DCG score for long-term compared to 36% for session-term profiles created using Session Track2014 dataset.

REFERENCES

Abri, S and Abri, R. 2020. Providing a personalization model based on fuzzy topic modeling. *Arabian Journal for Science and Engineering.*

Abri, S. et al. 2020. Group-based Personalization Using Topical User Profile. *UMAP '20 Adjunct Proceedings of the 28th ACM Conference on User Modeling, Adaptation and Personalization*. July 2020, pp 181–186.

Abri S. et al. 2020. A Classification on Different Aspects of User Modelling in Personalized Web Search, *4th International Conference on Natural Language Processing and Information Retrieval.*

Abri S. et al. 2020. Estimating Personalization Using Topical User Profile, *In 12th International Conference on Knowledge Discovery and Information Retrieval.*

Amer, N. et al. 2016. Toward word embedding for personalized information retrieval. *Neu-IR: The SIGIR 2016 Workshop on Neural Information Retrieval.*

Barla, M. and Bieliková, M. 2010. Ordinary Web Pages as a Source for Metadata Acquisition for Open Corpus User Modeling. *In: Proceedings of the IADIS International Conference WWW/Internet 2010*, pp. 227-233.

Bennett, P. et al. 2012. Modeling the impact of short- and long-term behavior on search personalization. *In: Proceedings of the 35th international ACM SIGIR conference on Research and development in information retrieval*, pp. 185-194.

Bougouin, A. et al. 2013. Topicrank: Graph-based topic ranking for keyphrase extraction. *In Proceedings of IJCNLP*, pp. 543–551.

Chirita, A. et al. 2005. Using ODP metadata to personalize search. *In: Proceedings of the 28th annual international ACM SIGIR conference on Research and development in information retrieval*, pp 178-185.

Chris, M. et al. 2015. Corpus- independent Generic Keyphrase Extraction Using Word Embedding Vectors.

Daoud, M. et al. 2009. A session based personalized search using an ontological user profile. *In: Proceedings of the 2009 ACM symposium on Applied Computing*, pp. 1732-1736.

Dredze, M. et al, 2008. Generating summary keywords for emails using topics. *In: Proceedings of the 13th International Conference on Intelligent User Interfaces*, pp. 199–206.

Gutwin, C. et al. 1999. Improving browsing in digital libraries with keyphrase indexes. *Decision Support Systems*, Vol. 27, No. (1-2), pp 81–104.

Hammouda, K.M. et al, 2005. CorePhrase: Keyphrase extraction for document clustering. *In: Proceedings of the 4th International Conference on Machine Learning and Data Mining in Pattern Recognition*, pp. 265–274.

Harvey, M. et al, 2013. Building user profiles from topic models for personalised search. I*n: Proceedings of the 22nd ACM international conference on Conference on information & knowledge management*, pp. 2309-2314.

Hulth, A., 2004. Combining machine learning and natural language processing for automatic keyword extraction. Stockholm University.

Hulth, A. and Megyesi, B.B. 2006. A study on automatically extracted keywords in text categorization. *In: Proceedings of the 21st International Conference on Computational Linguistics and the 44th Annual Meeting of the Association for Computational Linguistics*, pp. 537–544.

Karimi, S. and Abri, R. 2016. Improvement of Semantic Search Results with Providing an Updatable Dynamic User Model, *International Journal of Computer Applications(IJCA),* Vol. 155 , No. 4,pp. 7-14.

Liu, F. et al. 2004. Personalized web search for improving retrieval effectiveness. *IEEE Transactions on Knowledge and Data Engineering*, Vol. 16, No. 1, pp. 28-40.

Matthijs, N. and Radlinski, F. 2011. Personalizing web search using long term browsing history. *In: Proceedings of the fourth ACM international conference on Web search and data mining*, pp 25-34.

Medelyan, O. et al, 2009. Human-competitive tagging using automatic keyphrase extraction. *In: Proceedings of the 2009 Conference on Empirical Methods in Natural Language Processing*, pp. 1318–1327.

Mihalcea, R. and Tarau P., 2004. Textrank: Bringing order into texts. *In Proceedings of EMNLP 2004*, pp. 404–411.

Momtazi, S. and Lindenberg, F. 2016. Generating query suggestions by exploiting latent semantics in query logs. *Journal of Information Science*, pp 437-448.

Qiu, G. et al. 2007. Quantify query ambiguity using odp metadata. *In: Proceedings of the SIGIR '07*, pp. 697-698.

Santos, R. L. et al. 2010. Selectively diversifying web search results. *In: Proceedings of the CIKM '10*, pp. 1179-1188.

Sieg, A. et al. 2007. Web search personalization with ontological user profiles. *In: Proceedings of the sixteenth ACM conference on Conference on information and knowledge management*, pp 525-534.

Stuart, R., et al. 2010. Automatic keyword extraction from individual documents. *Text Mining: Applications and Theory*, pp. 1–20.

Tang, J. et al. 2010. A Combination Approach to Web User Profiling. *In: ACM Transactions on Knowledge Discovery from Data*, Vol. 5, No. 1.

Thuy, D. et al. 2010. Wingnus: Keyphrase extraction utilizing document logical structure. *In Proceedings of SemEval*, pp. 166–169.

Vicente-López, E. et al. 2014. Personalization of Parliamentary Document Retrieval using different User Profiles. *In: Proceedings of the 2nd International Workshop on Personalization in eGovernment Services and Applications.*

Vu, T. et al. 2015. Modelling time-aware search tasks for search personalisation. *In: Proceedings of the 24th International Conference on World Wide Web*, pp. 131-132.

Vu, T. et al. 2015. Temporal latent topic user profiles for search personalisation. *In: ECIR:37th European Conference on IR Research*, pp. 605-616.

Vu, T. et al. 2017. Personalised Query Suggestion for Intranet Search with Temporal User Profiling. *In: Proceedings of the 2017 Conference on Conference Human Information Interaction and Retrieval*, pp. 265-268.

Wei, C. et al. 2009. A Personalized Model for Ontology-driven User Profiles Mining. *2009 International Symposium on Intelligent Ubiquitous Computing and Education*, pp. 484-487.

Witten, IH. et al. 1999. Kea: practical automatic keyphrase extraction. *In: ACM conference on digital libraries*. New York, NY, USA, pp. 254-255.

Xiaojun, W. and Jianguo, X. 2008. Single Document Keyphrase Extraction Using Neighborhood Knowledge. *In AAAI*, Vol. 8. pp 855–860.

Yutaka, M. and Mitsuru, I. 2004. Keyword extraction from a single document using word co-occurrence statistical information. *International Journal on Artificial Intelligence Tools,* vol. 13, No. 1, pp. 157–169.

IDENTIFYING DIFFICULTIES IN THE KNOWLEDGE TRANSFER PROCESS IN GLOBAL SOFTWARE: A QUALITATIVE ANALYSIS

Franciney O. Lima, Victoria Carolina S. Mattos, Raquel F. V. Cunha, Alexandre S. Teixeira, Marcelo S. Ayres, Luis H. Pascareli, Fernando B. Pires and Bruno A. Bonifácio
Sidia Institute of Science and Technology
Manaus – Amazonas, Brazil

ABSTRACT

Due to increasing demand for new technologies, it is common in software projects to be necessary to incorporate new team members. However, when new hires join a company, they should learn about working process, organization structure, and company corporate culture. Therefore, companies should be adopting strategies to manage and transfer knowledge to better support newcomers. Sidia R&D Institute had to hire new members to increase our Project Leader team, consequence of a massive project demand. As we work in a distributed environment, we use Wiki as an alternative tool for sharing knowledge and for helping newcomers learn about our software development process. However, newer members reported great difficulty during Wiki usage. This paper reports results of a qualitative study aimed to identify the difficulties faced by new team members during wiki usage at Sidia R&D Institute, as well as identify actions that are often adopted to mitigate these difficulties. The study reveals that despite of wiki being important to improve knowledge transfer in Sidia team, newly PLs had difficulties to access wiki information caused by usability issues and lack of adequate knowledge management.

KEYWORDS

Qualitative Analysis, Grounded Theory, Knowledge Management, Knowledge Sharing

1. INTRODUCTION

As software development is increasingly globalized, it is common from massive, in software projects, incorporate new team members. However, newcomers, especially new hires, usually need more time to become acquainted with projects (Bao et al., 2019). During onboarding period, they face several difficulties and challenges such as misunderstandings process, learning curve, and other issues that cause expectation breakdowns (Avram, 2007). For this reason, knowledge management process must be organized and implemented in order to reduce technical and sociological difficulties.

In this context, companies have been adopting varying strategies to manage and transfer knowledge since, success can be difficult (Heredia et al., 2017). To better support newcomers in onboarding process, difficulties must be identified and understood.

Sidia is a R&D Institute located in Brazil that works collaborating with Samsung Mobile division, located in South Korea, and external stakeholders. Resulting from massive project demand, Sidia had to hire new members to increase team responsible to manage software development process, the Project Leader (PL) team. Despite initial training, new members still faced difficulties, even with the transfer of knowledge from more experienced colleagues to new members, while they are preparing for a project. This scenario generated great difficulty for knowledge management. To reduce these difficulties, we used Wiki as an alternative for sharing knowledge and for helping newcomers learn about our software development process. However, newer PLs reported great difficulty during Wiki usage, due to a large amount of information and difficult to use and explore wiki content.

This paper presents a qualitative analysis aimed to understand which knowledge transfer difficulties are faced by newer PLs. In previous work, we identified alternatives to improve knowledge management process and we identified usability issues of wiki (Cunha et al., 2020). In this paper, we aimed to identify newcomers' learning process and show suggestions applied to improve documentation on Wiki. To accomplish it, we use Grounded Theory (GT) procedures to better understand data results. Thus, we hope to assist companies to improve knowledge transfer and access information in GSD environment.

This paper is structured as follows: Section 2 provides some related work and description of our Company Sidia as well as the GSD setting where we are in. Section 3 describes study planning and design, which we describe how we conducted the survey, and briefly the previous study. In Section 4, we present results achieved. Section 5 concludes and shows some future directions we are planning to follow to continue improving onboarding process and knowledge transfer in the company.

2. BACKGROUND

Due to distributed settings, raises the question of how to speed up the learning of project's newcomers (Kroll et al. 2016). To some extent, newcomers usually need to learn social and technical aspects alone, exploiting existing information in mailing lists, source code repositories, and issue manager (Mahmood, 2015). Furthermore, newcomers may not receive enough training or may not have intimate knowledge of the practices they are normally trained to follow (Heredia et al.,2017).

In this context, tools are essential for collaboration among team members, enabling communication, and knowledge management with more effectiveness (Kanakis, 2019). For this reason, some tools can support as much communication, coordination, documentation as knowledge management, especially in GDS environment.

In this sense, several investigations have focused on understanding how tools can improve collaboration, communication and knowledge management. Due to cost reduction, companies have been adopting Wiki as alternative for knowledge management (Smite, 2017; Bao et al. 2019; Portillo-Rodriguez, 2012). According to related works, Wiki is important resource to knowledge management. However, when Wiki has several information, users can face difficulty to use and this scenario can be a problem during onboarding process.

Sidia is a R&D Institute, responsible for improvements on the Android Platform of Samsung products in all Latin America. Institute works collaborating with Samsung Mobile division, located in Korea, and external stakeholders provided by Mobile Network Operators (MNO) from other Latin countries (e.g., Brazil, Mexico, Chile, Peru). Each software project is managed by one PL, responsible to lead developers' team, managing requirements of each software version, negotiate deadlines, and update schedules for each project.

As we work in a distributed environment, we use Wiki as an alternative for sharing knowledge. In Wiki, we put information about working process, tools used, focal points of each MNO, stages of software development process etc. However, we observed that novice PLs faced great difficulty in using the Wiki due to a large amount of information, and difficulty to use and explore information access.

For this reason, we performed a survey with newcomers from our team. Our previous work relied on difficulties faced by newcomers to search for work process information in Wiki and show quantitative results considering perceived usefulness and perceived ease of use indicators within the Technology Acceptance Model – TAM (Cunha et al., 2020). Next Section presents the research conducted, findings, and how we use results to improve our Wiki pages.

3. IMPROVING WIKI THROUGH QUALITATIVE ANALYSIS

Due to massive projects demand, Sidia had to hire new members to increase headcount of PL team. As we work in GSD environment, initial trainings were not enough during onboarding period, hence newly PLs did not have knowledge of project management practices in company.

For this reason, we have been adopting Wiki as alternative tool to manage knowledge. In Wiki tool we have information since overview process until tutorials about tools usage and other working best practices. However, our team had strong difficult to use Wiki content information. In this case, we performed a survey using online questionnaire to understand difficulties faced by our newcomers. Thus, we design a study to analyze data collected. The previous study was detailed reported at Cunha et al. (2020). In this paper we will present qualitative results and improvements applied as contribution of previous work.

3.1 Quantitative Results

The goal of this study was to evaluate Wiki content to knowledge transfer from the perspective of new project leaders by Sidia. In this scenario we designed the study, to collect data using an online questionnaire.

Table 1. Previous study results (Cunha et al., 2020)

Experimental Design	Summary Results
Participants	We choose 24 volunteer participants of PL team. This participants were newly and have initial experience on Sidia project process.
Indicators	To evaluate quality of use and acceptance when participants interacted with wiki, we have analyzed perceived usefulness and perceived ease of use indicators within Technology Acceptance Model – TAM. This model is focused on aspects that are strongly correlated to user acceptance of a given technology.
Results	During study execution, we have applied a questionnaire asking for subjects' opinions towards their improvement. We available questionnaire during a week. We decide to collect information about frequency of usage Wiki due to understanding if information enabled in Wiki is adequate and useful to assist newcomers. Considering **ease of use**, 42% reported that they have difficulty with Wiki content presentation, and another 32% consider Wiki ease to find information. Considering useful perception, 76% of users reported as positive results.

Quantitative results were useful to identify difficulties, failures on training faced by newly PLs. In addition, we also decided to collect qualitative data regarding the participants' interaction with the Wiki. We made such decision aiming to obtain a more accurate result. Thus, we would be able to combine quantitative and qualitative data to better understand the identified problems. Next section we present qualitative analysis.

3.2 Qualitative Results

We gathered data from the follow-up questionnaire from each subject. We intended that questionnaires' data could assist us identifying and understanding which features could be improved to facilitate knowledge transfer, as well as which problems could be compromising the learnability. To analyze data collected we use procedures of Grounded Theory - GT (Mills et al. 2006). We use this method to build knowledge about improvements in Wiki and to identify relationship between subjects reported and some items.

We extracted qualitative data and coding using data reported by PLs. Then, codes found in questionnaires were grouped according to their properties, thus forming concepts that represent categories. For the analysis of inspector's interaction with technique, following categories were defined: Learning Strategies, Wiki Issues, Improvements and Ideas. Considering Learning Strategies category, we found important results to understand how newly PLs learning working process, see Figure 1.

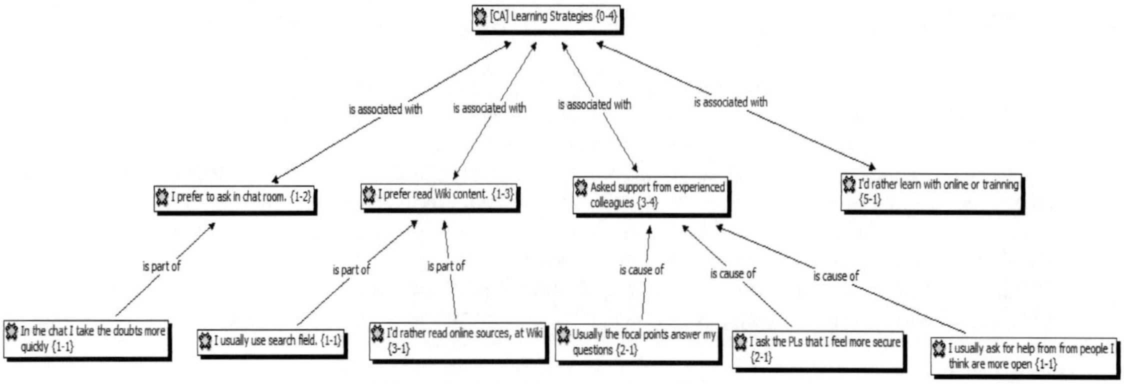

Figure 1. Points related learning strategies follow by newly PLs

About learning strategies, we identified four interactions category used by PLs. Some PLs related that prefer to learn with online or training. Some PLs prefer to ask for experienced PLs on chatroom. One participant related that *"In the chat I take the doubts more quickly"*. Another PLs prefer to read Wiki content using resources available in the tool. One participant said that "*I usually use search field*", an others participants related that *"I'd rather read online sources, at Wiki"*. In addition, most participants prefer to ask support for experienced colleagues. Some participants related that focal points of project have important role to support newly PL, as *"Usually focal points answer my questions"*; and others prefer asked colleagues that they feel more secure or open to receive correct response. For example, one participant said that *"I usually ask for help from people I think are more open"*. Thus, we can observe that despite trainings and content, newly PLs prefer ask for experienced colleagues. This scenario supports that we have to improve content to create best learning experience for newcomers.

Related to Wiki issues (Figure 2), we identified some problems that affect learning experience by newly PLs. Some PLs reported that improvements are related to usability issues. One participant said that *"Someone give review before page published in wiki"*. Another participant had strong difficulty to add new resources in Wiki, and said that *"I didn't find a way to write and add some HTML elements, like collapse sections.* This report allows us identify need to add plugins or add-ons to support new resources and contents.

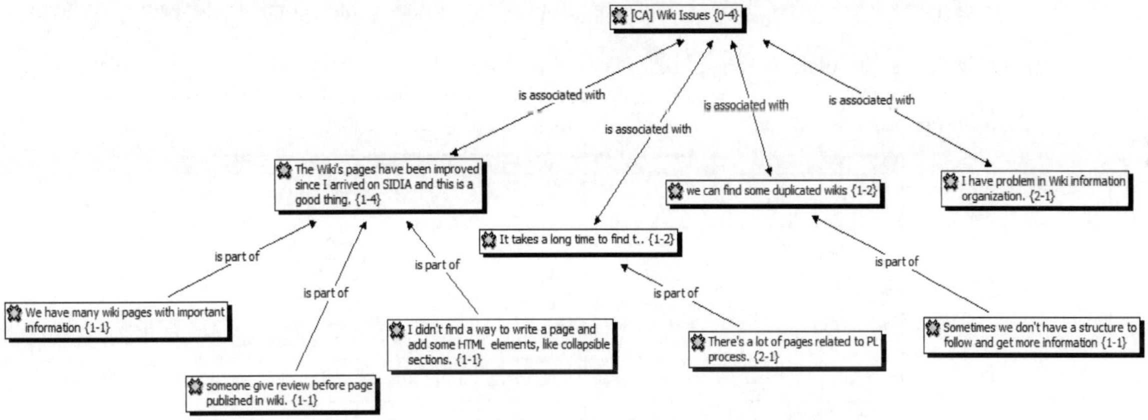

Figure 2. Wiki issues relations identified with qualitative analysis

Some participants reported that they found several pages duplicated as said one participant: *"Sometimes we don't have structure to follow and get more information"*. Another participant said that "*It's too difficult to find information on tool*", caused by Wiki organization. These factors may assist on improving the user experience when fixed. Considering information issue, one participant said that *"We have many pages with important information"*. These issues related usability and organization have been impacted negatively on PLs' interaction. In this case, these problems affect finding information desired by PLs.

Considering improvement and new ideas, most important contribution of this study was related usability improvements. These improvements are related to structural contents and topics suggested by subjects, see Figure 3.

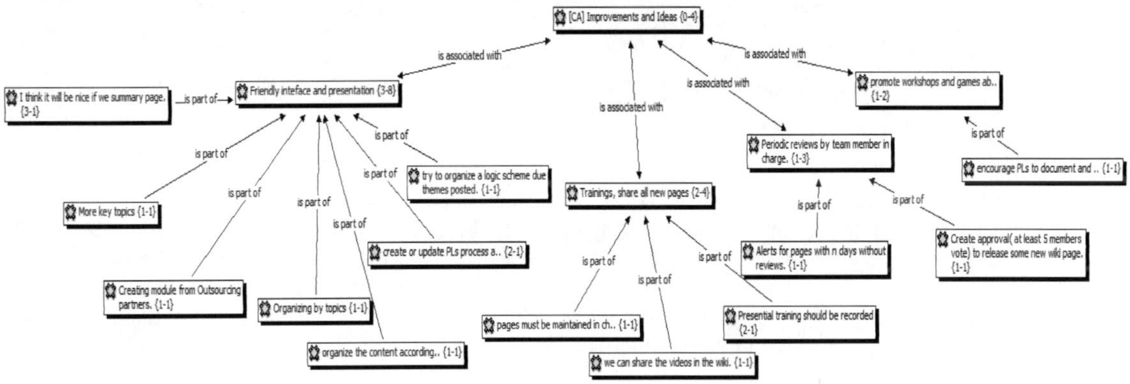

Figure 3. Improvements and ideas suggested by participants of study

This qualitative analysis was important to improve Wiki design and to elicit new requirements to be developed. In this context, some participants reported as suggestion to include an index page to facilitate searches. One participant said that *"I think it will be nice if we summary page"*. Other participant suggested *"try to organize logic scheme due theme posted"*. One participant for example suggested: *"More key topic"* and *"create or update PL process"*. In addition, some participants suggested to add new contents as online trainings, periodic review by specific team, alerts when pages have been updated and others improvements. One participant suggested *"Presential training should be recorded"* and *"we can share video training in wiki"*. Other participant suggested to have games and workshops to share and involve PLs, said that *"promote games and workshops"*. These findings were important to improve our training methods during integration phase of newly members. We use a tool to support record training, especially during pandemic period, that our team worked on home office scope. Next section presents contributions and new modifications developed after this case study.

3.2.1 Study Contributions

We used quantitative and qualitative results to improve Wiki content. Considering suggests gathered from participants' study, we created a backlog to better execution improvements. Main change was restructuring Wiki content presentation. Based on results we grouped information and contents based on common knowledge.

Initially Wiki was structured in one page, organized by topics. This organization caused strong difficult to find information. In this case, we created categories and grouped information as: processes, how-to and tutorials, useful information, organization links as showed Figure 4 below.

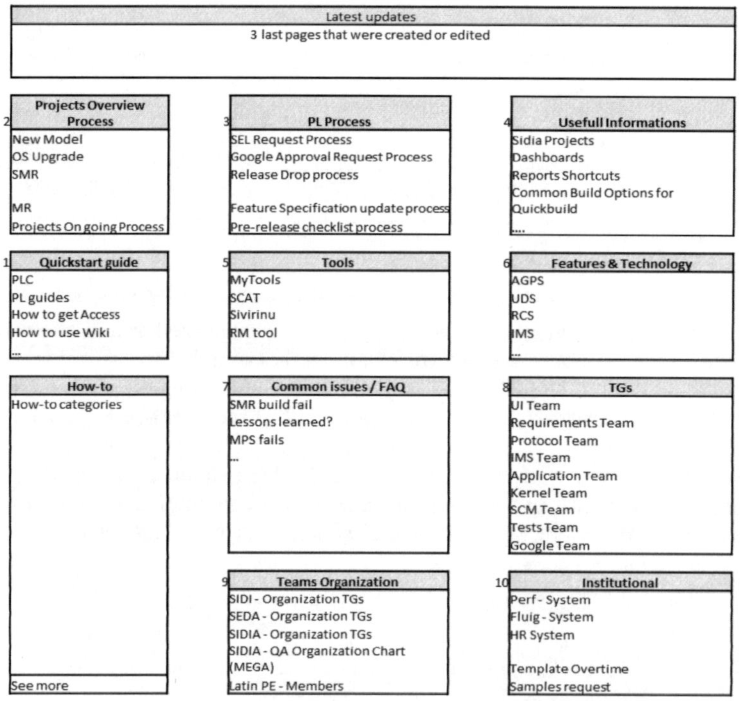

Figure 4. New Wiki structure organization

Figure 4 show new first organization approach adopted after of Wiki analysis. As main changes applied, we created sections based on common content aimed to improve learning during onboarding phase. In addition, we created index with order to better advice newly PLs which section order they should follow. Thus, we divided in chronological order for newly PLs. As improvement was created a specific group to evaluate changes and suggest changes. This group reorganize wiki organization and propose new order based on numbers (see Figure 4). In this case, first section is Project Overview, where newcomers can see all projects process executed by Sidia PL team. After that they can access specific process topics that they prefer, in section PL Process.

We also created common issues section. This section was created by experienced PLs with problems and project issues faced by them that can contribute to newly PLs. Other important change was how-to in specific section, and overview organization teams. As we work in GSD environment this section is important for PL know all team, know who is in charge for specific project (e.g. focal points, to assign issues etc.).

Another contribution was video training that we recorded and shared in specific Wiki page. In addition, we create a process to edit and share new Wiki pages. After this study, we have a specific team named as improvement process team, who is responsible to review and share new pages. We proposed also a template with good practices and content structure, following 5W2H method to facilitate learning, importance of each page and process related that page. The conclusion and future works are described on next Section.

4. CONCLUSION

This paper presented an extension study performed in Wiki, where we collected information about how newcomers learning about the working process at Sidia R&D Institute. Previous work, described in detailed at Cunha et al. (2020), presented quantitative results and overview about difficulties faced by newly PLs during onboarding process at Sidia, specifically about knowledge transfer by new hires members. In this paper, we presented a qualitative analysis results and improvements made as contribution of this study.

In this sense, in previous work we conducted an empirical study attended by 24 volunteer newly PLs from Sidia as participants. We used an online questionnaire with questions based on TAM, considering ease of use, usefulness and motivation and engagement. As results presented, we have observed that participants have difficulty using the wiki, for instance, to search for information on the work process, nomenclatures, teams responsible etc. In this paper we conducted a qualitative analysis, using procedures of Grounded Theory to better understand difficulties and define actions to apply as improvements. In this case, we divide our findings into three categories: Wiki issues, Learning Strategies and Improvements and Ideas.

Considering Wiki issues, we observed that most issues are related to usability and structure content. As improvement we restructured content dividing in section by common knowledge. Considering Learning Strategies, we could see that newly PLs learn most effectively with experienced colleagues. In this case, we proposed training recorded and share in specific page. Considering Improvements, we create a team which is in charge of controlling and managing wiki content and we are planning new action as games and workshops to improve integration by newly PLs. Thus, promoting more contribution by these newcomers in Wiki content presentation.

Based on these results we are redesigning Wiki content. However, another interesting aspect to be investigated, as future work is how to minimize the impact of developer misunderstanding during integration in the company. In our case, we applied Wiki, but it is possible to recommend a set of data analytics based on developer profiles learning. However, it is an aspect that still needs further investigation.

Thus, we will replicate this study after improvement and compare the results with this work. We expect with this experience report to show through practical examples as it is possible to improve the learning process by newcomers in GSD environment. In addition, we intend to encourage software development industry to improve knowledge transfer to improve newcomers' onboarding to better support difficulties faced by them.

ACKNOWLEDGEMENT

Our thanks to Sidia team and SAMSUNG Electronics of Amazon Ltda for partial support, in the terms of Informatics Law N° 8387/91.

REFERENCES

Avram, G. 2007. "Knowledge Wok Practices in Global Software Development," inECKM2007- Proceedings of the 8th European Conference on Knowledge Management, Barcelona, Spain, p 87-97.

Bao, L. et al., 2019. "A large scale study of long-time contributor prediction for GitHub projects," in: IEEE Transactions on Software Engineering, pp. 1 – 22, Vol 1.

Darja Šmite N. B. M. A. Š. C. W., 2017. "Software teams and their knowledge networks in large-scale software development," Information and Software Technology, pp. 71 - 86.

E. Hustad, 2014. "Knowledge networking in global organizations: the transfer of knowledge," in: SIGMIS Conf. on Computer Personnel Research: Careers, Culture, and Ethics in A Networked Environment, 299-239.

F. S. K. D. a. E. A. G. Kanakis, 2019. "Supporting a flexible grouping mechanism for collaborating engineering teams," in: Proceedings of the 14th International Conference on Global Software Engineering.

G. Android, "Android Security Bulletin," 10 02 2020. [Online]. Available: https://source.android.com/security/bulletin.

Heredia, A. et al, 2017. "Tool-supported continuous business process innovation: a case study in globally distributed software teams," European J. International Management, pp. 388 - 405.

H. O. Barbosa et al. 2019. "Uma Análise do Uso de Ferramentas em Desenvolvimento Distribuído de Software para Atualização da Plataforma Android, " in IADIS Americana WWW/Internet 2019, pp. 29- 38. Portugal.

Kroll, J. Mäkiö J. and Assaad, M. 2016. "Challenges and Practices for Effective Knowledge Transfer in Globally Distributed Teams - A Systematic Literature Review," In: 8th International Joint Conference on Knowledge Discovery, Knowledge Engineering and Knowledge Management (IC3K 2016).

Mills, J., Ann, B., Karen, F. 2006. The development of constructivist grounded theory. In: International Journal of Qualitative methods. Cap 5, Vol. 1, 25-35.

Mahmood Niazi et al, 2015. "Empirical investigation of the challenges of the existing tools used in global software development projects," IET software, vol. Vol 9, p. 135 – 143.

M. Chuttur, 2009. "Overview of the Technology Acceptance Model: Origins, Developments and Future Directions," Sprouts: Working Papers on Information Systems, vol. 9, nº Sprouts, pp. 9 - 37.

Portillo-Rodriguez et al., 2012. "Tools used in Global Software Engineering: A systematic mapping review," Information and Software Technology, vol. Vol 54, pp. 663 - 685.

ASSESSING JOB MARKET DYNAMICS USING ELK STACK

Gabriel Silva[1], Mário Rodrigues[2], Marlene Amorim[3], Angélica Souza[4], Marta Dias[3] and Armando Pinho[5]
[1]DETI, [2]ESTGA & IEETA, [3]DEGEIT & GOVCOPP, [4]DEGEIT, [5]DETI & IEETA
University of Aveiro, Campus Universitário de Santiago, Aveiro, Portugal

ABSTRACT

The adoption of digital technologies promises to accelerate the transformation and the agility of processes, work activities and revenue models. Yet, the promised gains come together with dramatic needs for qualified professionals who can effectively leverage the technology potential. Job contexts are being reshaped as new models for the interaction and integration of humans and technologies take shape.
To increase the readiness of the job market in this fast-changing context it is important that all stakeholders – companies, professionals, policy makers – are aware of the job market dynamics and needs. This can be observed from the collection of job announcements, but its high volume requires effective tools for analyzing and simplifying it in order to draw timely and correct conclusions.
ELK stack was used for dealing with the high volume of job announcements. ELK is a stable platform that can manage large quantities of data and the Kibana layer enables to rapidly explore data and create visualization dashboards. As job announcements have distinct formulations for similar roles, depending on the hiring company, this raises the necessity of establishing a common ground for comparing the job descriptions. In this work were mapped job descriptions to ESCO occupations. ESCO is an ontology published by the European Union and its occupations are job positions.
Results show that the ELK stack is a suitable tool for providing a visual interpretation on the job market dynamics. Moreover, the first experiments using natural language processing techniques and machine learning algorithms revealed an accuracy over 0.9 in mapping job descriptions to ESCO occupations. This result is very promising and shows that ESCO a good candidate as common ground to enable comparison of job market dynamics for distinct environments.

KEYWORDS

Natural Language Processing, Ontology, Data Overview, ESCO, ELK Stack, Job Market

1. INTRODUCTION

Digitalization is one of the most popular topics in the agendas of companies and policy makers. For companies, the adoption of digital technologies promises to accelerate the interconnectedness and the agility of processes, work activities and revenue models (Szalavetz, 2019). Yet, the promised gains come together with dramatic needs for qualified professionals who can effectively leverage the technology potential. Job contexts are being reshaped as new models for interaction and integration of human talent and technologies take shape, and as enormous volumes of data are generated at every operation (Freddi, 2018).

The demand for qualified professionals that can make sense of such accelerated and interconnected work systems is already evident, notably in the explosive growth of job announcements in social media and online platforms. The challenge lies in the fact that many of the professional profiles that are in growing demand require new qualifications, and unique combinations of technical and behavioural competences that are hard to find in the current job market (Chryssolouris et al., 2013, Jermans et al., 2020). Several of these new jobs, such as app developers, cloud computing specialists, data scientists, drone operators, data brokers, cyber security specialists, among many, were inexistent in the last decade. For both companies and professionals, this is a critical moment to make sense of the new professional profiles and demands that are emerging, in order to adjust recruitment and qualification and career strategies.

The popularity of online media for recruitment, and the abundance of job postings announced every day, offers a rich setting to learn about the characteristics of the new professional profiles that are in demand to meet the digitalization across all business sectors (Briscariu, 2019, Gelpi, 2019). Moreover, the understanding in the changes taking place in workforce demand is critical for the society, in order to develop detailed knowledge about the forthcoming skills requirements and support the development of adequate education and training programs in a timely manner. This study offers a contribution in such direction and for that it uses state of the art information visualization tools such as the ELK stack (ELK 2020). The study develops tools that allow for the extraction and the analysis of large volumes of data from online job announcements, with the purpose of advancing in the understanding about the emerging demands for competences and skills. The study offers a contribution to bring together the rich information about emerging demand for professional profiles that is scattered across new job announcements, and the existing structured knowledge about skills, competences, qualifications and occupations relevant for the EU labor market that is organized in ESCO (ESCO 2020), the European Skills, Competences and Occupations classification system.

In the next section it is discussed the related work, in section 3 is described the system developed followed by the achieved results and discussion in section 4. The document ends in section 5 with the relevant conclusions.

2. RELATED WORK

In this section literature related to either extracting job information from postings or resumes is presented as well as articles using frameworks such as ESCO.

In the article (Fernández-Sanz, Gómez-Pérez and Castillo-Martínez, 2017), the authors develop a framework called eSkills Match. The framework attempts to align the existing work done by the European Union with the European e-Competence Framework (e-CF), ESCO and the Information and Communication (ICT) Body of Knowledge (BoK) into a single model. This model uses e-CF as the reference framework, tries to relate the BoK directly with it. The authors also use ESCO and relate it with the e-CF framework through skills and knowledges. In the end the authors had a set of 10 ICT job profiles that were used to test the matching method with only 4 of these being present in the article. The authors identify the difficulties in matching different frameworks, requiring external validation from experts at times as well as the need to include more jobs.

In a second article (Chen, Zhang and Niu, 2018) the authors attempt to extract information from resumes. The authors identify two steps needed to extract information from resumes which are not standardized neither in format nor layout. The first step takes as input a resume where the raw text is extracted followed by identifying the composition of each line and using adaptive segmentation in order to output semi-structured data comprised of several key-value pairs. To help generate this data the authors design a novel feature called "Writing Style". The second step is called "Resume Facts Identification" where the previously generated semi-structured data is taken as an input, passed through a multiple category text classifier and the result is structured output resume data containing facts about the resume that was used as an input. The results are compared with PROSPECT and CHM with this method beating both in almost every test done with the added benefit of needing less hours of annotations.

A different approach to extracting information from resumes and converting it into structured data can be seen in (Celik Ertuğrul et al, 2013). An ontology-driven algorithm is used to extract information and match it with concepts. The methodology is based on concept-matching and ontological rules so that semantic analysis and data parsing can be performed on the resumes. Extracting information such as experience, features and business/education information and converting it onto an ontology. The authors propose two algorithms that can be used to accomplish this task and test them on both English and Turkish résumés.

E-Recruitment systems try and give the best possible match between candidates and job descriptions, in this article (Ahmed et al, 2019), the authors propose a new approach to building these systems. The system created extracts the job description text and segments with the help of dictionaries (that are a combination of rules and lists). This segmentation then passes through a Natural Language Processing (NLP) pipeline (sentence splitting, part-of-speech tagging, named entities extraction and compound words extraction) they are then sent to the "Context Builder" and "Enrichment" processes before being stored in the Knowledge Base. This approach is compared with other information extraction software such as OpenCalais and Alchemy and beats them both by quite a margin in all the metrics used (precision, recall and F1) and tests done (job title and requirement extraction).

3. DEVELOPED SYSTEM

Working with different data sources is always a challenging task. Every source has their own schema as well as attributes and naming conventions. A goal to create an adaptive system that could easily ingest data from any source was set at the beginning of this project. Instead of ingesting data from every Application Programming Interface (API) and adding the documents as they were onto the database system, the decision was to create a data model that these documents could be converted to. Figure 1 shows the flow of data in the system that was created.

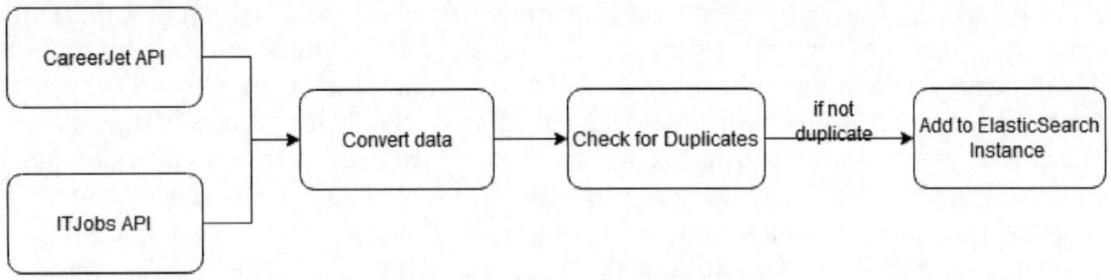

Figure 1. Data Information Flowchart

The creation of this shared data model allows for easier data crunching, inclusion of additional sources of data as well as duplicate detection since the model is the same. Overall, it allows for more control over the data and which fields can be used later for analysis. The whole system works with the ELK (ElasticSearch, Logstash, Kibana) stack (Bajer, 2017).

3.1 Data Sources

In order to develop this work, the first step taken was to find websites that had job offerings and see if there was an API provided so that data could be extracted and stored on our end. The websites considered were LinkedIn, CareerJet, ITJobs, Glassdoor, Stackoverflow, Indeed, Net-Empregos, and Sapo Empregos.

From these websites only CareerJet (CareerJet, 2020) and ITJobs (ITJobs, 2020) had APIs that provided listings to every job posted on their respective websites. LinkedIn also had an API that could be used; however, this would be against their terms of service meaning the accounts could be shut down at any time so it was not selected as a source for data extraction. Glassdoor, Stackoverflow and Indeed do have APIs available, however, there needs to be authorization for them to be used and to get an API key. The last two sources, Net-Empregos and Sapo Empregos, do not have an API that can be used and thus would require web-scrapping techniques in order to extract information. While this is an effective technique, changes on those websites could cause data extraction failures, which is not a desired outcome.

For early stage of development and testing just ITJobs and CareerJet are considered since they offer an API with direct access to the information displayed on their website. These websites offer information about a job posting such as: Posting Date, Company Information, Job Title, Job Description, Job Location among others.

Unfortunately, only ITJobs gives the complete Job Description which is the most useful thing, CareerJet cuts the Job description after a set number of characters making it so that web scrapping had to be used in conjunction with their API in order to get full descriptions and automate the whole process.

3.2 Data Model

Since every data source gives different fields with different names there was the decision to create a unified model under which it was possible to convert the results obtained from API calls to both ITJobs and CareerJet.

This Data model should be comprehensive and extensive but also easily expansible so that everything needed to feed both Kibana and the machine learning algorithms. It should also make use of all the information provided by each API.

Looking at the data gathered by both ITJobs and CareerJet the data model ended up having the following 14 fields: (1) Source - Website it came from; (2) Location - Location of the job; (3) Date Posted - Date in which the job was posted in a year, month, day format; (4) Job Posting - Link to where the job was posted; (5) Title - Job title; (6) Description - The job description written by the company; (7) Company - Name of the recruiting company; (8) Website - Recruiting company website; (9) Contact - Recruiting company contact; (10) Allow Remote - If the work can be done remotely; (11) Salary - Salary ranged the company posted with the job; (12) Type - Whether it's a full-time job or part time; (13) Contract - If the job is temporary or not; and (14) Number of Words - Number of words the job description had.

Having created this model, it is now needed to convert and standardize the data obtained from querying both the ITJobs and the CareerJet APIs. The response obtained by the ITJobs (ITJobs, 2020) API did not need much conversion to our proposed data model. The API returns almost every field in our model (some with different names), except for "Source" and "Job Posting", however, there were incomplete postings that did not contain every field, with the one that was missing the most being "Salary". Besides having to fill in the fields that were not provided the date also had to be converted to the format used by our model.

CareerJet (CareerJet, 2020) was the more troublesome API. The job description had a fix number of characters after which the whole description was truncated. This was solved using web scrapping. The API returned the link to the job posting which is then used to extract the whole job description. Besides the trucated job descriptions the API does not return a lot of information that would be useful in our model. CareerJet is lacking the following fields: Contact, Type, Allow Remote, and Contract. Some of these might be possible to get in the future with more web scrapping or by using NLP methods on the job description.

3.2.1 Handling Duplicates

In order to consider several data sources, it was crucial that our data extraction algorithm could handle duplicates since most of the times companies don't post only on a single website but instead post to several. The first step towards achieving duplicates detection was to make both the job title as well as the company name lower-cased. This was done so that in case the websites handled things differently, for example, some websites like to capitalize the beginning of every word in the title. After standardizing titles and company names, the date a job was posted is also looked at as a possible duplicate detection. The month check is to account for companies that post jobs at different points in time, which could have a multitude of reasons behind, such as, they need mor people to fill that role or because they haven't found anyone within a month time frame which could be significant to identify a lack of specialized employees in that area. Since ElasticSearch uses the Lucene search engine behind, a score is attributed to documents based on their similarity to the query. Having no control over how this similarity score is calculated, in this algorithm, every document returned by the query is looked at as a possible duplicate.

In short, the algorithm is as follows:

Algorithm 1: Job posting duplicate detection

Query ElasticSearch for documents with the same title as the new job
For: Every document retrieved from the query:
  If: New job posting title and company name do MATCH the job in the database **then:**
    If: Month the new job was posted MATCHES the month of the job in the database **then:**
      Return True
Return False

In case the algorithm returns a "True" value this means that there is already a job posting in ElasticSearch with the same exact title, from the same company and posted in the same month so this document will not be added. However, in case the algorithm returns a "False" value this means that ElasticSearch could not find any document like the new one so it should be added.

3.3 Data Presentation

The data presentation layer is done through Kibana in combination with an ElasticSearch instance of ELK (ElasticSearch, Logstash, Kibana) stack. ElasticSearch indexes every field of the documents making it easy for Kibana to quickly get the information needed to generate the graphs. Kibana offers the ability to create several types of graphs and join them in a single interactive dashboard that can be queried. It is a powerful tool that allows users to create easy to read dashboards and compare, for example, the performance of two different cities in an activity sector.

Figure 2 presents an example of dashboard with four areas containing distinct views. Each view is interactive and selecting an attribute in one make the others refresh and adapt to the new filter(s).

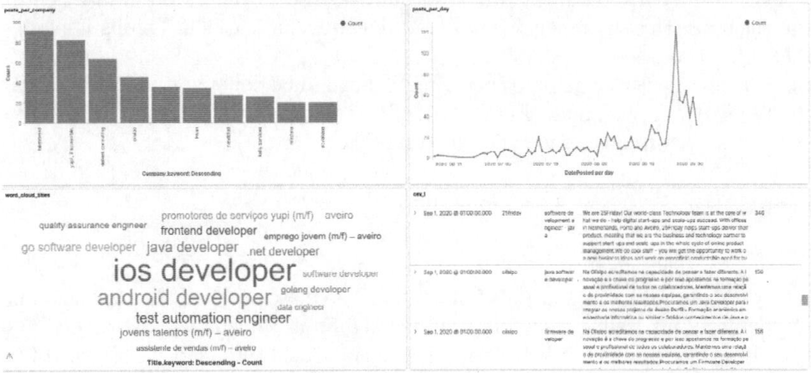

Figure 2. Example of a Dashboard

The dashboard allows an user to visualize the companies with the most job postings (top left bar graph), the number of job postings per day (top right graph), the most sought after job titles (bottom left) and a table visualization of the data that has date of the job posting, company, job title and recruitment description as well as number of words (bottom right).

With the same schema, these dashboards allow for users to select, for example, “ios developer” on the bottom left word cloud and the whole dashboards filters itself as seen in Figure 3.

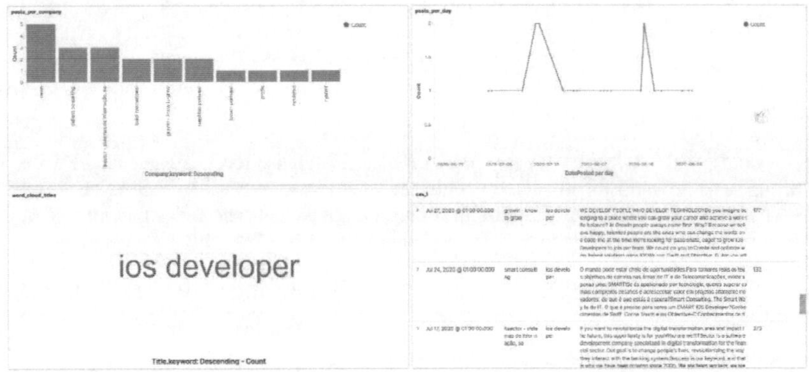

Figure 3. The updated dashboard when the user presses the term “ios developer” in the word cloud

4. RESULTS AND DISCUSSION

The system has been collecting data from ITJobs and CarrerJet for the past 5 months. We have limited the data collected to jobs proposals icluding the region of Aveiro, our region, just to not overload ITJobs and CarrerJet before we make sure that the developed system worked as designed. There was no optimization or specifically designed algorithm having this limitation into consideration.

4.1 Data

So far there are close to four thousand data points (3920) in 5 months with more being added weekly. The filtering algorithm has excluded more than two thousand job postings with each job posting containing between 200-300 words per description with the minimum being 57 words and the maximum being 490. When it comes to data sources, CareerJet has far more data, providing 3519 results while ITJobs has 409 results in our database. This discrepancy can be attributed to the fact that ITJobs is purely focused on job postings for IT roles.

Besides this there was also some pre-processing that had to be done. For our testing data we used a small sample from ITJobs, data corresponding to a week of postings. Some job descriptions had to be translated to English in order to maintain consistency with the rest of the offers.

4.2 Ontology

Each job gathered was classified as an ESCO occupation (European Skills, Competences and Occupations). ESCO describes 2942 occupations and 13485 skills linked to these occupations translated into 27 languages. The following protocol was implemented to train the algorithms to classify jobs as ESCO occupations. For each job posting that was gathered between days 11 and 18 of September 2020 an ESCO category was attributed manually. The manual classification was done by two people that independently classified each job posting, and a third person would choose a classification whenever the first two people did not agree. In the end, for the existing 58 job postings were assigned a total of 9 ESCO occupations, in which the jobs were classified as. However, the data was imbalanced with a few occupations having only 2 or 3 job postings associated with them while, for example, two other occupations have 16 and 14 job postings. Nevertheless, the experiment continued to assess if the approach is feasible and should be further investigated.

In Table 1 is visible an example of a job posting, with the description truncated, as well as the corresponding ESCO designation assigned to it. Table 2 shows the designations from ESCO as well as the labels representing each class used in the machine learning algorithm, alongside the number of samples for each designation.

Table 1. Example of a job announcement and the ESCO occupation assigned

Title	Description	ESCO Occupation
Scala engineer	Keywords: Scala, Java, CI/CDYears of experience: 3+ English level: Advanced ... we are hiring Scala Engineer for a long term contract role in Porto, Aveiro SKILLS AND EXPERIENCE:- Service-oriented architectures, design patterns and data structures;- Test automation, continuous integration and continuous delivery;- Working with relational …	Software and Application Developers

Table 2. ESCO occupations used, the label for each occupation and the number of samples for each occupation

ESCO Designation	Label	Number of samples
Software and Application Developers	0	16
Analytics Specialist	1	2
Back End Developer / Engineering	2	5
Data Engineer	3	2
DevOps Engineer / Cloud Computing	4	4
Frontend Engineer / Engineering	5	14
Hardware/Infrastructure Engineer	6	3
Javascript Developer / Engineering	7	8
Telecom specialists	8	4

After assigning an ESCO occupation to each data point, the data was prepared data by removing punctuation, stop words, and other irrelevant words or words that could influence the accuracy of the algorithms (such as the name of companies). Following the pre-processing step was the creation of a TF-IDF (Term Frequency-Inverse document frequency) matrix (Ramos, 2003).

The resulting matrix had 58 rows (one for each job) and 1531 columns (one for each word/feature considered) was used to test tree machine learning algorithms: (1) Support Vector Machines (SVM) without specific kernel; (2) k nearest neighbors (k-NN) considering a single neighbor as some classes have just two samples, and (3) decision tree with the default behavior of SKLearn toolkit (Pedregosa et al, 2011).

The algorithms performance was measured using the leave one out cross-validation (Berrar, 2019). This is suitable as our dataset is not very large altogether and the imbalance of the data prevented the usage of a k-fold cross validation. Results can be seen in Table 3 with the corresponding confusion matrixes in Figure 4.

Table 3. Accuracies obtained for each machine learning algorithm using leave one out cross-validation.

Algorithm	**Accuracy**
SVM	0.810
KNN	**0.948**
Decision Tree	0.879

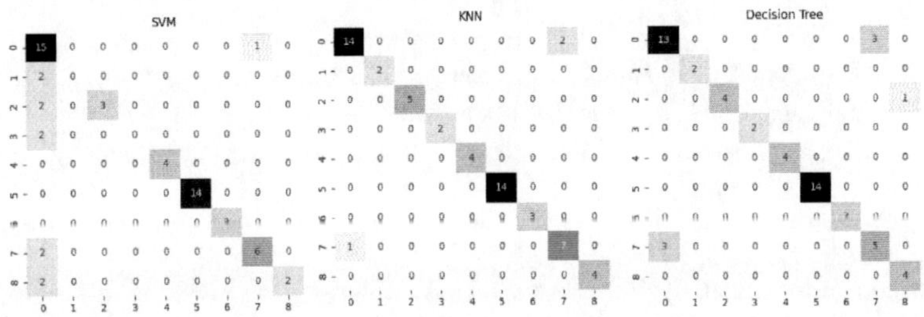

Figure 4. Confusion matrix for each machine learning algorithm. The meaning of each matrix label is in Table 2

5. CONCLUSION

This work shows that it is possible to have an accurate overview of the job market dynamics based on the collection of job offerings and by using tools such as the ELK stack to explore and visualize data. This can be done if two issues are considered carefully: (1) have a data model with the features required for a good data description; and (2) when using multiple overlapping sources, as it was our case since a company can advertise the same position in several places simultaneously, an adequate duplicate detection algorithm must be implemented. Here was considered that a similar job proposal in the same month is a duplicate and that after one month is a new job proposal for a similar position. A limitation of this job market overview is that, although this duplicate criterion is adequate for the companies interviewed in previous works (citation omitted due to blind review), we cannot guarantee that all companies have the same behavior and thus the dashboard will present some inaccuracies. However, these inaccuracies are not expected to be meaningful.

The machine learning experiment conducted shows that one can expect to achieve a uniform job description using an ontology such as ESCO. The uniformization of the job description is important for making possible the comparison of the job market dynamics across distinct regions, companies, time periods, etc. Moreover, considering ESCO, this would allow not only look at the job market, the ESCO occupations, but also to the competences more in need by the market, as ESCO relates occupations with qualifications and skills. This implies that with small changes, this platform will be able to show the qualifications and skills more in demand in each region, allowing the adoption of policies to mitigate possible gaps, and thus improving the competitiveness of region.

ACKNOWLEDGEMENT

This work was supported by National Funds through the Portuguese Foundation for Science and Technology (FCT—Fundação para a Ciência e a Tecnologia) within IEETA/UA R&D unit (UIDB/00127/2020) and GOVCOPP (project POCI-01-0145-FEDER-008540), funded by FEDER funds through COMPETE2020 - Programa Operacional Competitividade e Internacionalização (POCI).
"Aveiro STEAM city" project is co-funded by the European Regional Development Fund – ERDF, included in the "Urban Innovative Actions" programme. With a total budget of 6.115.915€ (4.892.732€ ERDF), the project is led by the Municipality of Aveiro in partnership with the University of Aveiro, Altice Labs, Instituto de Telecomunicações, INOVARIA and CEDES.

REFERENCES

Ahmed Awan, M.N., Khan, S., Latif, K. and Khattak, A.M., 2019. A New Approach to Information Extraction in User-CareerJet (2020). Available at: https://www.careerjet.com/ (Accessed: 30 September 2020)

Centric E-Recruitment Systems. *Applied Sciences*, *9*(14), p.2852.

Berrar, Daniel, 2019, Cross-Validation. In Encyclopedia of Bioinformatics and Computational Biology (Vol. 1, pp. 542-545).

Briscariu, R., 2019. The use of social networks sites in the recruitment process. Management Research and Practice, 11(4), 5-10.

Celik Ertuğrul, D., Karakas, A., Bal, G., Gultunca, C., Elçi, A., Buluz, B., and Alevli, M. 2013. Towards an Information Extraction System Based on Ontology to Match Resumes and Jobs. In *undefined* (pp. 333-338).

Chen, J., Zhang, C., and Niu, Z. 2018. A Two-Step Resume Information Extraction Algorithm. *Mathematical Problems in Engineering, 2018*, p.5761287.

Chryssolouris, G., Mavrikios, D., & Mourtzis, D. 2013. Manufacturing systems: skills & competencies for the future. Procedia CIRp, 7(2013), 17-24.

ELK (2020) Elastic Stack and Product Documentation. Available at https://www.elastic.co/guide/index.html (Accessed: 30 September 2020)

ESCO (2020) Available at https://ec.europa.eu/esco (Accessed: 30 September 2020)

Freddi, D. 2018, Digitalisation and employment in manufacturing. AI & SOCIETY, 33(3), 393-403.

Gelpi, A. (2019). Focus on social media as vital element of graduate recruitment campaigns. Recruiting & Retaining Adult Learners, 21(10), 12-12.

ITJobs (2020). Available at: https://www.itjobs.pt/ (Accessed: 30 September 2020)

Jerman, A., Pejić Bach, M., & Aleksić, A., 2020. Transformation towards smart factory system: Examining new job profiles and competencies. Systems Research and Behavioral Science, 37(2), 388-402.

Luis Fernández-Sanz, Josefa Gómez-Pérez, and Ana Castillo-Martínez 2017. e-Skills Match: A framework for mapping and integrating the main skills, knowledge and competence standards and models for ICT occupations. *Computer Standards & Interfaces, 51*, p.30 - 42.

M. Bajer 2017. Building an IoT Data Hub with Elasticsearch, Logstash and Kibana. In *2017 5th International Conference on Future Internet of Things and Cloud Workshops (FiCloudW)* (pp. 63-68).

Pedregosa, F., Varoquaux, G., Gramfort, A., Michel, V., Thirion, B., Grisel, O., ... & Vanderplas, J. (2011). Scikit-learn: Machine learning in Python. the Journal of machine Learning research, 12, 2825-2830.

Ramos, J., 2003, December. Using tf-idf to determine word relevance in document queries. In Proceedings of the first instructional conference on machine learning (Vol. 242, pp. 133-142).

Szalavetz, A. 2019. Industry 4.0 and capability development in manufacturing subsidiaries. Technological Forecasting and Social Change, 145, 384-395.

GETTING CLOSER TO THE THINGS WE ARE LOOKING FOR – A PROPOSAL FOR ASPECT-DRIVEN TEXT ANALYSIS

Kurt Englmeier and Matthias Schneider
Schmalkalden University of Applied Science, Faculty of Computer Science
Blechhammer, 98574 Schmalkalden, Germany

ABSTRACT

Locating facts in texts is still a challenge for retrieval systems. Instead of measuring the relevance of the entire text for a search query, the focus of our approach of fact retrieval and text mining is on spotting only essential parts of text. We propose to enrich search queries by aspects supporting highly precise retrieval. An aspect denotes the unique interpretation of a set of words that appear in close proximity. We conceive an aspect representation as a hierarchical structure composed by its semantic elements that, in turn, constitute the aspect's implicit meaning.

In this paper, we present the definition and application of aspect blueprints that serve as standardized representations of aspects. Our prototypical system Contexter operates on these blueprints and locates facts in texts. In a semi-automatic way, the system tries to detect variants of blueprints that the user can confirm or reject. Here, we illustrate our approach and system in the realm of economic information.

KEYWORDS

Information Retrieval, Text Analysis, Text Mining, Aspects, Named Entities, Bag of Words, Blueprints

1. INTRODUCTION

Whatever information retrieval system (IRS) we use to satisfy our information need, we more or less have the same recurring user experience: We enter a couple of keywords, probably select one or two additional search terms recommended by the system, and get an overwhelming list of retrieval results. Many times, we encounter the things we were looking for among the first entries on the list. At least, we assume that the list entries point to the information we require. Quite often, the cumbersome and awkward part of our search starts right here, when we have to sift through all presumably relevant documents in order to find the information we need. This process can get quite time-consuming when our required information is located somewhere in large documents. This performance can be acceptable for IRS when humans complete the retrieval process.

In text mining however, the measurement of relevance on document level is insufficient. Text mining tries to classify the content of a text on a more fine-grained level, i.e. on paragraph or even sentence level. Classifying a text on document level can be justifiable in the case of small texts, when its content covers only one or two contextual aspects. If a text covers a broad variety of aspects, its summarization in a single title or a handful of keywords may be not suitable for most text mining as well as information retrieval purposes.

Instead of summarizing the content of a text (or parts of it) by the most important keywords, we propose the assignment of aspect representations to texts on possibly the most fine-grained level. A hierarchical structure composed of terms describes the respective aspect together with its semantic subcomponents. Information retrieval or text mining processes operate on these aspect representations and enable the location (and extraction) of relevant text passages on a more fine-grained level, that is, on paragraph or sentence level. An interesting application area of our approach can be a Legal Tech system that identifies facts in documents like balance sheets, claims, complaints, or contracts and looks up the pertinent legal rules.

In this article, we illustrate our approach in the realm of fact retrieval in economic reports. The work presented here reflects the current state-of-work of our research group of the Schmalkalden University of

Applied Science. At first, we outline the theoretical and technical background of our approach. A fundamental set of aspect representations are handcrafted. These aspect blueprints may contain named entities, keywords or N-grams of words. We illustrate the syntax for the definition of blueprints and how our prototypical mining system "Contexter" operates on them in order to analyze and classify texts. We also describe the supervised learning processes for a semi-automatic approach to identify further useful aspect blueprints.

2. RELATED WORK

Our approach is designed around the paradigm of fact retrieval emphasizing natural language (Balasubramanian et al., 2007; Fuhr, 1992; Keikha et al., 2014; Kolodner, 1982) and the support of users in constructing more complex search queries (White et al., 2007; Nguyen et al., 2018).

A feature in a text is associated with a token delimited by white space. (Weiss, 2015, p. 27) Even though tokens reference mostly words, they can also address numerical data, codes, or symbols. Each feature denotes, thus, a particular and mainly unique meaning or aspect of a word. In some cases, it can be helpful to consider multiword features. "European Union" or "U.S. Dollar" are examples for multiword features. The corresponding tokens represent a unique meaning, but only when occurring together. Names of persons are also examples of multiword features. In contrast to the previous examples, the sequence of tokens addressing names need not necessarily be consecutive. There can even be a middle name that is referenced in one feature and omitted in the other, but both multiword features address the same person. The classification of text using multiword features has a long tradition (Acosta et al., 2011; Calzolari et al., 2002; Papka and Allan, 1998). From a different point of view, multiword features can also be considered as word n-grams or n-words (Huston et al., 2012).

An instrument that proved to be useful in our context are Bag of Words (BoW). They contain keywords indicating institutions like Wall Street, Dow Jones, or White House. We can imagine a variety of theme-specific BoWs (for locations, names, sentiments etc.) applicable in a given context (Woods, 1996).

The concept of feature, however, is not restricted to words. Named entities are probably the most essential ingredients for the composition of features. At first, in combination with words they identify common patterns in texts reflecting time, prices, distances, and the like. A currency, for example, is usually represented by a symbol or code. The temperature is usually indicated by a numerical expression with an adjacent symbol for degrees in Kelvin, Celsius, or Fahrenheit. Named entities also help to standardize factual information and to abstract away the different forms of expressions for essentially the same thing. Named entities indicate that is probably more suitable to talk about multi-*expression* features that refer to a series of text elements and indicate their meaning.

Named entity recognition (NER) may even take a special role in the identification of elements of BoWs, when special indicative terms appear in close proximity to words with particular characteristics, mainly proper names. Words such as "Mr." or "Health Senator" hint to names of persons. There are further indicative terms pointing to names. For example, the term "by" following the title of an article often leads the list of names authoring that article. The identification of proper names benefits from the analysis of sequential dependencies when bags of words can be produced automatically instead of manually. There are promising approaches to automatically identify names (and other important key expressions) in texts using conditional random fields (CFR) (Sha and Pereira, 2003) or hidden Markov Models (HMMs) (Freitag and McCallum, 2000). A conditional pattern, for example, can be a series of capital letters in parentheses following words starting with capital letters. This pattern may indicate organization names with their respective abbreviations, such as National Institute of Health (NIH) or Korean Electric Power Corporation (KEPCO).

The next important step in the analysis of text is the annotation of features according to the meaning they express (Cowie and Lehnert, 1996; Salton et al., 1997). Annotation has two roles: first, it adds a meaningful term to features, in particular when they contain numeric data. Such patterns, for example, represent dates, percentages, numerical data, distances, and the like. Second, the annotations themselves represent a feature that again can be part of multi-expression feature. When iteratively performed, annotation produces an increasingly more abstract representation of the content it addresses. The target application area of our approach, however, is the location of text passages that are strongly related. Legal information retrieval systems (Heo et al, 2017, for instance, try to find pertinent rules regulations for facts or issues mentioned in a complaint, claim, contract, etc.

3. ASPECTS AND THEIR BLUEPRINTS

3.1 The Representation Structure of Aspects

Features stand for a precise meaning represented by their constituting expressions. Aspects, on the other hand, denote the interpretation of text features (Singh and Croft, 2016). The expression "500 €" means a precise amount of money and "2.4 GW" a precise amount of energy. An aspect representation tries to interpret the content of its feature as precisely as possible. The amount of money, for instance, can be a price tag or a characteristic of a money transfer. The more surrounding information we take into account the more complex, but also the more correct gets the definition of an aspect and the interpretation of its constituting features. If a feature like "costs" is adjacent to the expression of the amount of money, then the features together constitute the aspect "price tag". The price tag, in turn, may stand for a bargain or its contrary. This again may be part of a purchase, which usually includes vendor, buyer and further characteristics.

With the growing integration of aspects, we achieve a hierarchy with the most abstract description on its top. Let us consider the aspect "investment in nuclear energy production". This aspect consists of the two parts "investment" and "nuclear energy production". The aspect "investment", in turn, may be composed by constituting elements such as "investor", "investment object", and "price". All of these aspects can be further detailed, and so on. For each aspect, we obtain more or less complex, hierarchical representations. Aspects on the fine-grained level of the hierarchy may cover a few adjacent features. With the growing level of abstraction, an aspect may span an entire phrase, paragraph, page, or even more. The aspect of the purchase of a real estate can easily span an entire document of a dozen of pages.

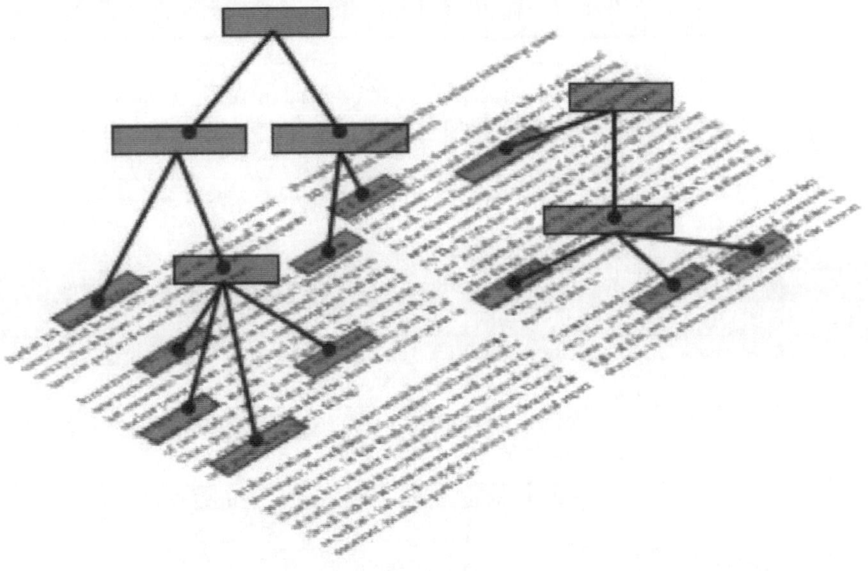

Figure 1. Schematic presentation of an aspect hierarchy and its subcomponents

The top-level aspect in a hierarchy of aspects represents a fact in an abstract way. It is obvious, that there may be many variations in the representation of this aspect. Variations even start on a fine-grained level. A named entity composed of a numerical expression with an adjoint currency symbol constitutes the aspect "price". There may exist as many variants of this aspect as exist currencies in the world. And even each currency can be denoted in multiple ways (e.g. "U.S. dollar", "USD", "$").

3.2 The Syntax of Aspect Blueprints

The aspect blueprint is the central element in our approach for a combination of text and fact retrieval and for the classification processes in text mining. In order to cover all variants of an aspect, we have to find a suitable blueprint that covers all its possible instances. As reflected in figure 1, the blueprint is basically a structure of expressions where each element may hold one or more

- keywords (in their stemmed forms, including their corresponding synonyms),
- references to BoWs,
- n-grams (as a series of adjacent features),
- named entities, or
- references to further aspects on a more fine-grained level.

Regular expressions are a powerful instrument to detect patterns in all kinds of unstructured data, not only in texts. However, they require special skills and are not easy to handle, in particular, when they are addressing complex, i.e. real-world, patterns. Nevertheless, regular expressions are key to flexible and powerful text analysis.

Our approach adopts regular expressions but shields the users from their complexity by hiding them in a set of labeled expressions starting with keywords, n-grams, and named entities representing things like name, social security number, distance, birthday etc. Instead of defining regular expressions, the users define their blueprints by resorting to these more basic expressions. The users then gradually define more complex expressions by integrating already existing blueprints. The syntax they use in order to define their blueprints is quite simple. It enables the user to describe adjacent elements of an aspect. A blueprint of an order, for example, lists the persons or organizations that act as sellers and buyers, the product, the date, and the price.

Table 1. Operators of the syntax to define aspect blueprint

Operator	Function
.	The dot indicates strong sequence (“followed by”). The expression indicated before the dot must be located before the one indicated after the dot.
,	Comma means weak sequence. Some indicated expressions (at least one) shall appear sequentially in the data. However, they may appear in any order (inclusive combination).
;	The semicolon is used to indicate an exclusive combination. Just one of the expressions ought to be located.
:	Labeling (annotation) operator: the name after the colon is assigned to expressions or a group of expressions.
(...)	Parentheses serve to indicate a group of expressions. Grouping only makes sense together with the labeling operator.
?	The question mark indicates that an expression or group of expressions is optional.
“*keyword*”	Keywords are indicated between quotation marks

The users may indicate the aspect of “decrease” by the following blueprint: `decrease="decline".fraction,time point.fraction.time point`. “fraction” stands for a named entity representing percentages and similar expressions. All representations of a single point in time are represented by the named entity “time point”. The keyword “declined” is a placeholder for all synonyms reflecting a decline. Before the Contexter system applies this blueprint to any text, the keywords are implicitly replaced by the stemmed versions of all their synonyms. Stemming is, of course, also applied to the target text beforehand. After the application of this blueprint a piece of text concerning a decrease is marked like this: "The share of nuclear energy in power generation has <decrease>declined from its peak of <fraction>17 percent</fraction> <time point>in <year>1996</year></time point> to around <fraction>ten percent</fraction> <time point>today</time point></decrease>".

A particular aspect can be expressed by different words, much like the type of numerical information (date, price, or growth rate, for instance) can be expressed in different syntactic forms. It is important that a unique title represents each aspect. Each blueprint, in turn, represents not only the semantic architecture of its meaning, but also the different syntactic facets its instances may take in texts.

Whenever an expression of a blueprint refers a specific keyword, all of its applicable synonyms need to be taken into consideration. However, not all possible synonyms are also applicable in every context. In an expression describing a certain amount of money like "to the tune of 12.65 billion U.S. dollars", none of the synonyms of the term "tune" is applicable in this context. In some occasions, it is thus recommendable to consider the applicability of synonyms by considering n-grams. Thorough n-gram analysis reveals, that "to the tune of" have synonyms like "to the amount of" or "add up to".

Figure 2 shows the representation of a piece of text referencing a broader aspect, namely an investment. At first, all instances that meet the qualities of an expression representing a price are identified and marked by the blueprint `price=?″price″.money. currency`. These instances are expected to be composed of an instance matching the blueprint (amount of) "money", a further one addressing the currency and an occasional (leading or trailing) word "price" (or a synonym expression such as "at a cost of"). The expression "price" is optional and thus leaded by a question mark. Keywords are stated in quotes. Internally they are mapped to their standardized (stemmed) forms. Terms without quotes thus refer to the blueprint elements or to BoWs. The dots stand for "close proximity" which can range from "immediately adjacent" to "next blueprint coverage".

In 2009, the UAE government commissioned Korean Electric Power Corporation (KEPCO) from South Korea to build four reactors with an output of 5.4 gigawatts (GW) at a cost of 28.2 billon U.S. dollars. This equates to a dedicated investment of 5,300 U.S. dollars per kilowatt.

<investment><time point>In <year>2009</year></time point>, the <buyer><body> UAE government</body></buyer> commissioned <seller><organization>Korean Electric Power Corporation (KEPCO)</organization></seller> from <region>South Korea</region> to build <plant>four reactors</plant> with an <output>output of <power>5.4 gigawatts (GW)</power></output> at a cost of <price>28.2 billion U.S. dollars</price></investment>. This equates to a dedicated <investment>investment of <price>5,300 U.S. dollars</price> <unit>per kilowatt</unit></investment>. No less than <price>18.7 billion U.S. dollars</price> of the total sum was financed with public money.

Figure 2. Section of a text and its representation after basic text patterns have been identified and accordingly annotated

4. THE SEMI-AUTOMATIC PROCESS OF TEXT ANALYSIS

In the first place, hand-crafted blueprints may appear outdated given the availability of so many powerful automatic information extraction systems that use machine-learning or similar techniques (Etzioni et al., 2008). We believe that the performance of the analysis process benefits from user intervention. The users are good in formulating hypotheses about the things they expect to encounter in texts. This can be the starting point for machines to step in and support the users. The support can take two fundamental forms: First, providing users with a language for the definition of aspect blueprints that is fast to learn and easy to handle and, second, a machine that takes the users' blueprints and automatically discovers further blueprints on its own.

The semi-automatic process takes the blueprints defined by the users, in fact, as seeds and tries to locate similar but new blueprints. The findings are presented to the users that confirm or reject the results of the automatic process. The first group of blueprint elements that benefit from automatic discovery are proper names, usually stored in the BoWs. Proper names pose, in general, a certain challenge to automatic text analysis. By applying identification rules inclined to CFR methods, we can automatically identify proper names to a certain extend. For instance, words starting with uppercase letters and immediately following special terms like "Premier ministre", "Mr.", or "the author" usually indicate that these words are proper names of persons. The system can identify names of organizations by applying suitable rules like the ones described here. Some BoWs (for countries, for instance) can also be imported from external sources. However, there always remain proper names in text that are not covered by external sources. These names need to be detected and added to the BoWs.

The more interesting learning process for our system targets the discovery of blueprints. Each set of blueprint elements is annotated by a title reflecting the overarching aspect of the elements. By repeatedly applying this process the blueprint gets more layers and covers a growing text area. The blueprint then resembles a hierarchy with a general representation of covered text on its top and growing specialized representations towards its bottom. In principle, the system takes the user-defined blueprints as seeds and tries to find further applicable blueprints that are similar to the seeds. This title summarizes the content of all blueprint components on its underlying layer. It thus abstracts away the content details of the sub-component layer it stands for. Each such blueprint can be a constituting element in the next layer of abstraction. If blueprints can be applied to text, they cover a certain text area. It can be a sentence, a paragraph, or a larger text section.

The basic idea of the semi-automatic process is that the system modifies existing blueprints on its own and test them against the text base. If the system finds text instances that match the modified blueprint, it reports this blueprint back to the users that confirm or reject it. When the users confirm a newly found blueprint is added to the collection of existing aspect blueprints. The system modifies the blueprint

- by trying to substitute its subcomponents one by one or
- by adding new subcomponents that the fringe of the blueprint (figure 3).

The process of substitution starts with blanking out a subcomponent. The remaining blueprint is then applied to the text base. Whenever it matches, the text passage between the subcomponent adjacent to the blanked-out subcomponent gets further investigated. The system tests if there is an already existing blueprint in the collection that can be applied to this piece of text and, thus, serves as new subcomponent.

Similarly, the system tests if it can add a blueprint at the fringes of the blueprint's text coverage. The coverage area can be a fraction of a phrase, an entire phrase, more than one phrase, or even one or more paragraphs. The system ventures out into the adjacent text, tries to find an applicable blueprint and considers it as new subcomponent. Depending on the size of the coverage area, the system explores the surrounding sentence, couple of sentences, or paragraph. The text, the system explores, may not be covered by another blueprint that has at least of one level of subcomponents. Texts covered by hierarchical compositions of blueprints are further limits for the system's exploration into yet uncovered text areas. Single aspect blueprints that are not building blocks of other blueprints may be added.

Eventually, the system presents all new blueprints to the users that, in turn, select the ones that make sense and reject the others. The probably more challenging task for the users is the selection of suitable, consistent, and unambiguous titles for the blueprints. Moreover, the title once defined by the individual user needs to be institutionalized. The titles of the blueprints reflect the semantic picture of all aspects an organization is dealing with in its information management. There are standardized concept hierarchies available like schema.org or the nomenclatures of statistical offices. However, they cover only small fractions of the information ecosystem addressed by an organization.

The share of nuclear energy in power generation has **<decrease>**declined from its peak of <fraction>17 percent</fraction> <time point>in <year>1996 </year></time point>**</decrease>** to around <fraction>ten percent </fraction><time point>today</time point>.¶

After adding new subcomponents:¶
The share of nuclear energy in power generation has **<decrease>**declined from its peak of <fraction>17 percent</fraction> <time point>in <year> 1996</year></time point> to around <fraction>ten percent</fraction> <time point>today</time point>**</decrease>**.¶

Figure 3. Example of the expansion of an already existing blueprint by examining the text area beyond the fringes of the actual text coverage

5. CONCLUSION

This paper presents the state of work of design and prototypical implementation of a text analysis system operating on aspect blueprints that can be defined by the users. It mainly uses named entity recognition and theme-specific BoWs to precisely spot facts in texts and, thus, enables retrieval of information on a very fine-grained level. The system has been tested on economic articles published by the German Institute of Economic Research (DIW). The objective was to locate and classify facts in these texts and to spot statements about the same facts across the further publications of the institute.

The application areas of the aspect blueprints are manifold and reach beyond spotting of relevant text sections. A further purpose is the identification of facts in texts and their representation in a distilled and standardized way. This facilitates the comparison of representations of related facts in different sources. Such a feature may be part of a Legal Tech application that analyses balance sheets, for instance, and locates in legal rules of balance sheets all sections that are pertinent to the statements in the sheets.

Our approach and our prototype are still work in progress, but we already noticed that our aspect blueprints have a certain proximity to ontologies. We use the blueprints for text interpretation on a basic level and gradually produce aspect hierarchies. However, we clearly see the necessity to add more functionality to blueprints, in particular, when parts of the schema address factual (i.e. numerical) information. Quite often, calculations can be helpful to check the plausibility of statements based on numerical information. The standardized representation of facts enables the opportunity to include (at least some decent) inference mechanisms. The representation of extracted instances can be used to link data processing features to the elements of the blueprints.

```
<decrease>
    <fraction>
        17 percent
    </fraction>
    <time_point>
        <year>
            1996
        </year>
    </time_point>
    <fraction>
        ten percent
    </fraction>
    <time_point>
        today
    </time_point>
</decrease>
```

```
<investment>
    <time_point>
        <year>
            2009
        </year>
    </time_point>
    <buyer>
        <body>
            UAE government
        </body>
    </buyer>
    <seller>
        <organization>
            Korean Electric Power Corporation (KEPCO)
        </organization>
    </seller>
    <region>
        South Korea
    </region>
    <plant>
        four reactors
    </plant>
    <output>
        <power>
            5.4 gigawatts (GW)
        </power>
    </output>
    <price>
        28.2 billion U.S. dollars
    </price>
</investment>
```

Figure 4. Section of a representation of a fact as annotated and extracted by the blueprint "investment" (see also figure 2)

After locating (and extracting) instances of a blueprint in the distributed texts the system transforms them into XML representations, suitable for further data analysis. The XML files in Figure 4 represent the two text examples discussed in our paper here. These features can, for instance, deduce a specific date that needs to be assigned with the element containing the word "today". Representing a text passage in machine-processable form like the one shown in figure 4 offers also the opportunity to extract all information concerning investments in nuclear energy power in order to prepare it for automatic reporting.

A further objective of our approach is a stronger involvement of humans in the development and management of text mining tools and, in general, to enhance the adoption of this technology on a broader scale. This involvement results in a more active role of the users in designing, controlling, and adapting the learning process that feeds, in this case here, the automatic detection of facts in text. The syntax for the definition of a blueprint is easy to learn. Even users without technical background are in the position to write definitions for aspect blueprints. In the next phase of the development of our prototype, the users will be involved more closely in the training of the semi-automatic processes to detect blueprints that come semantically close to existing definitions.

REFERENCES

Acosta, O.C., Villavicencio, A., and Moreira, V.P. (2011) 'Identification and Treatment of Multiword Expressions Applied to Information Retrieval', *Proceedings of the Workshop on Multiword Expressions: From Parsing and Generation to the Real World,* pp. 101-109.

Balasubramanian, N., Allan, J. and Croft, W.B. (2007) 'A comparison of sentence retrieval techniques', *Proceedings of the 30th annual international ACM SIGIR conference on Research and development in information retrieval*, pp. 813–814.

Calzolari, N., Fillmore, C.J., Grishman, R., Ide, N., Lenci, R., Macleod, C., and Zampolli, A. 'Towards Best Practice for Multiword Expressions in Computational Lexicons', *Proceedings of the Third International Conference on Language Resources and Evaluation (LREC 2002)*, pp. 1934-1940.

Cowie, J. and Lehnert, W. (1996) "Information Extraction". *Communications of the ACM* 39(1), pp. 80–91.

Etzioni, O., Banko, M., Soderland, S., and Weld, D.S. (2008) "Open information extraction from the web", *Communications of the ACM* 51(12), pp. 68-74.

Freitag, D. and McCallum, A. (2000) "Information Extraction with HMM Structures Learned by Stochastic Optimization", *Proceedings of the Seventeenth National Conference on Artificial Intelligence and Twelfth Conference on Innovative Applications of Artificial Intelligence*, pp. 584-589.

Fuhr, N. (1992) 'Integration of probabilistic fact and text retrieval', *Proceedings of the 15th annual international ACM SIGIR conference on Research and development in information retrieval*, pp. 211–222.

Heo, S., Hong, K., and Rhim, Y.-Y. (2017) "Legal Content Fusion for Legal Information Retrieval", *Proceedings of the 16th Edition of the International Conference on Articial Intelligence and Law*, pp. 277–281.

Huston, S., Culpepper, J.S., and Croft, W.B. (2012) 'Sketch-Based Indexing of n-Words', *Proceedings of the 21st ACM International Conference on Information and Knowledge Management,* pp. 1864-1868.

Keikha, M., Park, J.H., Croft, W.B. and Sanderson, M. (2014) 'Retrieving Passages and Finding Answers', *Proceedings of the 2014 Australasian Document Computing Symposium,* pp. 81–84.

Kolodner, J.L. (1982) 'Requirements for natural language fact retrieval', *Proceedings of the ACM '82 conference*, pp. 192–198.

Nguyen, A.T., Kharosekar, A., Krishnan, S., and Krishnan, S. (2018) 'Believe it or not: Designing a Human-AI Partnership for Mixed-Initiative Fact-Checking', *Proceedings of the 31st Annual ACM Symposium on User Interface Software and Technology*, pp. 189–199.

Papka, R. and Allan, J. (1998) 'Document classification using multiword features', *Proceedings of the seventh international conference on Information and knowledge management*, pp. 124–131.

Salton, G., Allan, J., Buckely, C., and Singhal, A. (1997) "Automatic Analysis, Theme Generation, and Summarization of Machine-Readable Texts", in: Karen Sparck Jones and Peter Willett, *Readings in Information Retrieval*, San Francisco: Morgan Kaufmann, pp. 478–483.

Sha, F. and Pereira, F., (2003) "Shallow Parsing with Conditional Random Fields", *Proceedings of the HLT-NAACL conference*, 2003, pp. 134-141.

Singh, M. and Croft, W.B. (2016) „Iterative Search using Query Aspect", *Proceedings of the 25th ACM International on Conference on Information and Knowledge Management*, pp. 2037-2044

Weiss, S.M., Indurkhya, N., Zhang, T. (2015) *Fundamentals of Predictive Text Mining,* 2nd edn. London: Springer.

White, R.W., Drucker, S.M., Marchionini, G., Hearst, M., and Schraefel, M.C. (2007) 'Exploratory search and HCI: designing and evaluating interfaces to support exploratory search interaction', *CHI '07 Extended Abstracts on Human Factors in Computing Systems*, 2007, pp. 2877–2880.

Woods, W.A., (1996) "Context-Sensitive Parsing". *Communications of the ACM 13(7)*, pp. 413–445.

ONTOLOGY-BASED HUMAN-MACHINE COLLECTIVE INTELLIGENCE ENVIRONMENT FOR DECISION SUPPORT

Alexander Smirnov and Andrew Ponomarev
St. Petersburg Federal Research Center of the Russian Academy of Sciences (SPC RAS)
Russian Federation, 199178, St. Petersburg, 14th Line, 39

ABSTRACT

The paper proposes the design of a computer environment aiming at the support of human-machine collective intelligence in decision-making problems. The environment supports two main processes taking place during the collective effort on a complex problem: process organization (planning the activities and the distribution of the responsibilities) and building a solution (plan implementation). To address the problem of human-machine interoperability, the environment leverages multi-aspect ontologies, allowing to represent the status of the process and information about the problem in a human- and machine-readable way. The proposed solution can be employed in building interoperable human-machine collaborative systems in variety of complex problem domains.

KEYWORDS

Human-Machine Systems, Human-In-The-Loop, Collective Intelligence, Collaboration, Decision Support

1. INTRODUCTION

Many real-life problems are too complex to be addressed by purely computer/software systems (even despite new promising developments in the area of AI). This is especially true, for example, for the problems arising in managing complex business or societal systems. Besides, decision-making is usually connected with some form of responsibility and accountability, but the ideas and technologies for algorithmic accountability, though being actively explored, are still not mature enough for practical uses. Therefore, human experts still are (and probably for a rather long time will be) an important part of many complex decision-making scenarios. However, human experts today usually are accompanied by the increasing use of AI tools and more and more sophisticated software agents.

In this paper, the problem of supporting human-machine collaboration in decision-making scenarios is explored in the following perspective. As the global communication technologies evolved, a new approach to building information processing applications has emerged, offered by crowdsourcing technology. Today, one can reach a huge (global) pool of potential experts and contributors, possessing all the skills and knowledge required for solving a particular problem. However, crowdsourcing is typically used for rather simple tasks (like, image or audio annotation), the possibility of using it for more complex problems is the subject of active research (Kittur et al., 2011; Retelny, Bernstein and Valentine, 2017; Valentine et al., 2017). Besides, in the vast majority of crowdsourcing applications, the participants are not able to communicate (the tasks issued to them, are so simple that communication and collaborative work are not usually reasonable).

This paper focuses on supporting the collective intelligence of dynamic (*ad hoc*) teams consisting of heterogeneous (human and machine) participants. In a sense, this research is positioned between classical group decision support systems (taking from them protocols for collective decision-making and agreement), modern crowdsourcing applications (taking from them the techniques addressing workforce on the on-demand basis), and multi-agent human-machine collaboration. Besides, the *ad hoc* teams (not necessarily in the Internet) are an interesting phenomenon, actively studied from the organization research point of view (Bechky, 2006; Faraj and Xiao, 2006).

The paper describes the conceptual organization of the human-machine collective intelligence environment, as well as some aspects of technical implementation. It also illustrates how different parts of the environment interact during the collective decision support scenarios.

The rest of the paper is structured as follows. Section 2 describes related research in a several areas influencing the concept and design of the environment. Section 3 describes the main ideas behind the proposed environment design and its mechanisms.

2. RELATED WORK

The problem of building environments allowing to access the resources of loosely connected people interacting via Internet is often discussed as one of the lines in crowdsourcing or crowd computing research. Despite the fact, that in most of the crowdsourcing platforms participants usually do their tasks independently, in crowdsourcing research there are continuous attempts being taken to adapt crowdsourcing to more complex problems and (these trend are related) to develop collaborative workflows (Retelny *et al.*, 2014). It has also been shown, that for complex problems pre-programmed workflows (typical for most of the crowdsourcing platforms) are too limited (e.g., (Retelny, Bernstein and Valentine, 2017)), therefore, the potential of crowdsourcing for complex work is tightly connected with the mechanisms of dynamic team formation, workflow adaptation. In particular, the papers (Retelny et al., 2014; Retelny, Bernstein and Valentine, 2017; Valentine et al., 2017) study the limitations of workflow-based solutions, and propose ways to overcome these limitations with a help of dynamic organizations from members of the crowd (one of them is called "flash organizations" (Valentine et al., 2017)). However, these papers address only problems of human collectives. In this research, however, we are building an environment where heterogeneous agents (human and software) would be able to collectively decide on the details of the workflow.

Collaborative decision-making is also actively explored in the area of computer-supported collaborative work (e.g., (Terveen, 1995; Elmarzouqi, Garcia and Lapayre, 2008)). The results of the Dicode project implemented within the framework of the European FP7-ICT program (Karacapilidis, 2014; Karacapilidis and Tampakas, 2019) deserve special attention. In the framework of the project, in particular, an ontological presentation of the argumentation process and a number of visual tools for working with a thus formalized set of interrelated arguments are proposed. The importance of these results lies in the fact that for sharing information about the problem by experts and software agents, it should have a structured representation, one of the options of which is a graph of the relationship of arguments. However, explicitly encoding all the arguments may be too difficult.

A high-level paper (Jennings et al., 2014) summarizes what is required to support human-machine collectives and current technological limitations for building them. In particular, the authors underline the need for the flexible autonomy of the agents, agile team-building, incentivization and accountability. The proposed environment account for all these prerequisites.

In a broader perspective, an important source line of research relevant for such an environment is the study of ad hoc teaming and collaboration in human collectives. Dynamic creation of (relatively) short-lived teams is typical in some areas of human activity. The findings of socio-psychological research of mechanisms allowing efficient composing and functioning of such teams can be useful for any computer-based environment supporting such teams (although, not all of them are directly applicable).

There are several important publications in this area. Faraj and Xiao (2006) analyze the coordination processes of medical trauma center where fast-response and error-free activities are essential requirements. They find two categories of coordination mechanisms employed in such organizations: expertise coordination practices (used most of the time, on the habitual patient's trajectory – reliance on protocols, plug-and-play teaming, community of practice structuring, knowledge sharing), and dialogic coordination practices (used for a problematic patient's trajectory – epistemic contestation, joint sense-making, cross-boundary intervention, protocol breaking). Bechky (2006) analyzes and describes coordination mechanisms of a filming crew (filming crews are usually collected for relatively short period of time from people most of whom previously didn't work together). Both papers underline flexible role-based distribution of responsibilities as a key to coordination in ad hoc teams.

Overall, there are following outcomes that can be derived from the analysis of the organization research, that may solve as requirements for the environment:

1) Research of social systems and current practices in designing such systems agree that the elements of self-organization are critical, especially when solving complex problems. Despite the fact that there are a number of works close to the proposed, there are currently no solutions supporting the collective intelligence formed by artificial intelligent software services and people.

2) An important mechanism for self-organization in dynamic human groups is role-based coordination (Retelny, Bernstein and Valentine, 2017; Valentine et al., 2017). Non-rigid role responsibilities structure has shown to be very effective in supporting collaboration in ad hoc teams. The concept of the role, therefore, should also be provided by the environment, as well as the mechanism of "switching" the software agent between the roles (if possible) and clarifying the specific content of the role within the framework of this team (Lhaksmana, Murakami and Ishida, 2018).

3) The manifestation of team self-organization can be structured using patterns (Gilbert et al., 2015), structures and coordination schemes that participants come to under certain conditions.

4) A formal representation of problem-related information is necessary, allowing one to track the cause of certain arguments or results (provenance) (Jennings et al., 2014; Karacapilidis and Tampakas, 2019), which is "understood" by both the participating people and the software agents. Therefore, information exchange infrastructure should not only allow all participants to get relevant information, but also to support accountability and provenance.

5) The environment should provide some incentive management mechanism allowing to reward participants (Jennings et al., 2014). It is crucial due to the openness of the environment.

3. COLLABORATION ENVIRONMENT DESIGN

The purpose of the environment is to leverage the coordination procedures between heterogeneous agents (in short-lived teams), allowing information exchange on two levels: information concerning the problem being solved (available data, opinions, arguments and models), and process information (role distribution, responsibilities and so on).

It should be noted, that the environment is inherently dedicated to decision support problems. Therefore, the design is influenced by decision-making methodologies (e.g., (Simon, 1979; Mann, Harmoni and Power, 1991; Guo, 2008)) and the workflow implemented by a team mostly corresponds to a typical decision-making process.

The proposed environment is discussed in this paper in two levels. First, conceptual design, which shows important concepts of the environment and how they interact during the problem-solving. Second, technological design, showing how (by what technologies and software components conceptual design is implemented).

The environment interacts with the following principal actors: end-user (decision-maker), participant, and service provider. End-user (decision-maker) uses the environment to get help in making a decision. He/she describes the problem and posts so that the problem description is visible to a specified community. Participant is an active entity (human or a software service) working on a problem given by the end-user. Finally, service provider develops, integrates to the environment, and supports software services that can act as participants working on some problem given by the end user. Service provider is also responsible for the deployed services, assuaging the problem of service accountability.

The core entities involved in most of the processes taking place in the environment are problem and team. Problem is introduced by an end-user and then is addressed by a team of participants. The description of a problem has a complex structure and representation. First of all, it contains not only information, specified by the end-user (initial statement), but also includes all the information produced by the team. So, during team's activity, the problem becomes more and more detailed. Second, to enable (at least, partly) effective interpretation by software agents, problem description is represented in a semi-structured way. In particular, machine readability is achieved via using ontologies. It is a crucial point in design. Since their introduction to the IT industry during Semantic Web initiative, ontologies proved themselves both quite efficient in solving interoperability problems and quite non-friendly for non-expert users. Still, we argue that for mixed human-machine teams, the ontologies provide a kind of *lingua franca*, acceptable by both human and software participants of the process. However, to make the use of ontologies easier for people, the environment makes the use of ontologies as implicit as possible by relying on three techniques:

- Implicit ontological representation of the structure of problem information. It means, that a human participant sees the problem description as a set of constraints, alternatives, criteria, alternative evaluations, arguments and so on, in other words, in terms that are widely used in decision-making literature and, in particular, by nearly every decision-making methodology. However, "under the hood" this structure is encoded with the decision-making ontology, therefore, software agents are also able to analyze the problem structure.
- Natural language processing. Using advances in this area it is possible to infer the role of some information pieces, its relationship with the goal and/or some line of argumentation and so on.
- GUI-based nudging participants to encode problem structure in an ontology-compatible way. Digital nudging (Schneider, Weinmann and vom Brocke, 2018) is a technique of growing importance, due to the fact that currently so many choices people do by interacting with virtual environments. In particular, nudging is quite effective alongside with the natural language processing of problem information, as it allows to ask user to disambiguate some terms and relations in the problem information.

The environment defines two basic ontologies, representing different aspects of the collaborative decision support:

- Decision-making ontology. This ontology defines main concepts that are used during decision-making (criterion, alternative, evaluation etc.) and interaction between them. The ontology is based on the analysis of existing decision-making methodologies and has been built in such a way to support majority of them.
- Collaboration and coordination ontology. It defines the concepts used in distributing work among team members (role, responsibility, dependency etc.).

The use of these ontologies allow artificial agents to 'understand' the processes taking place in the team and contribute to them. However, for the ontology-based decision-support agents, there is also a possibility to define a domain ontology and map it to the decision-making ontology. These ontologies (two generic and the domain one) capture orthogonal views on the decision-making process. To tie these views into a complex, consistent structure, we propose to use the apparatus of multi-aspect ontologies (Smirnov, Shilov and Parfenov, 2019). It allows connecting multiple conceptualizations (possibly, built using different formalisms); so that changes performed in one view (aspect) are automatically reflected in other views (aspects). For example, if the environment is used in smart tourism applications and the decision to be made is choosing a tourist route, then *route* (defined in the problem domain ontology) is equivalent to the *alternative* (defined in the decision-making ontology). The presence of these mappings allows the software participants of the decision support process to treat routes as alternatives (e.g., in visualizing them or building Pareto optimal set (Luc, 2008)). It also allows problem-specific services to contribute to the decision-making (e.g., estimate typical traffic of the route, its length). Obviously, these mappings between different aspects, joining aspect ontologies into a multi-aspect ontology are problem-specific and building these mappings is a part of problem definition.

The way problem information becomes richer and grows via interaction of agents, is implemented via 'blackboard' interactions. Particularly, with a help of ontology-based smart space technology (Roffia *et al.*, 2018). As the progress of a team on the problem is reflected by structural changes of ontological description of the problem, it allows to leverage ontology-based publish-subscribe mechanisms to intelligently perform some actions by software agents in response to particular situations during problem-solving.

Another core entity, as it was already mentioned, is a *team*. Team in the context of the environment is defined as a heterogeneous group (consisting of human participants and software services) working towards solution of a particular *problem*. Each problem has a team dedicated to it. Obviously, a participant may be a member of several teams, or not be a member of any team.

Initial team formation is based on the same principles that are used in most of the crowdsourcing platforms and knowledge networks (e.g., (Ahmad *et al.*, 2011)): each participant has a profile describing key specializations, problem-solving history, as well as the history of previous collaborations (with mutual evaluations). The initiative in this process is mixed in the sense that a contributor should send a proposal to the end-user, consisting of one or more team members (proposal may include several participants that already have some positive experience of working together), and end-user has to collect the initial team. However, decisions of the both parties – participants and end-users – are assisted by environment. The participants may choose to receive recommendations in case some problem touching his/her area of competences is posted. On the other hand, end-users may explore the description and history of all the participants mentioned in the proposals. If a team understands that it lacks some competencies or resources, it may create a new resource requirements, that are registered in the environment and resolved in a manner, similar to the initial team formation process (participants have to actively apply for the positions in the team, however, both sides are assisted by the environment mechanisms).

This doesn't fully apply to the software participants (services). As the throughput of software services is not as limited as the throughput of humans, and the execution is relatively cheap, software services are passively connected to any team and by the mechanisms of the environment (ontology-based publish-subscribe) are watching the processes taking place with the problem. There are two states a software service can be in with respect to a team (Figure 1): dormant and active. Initially, all services are in the dormant state and are waiting specific conditions during the problem-solving. If these conditions defined by a particular service are met, the service tries to activate, describing its purpose and terms of use. If the team agrees that the service is useful for the problem, the service is allowed to activate (change state to active) and become a member of the team. Otherwise, the service remains dormant. Active service may also be transferred to the dormant state by a decision of the team. Besides, the services can be accessed via a service catalog and activated manually by team members.

Active services can be used by the members of a team. The mechanics of their usage depends on the kind of a service. There are following types of services:

- Problem-solving service;
- External tool and database access service.

Problem-solving service accesses the problem information described in the form of ontology and natural text and can actively add information pieces to it. An example of such service is a statistics-based question answering service – if it detects a question about some facts (e.g., "How many people die from tuberculosis in the World in one year?") and can answer it in some form it adds an answer to the question. Another example is a service that derives from the problem information a current set of alternatives and their evaluations, builds a Pareto optimal set and adds it to the problem information.

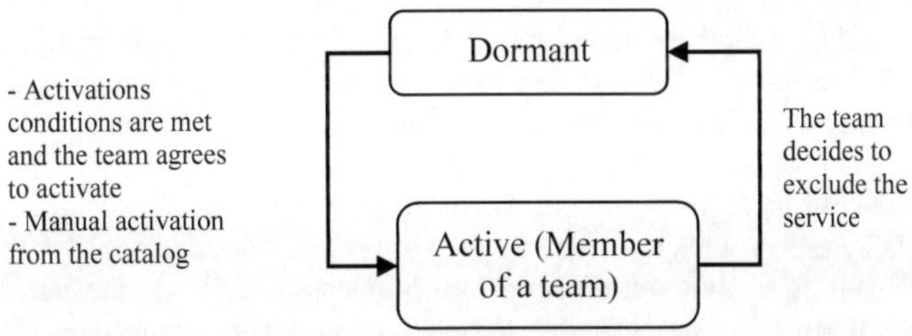

Figure 1. Service states with respect to a team

External tool and database access services in activated form only provide an access to a specified resource. For example, if a team need epidemic database, it can activate the service that grants access to this database and use it for queries.

Simultaneously two processes take place when team works on a problem: *solution preparation* and *decision support (re)organization*. Both of these processes are supported by mechanisms provided by the environment. Solution preparation is main productive process, during which problem is enriched with new information and artifacts created by team members. General scheme of the solution preparation process is driven by decision support methodologies (e.g., Simon's model (Simon, 1979), DECIDE (Guo, 2008), or GOFER (Mann, Harmoni and Power, 1991)). It should also be noted, that these methodologies provide the general scheme of the solution preparation, main stages that have to be performed, while execution of each stage is done via activities relevant to the problem at hand. For example if the environment is used by an organization to decide which motivation policy to implement for the workers, then the stage of Considering all the alternatives may contain a task of identifying relevant scientific publications about the effectiveness of motivation policies. The necessary activities (contents of the respective stage) are defined and enacted by the team itself, the environment allows to track these activities and connect their results with the problem definition and the concepts of decision-making ontology.

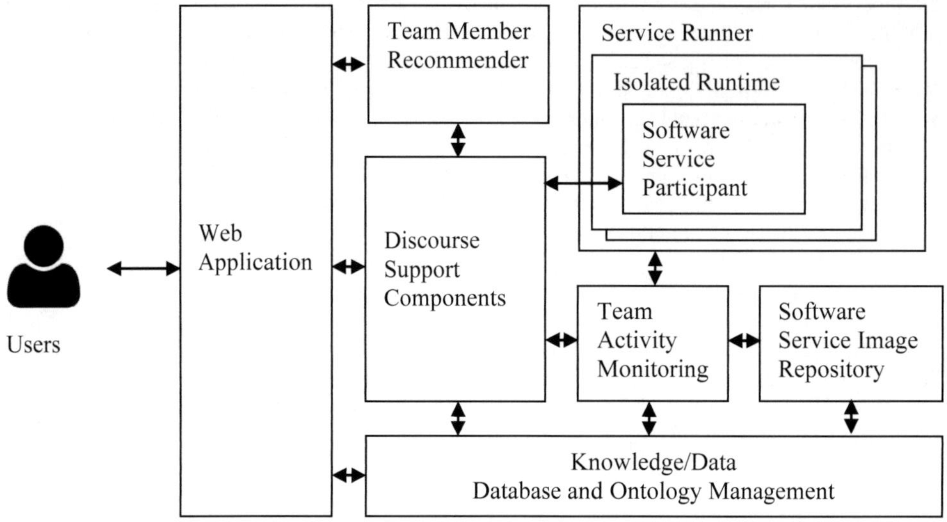

Figure 2. Technological design of the environment

Physically, the process of solution preparation can be viewed as adding information to the problem definition initially provided by the end-user (in the smart space). First, by adding explicit criteria and constraints (during the activities of initial stages – Define the problem and Establish the criteria), then by adding alternatives and their evaluations (later stages). The result of this process is fully detailed description of a problem situation, weighted alternatives and their estimated consequences – accepted by the end-user.

Decision support (re)organization process represents all the activities aimed on planning and organization of team work (e.g., deciding whether additional resources are required, assigning team member responsibilities, setting task deadlines and identifying new tasks to be solved in order to reach the goals of the whole process). Complex activities cannot be fully planned (and the literature review supports that), therefore, the team can adapt the plan as the solution process advances. General scheme of the decision support (re)organization process includes a number of activities: plan, refine, execute, observe, and reflect. During the Plan activity the team (or a responsible member of the team) builds a list of activities and assigns responsibilities using the features of the environment. If it is necessary, some plan items should be refined (this is especially the case when there are software services assigned to them). The planned activities are executed (this is actually a solution preparation process, described earlier); the results are observed and reflected on. If during the execution it turns out that some additional activities have to be performed, then the plan is adjusted and the cycle continues.

Technologically the environment (Figure 2) is implemented as a web application where each problem (and, therefore, a team) has its own workspace, supporting both informal text-based communication (similar to popular collaboration environments like Slack (*Slack - Official Site*, no date) or Mattermost (*Mattermost - Official Site*, no date)), but also have integrated 'nudging' modules allowing to tie the information into decision-making ontology formalized view, making it accessible for software services. Besides, humans can also browse the problem information in this structured ontology-based view and edit it if it is necessary.

The 'nudging' functionality is implemented as a set of Discourse Support Components, that maintain both the structured (ontology-based) and unstructured problem description and constantly perform mapping between them. Besides, these components provide an interface for other components of the system to access the contents and requirements of the team.

Team Member Recommender is responsible for performing assistance on finding team members for problems. It issues recommendations to participants who fit the active teams according to the implemented fit estimation models.

Software services are integrated into the collective intelligence environment in the following way. Service provider registers the service by specifying activation context, terms of usage and runnable image of a service (Software Service Image Repository component). The description is encoded via SPARQL-based declarative language to enable ontology-based subscription mechanisms. In order to preserve confidentiality of the team work, the services are run in an isolated way. Until their presence is accepted by the team, watching is done by the environment (on behalf of a service, particularly, by Team Activity Monitoring component). After the activation condition has been fired, a service instance is created from the runnable image and run in a new isolated container without internet access making sure that details of the problem will not be accessible by service provider who is not member of a team.

4. CONCLUSION

The paper addresses some conceptual and technological issues arising in creating dynamic collaborative systems for complex problems decision-support. Foremost, it addresses the issue of interoperability in heterogeneous (human and machine) collectives working on a decision support problem, and the issue of adapting the workflow (action plan) of a complex collaborative activity, which is important, as reasonably complex decision-support procedures cannot be designed in advance in the sufficient level of detail.

Based on the multi-disciplinary analysis of team coordination and collaborative systems research, the paper proposes a design of a novel class of environments, providing means for human-machine collective intelligence for decision support.

The issue of interoperability is addressed with the help of ontologies providing human- and machine-readable representation of the both problem- and process-related information. In particular, the environment leverages the idea of multi-aspect ontologies, allowing to connect problem domain and universal concepts of decision-making and team functioning in a problem-specific way.

Technologically, the environment derives many ideas from ontology-based smart space technology, providing a semantic shared space, readable and modifiable by team members. Smart space technology also serves as an interaction media, implementing indirect communication via publish/subscribe mechanism. In particular, this mechanism allows software team members to react to certain structures in semantic representation of the decision-making problem.

The proposed environment can be used to support decision-making in a variety of domains, where inherent complexity of the problems requires the symbiosis of human's creative potential, machine's information processing ability, and the flexibility in organizing the interactions between them.

ACKNOWLEDGEMENT

The research is funded by the Russian Science Foundation (project # 19-11-00126).

REFERENCES

Ahmad, S. *et al.* (2011) 'The jabberwocky programming environment for structured social computing', *Proceedings of the 24th annual ACM symposium on User interface software and technology - UIST '11*. New York, New York, USA: ACM Press, pp. 53–64. doi: 10.1145/2047196.2047203.

Bechky, B. A. (2006) 'Gaffers, gofers, and grips: Role-based coordination in temporary organizations', *Organization Science*, 17(1), pp. 3–21. doi: 10.1287/orsc.1050.0149.

Elmarzouqi, N., Garcia, E. and Lapayre, J.-C. (2008) 'CSCW from Coordination to Collaboration', in, pp. 87–98. doi: 10.1007/978-3-540-92719-8_9.

Faraj, S. and Xiao, Y. (2006) 'Coordination in fast-response organizations', *Management Science*, 52(8), pp. 1155–1169. doi: 10.1287/mnsc.1060.0526.

Gilbert, N. *et al.* (2015) 'Self-organizing dynamical systems', *International Encyclopedia of the Social & Behavioral Sciences*. Elsevier.

Guo, K. L. (2008) 'DECIDE: a decision-making model for more effective decision making by health care managers', *The Health Care Manager*, 27(2), pp. 118–127. doi: 10.1097/01.HCM.0000285046.27290.90.

Jennings, N. R. *et al.* (2014) 'Human-agent collectives', *Communications of the ACM*, 57(12), pp. 80–88. doi: 10.1145/2629559.

Karacapilidis, N. (ed.) (2014) *Mastering Data-Intensive Collaboration and Decision Making*. Cham: Springer International Publishing (Studies in Big Data). doi: 10.1007/978-3-319-02612-1.

Karacapilidis, N. and Tampakas, V. (2019) 'On the Exploitation of Collaborative Argumentation Structures for Inducing Reasoning Behavior', in *Proceedings of the 18th International Conference on WWW/Internet 2019*. IADIS Press, pp. 78–84. doi: 10.33965/icwi2019_201913L010.

Kittur, A. *et al.* (2011) 'CrowdForge: Crowdsourcing Complex Work', in *Proceedings of the 24th annual ACM symposium on User interface software and technology UIST '11*.

Lhaksmana, K. M., Murakami, Y. and Ishida, T. (2018) 'Role-Based Modeling for Designing Agent Behavior in Self-Organizing Multi-Agent Systems', *International Journal of Software Engineering and Knowledge Engineering*, 28(01), pp. 79–96. doi: 10.1142/S0218194018500043.

Luc, D. T. (2008) 'Pareto Optimality', in *Pareto Optimality, Game Theory And Equilibria. Springer Optimization and Its Applications, vol 17*. Springer, New York, pp. 481–515. doi: 10.1007/978-0-387-77247-9_18.

Mann, L., Harmoni, R. and Power, C. (1991) 'The GOFER course in decision making', in Baron, J. and Brown, R. V. (eds) *Teaching decision making to adolescents*. Hillsdale: Lawrence Erlbaum Associates, pp. 61–78.

Mattermost - Official Site (no date). Available at: https://mattermost.com/.

Retelny, D. *et al.* (2014) 'Expert crowdsourcing with flash teams', *Proceedings of the 27th annual ACM symposium on User interface software and technology - UIST '14*, pp. 75–85. doi: 10.1145/2642918.2647409.

Retelny, D., Bernstein, M. S. and Valentine, M. A. (2017) 'No Workflow Can Ever Be Enough: How Crowdsourcing Workflows Constrain Complex Work', *Proceedings of the ACM on Human-Computer Interaction*, 1(2), p. Article 89. doi: 10.1145/3134724.

Roffia, L. *et al.* (2018) 'Dynamic Linked Data: A SPARQL Event Processing Architecture', *Future Internet*, 10(4), p. 36. doi: 10.3390/fi10040036.

Schneider, C., Weinmann, M. and vom Brocke, J. (2018) 'Digital nudging', *Communications of the ACM*, 61(7), pp. 67–73. doi: 10.1145/3213765.

Simon, H. (1979) 'Rational Decision Making in Business Organizations', *American Economic Association*, 69(4), pp. 493–513.

Slack - Official Site (no date). Available at: https://slack.com/.

Smirnov, A., Shilov, N. and Parfenov, V. (2019) 'Building a Multi-aspect Ontology for Semantic Interoperability in PLM', in *Product Lifecycle Management in the Digital Twin Era. IFIP Advances in Information and Communication Technology*. Springer, pp. 107–115. doi: 10.1007/978-3-030-42250-9_10.

Terveen, L. G. (1995) 'Overview of human-computer collaboration', *Knowledge-Based Systems*, 8(2–3), pp. 67–81. doi: 10.1016/0950-7051(95)98369-H.

Valentine, M. A. *et al.* (2017) 'Flash Organizations', in *Proceedings of the 2017 CHI Conference on Human Factors in Computing Systems - CHI '17*. New York, New York, USA: ACM Press, pp. 3523–3537. doi: 10.1145/3025453.3025811.

A SURVEY ON THE STATE OF CLOUD ADOPTION IN MICRO & SMALL BRAZILIAN IT COMPANIES

Gabriel Costa Silva[1], Cesar Giovani Colini[2] and Elizandro Ferreira[2]
[1]*Universidade Tecnológica Federal do Paraná (UTFPR), Cornélio Procópio, Paraná, Brazil*
[2]*Micro and Small Business Support Service (SEBRAE), Pato Branco, Paraná, Brazil*

ABSTRACT

Micro & small companies are essential for Brazilian IT market. For instance, 95.5% of Brazilian software development companies are micro or small. Although cloud computing plays a key role in reducing infrastructure and personnel costs in small companies, little is known on the state of cloud adoption in micro & small Brazilian IT companies (MSBCs). If cloud adoption in MSBCs differs significantly from other companies around the world, MSBCs may need tailored training and tools. Moreover, these differences may limit MSBCs competitiveness in the global IT market. To understand the state of cloud adoption in MSBCs, we partnered with a regional IT association to conduct a survey with their 93 associated companies, from which we received 29 valid responses (31% response rate). Eighty-three percent of surveyed companies are currently using cloud, 65% of cloud users in our survey use more than one cloud provider, and 54% of current cloud users reported issues when using cloud services. Compared to related surveys, we did not find significant differences regarding perceptions and practices of cloud adoption. This result suggests that cloud adoption may not vary significantly with company size and region.

KEYWORDS

Vale Digital, SEBRAE, Context-Driven Research, SMEs

1. INTRODUCTION

A recent survey shows that Brazilian domestic market of software and services reached the 9th position (US$ 18.6 billion) in the 2017 world ranking, surpassing countries like Italy, Spain and India (ABES 2018). The same survey shows that 95.5% of Brazilian software development companies are micro (up to 10 empl.) or small (up to 100 empl.). As Richardson & Von Wangenheim (2007) explain, small companies differ from medium and large in that they lack sufficient staff for specialised tasks and have tight budget. Therefore, cloud computing plays a key role in small companies since its unique characteristics may help reducing infrastructure and personnel costs (Marston et al. 2011).

However, little is known on the state of cloud adoption in micro & small companies (Sahandi et al. 2013; Wood & Buckley 2015). Furthermore, industrial cloud surveys show no data on perceptions and practices of Brazilian companies (RightScale 2018; Capgemini 2012; NorthBridge 2016). This lack of information impedes understanding the extent to which cloud adoption in micro & small Brazilian IT companies (MSBCs) differs from other companies around the world. This understanding is essential for MSBCs since it: (i) enables benchmark against other companies; (ii) highlights regional differences; (iii) points out missing opportunities; and (iv) supports developing tailored tools.

Our research question asks whether perceptions and practices on cloud adoption in MSBCs differ significantly from other companies around the world. As sampling all MSBCs is an unrealistic goal because of the lack of a widely available list of all MSBCs (Baltes & Diehl 2016), we undertook a context-driven survey. As Briand et al. (2017) explain, context-driven research *"focuses on problems defined in collaboration with industrial partners and is driven by concrete needs in specific domains and development projects."* Therefore, we partnered with a regional IT association (Vale Digital[1]) to supporting the region where our university lies in. This strategy enables us to contribute to the development of the region, firstly, by diagnosing the state of cloud adoption in regional companies, and secondly, by providing appropriate training, consultancy and tools.

[1] http://valedigital.org.br

To address our research question, we conducted a survey research following rigorous guidelines (Section 2). We identified perceptions and practices of our respondents on cloud adoption, and issues faced when using cloud services (Section 3). When analysed against cloud surveys applied around the world, we observed that cloud adoption in MSBCs does not differ significantly from other companies although we could identify some interesting differences (Section 4). We present practical and research actions we are taking as our commitment with this context-driven survey, and explain the impact of our findings in our research question (Section 5). In Section 6, we discuss in detail several threats we identified. Finally, Section 7 concludes this paper.

2. SURVEY & PLAN EXECUTION

Due to the lack of established guidelines for empirical and survey research in cloud computing (Gholami et al. 2016), our study is mainly based on Kitchenham & Pfleeger (2008) guidelines as they enable rigorous survey preparation and execution. To encourage independent replications of this study, the questionnaires, the dataset, and the R instructions used to conduct and analyse this study are available online[2].

As Kitchenham & Pfleeger (2008) recommend, we used previously published cloud surveys (NorthBridge 2016; RightScale 2018; Emison 2014; Capgemini 2012) to construct our questionnaires. These published surveys were applied worldwide, targeting different company sizes. We also used the only two surveys targeting Small and Medium Enterprises (SMEs) (Sahandi et al. 2013; Wood & Buckley 2015) we could find.

From these surveys, we selected questions that could help answering our research question, and complemented our questionnaires with few questions we created to fully achieve our research goals. As recommended by Easterbrook et al. (2008), several questions included a short glossary to make clear to our respondents the meaning of terms we used in the survey, such as what we understand by service & deployment models. The research questionnaire consists of one open and 14 closed questions. Most closed questions present options from which our respondents could select one or more that apply in their companies. Cloud adoption questions target only companies that use or plan to use cloud services.

MSBCs are the target population of our survey. As most surveys (Kitchenham & Pfleeger 2008; Baltes & Diehl 2016), our survey uses a convenience sample since there is not a widely available list of all MSBCs. Unlike random sampling (probalistic), convenience sampling (non-probabilistic) obtains responses from participants that are available and willing to respond (Kitchenham & Pfleeger 2008). As this study is undertaken as a context-driven research (Briand et al. 2017), our sample consists of companies that belong to a Brazilian IT association in the South-west of Paraná state, called *Vale Digital*[3]. The rationale for this choice is that *Vale Digital* lies in the same region where our university is located. Thus, we can contribute to the regional development by diagnosing the state of cloud adoption in regional companies and by providing training, consultancy and tools to support these companies.

Vale Digital groups 93 IT companies of varied sizes and ages. These companies are organised into four federations according to the macro-region where they lie in. We note that cloud surveys classify micro & small companies in different ways (Sahandi et al. 2013; Wood & Buckley 2015; RightScale 2018; ABES 2018). The Brazilian Micro and Small Business Support Service (SEBRAE[4]) classifies a company size according to their number of employees. Whereas a micro company has up to 9 employees, a small company has up to 49 employees (SEBRAE & DIEESE 2015). This classification is used as reference from hereon.

To get the list of associated companies, we directly approached each federation of *Vale Digital* by phone. During the phone call, we explained our purpose and main benefits of our study. The author of this study used his credibility in the region to asking for the list of associated companies, as recommended by Smith et al. (2013). After the phone call, we sent an email formalising our request. All four federations provided a full list of associated companies, containing their phone number, email and a person to contact.

As recommended by Kitchenham & Pfleeger (2008), three researchers evaluated our questionnaires before we administered them. Suggestions given by researchers were analysed and the questionnaires were improved to the current version. To administer the questionnaires, we approached companies by phone to

[2] https://github.com/EmpiricalStudies/cloud-survey-valedigital.git
[3] http://valedigital.org.br
[4] https://www.sebrae.com.br/sites/PortalSebrae/canais_adicionais/sebrae_english

identifying an appropriate respondent then, we sent the questionnaires to respondents by email. To increasing participation in our survey, we followed recommendations summarised by Smith et al. (2013). Thus, in the email to the respondent, we briefly explained the purpose of our survey, their benefits both to the respondent and to the region where the company lies in, and ensured the confidentiality of individual results.

3. RESULTS

Whereas this section identifies current perceptions and practices of MSBCs, the next section analyses our findings compared with that identified by related surveys in companies around the world. Together, these findings answer our research question within the context of our study.

3.1 Company & Respondent Characterisation

From the ninety-three *Vale Digital* companies invited to our survey, forty responded to our online questionnaire (43% of response rate). However, we removed 11 responses from our dataset because they came from companies larger than micro or small. Thus, our sample consists of twenty-nine valid responses (31% of response rate). It is important to highlight that even after the data reduction the sample size is still within the acceptable rate reported in the literature (Sahandi et al. 2013; Smith et al. 2013).

The responses came from nineteen micro (65.5%) and ten small (34.5%) companies. These companies employ from 1 to forty people. Twelve companies (41.3%) have between 4 and 5 employees in total. Most companies (55.2%) are older than 6 years, and more than one-third of companies in our sample are older than 10 years. Whereas only 10% of micro companies are older than 10 years, this percentage increases to 80% for small companies -- which may suggest a correlation between company age and size.

Thirteen companies (44.8%) have software development as their main activity. Developing customisable software is the main activity of nearly one-third of our sample, followed by technical support, maintenance or other IT services (20.7%). Surveyed companies target seventeen different markets. Technology and Consulting & Services (55.2% each) are the main target markets, followed by retail (48.3%).

Owners, co-owners and CEOs quite often play technical roles in MSBCs. Not surprisingly, most (62%) of our respondents are co-owners (41%), CEOs (14%) or owners (7%). Only 38% of our respondents identified themselves as playing other roles in the company, namely: Director (24%), Developer (7%) and Manager (7%). We note that these 38% of respondents employ in total 11% more employees than the other ones. This may suggest that larger companies assigned the questionnaire response to their employees whereas the owners responded the questionnaire in smaller companies.

Respondents have different levels of knowledge regarding cloud computing. In our characterisation questionnaire, basic knowledge (level 1, 24.1%) and advanced knowledge (level 2, 27.6%) do not imply practical experience managing cloud services. On the other hand, knowledge plus practical experience (level 3, 20.7%), along with mastery (level 4, 27.6%) do imply. We note that the sample size of respondents with and without practical experience is similar.

3.2 Perceptions on Cloud Adoption

The vast majority (86.2%) of surveyed companies agree (34.5%) or strongly agree (51.7%) that using cloud computing leads to competitive advantages. This subset of companies is already cloud users or is planning to use cloud soon. Ten percent of companies that selected neutral to this question are already using cloud services. The only respondent that disagreed to this question (3.4%) has no plan to use cloud computing.

Cost reduction (37.9%), mobility & convenience in accessing applications (27.6%), and reduced capital expenditure in hardware, software, IT support or information security (24.1%) are the three major drivers of cloud computing adoption, according to our respondents. Reduced planning, maximising resource utilisation, and increased computing capacity were cited only once.

Lack of knowledge, advice or guidelines on cloud adoption, along with fear of security breaches are major (55.2%) barriers for cloud adoption in surveyed companies. Lack of trust, along with cost concerns are the second most cited concerns (31%). Vendor lock-in was the less cited concern although this is a frequent issue faced by surveyed companies already using cloud (Section 3.3).

Nearly half of our respondents (44%) disagree or strongly disagree that there is sufficient advice, support & training for assisting MSBCs when selecting cloud technologies. On the other hand, only 10% agree or strongly agree with the existence of sufficient advice, support & training for MSBCs. Forty-one percent of our respondents neither agreed nor disagreed with this question. We could not observe any significant demographics difference among respondents of this question.

Unauthorised access to or leak of information (51.7%), service unavailability (48.3%), and security breaches (44.8%) are the three major risks of using cloud computing, according to our respondents. We observed a correlation between knowledge on cloud and perceptions on risks since only 32% of respondents who pointed security concerns as risks of using cloud have practical experience using cloud services.

Finally, several respondents who pointed service unavailability as a risk of using cloud computing noted on the survey constant issues with the internet service availability. This may suggest a major concern with the internet service unavailability rather than the cloud service.

3.3 Practices on Cloud Adoption

Eighty-three percent of surveyed companies are currently using cloud, 14% are planning to use, and only one company (3.4%) has no plans of using cloud. Among companies that use or are planning to use cloud computing, 89% use or plan to use cloud computing for an existing project.

The only company that has no plans of using cloud is a micro sized, older than 10 years company with 4 employees that provides technical support, maintenance & other IT services. This company disagrees that cloud can offer competitive advantage to its users, and the respondent pointed having advanced knowledge on cloud. As we noted in Section 3.1, this knowledge level does not imply practical cloud experience.

Not only the cloud adoption is high, but also the interest in providing cloud services. Sixteen companies (55.2%) currently provide cloud services whereas 17.5% are planning to provide cloud services in the next 12 months. In addition, other 17.5% of companies are considering to provide cloud services in the future.

Only three companies (10.3%) have no plans to provide cloud services. All these three companies are micro sized companies, but they differ in their main activities - software development (on request), technical support, maintenance & other IT services, and other. Application servers is the main target for replacement with cloud service (28.6%), followed by backup (21.4%) and file storage (17.9%).

Taking into consideration only companies that are currently using or are planning to use cloud computing, modern technology, along with competitive price are deemed as important criteria to select cloud providers for 60.7% of our respondents. Provider location and time in the market were the less cited criteria (3.6%). We observed that two-thirds of companies (n = 10) that pointed technical support as an important criterion for cloud provider selection have no practical experience with cloud service. This might suggest that they need technical support to compensate their lack of practical experience.

Google (41.7%), Amazon (37.5%), and Microsoft alongside IBM (12.5% each) are the public cloud providers often used by cloud users in our survey. We noted that Google is preferred by companies using primarily SaaS services whereas Amazon is preferred by companies using primarily IaaS services.

Several cloud providers were cited only once (e.g., Heroku). In total, other providers are used by 54.2% of cloud users in our survey. We observed that 35% of cloud users in our survey use only one cloud provider whereas 65% of cloud users use more than one cloud provider. The practical knowledge on cloud computing is slightly greater (64%) on those who use more than one cloud provider than on those who use only one (50%), suggesting that practical experience may lead to confidence to use multiple providers.

Among companies that use or are planning to use cloud computing, 64% use or plan to use SaaS, followed by 54% for IaaS, and 29% for PaaS. Other service models correspond to 19%. Regarding the deployment model, companies using or planning to use cloud computing prefer the private model (39%). Yet, public and hybrid models (each) are used or planned to be used by 29%.

Fifty-four percent of current cloud users reported facing issues with cloud computing. The most often (always or usually happen) issues are vendor lock-in (37.5%) and lack of qualified staff (25%) whereas the less frequent (never or occasionally happen) are provider going out of business (100%), unauthorised access (96%) and loss of control (88%). Only one company reported having no issue at all. This is a micro sized company established between 6 to 10 years, with some practical knowledge on cloud. This figure increases to 3 when we consider never or occasionally had any issue.

We investigated the correlation between reported issues and the 3 major risks of using cloud computing (according to the perception of our respondents). Because only companies that are currently using cloud can inform the occurrence of issues, this analysis takes into account only companies that already use cloud.

We observed that 58% of companies that consider unauthorised access as a risk of using cloud computing have never had any issue with unauthorised access. The figure increases to 92% if we consider companies that never or occasionally had any issue with unauthorised access. Fifty percent of companies that consider service unavailability as a risk have never or occasionally faced this issue. Similarly, 60% of companies that pointed security as a risk have never or occasionally faced this issue.

No company that reported unauthorised access, service unavailability or security breach as risks of using cloud computing faced these issues often (i.e., always or usually happen). This might suggest that the perception of cloud risks is likely to be based on assumptions, perhaps prompted by the lack of knowledge, rather than result of real negative experiences. On the other hand, we should consider that company's perception on risks might be prompted by the damage size rather than by the frequency of issues.

We also investigated the correlation between the 2 most often (i.e., always or usually happen) reported issues faced by cloud users and the barriers they pointed for cloud adoption. Again, we consider in this correlation only companies that are currently using cloud computing.

No respondent that often faced vendor lock-in issues mentioned it as a barrier for adoption. In contrast, 64% of companies that are facing issues with the lack of qualified staff pointed a barrier related to the lack of knowledge (that could be resolved by having qualified staff).

4. ANALYSIS

This section analyses the results of our survey (Section 3) compared with related surveys. This section analyses the set of surveys used as primary basis for structuring the questions used in this study (Section 2). We use the most relevant topics presented in Section 3 criteria for analysing this and related surveys.

4.1 Drivers of Cloud Adoption

Cost reduction is deemed the main driver for cloud adoption in three out of five surveys. Furthermore, cost is one of the three most cited drivers in Emison and NorthBridge's survey. These results may suggest that cloud adoption is cost-driven. Like Sahandi, Alkhalil & Opara-Martins' survey, our respondents regard mobility and convenience in accessing applications as important drivers of cloud adoption. This may suggest that small companies have similar perceptions on cloud drivers, regardless of the country. On the other hand, scalability, which is among the most cited drivers in Emison, NorthBridge, and Sahandi, Alkhalil & Opara-Martins' surveys, does not appear in our survey as one of the most cited drivers. In fact, increased computing capacity (which is one facet of scalability) is the less cited driver in our survey. This may suggest that our respondents differ from others in that they are primarily interested in reducing their costs.

4.2 Cloud Adoption Barriers & Support

Like our survey, security concerns are among the most cited barriers for cloud adoption in related surveys. Similar to RightScale's survey, our respondents pointed out the lack of knowledge as an important barrier.

On the other hand, vendor lock-in is deemed as an important barrier for NorthBridge and Sahandi, Alkhalil & Opara-Martins' surveys, but it is the less cited barrier in our survey. Another major difference between ours and related surveys is that several barriers tie in our survey.

For instance, two barriers share the position of most cited barrier, and three barriers share the 3rd position. This may suggest that our respondents do not share a unified perception on cloud adoption barriers. As in the drivers of cloud adoption, perhaps this result is correlated with different knowledge of our respondents on cloud (Section 3.1). In addition, the RightScale's survey shows that the level of importance on cloud barriers decreases with higher cloud maturity (RightScale 2018).

Only our survey asked about the support for cloud adoption. However, Wood & Buckley (2015) note that most of their respondents "feel there is not enough advice, support or training available for SMEs," which is in line with our findings (Section 3.2). In addition, we observe that RightScale's survey points the lack of resources/expertise as one of the greatest barriers for cloud adoption - and this importance increases with lower cloud maturity (RightScale 2018). This might suggest that companies are not able to train their teams in the rate they need even when there is enough support for cloud adoption.

4.3 Cloud Risks & Adoption

Security-related concerns are among the most cited risks of using cloud services. We observe that respondents in our and in related surveys share similar opinions. For instance, *unauthorised access to or leak of information* is among the three most cited risks in Emison's survey. Service unavailability, our 2nd most cited risk, appears as the 3rd most cited risk in the Wood & Buckley's survey.

Apart from Sahandiet al. (2013) and Wood & Buckley (2015) that do not investigate the rate of cloud adoption, the cloud adoption rate varies from 76% (Capgemini) to 96% (RightScale). We could not observe a correlation between the date when the survey was undertaken and cloud adoption rate, although the latest RightScale's survey shows an increase in the cloud adoption rate.

4.4 Public Cloud Providers

Among related surveys, only RightScale and Emison's survey investigated the most used public cloud providers. Like our survey, Amazon, Microsoft and Google are among the most used public cloud providers. However, the order and adoption rates vary. Whereas Google features as the most used provider in our survey (41.7% of use), it features as the third most used in both RightScale and Emison's survey (18% and 29%, respectively). Microsoft, which features as the third most used provider in our survey (12.5% of use), features as the second most used in both RightScale and Emison's survey (45% and 48%, respectively). Finally, Amazon features as the second most used provider in our survey (37.5% of use) whereas it features as the most used provider in both RightScale and Emison's survey (64% and 62%, respectively).

RightScale's survey also shows the use rate of multiple cloud providers. Whereas 65% of our respondents are using more than one cloud provider, this figure decreases to 31% among RightScale's respondents. Taking into account only small & medium companies investigated in RightScale's survey, the figure increases to 33% - suggesting that the number of cloud providers used inversely increases to company's size.

5. DISCUSSION

Several findings suggest that the lack of qualified staff may be a relevant issue faced by MSBCs when adopting cloud. Firstly, the lack of knowledge, advice or guidelines is pointed as the main barrier for cloud adoption. Secondly, a large number of respondents disagree that there is sufficient advice, support & training for assisting their companies when adopting cloud technologies. Next, we observed a possible correlation between the level of knowledge on cloud and some perceptions and practices. Finally, we identified several differences between perceptions on risks and barriers when compared with real issues faced by cloud users.

As part of our commitment with this context-driven survey, we have been investigating cloud tools and platforms that could either facilitate the start of cloud beginners (Silva et al. 2018) or offer better performance (Ré et al. 2018). These studies offer valuable recommendations in the decision making on moving to/using the cloud. In addition, we are delivering cloud courses tailored to regional companies.

The research question driving our study asks whether perceptions and practices on cloud adoption in MSBCs differ significantly from other companies around the world. This investigation is critical for (i) enabling benchmark against other companies; (ii) highlighting regional differences; (iii) pointing out missing opportunities; and (iv) supporting the development of tailored tools.

Taking into account the results of our survey, when compared with companies in related surveys, MSBCs share similar perceptions on cloud drivers, barriers and risks. When compared only with SMEs, MSBCs face similar challenges, such as the lack of support for cloud adoption. MSBCs also share similar practices with companies in related surveys, such as wide SaaS adoption followed by IaaS, and their choice for cloud providers. Finally, cloud adoption rate in MSBCs is within the range identified in related surveys. These findings show that cloud adoption in MSBCs is in line with other companies around the world. Moreover, these findings suggest that cloud adoption may not vary significantly with company size and region.

However, we found several differences that may have been prompted by regional influences, company size, cloud maturity, and primary sector. These differences need further analysis, which we plan to undertake in future work by: (i) replicating an extended version of this survey covering different company sizes and regions in the Paraná state, Brazil; (ii) interviewing respondents to identifying reasons that led to their decisions; and (iii) evaluating the impact of our training and research activities over regional companies.

6. THREATS TO VALIDITY

Internal threats impact the cause-effect relationship. These threats might lead to an alternative cause for the effect (Wohlin et al., 2012). We identified three internal threats. First, the instrument used to collect data (Section 2) could introduce some flaws due to different perceptions on cloud concepts, and due to its length. To reduce this threat, we provided a glossary in our questionnaires to explain main cloud concepts. In addition, we tested the questionnaires with a group of researchers before administering them to the sample population. In our tests, no respondent exceeded 15 minutes, which we considered as acceptable.

Next, our respondents' answers may not correspond to their real practice (Section 3.3). As data was collected online, we have no means to validate responses. However, we should point out that our respondents' answers are in line with worldwide surveys in several cases. A future replication of this survey should also consider *in loco* interviews for identifying possible deviations from reality.

Finally, different company sizes, regions, primary sectors and respondents sampled in related surveys make it difficult to carry out a fair analysis. As related surveys do not show categorised data, we were unable to make a fair comparison. This may have impacted our conclusion.

External threats restrict generalisation beyond the scope of the study (Wohlin et al. 2012). We identified three external threats. First, the timelessness of our survey results is a possible threat. Several indicators may change rapidly in cloud surveys, such as the rate of cloud adoption (Emison 2014). On the other hand, drivers and barriers do not tend to change significantly to switch positions (Emison 2014). However, results were presented to companies as soon as we consolidated them. In addition, we have been working on these results since we finished the survey. Therefore, expected results of the context-driven research have been met.

Second, one can argue whether our sample is representative of the target population. When surveying software developers, Baltes & Diehl (2016) observe the lack of structured and systematic source of population representatives. Therefore, it is not uncommon to limit studies to a single group (Robillard 2009; Genero et al. 2003) - which is the case of our survey. To make the results of our survey valid to a group, we mitigated this threat by undertaking our survey as a context-driven research (Briand et al.2017). This enabled us to take full advantage of our survey results to contribute to regional MSBCs. In addition, our results can be regarded as a preliminary snapshot of the state of cloud adoption in MSBCs.

Finally, our sample may be considered small when compared with related surveys although our response rate is far above the minimum considered acceptable (Sahandi et al. 2013) and within the range often found in other surveys (Smith et al. 2013). Moreover, the literature emphasises that generalisation cannot be achieved by a single study, but independent replications are necessary to increase the confidence in empirical results and enable their generalisation beyond their initial context (Wohlin et al. 2012; Shull & Feldmann 2008; Kitchenham et al. 2002). Therefore, we understand that our results are indicative and cannot be widely generalised beyond *Vale Digital* before replication and extension by other researchers.

7. CONCLUSION

The survey reported in this paper shows evidence that perceptions and practices on cloud adoption in micro & small Brazilian IT companies (MSBCs) are in line with companies around the world. Although this suggests that cloud adoption does not vary significantly with the company size and region, we highlight that our findings are indicative and we do not claim for comprehensiveness or generalisation. Instead, by carrying out this survey as a context-driven research, we could devise tailored actions to helping regional MSBCs on addressing issues revealed by our survey. In addition, this study sheds some light to understand the state of cloud adoption in MSBCs, and its differences (or lack thereof) from other companies.

REFERENCES

ABES 2018, Brazilian Software Market: scenario and trends, Technical report, Associação Brasileira das Empresas de Software (ABES). URL:https://goo.gl/DkUjMF

Baltes, S. & Diehl, S. 2016, Worse Than Spam, in 'ESEM '16', ACM Press, New York, USA, pp. 1–6.

Briand, L., Bianculli, D., Nejati, S., Pastore, F. & Sabetzadeh, M. (2017), 'The Case for Context-Driven Software Engineering Research: Generalizability Is Overrated', *IEEE Software* 34(5), 72–75.

Capgemini 2012, Business Cloud: The State of Play Shifts Rapidly, Technical report, Capgemini. URL:http://goo.gl/oES9Vn

Easterbrook, S., Singer, J., Storey, M.-A. & Damian, D. 2008, Selecting Empirical Methods for Software Engineering Research, in 'Selecting Empirical Methods for SE Research', Springer London, chapter 11, pp. 285–311.

Emison, J. M. 2014, State of Cloud Survey, Technical report, InformationWeek. URL:http://goo.gl/GBx2NA

Genero, M., Piattini, M., Manso, E. & Cantone, G. 2003, Building UML class diagram maintainability prediction models based on early metrics, in 'METRICS, 2003', IEEE Comput. Soc, Sydney, pp. 263–275.

Gholami, M. F., Daneshgar, F., Low, G. & Beydoun, G. 2016, 'Cloud migration process - A survey, evaluation framework, and open challenges', *Journal of Systems and Software* 120, 31–69.

Kitchenham, B. A. & Pfleeger, S. 2008, Personal Opinion Surveys, in F. Shull, J. Singer & D. Sjøberg, eds, 'Guide to Advanced Empirical Software Engineering', Springer London, London, pp. 63–92.

Kitchenham, B. A., Pfleeger, S., Pickard, L., Jones, P., Hoaglin, D., El Emam, K. & Rosenberg, J. 2002, 'Preliminary guidelines for empirical research in SE', *IEEE TSE* 28(8), 721–734.

Marston, S., Li, Z., Bandyopadhyay, S., Zhang, J. & Ghalsasi, A. 2011, 'Cloud computing - The business perspective', *Decision Support Systems* 51(1), 176–189.

NorthBridge 2016, 2016 Future of Cloud Computing, Technical report, NorthBridge. URL:https://goo.gl/PnpjcR

Ré, R., Meloca, R. M., Roma, D. N., Ismael, M. A. d. C. & Silva, G. C. 2018, 'An empirical study for evaluating the performance of multi-cloud APIs', *Future Generation Computer Systems* 79, 726– 738.

Richardson, I. & Von Wangenheim, C. G. 2007, 'GuestEditors' Introduction: Why are Small Software Organizations Different?', *IEEE Software* 24(1), 18–22.

RightScale 2018, State of the Cloud Report, Technical report, Right Scale. URL:https://goo.gl/iq2Sh9

Robillard, M. P. 2009, 'What Makes APIs Hard to Learn?', *IEEE Software* 26(6), 27–34.

Sahandi, R., Alkhalil, A. & Opara-Martins, J. (2013), 'Cloud Computing from SMES Perspective: A Survey-based Investigation', *Journal of Information Technology Management* XXIV (1), 1–12.

SEBRAE & DIEESE 2015, Anuário do Trabalho na Micro e Pequena Empresa, Technical report, SEBRAE, São Paulo, SP. URL:http://goo.gl/jWw5tE

Shull, F. & Feldmann, R. L. 2008, Building Theories from Multiple Evidence Sources, in 'Guide to Advanced Empirical Software Engineering', 1 ed, Springer London, London, chapter 13, pp. 337–364.

Silva, G. C., Ré, R. & Silva, M. A. G. 2018, Evaluating efficiency, effectiveness and satisfaction of AWS and azure from the perspective of cloud beginners, in 'CASCON '18, ACM, Markham, Ontario, Canada, pp. 114– 125.

Smith, E., Loftin, R., Murphy-Hill, E., Bird, C. & Zimmermann, T. (2013), Improving developer participation rates in surveys, in 'CHASE', IEEE, pp. 89–92.

Torchiano, M., Di Penta, M., Ricca, F., De Lucia, A. &Lanubile, F. 2011, 'Migration of information systems in the Italian industry: A state of the practice survey', *Information and Software Technology* 53(1), 71–86.

Wohlin, C., Runeson, P., Höst, M., Ohlsson, M. C., Regnell, B. & Wesslén, A. 2012, *Experimentation in Software Engineering*, Springer.

Wood, K. & Buckley, K. (2015), Reality Vs Hype – Does Cloud Computing Meet the Expectations of SMEs?, in 'CLOSER '15', SCITEPRESS, Lisbon, Portugal, pp. 172–177.

DYNAMICALLY PRIORITIZED VIRTUAL-NETWORK MONITORING ACCORDING TO LIFECYCLE OF VIRTUAL MACHINES IN LARGE SCALE DATA CENTER

Hideki Okita[1], Hayato Hoshihara[2], Norihisa Komoda[3] and Toru Fujiwara[3]
[1]Research and Development Group, Hitachi, Ltd., 1-280 Higashi-Koigakubo, Kokubunji, Tokyo, 185-8601, Japan
[2]IoT & Cloud Services Business Division, Hitachi, Ltd., 6-26-3 Minamioi, Shinagawa-ku,, Tokyo, 140-0013, Japan
[3]Graduate School of Information Science and Technology, Osaka University, 1-5 Yamadaoka, Suita, Osaka, 565-0871, Japan

ABSTRACT

We propose a life cycle-based dynamic virtual network monitoring system that focuses on the varying failure rate in the life cycle of the VM and selects the target device for dynamic and continuous network monitoring. When using a combination of server monitoring with ping and network connection check with Ethernet OAM, the system sets higher priorities to the port connected to a long running server, and the port within a certain time after the connection change or virtual machine addition is set. The system then selects the ports from the higher priority port to be monitored by Ethernet OAM. As a result of the evaluation by the simulation, by dynamically selecting the port to be monitored for Ethernet OAM using the proposed method, it was confirmed that the average locating time of the VM failure is reduced by 2.2% compared to the conventional method. In the data center for cloud services running many VMs, it is possible to shorten the recovery from VM failure while suppressing the number of objects monitored by Ethernet OAM by using this method.

KEYWORDS

Virtual Network, Network Management, Data Center, Cloud Service, OAM

1. INTRODUCTION

As cloud services are applied to wider business fields, the demand for stable operations of IT systems in data centers that provide cloud services is growing. It requires not only higher reliability of the IT systems and but also rapid recovery to the normal state at the failures of the IT systems. The rapid recovery requires not only rapid detection of the failures and but also rapid locating the points of failure among various devices such as servers and network switches in data centers.

The load on administrators to manage the devices increases as the number of monitored devices in IT systems increases. The number of monitored devices is increasing especially in the data centers of cloud service providers and large companies due to the adoption of server virtualization technologies which enables to deploy multiple logical servers, called virtual machines (VMs), on a physical server. Also, network function virtualization (NFV) which virtualizes networks by virtual network function (VNF) is introduced in data centers. Network devices such as proxy servers, firewall devices, load balancers, and WAN optimization devices are running as VMs on servers (Luizelli, M.C. et al, 2015).

Communication protocols are standardized and widely used to monitor remotely server availability and network connectivity in data centers. In particular, ICMP (Internet Control Message Protocol) is the standard protocol for network management systems to monitor servers and network devices in TCP/IP networks by exchanging monitoring packets, well known as 'ping' (Postel, J., 1981).

Also, Ethernet OAM (Operations, Administration and Maintenance) is developed to monitor connectivity in Ethernet-based wide-area networks (WANs) (McFarland, M. et al, 2005). IEEE802.1ag (IEEE 802.1 WG, 2007) and ITU-T Y.1731 (ITU-T, 2015) are defined as the standard of Ethernet OAM. Ethernet OAM functions are generally implemented in network devices. Ethernet OAM supported devices transmit and receive continuously monitoring frames each other to check connectivity.

However, as monitored devices increase, more resources are necessary for monitoring systems although the resources of the monitoring system available for these monitoring processes are limited. Therefore, the data centers of cloud service providers and large enterprises require a network-based monitoring method that provides short average failure locating time for many VMs with less resources.

In this paper, we focus on the varying VM failure rates for each stage of the lifecycle of the monitored VMs. We propose a method to model the varying failure rate of the VM and to elect the target to focus on based on the failure rate. The following sections of this paper are constructed as follows. Section 2 describes related research works to monitor virtual networks. Section 3 describes an efficient virtual network monitoring system based on the life cycle of physical servers and VMs in the data center. Section 4 describes the evaluation results of the effectiveness of the proposed method by simulation. In addition, we examine the characteristics of the assumed model parameters when they are different from the model parameters being monitored.

2. RELATED WORK

The network problem is a major factor of service failures and accounted for 76% of the failure factors according to the failure analysis in a large-scale Internet service (Oppenheimer, D. et al, 2003). Also, the failures due to network problems are not insignificant according to the investigation results of the research institution (Schroeder, B. and Gibson, G.A., 2006) and the survey result in a commercial data center (Birke, R. et al, 2014).

Anomaly detection methods for network devices based on passive measurement realize precise and sensitive failure detection by using various statistical information (Tang, Y. et al, 2005; Gomes, R.L. et al, 2016; Katzela, I. and Schwartz, M., 2015; Liu, D. et al, 2013; Thottan, M. and Ji, C., 2003; Lakhina, A. et al, 2005; Mi, H. et al, 2013), although those require more monitoring resources of the network monitoring systems. From the active measurement viewpoint, a framework for achieving proactive network management is developed to predict exceptions in IP/MPLS networks by using OAM functions (Dini, P. et al, 2004). Also, a framework to integrate service-level monitoring with fault management using Ethernet OAM is developed for interconnected networks of Ethernet service providers so that they can identify rapidly the root cause in the networks (Varga, P. and Moldovan, I., 2007). However, these studies focus on networks with fixed monitoring targets for network service providers.

Also, the number of network end points that a network switch can monitor with Ethernet OAM at once is limited to at most tens due to the limitation of hardware resource such as a CPU of the network switch. As the number of monitored end points increases, the network switch receives more Continuous Check (CC) messages from the end points. It causes increasing CPU usage of the network switch to process the messages. For example, the maximum number of the monitored end points that a network-switch product can monitor in a network is set to 100 in default.

Therefore, the data center of a large-scale cloud service provider that creates and runs thousands of VMs and hundreds of thousands of VLANs, can not set all VMs and VLANs to be monitored with Ethernet OAM at the same time. As a result, while ping is used for all servers, the Ethernet OAM is used for limited servers. Therefore, servers that are not monitored with Ethernet OAM must be performed the connection check of the corresponding network part again once the failure of the server is detected at the service level by ping. There is a problem that it takes time to isolate the failure cause between the server and the network.

3. DINAMICALLY PRIORITIZED VIRTUAL NETWORK MONITORING

3.1 Method Overview

In this paper, we propose a new method of monitoring to reduce the average server failure locating time. Figure 1 shows the failure management in the method in a data center with Ethernet OAM and ping. Usually, there are two types of administrators in a data center; server administrators who use ping to monitor servers and network administrators who use Ethernet OAM to monitor networks in the data center. They should cooperate to clarify the root cause of service failures in the data center. When a server administrator detects a service failure by missing responses of ping messages from a monitoring server, the root cause of the failure is not yet clarified. A network administrator thus explores the Ethernet OAM monitoring point (MEP: Maintenance End Point) of the port that the server is connected. If the network administrator finds a failure with Ethernet OAM, the cause of the service failure exists in the network side. On the other hand, if Ethernet OAM does not detect a failure, it is considered that the cause of the service failure exists in the server side.

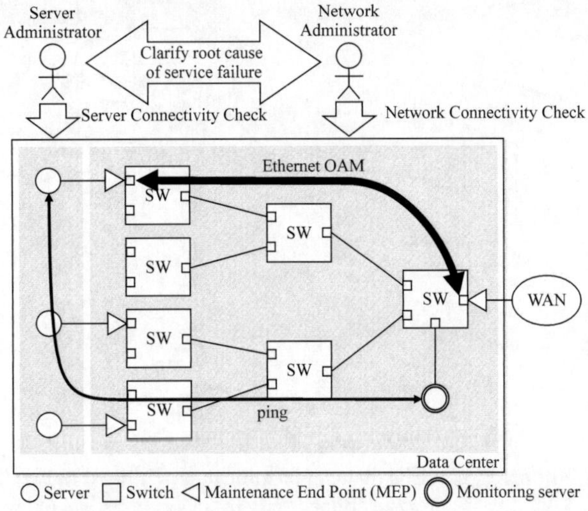

Figure 1. Failure Management of Data Center with Ping and Ethernet OAM

We introduce a new concept of dynamically selecting VMs to be monitored based on the stage of the VM lifecycle. In the past, the monitoring priorities of VMs are fixed throughout the lifecycle. However, when an IT system deploys a new physical server to activate a VM and changes its settings, if the elapsed time since it was activated is long, the hardware running the VM is likely to fail. Therefore, by increasing the allocation monitoring resources for VMs in such stage, and by decreasing the allocation monitoring resources for VMs in other stages, it is possible to shorten the average failure detection without increasing monitoring resources.

In order to select the monitored port, it is necessary to define and calculate the priority which changes in the time series according to the stage of the life cycle for each VM as an indicator of the selection. Therefore, the monitoring priority of the VM is changed according to the time series change of failure rate per VM. The pattern of failure rate for the operating time of a typical hardware including HDD on the server in the data center follows the so-called bathtub curve. The failure rate showed a high value early, decreased and eventually stabilized to a low value over time, and the high value is again shown by wear at the end of the life cycle (Yang, J. and Sun, F.B., 1999; Schroeder, B. and Gibson, G.A., 2007). Therefore, since the initial failure rate is high at the time of the introduction of the server, the monitoring priority of the VM running on the server is high, and the priority due to the initial failure is lowered over the period. On the other hand, the monitoring priority rises due to hardware wear over time.

Figure 2 shows which VMs in the data center are selected for monitoring based on the monitoring priority calculated for each VM, and also shows the time variation of the selected VM combinations. The four graphs of the left part of Figure 2 show the time variation of the monitoring priority for each of the four VMs. In addition, the thick lines of each graph represent the state in which the VM was selected for monitoring.

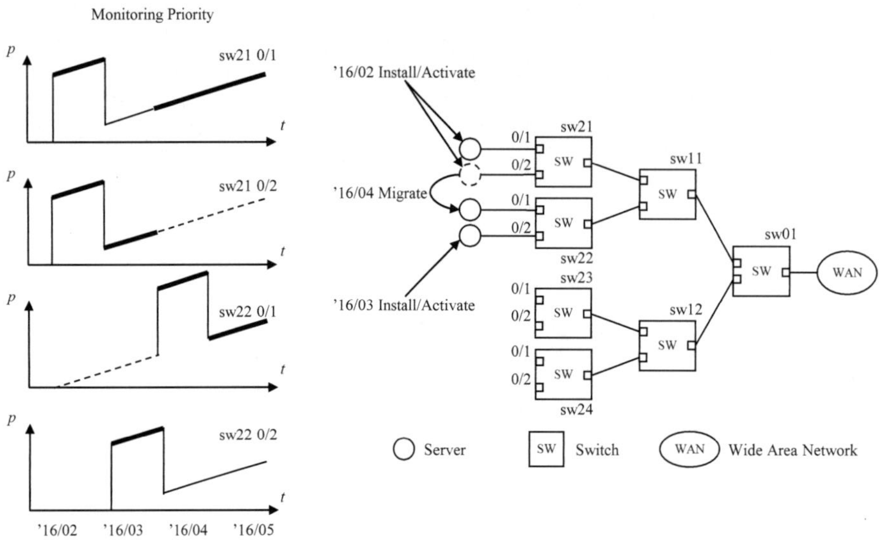

Figure 2. VM Monitoring Priority

In this example, the number of MEPs that can be allocated is limited to two. Two MEPs are first allocated to the network switch SW21 to monitor the connectivity to the ports connected to two servers when the servers activated two VMs at Feb. '16. When the third server with a VM is connected to the network switch SW22 at Mar. '16, the port that connects the first server is excluded from the monitored ports. And the port that connects the third server is added to the monitored ports. In addition, when the VM on the second server moves to the third server at Apr. '16, the priority of the port of the network switch SW22 that the third server is connected is increased to reflect the rise of the failure rate due to the configuration change, and the port is added to the monitored ports. At the same time, the port of the network switch SW21 connecting the first server is added again to monitored ports as the failure rate of the first server rises.

3.2 Port Monitoring Priority

To prioritize the above mentioned monitored ports, the proposed method calculates the port monitoring priority for each port of the switch in the network based on the total failure rate. The port monitoring priority p can be expressed as the following equation using the server wear failure rate $\lambda_{wear}(t)$, server initial failure rate $\lambda_{init}(t)$, and server change-derived failure rate $\lambda_{chg}(t)$.

$$p = 1 - (1 - \lambda_{\text{wear}}(t))(1 - \lambda_{\text{init}}(t))\left(1 - \lambda_{\text{chg}}(t)\right)$$

The method calculates the failure rate of the server wear-out failure $\lambda_{wear}(t)$ as following. Since the components of the server wears out as time goes on, the failure rate increases as well. The parameters a and t_1 represent the speed of wear-out and the time when the server has been deployed, respectively.

$$\lambda_{\text{wear}}(t) = \begin{cases} 1 - e^{-a(t-t_1)} & (t \geq t_1) \\ 0 & (t < t_1) \end{cases}$$

The method then calculates the server initial failure rate $\lambda_{init}(t)$ from the uptime of the server. The failure rate $\lambda_{init}(t)$ of a server is assumed to follow the following equation. Since the initial failure decreases as time goes on, the failure rate decreases as well. The parameter σ_{init} indicates the speed of stability of the server. By such an expression, it expresses the state that the service failure occurs due to a configuration error for a certain time since the server has been deployed or changed or a virtual machine is deployed on the server.

$$\lambda_{\text{init}}(t) = \frac{W_{\text{init}}}{\sqrt{2\pi}} e^{-\frac{(t-t_1)^2}{2\sigma_{\text{init}}^2}}$$

Then, this method checks whether the selection port is moved from the server connection change information, and that the date and time are entries prior to the specified times. If there is an appropriate entry, we calculate the failure rate $\lambda_{chg}(t)$ from the server change based on the elapsed time since the server connection occurred for each entry. If there is no entry, this method proceeds without calculating the failure rate $\lambda_{chg}(t)$ of the server changes. The failure rate $\lambda_{chg}(t)$ is expressed as a failure rate that combines the failure rates caused by individual connection changes as following. The failure rate caused by each connection change is represented by a normal distribution centered on $t = t_m$ (m = 0, 1, 2, ...) which is the timing of mth connection change.

$$\lambda_{chg}(t) = W_{chg} - W_{chg} \prod_{m} \left\{ 1 - \frac{1}{\sqrt{2\pi}} e^{-\frac{(t-t_m)^2}{2\sigma_{chg}{}^2}} \right\} (m = 0,1,2,\cdots)$$

3.3 MEP-enabled Port Selection

The network monitoring system using the proposed method chooses which port of the network switch of the data center is monitored for the Ethernet OAM based on the abovementioned port monitoring priority. The network monitoring system, based on the port monitoring priority calculated in the manner described above, selects the port to be monitored of all ports connected to the server. In this case, the system selects the monitored port so that it does not exceed the maximum programmable MEP number of each switch.

4. EVALUATION OF MONITORING EFFICIENCY

4.1 Evaluation Method

By simulation, we compared the average failure locating time of each server in the following three cases; (1) dynamically changed monitoring by Ethernet OAM based on the proposed method, (2) fixed monitoring the server running an important application, and (3) ping without Ethernet OAM. For this simulation, a small-scale discrete event network simulator was developed in C++. When this simulator is started, the object of the network node with the start-up time information is generated for each server. For each time step, the simulator checks if server failure happened or not for each object based on its uptime, configuration changes and the probability distribution of server failure. Also, it selects dynamically the objects that are monitored by using Ethernet OAM with MEP from all objects according to the proposed method in case (3). At the same time, the simulator checks if the server failures are detected with Ethernet OAM. If MEP is configured for a network node in failure, the Ethernet OAM detects quickly the failure. On the other hand, if MEP is not configured, the failure is detected by ping as usual. Based on the results, the simulator calculates the average failure locating time for the entire data center. The parameters of the implemented simulation are shown in Table 1.

Table 1. Simulation parameters

Parameter	Value
Number of nodes	1,000
Simulation duration	5 years
Simulation step interval	7 days
Server connection change frequency	Once in 100 days
Ethernet OAM CC interval	1 minute
Ping interval	15 minutes
Wear-out failure gradient a	1.0e-9
Initial failure rate amplitude W_{init}	0.0125
Initial failure rate standard deviation σ_{init}	8.0e4
Change failure rate amplitude W_{chg}	0.05
Change failure rate standard deviation σ_{chg}	8.0e4

4.2 Evaluation Results

We evaluate the improvement of the server failure locating time and the server failure detection rate by the proposed method. The server failure locating time is composed of the time that the monitoring system took for detecting a server failure by ping and the time that a network administrator took for identifying the network-side or the server-side as the cause of the server failure by using Continuity Check (CC) or Loop Back (LB) functions of Ethernet OAM. The server failure detection rate is defined as the percentage of servers that have been set to be monitored by using CC of Ethernet OAM with MEP among the servers that failed at the data center during the simulation.

Table 2 shows the simulation results of the server failure locating time and the server failure detection rate by the monitoring system. It shows, per server replacement rate, the number of failures, the server failure detection rate in the conventional method, and the server failure detection rate in the proposed method. As the server replacement rate increases, the number of total failures is reduced from 1357.65 to an average of 213.47. The average running time of the server is shortened as the server replacement rate increases. The server failure decreased since the servers were replaced before the server failure occurs due to the wear. The server failure detection rate represents the rate of the server that MEP is configured to the corresponding port and the system has detected the failure quickly by Ethernet OAM, of all the servers that failed through the simulation period. The MEP number was set to 16, and the server replacement rate was 10% per week to 50% per week every 10%. The average value of the server failure locating time was calculated by executing the simulation 100 times for each of the five server replacement rates.

The results of average server failure locating time were 754 seconds for ping only case, 749 seconds for the conventional method case and 732 seconds for the proposed method case, respectively. The change in server replacement rate did not affect the average server failure locating time or the average server failure detection rate. The proposed method reduced the average server failure locating time by 2.8% and 2.2% compared to the conventional method case and ping only case, respectively. Also, the proposed method improved the server failure detection rate by 5.32 points in average compared to the conventional method. It can be said that the proposed method increases the average server failure detection rate in data center and reduces the average server failure locating time regardless of the server replacement rate.

Table 2. Server failure locating time and server failure detection rate

Server change rate	Failures	Server failure locating time			Server failure detection rate	
		(1) Proposed	(2) Conventional	(3) Ping only	(1) Proposed	(2) Conventional
10%/week	1357.65	732.69 sec.	748.93 sec.	754 sec.	6.79%	1.61%
20%/week	700.13	731.85 sec.	748.89 sec.	754 sec.	7.05%	1.63%
30%/week	444.97	732.57 sec.	749.04 sec.	754 sec.	6.83%	1.58%
40%/week	307.11	732.30 sec.	749.29 sec.	754 sec.	6.91%	1.50%
50%/week	213.47	731.99 sec.	748.75 sec.	754 sec.	7.01%	1.67%

Also, in order to investigate the effect on the average server failure locating time by the number of MEPs, under the server replacement rate 20% per week, in the case of the number of MEPs of 8, 16, 32, 64 and 128, each of the simulation is performed 100 times, In each case, the average server failure locating time was measured. The results of this measurement are shown in Figure 3. As a result of this measurement, the average of about 700 server failures occurred in this evaluation. When the number of MEP is increased from 16 to 128 for these server failures, the average server failure locating time was shortened from 749 seconds to 713 seconds when the server was monitored by the Ethernet OAM in the conventional method. On the other hand, when monitoring the server by Ethernet OAM in the proposed method, the average server failure locating time was shortened from 732 seconds to 644 seconds In addition, the average server failure detection rate is improved from 1.6% to 13% in the case of the conventional method. Also, it is improved from 6.9% to 35% in the case of the proposed method. In the case of the proposed method with 128 MEPs, the Ethernet OAM can identify rapidly the failure factor for about one-third of all server failures.

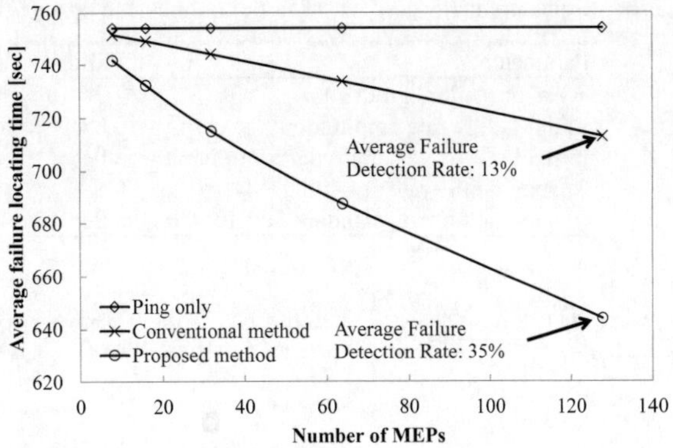

Figure 3. Server Failure Locating Time for the Numbers of Configured MEP

4.3 Sensitivity Analysis

The effect on the server failure detection rate is shown in the left part of Figure 4 when the parameter W_{init} which indicates the magnitude of the initial failure and the amplitude of the change failure used to estimate the server failure rate is different from the actual value. In addition, the right part of Figure 4 shows the effect of the parameter σ_{init} which represents the deviation in the time axis of the initial failure and the change failure used to estimate the server failure rate is different from the actual value. Even if the estimated value of the variance σ_{init} or amplitude W_{init} is shifted from the actual value, there is no significant change in the evaluation result of the server failure detection rate even in the case of the conventional method and the proposed method.

The result of the sensitivity analysis is described similarly under the environment where the occurrence of the wear-out failure is low, and the initial failure and the change failure are dominant. The simulation parameters which affects the server failure rate is shown in Table 3. The simulation parameters were set so that server failure rate due to the initial server deployment or the change of the server's connection can exceed the server failure rate caused by wear-out failure. The effect of the parameter W_{init} on the magnitude of the initial failure and the amplitude of the change failure is different from the actual value used to estimate the server failure rate is shown in the left part of Figure 5. In addition, the effect of the parameter σ_{init} on the size of the variance of the time axis of the initial failure and the change failure used to estimate the server failure rate is different from the actual value is shown in the right part of Figure 5. In the case of the proposed method, the server failure detection rate has changed significantly when the deviation σ_{init} is shifted. Specifically, when the ratio of the estimated value of σ_{init} to the actual deviation σ_{init} is 0.5 or less, the server failure detection rate is almost unchanged from the conventional method. On the other hand, when the ratio of deviation σ_{init} is 1 or more, the proposed method exhibits a higher server failure detection rate of about 2.5 points compared to the conventional method.

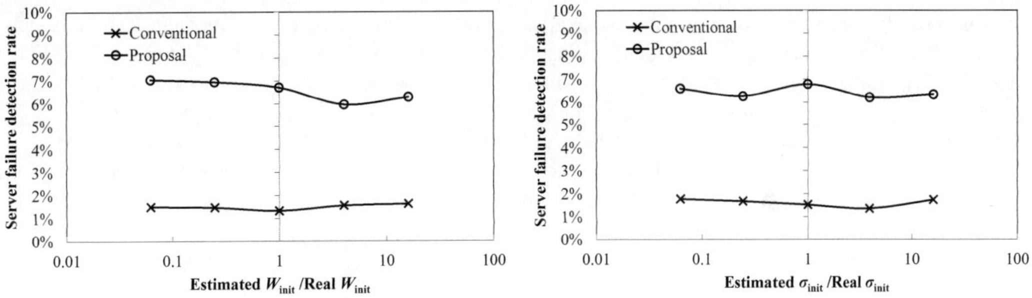

Figure 4. Sensitivity Analysis for W_{init} (Left) and for σ_{init} (Right)

Table 3. Simulation parameters in the case where initial failures and change failures are dominant

Parameter	Value
Wear-out failure gradient a	2/3e-10
Initial failure rate amplitude W_{init}	0.05
Initial failure rate standard deviation σ_{init}	5.0e5
Change failure rate amplitude W_{chg}	0.05
Change failure rate standard deviation σ_{chg}	5.0e5

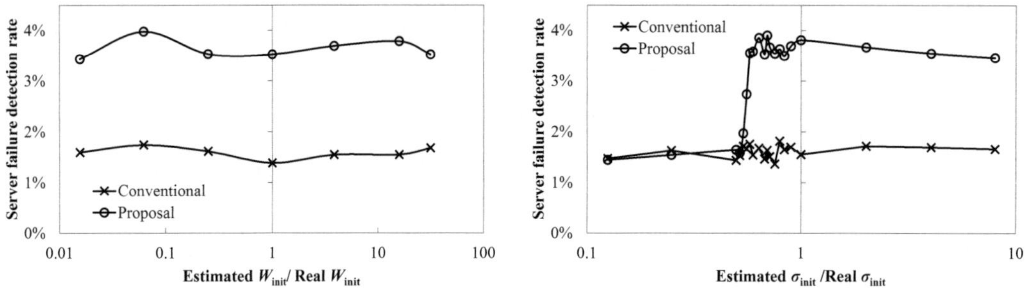

Figure 5. Sensitivity Analysis for W_{init} (Left) and for σ_{init} (Right) in Less Wear-Out Failure Case

5. DISCUSSION

As shown in Figure 3, the average server failure detection rate can be improved from about 7% to 35% when the number of MEPs activated in the network of data centers running 1000 servers is increased from 16 to 128. Therefore, the number of MEPs should be determined according to the target of the failure detection rate or the failure locating time of the data center. Also, we consider the results of the above sensitivity analysis for the case when the initial failure and change failure is dominant. If the ratio of the deviation σ_{init} of the estimated server failure rate to that of the actual server failure rate is less than 0.6, the server failure detection rate of the proposed method decreases to the same level with that of the conventional method. The cause of this behavior can be considered as follows. It is considered that if the actual value of the variance is greater than the estimate, it is more likely that a server that is not set as a monitored target by a MEP will fail. As a result, it is thought that it is the same as the case where the monitored targets by MEPs are selected substantially randomly. To avoid this problem, it is necessary to accurately calculate the deviation σ_{init} of the actual server failure rate in advance based on the failure history of servers in a data center in the past as much as possible.

6. CONCLUSION

We proposed a new network monitoring method which coordinates server management and network management. Specifically, we developed a lifecycle-based dynamic virtual network monitoring system that dynamically changes the server to be monitored with Ethernet OAM according to the server failure rate estimated based on the uptime and configuration changes of the server. As an evaluation result by the network simulator, the server failure locating time was reduced by 2.2% compared to the conventional method of setting fixed monitored targets. It can be said that coordinating server management and network management makes efficient the failure management in the large-scale data center.

REFERENCES

Birke, R. et al, 2014. Failure analysis of virtual and physical machines: Patterns, causes and characteristics. *Proceedings of 2014 Annual IEEE/IFIP International Conference on Dependable Systems and Networks (DSN'14)*, Atlanta, U.S.A.

Dini, P. et al, 2004. IP/MPLS OAM: Challenges and directions. *Proceedings of IEEE International Workshop on IP Operations and Management*, Beijing, China.

Gomes, R.L. et al, 2016. Software defined management of edge as a service networks. *In IEEE Transactions on Network and Service Management*, vol.13, no.2, pp.226–239.

IEEE 802.1 WG, 2007. IEEE Std 802.1ag-2007 virtual bridged local area networks, amendment 5: Connectivity fault management. *IEEE Standards*, IEEE Std 802.1ag-2007.

ITU-T, 2015. Operation, administration and maintenance (OAM) functions and mechanisms for Ethernet-based networks. *ITU-T Recommendation*, ITU-T G.8013/Y.1731.

Katzela, I. and Schwartz, M., 2015. Schemes for fault identification in communication networks. *In IEEE/ACM Transactions on Networking*, vol.3, no.6, pp.753–764.

Lakhina, A. et al, 2005. Mining anomalies using traffic feature distributions. *Proceedings of ACM SIGCOMM 2005*, Philadelphia, U.S.A.

Liu, D. et al, 2013. Network traffic anomaly detection using clustering techniques and performance comparison. *Proceedings of IEEE CCECE 2013*, Regina, Canada.

Luizelli, M.C. et al, 2015. Piecing together the nfv provisioning puzzle: Efficient placement and chaining of virtual network functions. *Proceedings of 14th IFIP/IEEE International Symposium on Integrated Network Management (IM 2015)*, Ottawa, Canada, pp.98–106.

McFarland, M. et al, 2005. Ethernet oam: Key enabler for carrier class metro ethernet services. *In IEEE Communications Magazine*, vol.43, no.11, pp.152–157.

Mi, H. et al, 2013. Toward finegrained, unsupervised, scalable performance diagnosis for production cloud computing systems. *In IEEE Transactions on Parallel and Distributed Systems*, vol.24, no.6, pp.1245–1255.

Oppenheimer, D. et al, 2003. Why do internet services fail, and what can be done about it?. *Proceedings of 4th USNIX Symposium on Internet Technologies and Systems (USITS'03)*, Seattle, U.S.A.

Postel, J., 1981. Internet control message protocol (ICMP). *IETF RFC*, RFC 792.

Schroeder, B. and Gibson, G.A., 2006. A large-scale study of failures in high-performance computing systems. *Proceedings of 2006 International Conference on Dependable Systems and Networks (DSN'06)*, Philadelphia, U.S.A.

Schroeder, B. and Gibson, G.A., 2007. Disk failures in the real world: What does an MTTF of 1,000,000 hours mean to you?. *Proceedings of FAST'07*, San Jose, U.S.A.

Tang, Y. et al, 2005. Active integrated fault localization in communication networks. *Proceedings of 9th IFIP/IEEE Interna tional Symposium on Integrated Network Management (IM 2005)*, Nice, France, pp.543–556.

Thottan, M. and Ji, C., 2003. Anomaly detection in IP networks. *In IEEE Transactions on Signal Processing*, vol.51, no.8, pp.2191–2204.

Varga, P. and Moldovan, I., 2007. Integration of service-level monitoring with fault management for end-to-end multi-provider ethernet services. *In IEEE Transactions on Network and Service Management*, vol.4, no.1, pp.28–38.

Yang, J. and Sun, F.B., 1999. A comprehensive review of hard-disk drive reliability. *Proceedings of Annual Reliability and Maintenability Symposium (RAMS)*, Washington, DC, U.S.A., pp.403–409.

USE OF WEB 2.0 IN CULTURAL HERITAGE

Lola García-Santiago and María Dolores Olvera-Lobo
Department of Information and Communication Sciences, University of Granada, Spain
Faculty of Translation and Interpreting. Calle Buensuceso 11 Despacho 11. Granada (Spain) 18071

ABSTRACT

As example of digital humanities in this paper the presence of institutional websites for heritage assets on relevant social media and Web 2.0 tools was analysed (social tools, Wikipedia and blogs). It was studied if new forms of cultural communication are being used as actual communication ways. The presence of institutional profiles was analysed on the following social networks: Facebook, Twitter, Google+, YouTube, Vimeo, Instagram, Flickr, Pinterest, TripAdvisor and FourSquare. Furthermore, it was identified the presence of heritage assets in the "Google Arts & Culture" project of the Google Cultural Institute as a new digital cultural resource. Results heterogeneous have been obtained and have been detected lacks in the adaption web 2.0. Wikipedia is the web 2.0 tool more used and only the 50% of the cases use Facebook or Twitter –most of them governmental institutions which manage cultural assets-. Image-based social networks are used but not in a usual way.

KEYWORDS

Digital Humanities, Web 2.0, World Cultural Heritage, Google Arts & Culture, Social Networks

1. INTRODUCTION

The concept denominated by the sociologist Zygmunt Bauman (2003) as liquid modernity is in constant evolution and adaptation to change. In the context we refer to in this work, the need for constant access to information demands the usage and appropriate management of the tools available on the Web 2.0 for a dissemination of content in accordance with the times we live in. Social media sites disseminate and share content in a community manner in the hope of feedback on the part of members. Institutions wishing to increase the expansion of the information they produce, along with their own presence and visibility, need to integrate with this group. It is for this reason that there is a progressive aware of what good digital identity management implies for improving visibility and facilitating participation and contact with users.

From the perspective of digital humanities, it is worth asking how the dissemination of information on cultural heritage is being implemented. In this regard, initiatives such as Google Arts & Culture, proposed by the Google Cultural Institute (2020) and to which reference will be made further on, are of great interest. Likewise, with increasing frequency, the bodies themselves are responsible in one way or another for the dissemination of information on heritage, mainly public bodies or non-profit governmental cultural institutions, which endeavor to create a digital identity and reinforce the on-line presence of cultural assets (García-Santiago and Olvera-Lobo, 2018). Social media in general and particularly social networks, unquestionably have a prevailing role in this task.

Therefore, given the enormous repercussion that heritage has on the cultural identity of towns, economic sectors involved in local development, or tourism, among many other factors, it is essential to be aware of the influence of the aforementioned communication structures (Jiménez-Orellana, 2016 and Rojas Castro, 2016). The analysis of how the digital identity of our heritage assets and the dissemination of information on them contributes to better knowledge of the function and optimum usage of these new technological and communicational tools.

Web 2.0 is the name given to the group of applications that take into account the effects of network interaction and exploit them via the participation and information generated on the part of users and consumers. That is, the Web is seen as a large platform where you can participate, share, interact and cooperate via programs executed online and used by multiple users at the same time (Castelló Martínez, 2010; Viñarás Abad, 2010;O'Reilly, 2005).

Web 3.0 takes it one step further. This term, which has not had much effect up to now, puts forward a more commitment concept of the Internet, in the sense that it advocates the common good and sustainable development of the Web. The idea behind Web 3.0 is therefore to extend the benefits of Web 2.0 to more people –encouraging accessibility and the use of mobile devices–, more functions and more applications, affording it more human meaning and a greater social and environmental impact.

2. METHODOLOGY

The study sample is comprised of 45 assets recognized by Unesco as World Heritage located in Spain, the European nation with the highest number of assets distinguished as such, until March 2018. In a manual processing, the institutional website for each of the heritage assets was identified, via consultations made via Google web search. The queries were considered from the denomination used by Unesco for each heritage asset, such as for example "Silk Exchange of Valencia" - and/or a variation on its name, if this turned out to be more recognizable. This is the case, for example, of "Pre-Romanesque Asturian" instead of "Monuments of Oviedo and the Kingdom of the Asturias", which is the denomination adopted by Unesco. The name of a heritage asset therefore frequently covers various monuments, places or assets. Thus, there are different cases of heritage assets with a "collective denomination" such as the "Historic City of Toledo" and the Monastery and Site of the Escorial, Madrid". In these examples it was necessary to locate and compile as many websites as subdivisions that resulted from said denomination. Commercial pages were excluded from the sample, and we selected those originating from some type of preferably public, private or mixed entity that guaranteed its legitimacy. As a result of this phenomenon, of the 45 assets classified by Unesco as cultural World Heritage, we analyzed 71 URLs of institutional websites that showed contents on the asset in the form of a simple web page or homepage, or in the form of a group of them for presenting different aspects of the heritage asset in a single documental unit called an institutional domain. If the group of pages is extremely voluminous, it may be an independent website under a domain such as .org, .es, etc. and with a structure such as, for example, *www.website.topleveldomain.* This step requires a human review and consequently it is not possible to be done automatically.

The presence of institutional profiles was analyzed on the following social networks: Facebook, Twitter, Google+, YouTube, Vimeo, Instagram, Flickr, Pinterest, TripAdvisor and FourSquare. Furthermore, where appropriate, we studied the existence of links from the heritage asset websites to these social profiles. In addition, Wikipedia entries and the existence of blogs relating to these cultural assets were identified, along with their presence on the Google Institute project.

The social networks –the most popular social media type– the analysis focused on were Facebook, Twitter, Google+, YouTube, Vimeo, Instagram, Flickr, Pinterest, TripAdvisor and FourSquare. On the one hand, we checked to see whether the institutional URLs of the cultural assets had a profile on these networks. In addition, we have explored if web pages of the sample are linked more if they have official profile on any of the different social networks and media of the cultural assets.

Furthermore, entries corresponding to heritage assets in the study sample were identified on Wikipedia, another of the social mediums that enjoys extensive acceptance and popularity amongst Web 2.0 users. We also analysed blogs. In this manner, in addition we were able to specify the use made of this Web 2.0 tool. We also determined which structure and content characteristics these blogs presented.

In parallel, we carried out searches in Google Arts & Culture from the denomination of each asset and identified the type of information collected in this Google Cultural Institute tool.

3. RESULTS

The data obtained from an analysis of the presence of institutional web pages of the sample heritage assets on the different social media sites reveal, overall, that 13% of the web pages considered do not yet have a Web 2.0 presence, even where the institution responsible for the management of the heritage asset does. This 13% of URLs correspond to 7 assets, that is, 15.6% of the sample, which are not totally or partially represented on any social media considered in the study. By way of example, this is the case for the "Historical City of Caceres", which, as the collective denomination it is, has 4 URLs that represent it. However, only one of its

URLs, –that corresponding to a part of this heritage asset, specifically the Church of san Francisco Javier–, is found to be represented on the Web 2.0 (in other words, a mere 25% of the total information on the heritage asset in question).

Figure 1 shows the results relating to the presence on social networks of the different institutional websites. From the social media used, 68% of the assets included in the sample have a presence on Wikipedia, followed by the social networks Facebook and Twitter. In contrast, the least used social networks are those that collect opinions and ratings both on the part of users and of any other person who wishes to express their comments, as in the case of TripAdvisor and Foursquare. The use of audiovisual formats is even more in the minority on the part of institutions on social networks such as Pinterest and Vimeo.

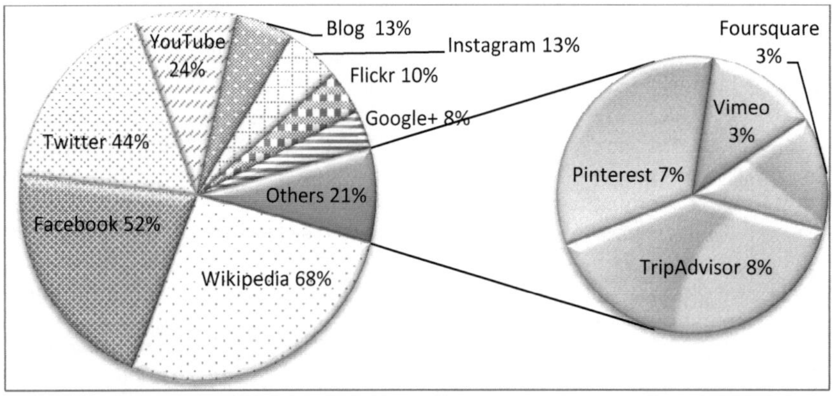

Figure 1. Web 2.0 presence of World Heritage (% of URLs)

As mentioned, on occasions there are more than one URL for a heritage asset where it is a monument complex containing various elements, that is, it has a collective denomination. For this reason, as a complement to the previous analysis, we considered the total or partial Web 2.0 presence of the heritage assets themselves (Figure 2) regardless of the number of URLs of each asset which is shown in former figure 1.

Again, the social media site most used by the World Heritage assets included in our study sample is Wikipedia, with 73% of the cases with a presence on this collaborative encyclopedia.

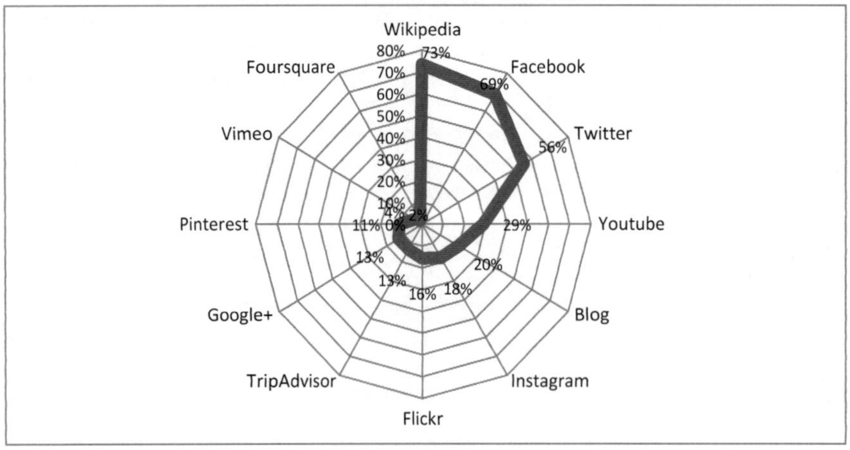

Figure 2. Total or partial presence on social media sites analysed (% 45 assets)

We also analysed the intensity of the presence of each asset on the different platforms mentioned –both those referring to social networks, and Wikipedia, blogs and Google Arts & Culture– from the number of platforms on which their institutional URLs were present.

Table 1. Social platforms employed by the assets

Number of platforms	None	1	2	3	4	5	6	7	8	9
Percentage of use	13%	31%	14%	14%	13%	4%	6%	3%	1%	0%

Table 1 shows the usage frequency of these platforms, that is, on how many of them the institutions have included a profile that links to the heritage asset websites. In this regard, attention should be drawn to the fact that over 70% of the URLs have institutional profiles on 1 (31%), 2 (14%), 3 (14%) or, even 4 (13%) social media sites. Furthermore, 14% of these boast a profile on 5 or more platforms. The heritage asset corresponding to the Alhambra of Granada particularly stands out; with a presence extending to all of the popular media used currently –a total of 10–. Apart from this exception, no asset is found on all of the platforms. This circumstance is undoubtedly influenced by the fact that tools such as TripAdvisor and FourSquare focus mainly on the opinions and comments of their users and/or visitors to the assets in question –their prime objective– rather than the institutions responsible for the management to these assets.

Focusing only the URLs which have an institutional profile on Twitter or Facebook, 79% of the cases analysed had a presence on both. On the contrary, 18% only having a Facebook profile and 3% only a Twitter profile. Besides, we have characterized the presence of cultural heritages which have Facebook and/or Twitter profiles according to the bodies responsible for each heritage asset (table 2). The highest presence on the aforementioned social networks is maintained by institutional URLs of the heritage assets managed by the central or regional administration, either individually or via consortiums between various bodies.

Table 2. Presence of Facebook and/or Twitter profiles

Type of institution	Governmental	Consortium	Municipal	Foundation	Religious	Private	Association
Facebook/Twitter use	37%	24%	26%	11%	5%	5%	3%

In relation to the presence of profiles of the sample URLs on the audiovisual networks, the use of video platforms –YouTube and Vimeo– is higher, with 25% of the institutional websites present on these, compared to 19% with a profile on the static image based sites Flickr, Instagram and Pinterest. Specifically, 24% of the sample URLs had a YouTube profile, compared to 3% for Vimeo. There was only one case where both platforms were used to increase presence on networks.

We studied this phenomenon for 45 assets and analysed whether there were great differences. It was possible to verify that 19% of the heritage assets recognised as World Heritage in Spain by Unesco have a profile on image-based social networks. 13% of these assets are represented on Instagram, and 7% on Pinterest. In relation to the usage frequency of these image-based social media sites (Table 3), it is observed that 57% of the assets have a profile on one of these platforms, whereas just 7% use all three.

Table 3. Heritage assets with profiles on image-based social networks

Number of image platforms	1	2	3
Percentage of use	57%	36%	7%

Something similar occurs with the video format, where a mere 6% of heritage assets that make use of video-based social media sites use the two platforms studied, YouTube and Vimeo.

As it was announced in methodology, we explored if web pages of the sample are linked more if they have official profile on any of the different social networks and media of the cultural assets.

In this regard, we carried out a quantitative analysis with the purpose of determining to what extent the inclusion of profiles on platforms of a generalist nature, such as Facebook and Twitter, affect links received (inlinks) by the institutional web pages. To achieve this, we made pertinent queries on the Google search engine and counted the number of permanent links originating from other websites to the URLs in the sample. According to the results obtained, attention may be drawn to the fact that 30% of the institutional URLs of the heritage assets with a profile on at least one of the two platforms has a high number of links originating from other websites (Figure 3), compared to those that do not make use of these social networks.

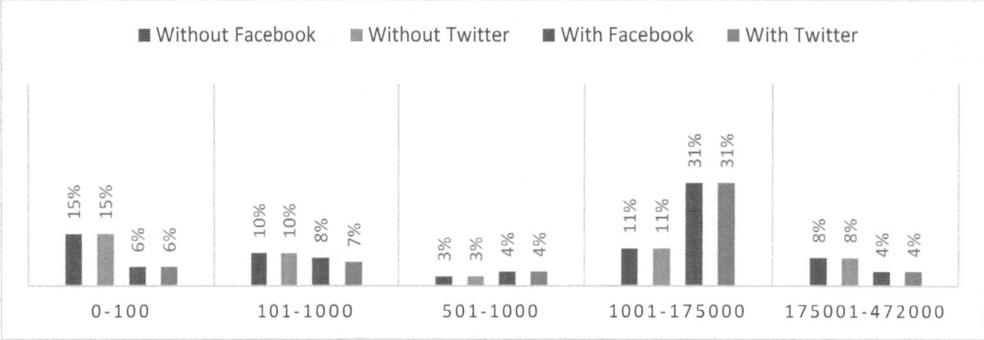

Figure 3. Relationship between inlinks to WebPage and Web 2.0 presence

The blogs analysed reveal differences in design. 55.5% of the blogs show a traditional design with the periodical inclusion of news and articles, compared to the other 44.4% which organise content by sections. The content of the blogs is in the Spanish language, with there being only two examples of information in other languages (English, French and Catalan). The greatest proportion of blogs includes images, articles with content and historical data. Others add sections that encourage frequent visits with novelties in actions relating to the heritage asset or events.

Just 12.5% of the sample URLs corresponding to World Heritage assets have their own blog, compared to 84.5% which have none. Additionally, 3% of blogs refer to the institution responsible for the management of the cultural asset, rather than simply the asset itself.

Finally, we have discovered that only 7% of the assets included in the sample are represented on this Google tool. Each entry displays audio-visual information on the heritage asset in general or on several of the numerous cultural aspects of interest. It links to current or past exhibitions accessible through web resources. Its main information sources are National Libraries and Museums. It also facilitates links to Wikipedia and other resources belonging to the company, such as Google Maps, for information on the location of the heritage asset, or virtual views via Street View. Interest in its geolocation is probably the reason for the cases included in this tool being architectural ensembles within municipalities.

4. CONCLUSION

This study confirms the heterogeneous efforts and strategies being carried out by institutions in the social media sphere. However, it also leaves no doubt that there is work left to do in terms of this aspect. Liquid modernity use web 2.0 as usual way to inform and search news. From the perspective of digital humanities, it is worth asking how the dissemination of information on cultural heritage is being implemented. This is the case both regarding the use of Web 2.0 tools and the management of content created for the public. Cultural entities, therefore, should mark the communication and publicity of their content as one of their priorities. In this regard, they are equally obliged to establish and develop a clear, defined strategy for building their digital identity. It is therefore recommendable for those responsible for the dissemination of cultural heritage to make a correct choice regarding the specific communication channel or channels using the language and form of expression adapted accordingly. Accordingly, the choice of social media sites to be used, and even the regular maintenance of the greatest number of them taking into account their specific features, requires professionals dedicated to this task.

In addition, attention must be drawn to the disconnection between the Google Arts & Culture project and any other social medium without any link that permanently links or connects this resource with the website or with a social profile.

The study carried out highlights a digital identity still lacking for heritage assets as autonomous entities, as they are integrated into the generic profile of the institution responsible for them. As has also been mentioned and in light of these results, it is clear that there is still a long way to go to extend this predisposition to the majority of these managing bodies in developing the communicative task via Web 2.0 social media sites effectively, for example taking advantage of audiovisual facilities and social networks, or adopting a multilingual focus in informative resources.

The function of some of these platforms is aimed at tourism in general and cultural tourism (for example TripAdvisor), while others are used as a way of dissemination and interaction with potential visitors. In the future, it is expected to monitor the evolution of the use of these media by these institutions.

We still continue doing research on the development of methodologies that facilitate the automation of data harvesting processes. After carrying out this research we can confirm that the methodology used in this work is adequate for this type of study. Thus, for example, it is capable of being applied in similar analyzes focused on proprietary social networks that do not allow the use of APIs, nor dumping, nor automatic data storage. However, it also has limitations such as the time required to collect and organize the data. Future work will continue to expand this line of research and it is planned to apply automatic information harvesting systems to compare their effectiveness. In addition, the user's perspective will be incorporated regarding the impact caused on them by the communications –both textual and audiovisual– that take place through social media.

REFERENCES

Bauman, Z. 2003. *Modernidad líquida*. Fondo de Cultura Económica, México DF

Castelló Martínez. A. 2010. Una nueva figura profesional: el Community Manager. *Pangea* Vol.1. http://revistapangea.org/ (last consultation: 19 October 2017).

Cohen, J. (Ed.). 1996. Special Issue: Digital Libraries. Communication ACM. Vol. 39, No.11.

García-Santiago, L. and Olvera-Lobo, M.D. 2018. Mexican World Heritage information on the web: Institutional presence and visibility. *Information Development*, Vol.34, No. 3, pp 261-279.

Google Cultural Institute. 2017. Available at: https://artsandculture.google.com/ (last consultation: 31 August 2020).

Jiménez-Orellana, L.J.2016. Museo y comunicación 2.0. Situación en España. *Documentación de las Ciencias de la Información*, Vol.39, pp. 177-203.

O'Reilly, Tim. 2005. Web 2.0: compact definition. Available at: http://radar.oreilly.com/2005/10/web-20-compact-definition.html. (Last consultation: 31 August 2020).

Rojas Castro, A. 2016. Big Data in the Digital Humanities. New Conversations in the Global Academic Contex In: Smart culture. *Analysis of digital trends: AC/E Digital culture annual report 2017*. DOI: http://dx.doi.org/10.17613/M6434X

Viñarás Abad, M et al. 2010. La comunicación corporativa de los museos en España a través de la comunicación 3.0: cuatro años de evolución comunicativa en la Red. In: *II Congreso internacional comunicación*, Salamanca, España. Vol. 3. http://giovannipf.260mb.net/comunicacioncorporativa.pdf?i=1

RAISING THE VOICE: EXPLORING ANTECEDENTS OF VOICE-ACTIVATED ASSISTANT USAGE INTENTION

Maria Madlberger and Jacquelyn O'Neill
Webster Vienna Private University
Praterstrasse 23, 1020 Vienna, Austria

ABSTRACT

Voice-activated assistants have become popular devices for a hands-free interaction with information systems. Despite a growing body of research, comprehensive models on usage intention especially in a commercial context have been under-researched. This research in progress explores antecedents of attitude and usage intention of voice-activated assistants through multiple theoretical lenses, including the Technology Acceptance Model, the Unified Theory of Acceptance and Use of Technology, Social Exchange Theory, and privacy concerns. The result is a conceptual framework consisting of six propositions on the impact of perceived usefulness, perceived ease of use, social influence, trust, and privacy concerns on attitude towards voice-activated assistants and their usage intention.

KEYWORDS

Voice-Activated Assistants, Voice-Activated Technology, Usage Intention, Attitude

1. INTRODUCTION

The interaction between users and information systems (IS) has experienced a transformative innovation with the development of voice-activated technologies and voice-activated assistants (VAAs). Such systems allow for an altered process of retrieving and exchanging information, making commands, and conducting online transactions. Instead of typing, clicking, and reading, users interact by speaking and listening which enables a hands-free interaction with an IS (Guy, 2018). With a growing performance, the usage of VAAs is expected to increase in the future (Burbach et al., 2019). Leading IT companies, such as Amazon, Google, Apple, and Microsoft, have developed proprietary VAA systems and hardware to interact with their customers.

The increasing comfort and continuously improving performance of voice-activated technologies has contributed to a growing popularity of VAAs among users. In 2019, 71 percent of U.S. millennials have used VAAs daily, 46 percent of them at least five times a day (Jindal, 2019). Across all age groups, 19 percent of U.S. users are using voice technologies daily (Olsen and Kemery, 2019). Almost half of online shoppers stated in a survey to be willing to use VAAs to locate products, compare prices, get help, or for self-checkout (Kinsella and Mutchler, 2018). In another survey, 34.9 percent of respondents stated to have made purchases through VAAs in 2019 and additional 27.4 percent intended to do so in the future (Olsen and Kemery, 2019).

The substantial change of interaction patterns between users and IS with VAAs calls for an enhanced understanding of its adoption drivers. Given the novelty of the technology, research in this area is still scant and largely dominated by research on adoption in general. The studies by Simon and Paper (2007), Burbach et al. (2019), and Liao et al. (2019) identify general drivers of adoption of voice-activated technologies and suggest that factors found in IS research on technology adoption are applicable in this context. However, two research gaps can be identified in the current literature: First, the application of VAAs within the specific context of commercial applications, especially online shopping, is under-researched. However, the wide-spread availability of commercial VAA, such as Amazon's Alexa, and the increasing relevance of omni-channel business raise the relevance of this research avenue. The study by Moriuchi (2019) provides first insights into this issue by investigating drivers of loyalty to companies that interact via VAAs with its customers. Second, IS research has revealed that drivers of technology adoption cannot be explained through one theoretical lens only. To account for the complexity of drivers of technology adoption, scholars have developed comprehensive frameworks that draw on a multitude of theories to capture relevant antecedents that are spanning across single theories (Venkatesh et al., 2003). Our research follows this notion and seeks to develop a conceptual framework that addresses key drivers of VAA usage in a commercial context from various seminal theories' views. Hence, this study addresses the following research question:

What antecedents are influencing users' attitudes and usage intention of VAAs in a commercial context?

This research in progress develops a conceptual framework grounded in seminal theories on technology adoption. It will be empirically tested with survey data in the next stage of the research. The framework seeks to investigate the applicability of known IS adoption drivers within the context of VAA with a specific emphasis on VAA's implications for user interaction and the commercial usage context of online shopping.

2. LITERATURE REVIEW

2.1 Technology Adoption

Research on factors that drive users' adoption of IS is comprehensive. The most widely acknowledged theory on IS adoption drivers is the Technology Acceptance Model (TAM) (Davis, 1989) which is based on Ajzen (1991)'s Theory of Planned Behavior (TPB). The TPB posits that behavior and its immediate antecedent, behavioral intention, are impacted by attitude towards that behavior, subjective norms, and perceived behavioral control. The original TAM is an extension of the TPB and specifically relates to the context of IS adoption by considering the impact of perceived usefulness and perceived ease of use on attitude and adoption intention (Davis, 1989). This impact has later been confirmed frequently and was complemented by additional factors. In an effort to consolidate the numerous partly overlapping theoretical frameworks that explain users' adoption of IS, scholars have unified a total of eight IS adoption models, including the above-mentioned TAM, to elaborate the Unified Theory of Acceptance and Use of Technology (UTAUT2) that explains the acceptance of technology by individual end-users (Venkatesh et al., 2012). It contributes four main constructs, i.e., performance expectancy, effort expectancy, social influence, and facilitating conditions.

The human-likeness of speech-based interaction with VAAs calls for the inclusion of theories that consider the interaction with IS in a social context. In this respect, the social exchange theory has suggested trust as a key construct that drives adoption behavior in many IS contexts, including the TAM (Gefen, 2002). Trust in IS can be considered either similar to trust in humans or different from it whereby the human-likeness of interaction with VAAs suggests that users' trust in VAAs rather resembles trust in humans than computers (Seeger et al., 2017). Derived from trust as a belief about others' benevolence, information privacy concerns are closely related to trust (Kumar et al., 2018). Information privacy concerns relate to individuals' worries about companies' potentially opportunistic practice of collecting and using personal information (Smith et al., 1996) which is relevant in a comprehensive exchange of information with VAAs.

2.2 Voice-Activated Assistants

VAAs are based on voice-activated technologies that consist of software agents which carry out tasks by communicating with users by natural language (Jiang et al., 2015). The technological basis are automatic speech recognition software systems which process the speech, analyze the speech pattern, match it with possible words, and finally create a text (O'Shaughnessy, 2003). A largely distinctive characteristic of voice-activated technologies and VAAs is the naturality of interaction between users and the IS, making a conversation with VAAs very similar to communication with human individuals and enhancing the perceived human-likeness of VAAs (Robert, 2017). Due to hands-free interaction, VAAs also help increase the convenience for users (Bentahar and Wakefield, 2018). VAAs also imply various factors that are perceived as downsides by users. One key issue is privacy concerns that are triggered by the sensitivity of exchanged information as well as the risk of dissemination of private information to unauthorized audiences (Feng et al., 2017). Further, trust in VAAs can be negatively affected if the IS does not understand or misinterprets users' speech (Jiang et al., 2013). Overall, by interacting with free speech instead of selecting pre-determined menu entries or typing commands in a certain syntax (Guy, 2018), VAAs are perceived more human-like and hence users will exhibit different expectations, attitudes, and usage intentions towards VAAs compared to other IS.

3. RESEARCH FRAMEWORK

The proposed research framework is largely grounded in an extended TAM that includes drivers of IS acceptance derived from the TPB (Simon and Paper, 2007), UTAUT (Burbach et al., 2019, Wagner et al.), and social exchange theory by including trust and privacy concerns (Kumar et al., 2018).

The original TAM considers perceived usefulness and perceived ease of use as key beliefs about IS as predictors of attitude towards the IS. In the context of VAA, both variables need to be understood against the background of their human-likeness. Research on drivers of acceptance of voice-activated technology has shown that users humanize the related IS but are still aware that they are non-human, turning the TAM-related perceived usefulness and perceived ease of use still influential for their acceptance (Moriuchi, 2019, Simon and Paper, 2007). Therefore, we draw on the predictors of the original TAM and propose:

Proposition 1: Perceived usefulness has a positive impact on users' attitude towards using VAAs

Proposition 2: Perceived ease of use has a positive impact on users' attitude towards using VAAs.

Social influence denotes the extent to which individuals' beliefs are influenced by others. Being discussed as subjective norm, this factor is a driver of behavioral intention according to the TPB. IS research based on the UTAUT has shown that this impact applies to the acceptance of IS (Venkatesh et al., 2003). Research on adoption drivers of voice-activated technologies has shown that perceptions of social norms also apply to this type of technology (Simon and Paper, 2007) so that we assert:

Proposition 3: Social influence has a positive impact on users' attitude towards using VAAs.

Trust is a key driver of IS adoption. With an increasing sophistication and resulting uncertainty about the IS in question, trust is gaining relevance. It has been found to be particularly crucial in an e-commerce setting (Kim et al., 2008) where purchase transactions are being carried out. In the context of VAAs, Nasirian et al. (2017) identified the impact of trust on usage intention. Based on these indications, we posit:

Proposition 4: Trust has a positive impact on users' attitude towards using VAAs.

The interaction with VAAs involves the transmission of a large variety of information including private conversations. The underlying artificial intelligence applications enable voice-activated technologies to obtain extensive information about the users through machine learning. Current findings on users' concerns on privacy and security related to VAAs are mixed; one the one hand, studies show a low level of concerns expressed by active VAA users (Pradhan et al., 2018), on the other hand, they have turned out to be a significant adoption barrier (Liao et al., 2019). Since actual users may differ from non-users in terms of privacy and security concerns, we posit that users' privacy concerns can show a negative influence on individuals' VAA adoption decision.

Proposition 5: Privacy concerns have a negative impact on users' attitude towards using VAAs.

In line with the TPB as well as a multitude of studies on behavioral intention, we posit that attitude determines the user's affection about a behavior which predicts behavioral intention. Hence, we suggest:

Proposition 6: Users' attitude towards using VAAs has a positive impact on users' intention to use VAAs.

4. CONCLUSION

To empirically test the conceptual research framework a quantitative survey among Internet users is the following stage in the study at hand. By means of a representative sample that will consist of Internet users, the significance of the proposed impacts as well as the overall explanatory power of the model will be tested in a structural model. In addition to the empirical testing of the conceptual framework, control variables such as socio-demographic factors and online purchasing experience will be included. Upon empirical validation, we hope that the conceptual framework will provide a more comprehensive understanding of antecedents of usage intention of VAAs.

REFERENCES

Ajzen, I., 1991. The Theory of Planned Behavior. *Organizational Behavior and Human Decision Processes,* Vol. 50, pp. 179-211.

Bentahar, A. and Wakefield, C.C., 2018. *Voice Search: The New Search Engine,* CreateSpace Independent Publishing Platform.

Burbach, L. et al., 2019. "Hey, Siri", "Ok, Google", "Alexa". Acceptance-Relevant Factors of Virtual Voice-Assistants. 2019 IEEE International Professional Communication Conference (ProComm), Aachen, Germany.

Davis, F.D., 1989. Perceived Psefulness, Perceived Ease of Use, and User Acceptance of Information Technology. *MIS Quarterly,* Vol. 13, pp. 319-340.

Feng, H. et al., 2017. Continuous Authentication for Voice Assistants. Proceedings of the 23rd Annual International Conference on Mobile Computing and Networking, pp. 343-355.

Gefen, D., 2002. Reflections on the Dimensions of Trust and Trustworthiness among Online Consumers. *ACM Sigmis Database* Vol. 33, No. 3, pp. 38-53.

Guy, I., 2018. The Characteristics of Voice Search: Comparing Spoken with Typed-in Mobile Web Search Queries. *ACM Transactions on Information Systems,* Vol. 36, No. 3, pp. 1-28.

Jiang, J. et al., 2015. Automatic Online Evaluation of Intelligent Assistants. Proceedings of the 24th International Conference on World Wide Web. pp. 18-22.

Jiang, J. et al., 2013. How Do Users Respond to Voice Input Errors? Lexical and Phonetic Query Reformulation in Voice Search. Proceedings of the 36th international ACM SIGIR Conference on Research and Development in Information Retrieval pp. 143-152.

Jindal, A., 2019. Voice Technology Adoption Will Skyrocket - but Only If Performance Keeps Up. *Forbes,* February 22, https://www.forbes.com/sites/appdynamics/2019/02/22/voice-technology-adoption-will-skyrocketbut-only-if-performance-keeps-up/#1d3a93f25127.

Kim, D.J. et al., 2008. A Trust-Based Consumer Decision-Making Model in Electronic Commerce: The Role of Trust, Perceived Risk, and Their Antecedents. *Decision Support Systems* Vol. 44, No. 2, pp. 544-564.

Kumar, S. et al., 2018. Interplay between Trust, Information Privacy Concerns and Behavioural Intention of Users on Online Social Networks. *Behaviour & Information Technology,* Vol. 37, No. 6, pp. 622-633.

Liao, Y. et al., 2019. Understanding the Role of Privacy and Trust in Intelligent Personal Assistant Adoption. Information in Contemporary Society - iConference 2019.

Moriuchi, E., 2019. Okay, Google!: An Empirical Study on Voice Assistants on Consumer Engagement and Loyalty. *Psychology & Marketing,* Vol. 36, No. 5, pp. 489-501.

Nasirian, F. et al., 2017. Ai-Based Voice Assistant Systems: Evaluating from the Interaction and Trust Perspectives. Twenty-third Americas Conference on Information Systems, Boston, MA. pp. 1-10.

O'Shaughnessy, D., 2003. Interacting with Computers by Voice: Automatic Speech Recognition and Synthesis. *Proceedings of the IEEE,* Vol. 91, No. 9, pp. 1272-1305.

Olsen, C. and Kemery, K., 2019. Voice Report 2019 BingAds. https://advertiseonbing-blob.azureedge.net/blob/bingads/media/insight/whitepapers/2019/04%20apr/voice-report/bingads_2019 voicereport.pdf.

Pradhan, A. et al., 2018. "Accessibility Came by Accident": Use of Voice-Controlled Intelligent Personal Assistants by People with Disabilities. Proceedings of the 2018 CHI Conference on Human Factors in Computing System. pp. 1-13.

Robert, L.P., 2017. The Growing Problem of Humanizing Robots. *International Robotics & Automation Journal,* Vol. 3, No 1.

Seeger, A.-M. et al., 2017. When Do We Need a Human? Anthropomorphic Design and Trustworthiness of Conversational Agents. Proceedings of the Sixteenth Annual Pre-ICIS Workshop on HCI Research in MIS. pp. 1-6.

Simon, S.J. and Paper, D., 2007. User Acceptance of Voice Recognition Technology: An Empirical Extension of the Technology Acceptance Model. *Journal of Organizational and End User Computing,* Vol. 19, No. 1, pp. 24-50.

Smith, H. et al., 1996. Information Privacy: Measuring Individuals' Concerns About Organizational Practices. *MIS Quarterly,* Vol. 20, No. 2, pp. 167-196.

Venkatesh, V. et al., 2003. User Acceptance of Information Technology: Toward a Unified View. *MIS Quarterly,* Vol. 27, No. 3, pp. 425-478.

Venkatesh, V. et al., 2012. Consumer Acceptance and Use of Information Technology: Extending the Unified Theory. *MIS Quarterly,* Vol. 36, No. 1, pp. 157-178.

Wagner, K. et al. 2019. Is It Human? The Role of Anthropomorphism as a Driver for the Successful Acceptance of Digital Voice Assistants. *52nd Hawaii International Conference on System Sciences (HICSS).* Hawaii, HI.

PARTICIPATORY GOVERNABILITY UNDER DEVELOPMENT: THE INSTITUTION OF CITIZEN PARTICIPATION AS THE BASIS FOR THE DESIGN OF THE "GOVERNMENT AS A PLATFORM" IN DEVELOPING COUNTRIES

Kirill Neverov
Saint Petersburg State University, 7-9 Universitetskaya Emb., St Petersburg 199034, Russia

ABSTRACT

An important point of the government as a platform is coordination with actors traditionally external for public administration (citizens, business) through shared software, data, and collaborative services. Unlike e-government, the focus in digital government is shifting to citizen participation: digital government focuses on services, functions and governance through citizen involvement. The key point here is the interaction of man and technology: the implementation design is a set of principles, methods and norms of interaction between man and technology, that is, a techno-ecological system. The main thesis of the study is the following proposition: the institution of participation is the basis of the design of the "government as a platform" due to the deep foundations of Web 3.0 technology, which encourage participation and have a collaborative nature. Participatory governance is inherent in digital governance. In our study, we strive to demonstrate how the factors determining the classification of countries as developing affect the participatory governability, implemented through the government as a platform. In this study, we adhere to the Lean Government approach.

KEYWORDS

Participatory Governability, Digital Government, Latin America

1. INTRODUCTION

The digitalization of public administration is not so much reduced to literally introducing modern information and communication technologies (ICT) and new digital technologies (Internet of Things, Big Data analysis, AI, etc.) into the practical activities of executive bodies. The key point here is the interaction of man and technology: the implementation design is a set of principles, methods and norms of interaction between man and technology, that is, a techno-ecological system.

The key characteristic of the introduction of digital government on the basis of the concept of "government as a platform" is political design. The design of implementing digital government can be considered as an essential characteristic of public administration, determining the interrelation of processes and technologies of control from below to control from above (thus, the design is determined by the interrelation of control technologies from above and below). The implementation design also implies the principles embodied in digitalization and implemented through the "government as a platform": ethical principles (openness, citizen awareness, understandability for citizens), values, interaction with citizens, their participation, etc.

The main thesis of the study is the following proposition: the institution of participation is the basis of the design of the "government as a platform" due to the deep foundations of Web 2.0 technology, which encourage institution of participation and have a collaborative nature. Therefore, participatory governance is inherent in digital governance.

The term governability in our study is revealed in the context of the concept of a "coordinating state", suggested in previous study (Smorgunov et al. 2019), the main idea of which is that the authorities in the new conditions, although they retain a central role in the processes of policy development and implementation, but increasingly perform the function of coordinating network interactions.

If we refer to the technological side of the implementation of government as a platform, then the basis here is such technologies and concepts as artificial intelligence, blockchain and distributed ledger technology, smart contracts. Internet of Things and Big Data analysis are also on the agenda (Ovanessoff A., Plastino E. 2017) (Webfoundation.org 2020.) (MIT Technology Review Insights 2020) (Rodríguez P. et al 2017.) (Ordoñez L.A.T. et al. 2019.) (Moura, Ph., Nicoletti, S. 2018.)

Under terms "developing state" or "developing country" we mean a country with a less developed industrial base (industries) and a low Human Development Index (HDI) relative to other countries (O'Sullivan, Sheffrin, 2003). It is assumed that the problems that states need to solve will also determine the design of implementation and the nature of citizen participation, as well as the forms in which they are clothed.

2. GOVERNMENT AS A PLATFORM (GAAP)

The concept of a government as a platform (GaaP) is based on the deep foundations of Web 2.0 and Web 3.0 technology of a collaborative nature, which are reflected in Gov.2.0 and Gov.3.0 (O'Reilly, T. 2010).

Therefore, from a public value perspective, the key challenge of the GaaP is to enable, control, and govern the dynamic combination of the needed resources, routines, and structures to adapt and respond to emerging and unpredictable citizens' needs, so that all the different values and expectations are simultaneously and dynamically fulfilled (Cordella, A., Paletti, A. 2019).

Platforms can be seen as a kind of regulated environment, allowing developers, users and others to interact with each other, to distribute data, services and applications, allowing governments to more easily monitor what is happening and promote innovation in public policy (except other areas). Since the platforms are not isolated, their integration with each other and other systems, ensuring their interoperability is a problem, since everything is connected to everything in the network (Janssen, M., Estevez, E. 2013).

The network approach leads to cooperation in the governance process, while its adoption depends on the willingness of government departments. Networks of actors foster participation, which affects regional development, forming a community. The platform acts as a playground for public participation and collaboration. The participation of citizens in the governance process, their involvement affects the perception of citizens by the government, and the modules of the government as a platform allow citizens to feel part of the process from which they were removed in the traditional offline format of public administration (Verma, R. K. et al 2017).

For the approach of "lean government" (l-Government), which is the philosophy of a minimal state, inherent the reduction of the administrative burden and the focus on efficiency while pursuing enhanced services and innovation, and orchestrating networks which are enabled by platforms. The general idea of l-Government is that platforms play a key role in connecting developers, content providers, government agencies, and service providers and users (Janssen, M., Estevez, E. 2013).

Digitalization implies the emergence of a new form of governability, which is essentially a network effect, which is the result of an increasing number of participants in network (Smorgunov, L. 2019. Participatory...). Openness improves efficiency in terms of increasing new participating projects. The network effect works here: the more participants, the higher the network efficiency at lower costs for individual participants. Promoting innovation is also an essential feature of platform openness (O'Reilly, T. 2010). For governments, integration with other platforms is necessary because users tend to use multiple platforms, and the added value of the platform can be enhanced by offering a seamless interconnection between the platforms (Janssen, M., Estevez, E. 2013).

Digital governability combines two multidirectional movements: control from above (from the state) and control from below (horizontal level of control, control of citizens by citizens / civil control). Control from above means "the ability of large organizational systems (states, TNCs, etc.) based on processing large amounts of data about citizens not only to control, but to use in the directions necessary for these systems, that is, to control the behavior of large masses of people (through disclosing of human space) (Smorgunov L.

2019. Institutionalization of...). Control from below is manifested through "increased governability through self-observation, social control and self-censorship. The essence of governability here is programming human behavior through network identification as an accessory (Smorgunov L. 2019. Institutionalization of...).

3. INSTITUTION OF PARTICIPATORY GOVERNABILITY IN DEVELOPING STATES

The following cases were selected for the study: Argentina, Bolivia, Brazil, Uruguay. These countries are included in the list of developing countries according to the UN version (United Nations Homepage 2020. The World Economic...). Two of them relate to fuel-exporting countries - Bolivia and Ecuador [25, p.167]. The programs of digital development of countries, the platform of digital government were analyzed. The following digitalization programs are analogues of EU's ISA2 programs. However, their negative side is a lack of technological details – these programs are more for policy-makers, than for engineers. Technical documentation is not available in free access.

The choice of cases was determined by development indicators (human development index, GDP) and the level of digitalization of public administration. HDI rankings are: Bolivia – 114, Brazil – 79, Uruguay – 57 (United Nations Homepage 2020. 2019 Human Development...) Ranking by estimated GDP in 2020: Bolivia – 88, Brazil – 8, Uruguay – 94 (International Monetary Fund 2020). Ranking in UN EGDI: Bolivia – 97, Brazil – 54, Uruguay – 26 (United Nations Homepage 2020. UN E-Government...). Ranking in UN E-Participation Index: Bolivia – 90, Brazil – 18, Uruguay – 29 (United Nations Homepage 2020. UN E-Government...).

The key guiding document for Argentina's digital government efforts is its Digital Agenda 2030, which was formally implemented in December 2018 after a development process secured through the participation and support of all relevant ministries. It provides a government-wide project and principles-based vision for the digital transformation of the public sector. The Digital Agenda is an important umbrella policy document and represents a significant step forward in establishing a common vision and goals. It moves Argentina closer to meeting the OECD Recommendation of the Council on Digital Government Strategies; however, it does not constitute a full digital government strategy in itself. The permanent adoption of digital technologies should accelerate the transformation of the Government, allowing the construction of a modern, efficient, transparent, close to the citizen, simple, trustworthy and participative State» (Gob.ar 2020), as well as subsection 2 "Government and open data": «Promote a collaborative and participative government. Create instances of dialogue between the Government and society. Promote innovation in the public sector through initiatives for the co-creation of public policies between citizens, the State and the rest of the nations (Gob.ar 2020).

The key guiding document for Bolivia's digital government is its Plan de Implementación de Gobierno Electrónico 2017 – 2025 (Plan of Implementation of Digital Government 2017 – 2025). In the section "Open Government of Participation" the following strategy is spelled out: "Deepening, through the use of Electronic Government tools, the processes of participatory governability and social control of citizens on issues of interest, generating greater interaction of dialogue between the population and the State. Institution of participation and social control are two fundamental pillars of the way in which State policy is built and directed. In this sense, ICTs can help to deepen the full exercise of the right to participation and social control individually and collectively. The spectrum of citizen participation will be expanded with the use of electronic government tools and digital media, through which the State will collect and interact around the requirements and proposals of citizens" (Gob.bo 2020).

Brazil implements the Brazilian digital transformation strategy and the Effective Brazil strategy. In particular, the following steps are spelled out in them: implementation of the Government Open Data Policy, in cooperation with other governmental bodies, aiming to consolidate a culture of transparency, social participation, accountability, research, innovation and entrepreneurship, through the use of free, reliable public data in open formats, made available in the Open Data Portal; expanding social participation on public services and policy life cycles; existence of a social participation digital platform as a locus of excellence for dialogue between government and civil society. Its objective ought to be the promotion of public interaction, publication of policy-related content, and access to online communication and debate tools; to consolidate the Digital Government Platforms: Data Analysis Platform, Data and System Interoperability Platform,

Transparency Portal, Government Open Data Platform, and the Digital Citizen Participation Platform; to maintain and improve a digital social participation platform as a place of excellence for dialogue between government and civil society (Gov.br 2020).

The key documents for digital transformation in Uruguay are Agenda Digital 2020 (Digital Agenda 2020) and Plan de Gobierno Digital 2020: Transformación con equidad (Plan of Digital Government 2020: Transformation with justice). In terms of participation, documents contain the following information: encourage different ways of approaching the relationship between citizens and the State, promoting transparency, accountability, citizen participation and the development of better services, generating direct contact channels with people and improving the quality of care in the services provided; deepen the open government culture, implementing e-participation mechanisms at 100% of central government agencies and increasing by 100% the offer of open government data; build secure environments and trust-based forms of interaction, in order to promote full participation in the information society; articulate multi-stakeholder actions and enhance their cooperation through a National Cybersecurity Operations Centre (SOC Nac) through public-private participation (Uruguaydigital.uy 2020.).

ICT perspectives in Latin America are huge due to level of urbanization (in 2019 80,87% of the total population of Latin America & Caribbean lived in urban areas and cities (Statista 2020)) and Internet coverage (almost 70% of Latin America's population have access to the Internet, which is 58,8% of world Internet users [9]). However, despite of potential, brain drain and lack of qualified human resources in ICT is still a problem for Latin American digitalization programs (Insead.edu 2020).

4. CONCLUSION

Thus, we can conclude that the developing countries of Latin America are inclined to carry out a digital transformation and form a government as a platform based on a design that involves participatory governability. The collaborative components that are embedded in the nature of digital technologies, which make it possible and stimulate the participation of citizens in the production of public services, in the case of developing countries make it possible to involve in the public policy the categories of citizens who were previously out of state attention (Bottom of the Pyramid) and increase the state's stinginess in the eyes of citizens through the formation of a positive algorithm of political behavior due to the active involvement of citizens in the field of political decisions that are of public importance and reflect public interest. The government as a platform, being in itself a social value, allows you to create a new social value through involving citizens, civil society, public institutions, non-commercial institutions and business representatives in the interaction. The factors relating the states to developing ones can be considered in two ways: on the one hand, they are an obstacle to the transformation of state administration into a digital government due to the obvious high cost of such undertakings; on the other hand, the restructuring of the traditional hierarchical vertical centralized state platform format will reduce corruption by minimizing public administration, more efficiently redistribute available funds in accordance with the request of citizens, modify policies faster and with accuracy. Participatory governance is changing not only the public administration system, but also the political thinking of society.

ACKNOWLEDGEMENT

The author disclosed receipt of the following financial support for the research, authorship, and/or publication of this article: This work was supported with a grant from the Russian Science Foundation (grant 19-18-00210 "Political ontology of digitalization: Study of institutional bases for digital forms of governability").

REFERENCES

Cordella, A. and Paletti, A., 2019. Government as a platform, orchestration, and public value creation: The Italian case. *In Government Information Quarterly,* Vol. 36, №4, pp. 1-15;

Gob.ar, 2020. *Agenda Digital Argentina 2030.* [online] Available at: http://servicios.infoleg.gob.ar/infolegInternet/anexos/315000-319999/318677/res138.pdf [Accessed 15 June, 2020];

Gob.bo, 2020. *Plan de Implementación de Gobierno Electrónico 2017 – 2025.* [online] Available at: https://agetic.gob.bo/2-plan-de-implementacion-de-gobierno-electronico.pdf [Accessed 15 June, 2020];
Gov.br, 2020. *Brazilian digital transformation strategy.* [online] Available at: http://www.mctic.gov.br/mctic/export/sites/institucional/sessaoPublica/arquivos/digitalstrategy.pdf#:~:text=The%20role%20of%20the%20Brazilian,prosperous%2C%20free%20and%20fair%20society [Accessed 15 June, 2020];
Insead.edu, 2020. *The Global Talent Competitiveness Index 2020.* [online] Insead.edu. Available at: https://www.insead.edu/sites/default/files/assets/dept/globalindices/docs/GTCI-2020-report.pdfp.42 [Accessed 13 Sept, 2020];
International Monetary Fund, 2020. *World Economic Outlook Database, October 2020.* [online] IMF.org. Available at: https://www.imf.org/en/Publications/WEO/weo-database/2020/October [Accessed 01 Nov, 2020];
Janssen, M. and Estevez, E., 2013. Lean government and platform-based governance-doing more with less. *In Government Information Quarterly*, Vol.30 (SUPPL. 1), S1-S8;
MIT Technology Review Insights, 2020. *The global AI agenda: Latin America.* [online] MIT Technology Review Insights. Available at: https://mittrinsights.s3.amazonaws.com/AIagenda2020/LatAmAIagenda.pdf [Accessed 10 Sept, 2020];
Moura, Ph. and Nicoletti, S., 2018. *Making smart cities and IoT a reality in Latin America: a quick guide for decision-makers.* [online] Gsma.com. Available at: https://www.gsma.com/latinamerica/wp-content/uploads/2018/11/IoTGuide-ENG.pdf [Accessed 10 Sept, 2020];
O'Reilly, T., 2010. *Government as a Platform.* [online] MIT Press Journals. Available at: https://www.mitpressjournals.org/doi/pdf/10.1162/INOV_a_00056#:~:text=Government%20information%20and%20services%20can,an%20improved%20approach%20to%20governance [Accessed 15 June, 2020];
Ordoñez L.A.T. et al., 2019. Approach to Blockchain and Smart Contract in Latin America: Application in Colombia. *In Communications in Computer and Information Science*, Vol.1052, pp. 500 – 510;
O'Sullivan, A. and Sheffrin, S.M., 2003. *Economics: Principles in Action.* Upper Saddle River, New Jersey;
Ovanessoff A. and Plastino E., 2017. *How Artificial Intelligence Can Drive South America's Growth.* [online] Accenture.com. Available at: https://www.accenture.com/_acnmedia/pdf-49/accenture-how-artificial-intelligence-can-drive-south-americas-growth.pdf [Accessed 10 Sept, 2020];
Rodríguez P. et al, 2017. *Using Big Data and its Analytical Techniques for Public Policy Design and Implementation in Latin America and the Caribbean.* [online] Inter-American Development Bank. Available at: https://publications.iadb.org/en/using-big-data-and-its-analytical-techniques-public-policy-design-and-implementation-latin-america [Accessed 10 Sept, 2020];
Smorgunov L., 2019. Institutionalization of Governability and the Problem of Veillance in the Space of Digital Communications. *In South-Russian Journal of Social Sciences*, Vol. 20, №3, pp. 62-75;
Smorgunov L.et al., 2019. Evolution of the Concept of Governability in the Context of Dizitalization. Proceedings of the International Conference ICT, Society and Human Beings 2019, Smart Cities 2019 and Web Based Communities and Social Media 2019. Porto, Portugal, p. 281-285;
Smorgunov, L., 2019. Participatory governability under digitalization conditions: network ef-fect and institutions. *In The Caspian region: Politics, Economics, Culture*, Vol. 4, № 61, pp. 43-49;
Statista, 2020. [online] Available at: https://www.statista.com/statistics/699089/urbanization-in-latin-america-and-caribbean [Accessed 13 Sept, 2020];
United Nations Homepage, 2020. *2019 Human Development Index Ranking.* [online] United Nations. Available at: http://hdr.undp.org/en/content/2019-human-development-index-ranking [Accessed 01 Nov, 2020];
United Nations Homepage, 2020. *The World Economic Situation and Prospects 2020.* [online] United Nations. Available at: https://www.un.org/development/desa/dpad/wp-content/uploads/sites/45/WESP2020_FullReport.pdf [Accessed 15 June, 2020];
United Nations Homepage, 2020. *UN E-Government Knowledgebase.* [online] United Nations. Available at: https://publicadministration.un.org/egovkb/en-us/Data-Center [Accessed 01 Nov, 2020];
Uruguaydigital.uy, 2020. *Plan de Gobierno Digital 2020: Transformación con equidad.* [online] Available at: https://uruguaydigital.uy/wps/wcm/connect/urudigital/ff2fba97-7871-474e-85ec-a43a75ef3376/Descargar+Agenda+Digital+2020+-+original.pdf?MOD=AJPERES&CONVERT_TO=url&CACHEID=ff2fba97-7871-474e-85ec-a43a75ef3376, ast accessed 2020/06/15 [Accessed 15 June, 2020];
Verma, R. K. et al, 2017. Government portals, social media platforms and citizen engagement in India: some insights. *In Procedia Computer Science*, Vol. 122, pp.842-849;
Webfoundation.org, 2020. *How Are Governments In Latin America Using Artificial Intelligence? A proposal for effective and legitimate implementations of AI systems in the public sector.* [online] Available at: http://webfoundation.org/docs/2018/07/AI-in-Latin-America_Overview.pdf [Accessed 10 Sept, 2020].

USING SEMANTIC RELATIONSHIPS TO ENHANCE NEURAL WORD EMBEDDINGS

Yanqin Yin, Xiaodong Sun, Huanhuan Lv, Pikun Wang, Hongwei Ma and Dongqiang Yang*
School of Computer Science and Technology, Shandong Jianzhu University, Jinan 250101, China

ABSTRACT

Neural language models have significantly improved current natural language understanding tasks. However, distributional semantics, derived from neural language models is less competitive in computing semantic relatedness or similarity than other taxonomy-based methods. Although current researches seek to exploit the handcrafted semantic knowledge in ontology to improve distributional semantics, they often ignore distinguishing different functions of semantic relationships in updating or retrofitting neural word embeddings. This paper proposes retrofitting neural word embedding through semantic relationships encoded in semantic networks such as WordNet and Roget's thesaurus. We employ the hypernym/hyponym relationships to modify the asymmetric distance measure in retrofitting neural embeddings, which can fully transfer the hierarchical semantic information contained in semantic networks. In the evaluation with the gold-standard data sets, our method achieved the Spearman correlation value of 0.80, which is about 8% higher than the state-of-the-art methods in the literature.

KEYWORDS

Neural Network Word Embeddings, Semantic Relationship, Semantic Similarity

1. INTRODUCTION

The Neural Network Word Embeddings (NNWEs), learned from the word co-occurrence prediction, have become a cornerstone of current language technologies, and the improvement on their capacities of semantic computing can further benefit other applications such as information retrieval and word sense disambiguation. NNWEs are less capable in distinguishing semantic similarity and relatedness than other taxonomy-based methods. It may hinder downstream NLP tasks, especially in applications of dealing with lexical semantics such as word sense disambiguation and natural language understanding.

The existing methods mainly post-processed NNWEs with semantic constraints to enhance their distributional semantics (Bojanowski et al., 2017, Nguyen et al., 2016). The semantic constraints are mainly retrieved from external knowledge bases, e.g. WordNet (Miller, 1995), PPDB (Ganitkevitch & Callison-Burch, 2014) and Roget's thesaurus (Kipfer, 2009). The post-processing methods such as Retrofitting (Faruqui et al., 2015), Counter-fitting (Mrkšić et al., 2016) and LEAR (Vulic & Mrksic, 2018) significantly improved NNWEs in lexical semantic computation (Vulic et al., 2017a, Vulic et al., 2017b). However, while taking into account semantic transitivity contained in the hypernym/hyponym (IS-A) relationships, they updated NNWEs with identical weights on both semantically close and distant concepts that are within a certain distance in the IS-A hierarchy, which can potentially dampen the impacts of these hand-crafted semantic relationships.

Inspired by previous works on semantically post-processing and enhancing NNWEs, this paper investigates how to improve NNWEs by integrating the IS-A hierarchy into a distributional semantic space. We propose a method of direct hypernym update (DHU in short) to retrofit NNWEs. DHU employs different semantic relationships different from LEAR. LEAR imposes the same weights on the concepts within one or more links distance in the IS-A hierarchy. It will inevitably feed inaccurate semantic constraints into NNWEs, and often results in miscalculating distributional similarity.

* Correspondence author: ydq@sdjzu.edu.cn

We firstly extract both synonymous and direct hypernym relationships from semantic networks, and then update NNWEs with them individually. By forcing a target word to only approach the semantically adjacent words, we can avoid the common problem of semantic incomprehension caused by cross-level use of IS-A relationships in LEAR. Experimental results show that DHU can significantly improve NNWEs in computing distributional semantics.

2. DHU RETROFITTING

Similar to the ATTRACT-REPEL (Mrkšić et al., 2017) and Counter-fitting (Mrkšić et al., 2016) models, we first extract semantic constraints from semantic networks, and then construct a novel retrofitting model using the direct hypernym constraints to improve NNWEs.

Let V be a dictionary of word embeddings. The injected external constraints include synonym constraints S, antonym constraints A and direct hypernym constraints DH. These constraints are processed as mini-batches such as B_S, B_A and B_{DH}. In these sets, the word pair (x_l, x_r) corresponds to a vector pair (X_l, X_r). A mini batch of k_1 word pairs is given by $B_S = [(X_l^1, X_r^1), \cdots, (X_l^{k_1}, X_r^{k_1})]$. Its negative example is $T_S = [(t_l^1, t_r^1), \cdots, (t_l^{k_1}, t_r^{k_1})]$, same as similarity for B_A and B_{DH}. The whole update process is as follows:

(1) Synonymy Attract:

$$S(B_S, T_S) = \sum_{i=1}^{k_1} \left[\tau(\delta_{syn} + cos(X_l^i, t_l^i) - cos(X_l^i, X_r^i)) + \tau(\delta_{syn} + cos(X_r^i, t_r^i) - cos(X_l^i, X_r^i)) \right] \quad (1)$$

$\tau(x) = max(0, x)$ is the hinge loss function, δ_{syn} is the attract margin which determines how much closer these vectors should be to each other than to their respective negative examples.

(2) Antonymy Repel:

$$A(B_A, T_A) = \sum_{i=1}^{k_2} \left[\tau(\delta_{ant} + cos(X_l^i, X_r^i) - cos(X_l^i, t_l^i)) + \tau(\delta_{ant} + cos(X_l^i, X_r^i) - cos(X_r^i, t_r^i)) \right] \quad (2)$$

(3) Vector Space Preservation:

$$R(B_S, B_A) = \sum_{X_i \in V(B_S \cup B_A)} \lambda_{reg} \left\| X_i - X_i \right\|_2 \quad (3)$$

where λ_{reg} is the $L2$ regulation constant and $\hat{X}_i$ denotes the original word vector for word x_i.

(4) Direct Hypernym Update

$$DH(B_{DH}) = \sum_{i=1}^{k_3} \frac{|x| - |y|}{|x| + |y|} \quad (4)$$

The full cost function is given by the sum of above the four formulas:

$$C = S(B_S, T_S) + A(B_A, T_A) + DH(B_{DH}) + R(B_S, B_A, B_{DH}) \quad (5)$$

3. EXPERIMENT SETUP

3.1 NNWEs

We tested DHU with three widely used NNWEs:
1) GloVe Common Crawl-300D[1] (GloVe)
2) GoogleNews-Vectors-Negative300-SLIM[2] (W2V-SLIM)
3) Paragram[3](300D)

1 https://nlp.stanford.edu/projects/glove/

2 https://github.com/eyaler/word2vec-slim

3 https://www.cs.cmu.edu/~jwieting/

3.2 Semantic Constraints

The synonymous, antonymous, and direct hypernym constraints were extracted from the two well-known semantic resources: WordNet and Roget's thesaurus. Among them, the synonymous constraints consist of 909,302 pairs and 554,507 pairs of synonyms, respectively; the antonyms are 465,406 pairs and 39,283 pairs. The direct hypernym constraints were taken only from WordNet, having a total of 320,586 pairs.

3.3 Hyper-parameters Optimization

To speed up the training process, we used AdaGrad (Duchi et al., 2011) to iteratively train the NNWEs. We set the initial learning rate to 0.05. The experimental hyper-parameters were optimized through grid search, i.e. $\lambda_{reg} \in [10^{-3}, 10^{-4}, \cdots, 10^{-10}]$, $\delta_{syn}, \delta_{ant} \in [0, 0.1, \cdots, 0.9, 1]$, and $k_1, k_2, k_3 \in [32, 64, 128, 256]$. By fine-tuning on the gold-standard data set of WordSim-353-similarity (Agirre et al., 2009), we achieved the optimal hyper-parameter values, i.e. $\lambda_{reg} = 10^{-9}$, $\delta_{syn} = 0.6$, $\delta_{ant} = 0.0$, and $k_1, k_2, k_3 = 128$.

3.4 Results and Analysis

To evaluate DHU on retrofitting NNWEs, we used the public data sets of SimLex-999 (Hill et al., 2015) and SimVerb-3500 (Gerz et al., 2016) as the tests sets. The Spearman rank correlation coefficient was calculated to show how close NNWEs can approach in comparison with human similarity ratings.

Figure 1 summarized retrofitting results of GloVe, W2V-SLIM, and Paragram on the above test sets. The retrofitting methods, in turn, are Retrofitting, Counter-fitting, LEAR, and DHU.

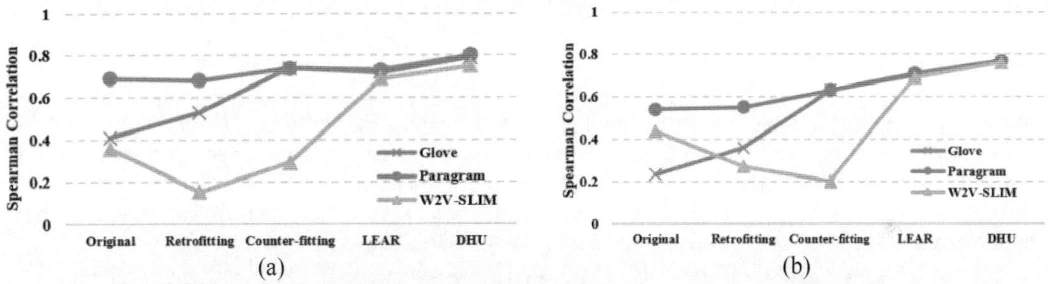

Figure 1. The performance of retrofitting word embeddings (a) SimLex-999 and (b) SimVerb-3500

The Retrofitting method significantly improved GloVe, but it could not work on Paragram and W2V-SLIM. It suggested that since Paragram was semantically initialized, and W2V-SLIM filters out synonymous concepts, which could restrict the retrofitting effects. The Counter-fitting results indicated that injecting both synonymous and antonymous constraints can significantly improve semantic similarity prediction.

Compared with Counter-fitting, LEAR achieved a relatively better result, which may indicate that injecting the IS-A constraints may be beneficial to enhance NNWEs. However, LEAR also introduced the IS-A hierarchical relationships without explicitly distinguishing their semantic differences in updating NNWEs, which may be detrimental to Paragram.

Our DHU method greatly improved the three NNWEs, partly because semantic distance under the direct hypernyms are relatively short, which are more reliable to function as semantic constraints; partly because DHU can take into account both the asymmetry of semantic relationship and directionality of semantic transferability between hypernyms and hyponyms (Marathe & Hirst, 2010). Given the increase of path length, concept similarity may decrease significantly while traversing along IS-A relationships. The hypernym constraints in DHU were retrieved from their directly adjacent words in WordNet, which may be beneficial to updating NNWEs. The experimental results also show that DHU can reduce uncertainty caused by the multi-level semantic transferability issues in LEAR.

To analyze semantic representations after retrofitting NNWEs, we adopted the TSNE method (Laurens & Hinton, 2008) to visualize GloVe.

In Figure 2, the similar words represented in GloVe are relatively sparse in the reduced 2-dimensional space. After retrofitting by LEAR, although the distance between *cat* and *cats* is shortened, the distance between cat and its synonyms was pushed further away. After the DHU retrofitting, *bobcat* along with *cat* was pulled closer than them in the LEAR retrofitting. DHU also added *cheetah*, *leopard*, *panther* and *lynx* to the top 5 distributional similar words of *cat*. These words belong to feline and have direct hypernym relationship with *cat*. They are semantically closer to *cat*. The semantic space after the DHU retrofitting, shown in Figure 2-(c), is more compact, which highlights the effectiveness of DHU.

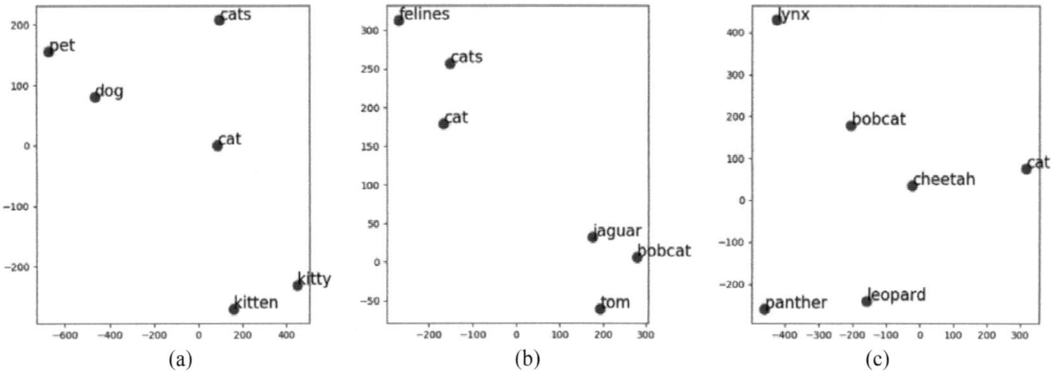

Figure 2. Demo of word positions in a 2-D space. We show the word *cat* and its top 5 distributional similar words in different neural embeddings an example to show the top 5 words are similar to *cat*.
(a) Original GloVe (b) GloVe after the LEAR retrofitting (c) GloVe after the DHU retrofitting

4. CONCLUSION

This paper proposed a novel retrofitting method of DHU to enhance NNWEs. Through injecting the direct hypernym constraints into NNWEs, we addressed the semantics disappearance after a multi-level traverse of IS-A relationships. DHU can effectively merge semantic knowledge into NNWEs. In the future study, we will seek different ways of incorporating other semantic relationships such as meronym-holonym (HAS-A) into NNWEs.

ACKNOWLEDGEMENT

This research was supported by the National Social Science Foundation of China (Grant No. 17BYY119).

REFERENCES

Agirre, E., Alfonseca, E., et al., 2009. A Study on Similarity and Relatedness Using Distributional and WordNet-based Approaches. *Proceedings of NAACL*. Boulder, Colorado, Association for Computational Linguistics, 19-27.

Bojanowski, P., Grave, E., et al., 2017. Enriching word vectors with subword information. *In Transactions of the Association for Computational Lingus.* 5, 135-146.

Duchi, J. C., Hazan, E., et al., 2011. Adaptive Subgradient Methods for Online Learning and Stochastic Optimization. *Journal of Machine Learning Research.* 12, 7, 2121-2159.

Faruqui, M., Dodge, J., et al., 2015. Retrofitting word vectors to semantic lexicons. *Proceddings of NAACL*. Denver, Colorado, Association for Computational Linguistics, 1606-1615.

Ganitkevitch, J. and Callison-Burch, C., 2014. The Multilingual Paraphrase Database. *Proceddings of the Ninth International Conference on Language Resources and Evaluation*. Reykjavik, Iceland, European Language Resources Association, 4276-4283.

Gerz, D., Vulic, I., et al., 2016. SimVerb-3500: A Large-Scale Evaluation Set of Verb Similarity. *Proceddings of EMNLP*. Austin, Texas, Association for Computational Linguistics, 2173-2182.

Hill, F., Reichart, R., et al., 2015. Simlex-999: Evaluating semantic models with genuine similarity estimation. *arXiv: Computational Linguistics.* 41, 4, 665-695.

Kipfer, B. A., 2009. *Roget's 21st Century Thesaurus.* Random House US, US.

Laurens, V. D. M. and Hinton, G., 2008. Visualizing Data using t-SNE. *Journal of Machine Learning Research.* 9, 2605, 2579-2605.

Marathe, M. and Hirst, G., 2010. Lexical Chains Using Distributional Measures of Concept Distance. *International Conference on Intelligent Text Processing and Computational Linguistics*. Berlin, Heidelberg, Springer, 291-302.

Miller, G. A., 1995. WordNet: a lexical database for English. *Communications of the ACM.* 38, 11, 39-41.

Mrkšić, N., Séaghdha, D. O., et al., 2016. Counter-fitting word vectors to linguistic constraints. *arXiv preprint arXiv: 1630.00892.*

Mrkšić, N., Vulić, I., et al., 2017. Semantic Specialization of Distributional Word Vector Spaces using Monolingual and Cross-Lingual Constraints. *In Transaction of Association for Computational Lingusitics.* 5, 8, 309-324.

Nguyen, K. A., Walde, S. S. I., et al., 2016. Integrating distributional lexical contrast into word embeddings for antonym-synonym distinction. *Proceddings of the 54th Annual Meeting of the Association for Computational Linguistics*. Association for Computational Linguistics, 454-459.

Vulic, I. and Mrksic, N., 2018. Specialising Word Vectors for Lexical Entailment. *Proceddings of NAACL*. New Orleans, Louisiana, Association for Computational Linguistics, 1134-1145.

Vulic, I., Mrksic, N., et al., 2017a. Cross-Lingual Induction and Transfer of Verb Classes Based on Word Vector Space Specialisation. *Proceddings of EMNLP*. Copenhagen, Denmark, Association for Computational Linguistics, 2546-2558.

Vulic, I., Mrksic, N., et al., 2017b. Morph-fitting: Fine-tuning word vector spaces with simple language-specific rules. *Proceedings of the 55th Annual Meeting of the Association for Computational Linguistics* Vancouver, Canada, Association for Computational Linguistics, 56-68.

TOWARDS A CONCEPT FOR STREAMLINING GAME DESIGN OF AN EXISTING SERIOUS GAME AND PRELIMINARY EVALUATION

Daniel Atorf[1], Ehm Kannegieser[1] and Marlene Dillig[2]
[1]*Fraunhofer IOSB, Fraunhoferstr. 1, 76197 Karlsruhe, Germany*
[2]*Hochschule Furtwangen University, Robert-Gerwig-Platz 1, 78120 Furtwangen, Germany*

ABSTRACT

This paper elaborates on a process to streamline the game design of the existing serious game Lost Earth 2307. Previous evaluations of the game revealed issues in terms of usability on the one hand and new requirements, such as motivation, accessibility via web and shorter gameplay, on the other hand. Based on the findings and the new requirements, the modification of the initial game design and the methods used are presented and elaborated. Furthermore, the question whether the resulting streamlined concept provides motivation and improves on usability is discussed. A subjective evaluation of this question is shown, followed up by presenting a preliminary study on a prototype implementation. The paper depicts the setup of the study using SUS and Flow Short Scale questionnaires and reports about the results and discusses the outcomes.

KEYWORDS

Digital Game-Based Learning, Game Design, Gamification, Usability, Preliminary Study

1. INTRODUCTION

The serious game Lost Earth 2307 was developed for teaching on how to analyze aerial and satellite images and on how to formally report on identified objects by using specific terms. This training domain is rather complex to teach, therefore individual training courses last several months and trainers have a high interest in keeping the students motivated over a long time. The game addresses this need by following the ideas of Digital Game Based Learning (Prensky 2007) and Immersive Didactics (Bopp 2006). It is integrated into the course as an optional element in the informal learning phase where students have to intensify their knowledge.

The game was evaluated iteratively during development, focusing on the learning outcome, on game functionality and user experience (Atorf et al. 2019a). Additional on site evaluation of immersion and usability showed that the learnability of the game was an issue. A pedagogical agent was implemented in order to improve learnability. However, a study on this implementation indicated, that the usability in Lost Earth 2307 should generally be improved (Atorf et al. 2019b). Usability issues greatly interfere with immersion, thus preventing acceptance and good learning outcomes (Cheng et al. 2015).

Further on site evaluation and reviews confirmed the described findings on usability. In addition, the requirements evolved on behalf of trainers and students. A main issue was that the overall time needed to complete a mission. The initially requested type of task had to cover actions on each step of the image exploitation process cycle, which potentially required several hours to complete. However, in the informal learning phase the game was one optional element of many. Thus, there was not enough time for students to play "just another mission" in addition to their regular exercises. Therefore, missions in the game need to evolve into smaller and more accessible tasks while keeping the major learning goals. In addition to this, the overall motivation to play the game and the retention rate should be improved further, as well as increasing the accessibility, meaning the game to evolve from a monolithic desktop application towards a web based and more mobile-like application.

In conclusion, these new requirements and the results of the previous studies and evaluations implicated a need for adapting the initial game Lost Earth 2307 in terms of gameplay, motivation, usability and accessibility, which can be summarized as streamlining the game. Hence, this paper focuses on developing a concept for a streamlined version of the existing game, addressing the findings of the previous studies and the new requirements, while staying true to initial learning goals and to basic game elements. A preliminary analysis of the streamlined concept and a preliminary study on usability and immersion on a prototype are discussed and their implications on future developments are reviewed.

2. METHOD & IMPLEMENTATION

2.1 Method for Streamlining the Concept

To address the new requirements and remaining a motivating, immersive game experience, while achieving the learning outcomes, the initial concept of Lost Earth 2307 was modified according to the new streamlined concept. (Yusoff et al. 2009) provide a framework for ensuring effective learning outcomes when creating serious games. The framework is derived from the input-process-outcome game model discussed by (Garris et al 2002) and presents several major components a serious game should consider (see Figure 1).

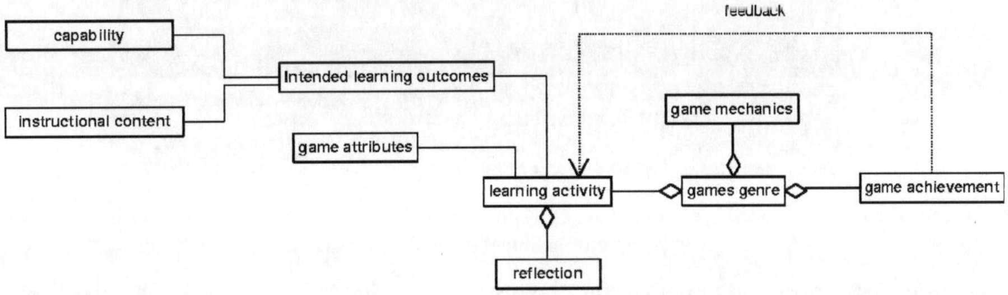

Figure 1. Yusoff et al. framework for serious games shown as a structural class diagram

An effective serious game should consider all components of the framework. A key component is the intended learning outcome. This is a combination of the intended capability and the instructional content (subject matter). Learning activity is key as well, because the activities within the game are what keeps players engaged and immersed. Along with the other components: reflection, game mechanics, game genre, game achievement, game attributes and a feedback loop an effective serious game is formed.

However, this method only shows whether all components are included in the serious game and gives an orientation, which attributes to develop. To analyze, whether the resulting serious game is motivating or not, the Octalysis Gamification Framework (Chou 2015) was used. It contains nine core drives to describe the source of engagement within the components and attributes of a gamification environment (see Figure 5, including results of the analysis).

2.2 Implementation

Streamlining the concept of Lost Earth 2307 followed Yusoff's serious game framework and Chou's Octalysis framework (Yusoff et al. 2009, Chou 2015). This chapter describes the main, streamlined elements and shows their contribution with regard to Yusoff.

A major streamlined element was replacing the initial task by smaller and quicker task types, thus by different types of missions. As stated before, a mission in the initial game always contained a complete image exploitation task, which generally took several hours to complete. Subsets of this process can now be asked using smaller tasks separately. For example, tasking of a sensor is now a stand-alone mission (was a mandatory part of the whole mission before) and labeling objects in imagery is now broken down into more suitable mission types such as multiple choice (see Figure 2 left), multiple response assessments and hot spot exercises (see Figure 2, right). All these new kinds of tasks allow players to perform a mission in a much shorter time than in the original game while still supporting the major learning objectives.

Figure 2. Examples for small tasks (left: multiple choice; right: hot spot)

The feedback loop after completing a mission was adapted respectively to the new task types. The new task types also lead to altering the mission sequence logic. This contributes to the game mechanics and feedback component of the serious game framework, whereas the new tasks itself contribute to the learning activity and to the need for quicker gameplay.

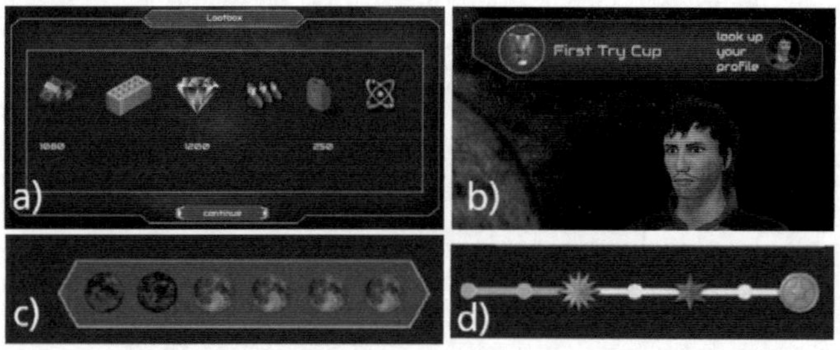

Figure. 3. Examples for achievements (a: loot box; b: trophy for completing first mission; c: learning progress visualized by liberated colonies; d: career progress)

To increase motivation additionally, the game achievements were improved, as previous evaluations showed that additional rewarding elements would be beneficial for keeping players immersed. Hence, another streamlined element was introducing further achievement elements following ideas of (Zichermann and Cunningham 2011): Trophies as recognition for achievement, loot boxes for surprise gifting, visualization of the learning progress and enhanced scoring of a mission in form of an accumulated progress bar visualizing a career with milestones were implemented in the prototype (examples see Figure. 3). Associated to the achievements a new game mechanic was introdued, which is feeding Zichermanns ideas of collecting and customization: A player is now able to spend resources in order to enhance his personal room (see Figure 4).

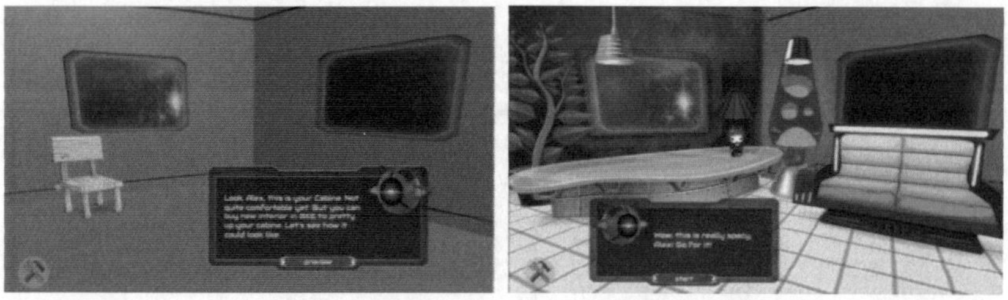

Figure. 4. Enhancing the personal room (left: initial state; right: fully enhanced)

These enhancements on the achievements contribute to Yusoff's game achievement and game mechanics components and specifically add to a more motivating gameplay.

To further address shorter gameplay and accessibility, some game mechanics were simplified. Especially the initially quite complex resource cycle was reduced to purchasing objects, which are required to start important missions. These simplifications correlate with adjustments to the general user interface. The user interaction is now designed to support gameplay via web and on mobile devices.

From a technology perspective, the game engine was switched from Havok Vision to Unity. This allowed easy web based deployment as well as mobile deployment while allowing to port core code from the original game. This web based approach allows playing the game in a web browser instead of installing a desktop application which increases the requirement for improved accessibility.

3. ANALYSIS AND PRELIMINARY STUDY

3.1 Analyzing the Streamlined Concept with Octalysis

With the streamlined concept of Lost Earth 2307 considering all components of Yusoff's serious game framework and implementing presumably motivating elements, the next step was to analyze the prototype implementation in terms of fun and motivation using Chou's Octalysis framework (Chou 2015). Each of the eight core drives were reviewed and assigned relevant game elements, resulting in a score for each core drive (see Figure 5).

The general evaluation outcome of the Octalysis tool was "*Proud of You / Good Motivation. [...]*". Hence, the prototype implementation of the streamlined concept seems to be fun and motivating according to the Octalysis framework.

Figure 5. Result of Octalysis analyzation of the protoype implementation

3.2 Setup of Preliminary Study

The results of the Octalysis framework were positive on the one hand, but quite subjective on the other. In order to get a more objective opinion whether the prototype implementation of the concept is heading into the right direction in terms of immersion and usability, a preliminary study was conducted.

(Kannegieser et al. 2019) propose that experiencing flow state compares to experiencing the Total Immersion state of (Cheng et al. 2015). Thus, for measuring the state of immersion the Flow Short Scale questionnaire (FSS) by (Rheinberg et al. 2003) was used. Usability was evaluated using the System Usability Scale (SUS) questionnaire by (Brooke 1996).

The setup of the study followed five steps: First, introducing the participant to the procedure. Second, elicit general data (gender, gaming experience, etc.). Third, playing the prototype of the streamlined concept on a provided laptop, monitored as a 'Think Aloud Session', where participants were asked to verbalize what happens inside their head (Albert and Tullis 2013). Fourth, presenting the FSS questionnaire directly after playing the prototype to capture the first impressions of immersion and last but not least answering the SUS questionnaire.

Nine subjects participated in the study, three of whom were female and five of whom were male. The subjects were not members of the target group. However, as stated in a previous study, improving general usability and immersion is mostly independent of the initial target group (Atorf et al. 2019b). All subjects had gaming experience and mainly played games on desktop computers. The tasks were customized for the study so that non image exploitation experts were able to complete the missions.

3.3 Results of the Preliminary Study

Regarding the evaluation of the Flow Short Scale questionnaire, statements "*3. I did not notice time passing*" and "*6. I am totally absorbed in what I am doing*" showed interesting results (see Figure 6). Five subjects agreed that statement 3 does fully apply. For five subjects statement 6 was nearly true and for three subjects it did fully apply. For statement "*5. My mind is completely clear*" and for statement "*7. The right thoughts/movements occur of their own accord.*" five subjects each affirmed level 5 on the Likert-scale.

All further statements of the Flow Short Scale varied widely in the results, so that no clear indications could be derived. However, the answers on statement 3 and 6 indicate, that some participants might have experienced a state of flow.

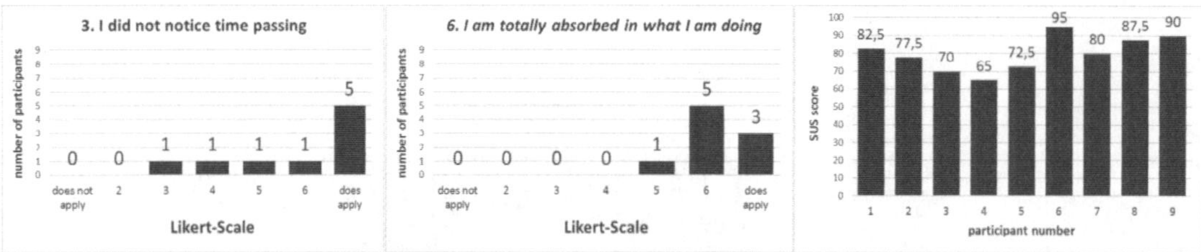

Figure 6. Evaluation of FSS questionnaire, statement three and six, as well as SUS questionnaire

Regarding usability, the highest SUS score was 95 and the lowest was 65. A score of 68 is commonly accepted as at least "good" usability (Bangor et al. 2009). Thus, eight of the nine participants acknowledged good usability for the prototype (see Figure 6). Monitoring the 'Think Aloud Session' revealed specific hurdles while using the prototype. As an example, for some participants it was not clear enough how to exchange resources. However, unlike in the original game, no show-stopping usability issues were monitored. In addition, each SUS score in this preliminary study is better than the average SUS score of the original game, which was 50 (usability issues of original game and SUS scores see Atorf et al. 2019b).

Item 1 of the SUS questionnaire is "I think that I would like to use this game frequently.". This item is of interest for determining a player's motivation to return to the game. Six out of the nine participants agreed or strongly agreed to the statement of item 1, although all participants were not members of the target group. This indicates, that some of these non-experts had fun playing the game and are willing to play again.

3.4 Discussion

The results of the Flow Short Scale questionnaire indicate that some participants might have experienced a state of flow. However, the number of subjects is far too low to make general assumptions. Furthermore, the gaming phase being limited to 20 minutes is creating a difficult environment for reaching a flow state at all. Hence, measuring flow as the optimum state of immersion seems not ideal within this setup and further evaluations should consider using the dedicated immersion questionnaires by (Cheng et al. 2015) to capture the level of immersion in more detail.

Regarding usability, the findings point towards an acceptable implementation for most of the participants. Nevertheless, the low number of subjects interdicts general conclusions. Nonetheless, some participants would like to play the game again.

4. CONCLUSION

The paper presented a process on how to streamline the game design of an existing serious game and how the prototype implementation was evaluated by a preliminary study. At first, the initial game design was modified by addressing the findings of previous evaluations and following the serious game framework by Yusoff. The resulting streamlined concept was analyzed in terms of motivation and fun, using the Octalysis framework. A preliminary study evaluated usability and immersion of the prototype implementation. The findings indicated that the streamlined concept seems to be on the right track regarding motivation and usability. However, the study was preliminary and lacked a suitable number of participants.

In general, the presented method for streamlining an existing game design seems to work. Gameplay is shorter and more accessible in comparison to the original game implementation, because of the improved SUS score and because of using a web based deployment. Future work will focus on improvements to usability and motivational elements, based on the findings of the preliminary study. These further improvements will be evaluated subsequently in qualified studies.

REFERENCES

Albert, W., Tullis, T., 2013. *Measuring the user experience: collecting, analyzing, and presenting usability metrics*. Morgan Kaufmann, Waltham.

Atorf D. et al, 2019a. Balancing Realism and Engagement for a Serious Game in the Domain of Remote Sensing. *In Games and Learning Alliance, Proceedings of the 7th International Conference*, GALA 2018, pp.146-156.

Atorf D. et al, 2019b. Study on Enhancing Learnability of a Serious Game by Implementing a Pedagogical Agent. *In Games and Learning Alliance, Proceedings of the 8th International Conference*, GALA 2019, pp.158-168. Springer Nature CH.

Bangor, A. et al. 2009. Determining What Individual SUS Scores Mean: Adding an Adjective Rating Scale. *In Journal of Usability Studies*, Volume 4, Issue 3, pp. 114-123.

Bopp, M. 2006. Immersive Didaktik und Framingprozesse in Computerspielen. *In Neitzel, B. and Nohr, R.F. Das Spiel mit dem Medium. Partizipation-Immersion-Interaktion. Zur Teilhabe an den Medien von Kunst bis Computerspiel*, pp. 170-186, Schüren, Marburg.

Brooke, J. 1996. SUS - A quick and dirty usability scale. *In Usability Evaluation in Industry*. Routledge.

Cheng, M.-T. et al. 2015. Game Immersion Experience: Its Hierarchical Structure and Impact on Game-based Science Learning. *In Journal of Computer Assisted Learning*, Vol 31, Issue 3, pp. 232–253.

Chou, Y. 2015. *Actionable Gamification: Beyond Points, Badges, and Leaderboards*. California, Octalysis Media.

Garris, R. et al. 2002. Games, Motivation, and Learning: A Research and Practice Model, *In Simulation & Gaming*, vol. 33, pp. 441-467.

Kannegieser, E. et al. 2019. Conducting an Experiment for Validating the Combined Model of Immersion and Flow. *In Proceedings of the 11th International Conference on Computer Supported Education*, Vol 2, pp. 252-259.

Prensky, M. 2007. *Digital Game-Based Learning*. Paragon House, St. Paul.

Rheinberg, F. et al. 2003. Die Erfassung des Flow-Erlebens. *In Diagnostik von Motivation und Selbstkonzept*. Göttingen: Hogrefe, pp. 261–279.

Yusoff, A. et al. 2009. A Conceptual Framework for Serious Games. *In 2009 Ninth IEEE International Conference on Advanced Learning Technologies*, pp. 21-23.

Zichermann, G., Cunningham, C. 2011. *Gamification by Design: Implementing Game Mechanics in Web and Mobile Apps* (1st ed.). O'Reilly Media, Sebastopol, California.

AN E-TUTOR TOOL FOR GRAMMATICAL ERROR CORRECTION

Xiaodong Sun, Yanqin Yin, Huanhuan Lv, Pikun Wang, Hongwei Ma and Dongqiang Yang*
School of Computer Science and Technology, Shandong Jianzhu University, Jinan 250101, China

ABSTRACT

Intelligent language learning tools have evolved into an inevitable aid for ESL/EFL (English as second or foreign language) learners to improve their linguistic skills. By functioning as a machine translation task, automatic grammatical error correction (GEC) has made significant progress with the help of deep neural networks, but its accuracy and coverage rates on different error types have not been fully satisfactory in practice. This paper designs an e-Tutor tool for GEC to help ESL/EFL learners automatically inspect and correct their grammatical errors in writing. One of the core research tasks in GEC is how to improve its generalizability while dealing with more complex error types. In the paper, we propose a novel data augmentation method to add artificial noise to native English corpora during training a neural translation model for GEC. To improve the output quality of GEC, we also design a re-editing module, which mainly consists of a statistical language model, along with a grammatical error detection classifier, in validating each sentence generated by GEC. Experiment results on GEC show that our e-Tutor tool can achieve state-of-the-art performance on the CoNLL-2014 dataset.

KEYWORDS

e-Tutor Tool, Data Augmentation, Grammatical Error Correction

1. INTRODUCTION

The goal of GEC is to take learners' erroneous sentences as input, translating or converting them into grammatically correct ones. Early research methods on GEC were based on grammatical rules and linguistic statistics. For example, Gamon et al. (2008) used a rule-based n-gram language model in correcting prepositions and qualifiers errors for ESL/EFL learners. Junczys-Brockett et al. (2006) proposed to adopt the statistical machine translation model into the GEC task, and their method was to automatically translate erroneous sentences into the correct ones that can satisfy the grammatical requirements for native English. Current studies usually take GEC as a neural machine translation (NMT) process and focus on architectural design of deep neural networks to realize the NMT's encoder-decoder pipeline.

In spite of recent breakthroughs in deep language processing (Torfi *et al.*, 2020), GEC is still a challenging task, partly due to the diversity of grammatical error types in learner language as ESL/EFL, and partly due to the complexity of interaction among multiple errors co-existing in context. Therefore, how to synthesize more learner data to feed and train a NMT model is key to enhance the generalizability of GEC while dealing with new or complex errors. To solve the problem of data scarcity on manually annotated learner corpora, Kiyono et al. (2019) proposed a data augmentation method that pre-trained a NMT model using artificially generated learner data. Katsumata and Komachi (2019) also showed that the training process of NMT required a large amount of learner data to deliver an effective GEC tool, and generating pseudo learner data can assist GEC to improve NMT's generalizability.

In the paper, we propose a novel method to automatically construct the learner dataset for training a NMT model for GEC. First, for a word (i.e., a verb or noun), we generate all of its inflected forms, which are then collected into its confusion set. The spelling candidate set, generated by the Aspell (Grundkiewicz *et al.*, 2019), is also combined with the confusion set to jointly synthesize spurious training data. We also introduce a two-stage processing for GEC: after training a NMT-based module with the synthesized data, we conduct the first-round GEC with it; we run the second-round GEC with a rule and statistical language module. The hybrid use of multiple correction methods can significantly improve our e-Tutor's performance on GEC.

* Correspondence author, ydq@sdjzu.edu.cn

2. E-TUTOR DESIGN

2.1 Architecture

Our e-Tutor architecture consists of three modules: pseudo data generation, NMT, and re-editing, as shown in Figure 1. Briefly, apart from pseudo data generation, the NMT-based GEC module has multiple layers of deep neural networks working as an encoder and decoder pipeline. Given the candidate sentences yielded from the NMT module, the re-editing module rectifies them with a rule-based punctuation checker and a language statistics-based misspelling corrector. Finally, a binary classifier on grammatical error detection selects an optimal sentence as output.

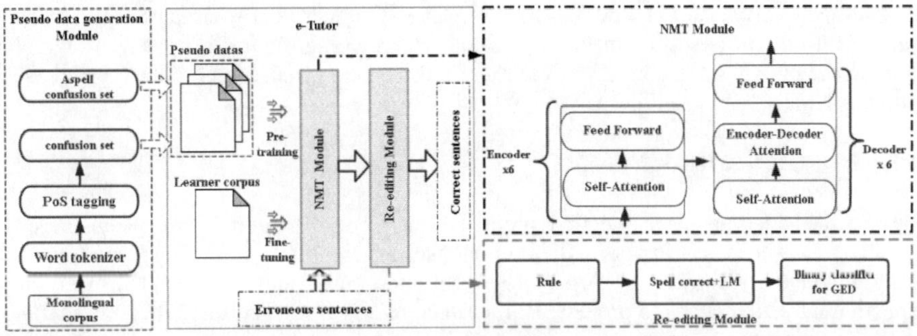

Figure 1. The e-Tutor workflow

2.2 Generating Pseudo Data

To improve the generalizability of NMT-based GEC, Grundkiewicz et al. (2019) suggested an unsupervised way of generating learner data. They first constructed a confusion set for a target word in a grammatically correct sentence using a spelling checker, and then replaced the target word with each word in the confusion set to produce spurious sentences for expanding the training data. Inspired by Grundkiewicz et al (2018), we design a novel way of data augmentation for GEC. Specifically, we first randomly select some words to introduce the token level of artificial errors, which consist of 15% of words in a native corpus. To improve the robustness of GEC on misspelling, one of the typical errors in ESL/EFL learners, we randomly conduct a character-level editing (i.e., insertion/deletion/replacement/swap) on 5% of words in a native corpus. The whole process of data augmentation is depicted as follows:

Rule 1: According to the established verb or noun transformation table, we first locate the inflected forms of a target word in a native sentence. We then select each of its inflected forms to replace it to form a learner sentence. If the target word has no inflection available, a candidate word in its spelling confusion set is randomly selected to replace it.

Rule 2: Randomly delete a word.

Rule 3: Randomly insert a word after a selected word.

Rule 4: Randomly swap with the next word.

Rule 5: Randomly change the case of the initial character in a word.

2.3 Re-Editing

To improve the correction quality of e-Tutor, we re-edit the candidate sentences, translated from the NMT-based GEC, with the following procedures:

1. A rule-based punctuation checker. The first letter of each sentence should be capitalized, and double punctuations and spaces should be removed.

2. Statistical spelling correction. For a target word, we first use Aspell (Grundkiewicz *et al.*, 2019) to yield its spelling variants. After replacing the target with its variants to form a new cluster of candidate sentences, we run a N-gram Language Model (NLM) to rank them and output the sentence with the highest possibility. We calculate statistical information from corpora to estimate the distributional probability of

n-grams. In the experiment, we used the Kenlm (Heafield, 2011) toolkit to train a N-gram language model (i.e., n=6) on the Gutenberg corpus (Lahiri, 2014).

3. Grammatical Error Detection (GED). We also train a binary classifier with BERT (Devlin *et al.*, 2019) on the CoLA dataset (Warstadt *et al.*, 2019) to assist error detection.

3. EXPERIMENTS

3.1 Learner Corpus

The existing learner corpora include FCE v2.1 (Dale and Kilgarriff, 2011), Lang8 (Mizumoto et al., 2011), NUCLE (Dahlmeier et al., 2013), and W&i+LOCNESS (Granger, 2014; Bryant et al., 2019). The types of errors that ESL/EFL learners often make are related with spelling, nouns, subject-verb agreement, and verb forms, among the others. To accurately cover more error types, we also used NUCLE and W&i+LOCNESS for fine-tuning NMT.

3.2 Data Augmentation

To generate pseudo learner data, we first preprocessed Google Billion Word Benchmark (Chelba et al., 2014), a public news corpus. After normalizing punctuations and limiting sentence length up to 80 words, we ran PoS tagging on the preprocessed corpus. For verbs and nouns, randomly selected, we replaced them with their respective inflection forms to produce learner data, as shown in Table 1. Since misspelling is one of the common grammatical mistakes, we also used Aspell to generate misspellings for a target word and stored them in its corresponding confusion set. Table 1 shows the inflection and misspelling confusion sets for a target word, after we conducted PoS tagging and lemmatization with NLTK and Aspell.

Table 1. Basic rules for generating a confusion set

	Tag	Explanation	Inflection confusion set
V	VB	Verb, the base form	*accept: accepts, accepting, accepted*
	VBD	Verb, past tense	
	VBG	Verb, gerund or present participle	
	VBN	Verb, past participle	
	VBP	Verb, non-3rd person singular present	
	VBZ	Verb, 3rd person singular present	
N	NN	Noun, singular or mass	*devote: devotion, devotions*
	NNS	Noun, plural	
	NNP	Proper noun, plural	
	NNPS	Proper noun, plural	
		Word	**Spelling confusion set**
		doing	*ding, dding, Dion, dingo, dingy*
		future	*Futures, feature, suture, future's*
		have	*Heave, Havel, haven, haves, gave*

3.3 Transformer Model

The NMT in the paper mainly employs the Copy-Augmented Transformer (Zhao *et al.*, 2019) model to build an encoder-decoder for GEC. The Copy-Augmented Transformer can determine whether to copy or generate a word in the correction process; only a few words in an erroneous sentence needs to be corrected, and most of the remaining ones are directly copied into the original positions in the sentence. The final probability distribution for a newly generated word is the weighted fusion of the decoding probability $p_t^{gen}(w)$ and copy probability p_t^{copy}. q_t is the mapping of the hidden state of decoding at time *t*. The keys and values are packed together into matrices K and V. *K, V* are different transformations of the hidden state of the input code. *W* stands for the parameter matrix.

$$P_t(w) = \left(1 - \alpha_t^{copy}\right) * p_t^{gen}(w) + \left(\alpha_t^{copy}\right) * p_t^{copy}(w) \quad (1)$$

$$\alpha_t^{copy} = sigmoid\left(W^T \sum((q_t^T K)^T \cdot V)\right) \quad (2)$$

$$P_t^{copy}(w) = softmax((q_t^T K)^T) \quad (3)$$

$$q_t, K, V = h_t^{trg} W_q^T, H^{src} W_k^T, H^{src} W_v^T \quad (4)$$

3.4 Fine-Tuning

To improve adaptability and recall rate of our Transformer-based GEC, which had been trained with our pseudo learner data, we combined the training datasets of NUCLE and W&I+LOCNESS to fine-tune it. After that, the GEC outputs were ranked and re-edited with the rule and statistics-based correctors, together with the BERT-based GED to yield the final result.

Table 2. CoNLL-2014 test set results

Model	CoNLL-2014(M^2score)		
	Pre.	**Rec.**	$F_{0.5}$
Chollampatt and Ng (2018) with Multilayer Convolution Neural Network (4 ensemble models), Rescoring, Spell Check, Learner corpus	65.5	33.1	54.8
Grundkiewicz and Junczys-Dowmunt (2018) with SMT, NMT, LM, Learner corpus	66.8	34.5	56.3
Lichtarge *et al.* (2019) with Transformer, best Ensemble, Learner corpus, Data augmentation	66.7	43.9	60.4
Commercial APP: Ginger API [1]	12.8	16.6	13.4
Our e-Tutor model after pre-training	58.5	28.0	48.0
plus fine-tuning	70.4	39.6	60.9
plus re-editing	**70.7**	40.2	**61.4**

4. RESULTS AND ANALYSIS

We evaluated e-Tutor using M^2 score (Dahlmeier and Ng, 2012) on the CoNLL-2014 test set, and its results are shown in Table 2. It clearly indicates that just using the synthetic pseudo-data for pre-trainingthe transformer-based model can achieve a decent performance, and e-Tutor can reach 48.0% on $F_{0.5}$. To cover more error types, we used the existing high-quality learner corpora to fine-tune the model. The results show that the model gained significant improvements on precision (70.4%), recall (39.6%), and $F_{0.5}$ (60.9%) in contrast with the pre-training process, exceeding most of published results in Tabel 2. Furthermore, after the comprehensive use of multiple error correction methods in re-editing, the precision rate of e-Tutor increased from 58.5% to 70.7%.

We also compared e-Tutor with a commercial GEC application: Ginger on the CoNLL-2014 test set. The results show that the e-Tutor tool significantly improved the GEC performance and has potential to be an effective tool for ESL/EFL learners.

5. CONCLUSION

It is a challenging task to develop a computer-assisted language learning (CALL) tool. We designed a data augmentation method to enhance the generalizability of NMT-based GEC, which can be further improved with the specific re-editing process. In future work, we will explore a more effective data augmentation method in training GEC models. To improve GEC accuracy, we will try to build up dedicated modules to separately deal with different error types.

[1] https://github.com/zoncoen/python-ginger

ACKNOWLEDGEMENT

This research was supported by the Humanity and Social Science Foundation of China Ministry of Education (Grant No. 15YJA740054).

REFERENCES

Brockett, C. et al., 2006, Correcting ESL Errors Using Phrasal SMT Techniques. *Proceedings of the 21st International Conference on Computational Linguistics and the 44th Annual Meeting of the Association for Computational Linguistics.* Stroudsburg, USA, pp 249-256.

Bryant, C. et al., 2019, The BEA-2019 Shared Task on Grammatical Error Correction. *Proceedings of the 14th Workshop on Innovation Use of NLP for Building Educational Applications. Association for Computational Linguistics.*

Chelba, C. et al., 2014, One billion word benchmark for measuring progress in statistical language modeling. arXiv preprint arXiv:1312.3005.

Dahlmeier, D. et al., 2013, Building a Large Annotated Corpus of Learner English: The NUS Corpus of Learner English. In *Proceedings of the eighth workshop on innovative use of NLP for building educational applications*, pages 22–31.

Dahlmeier, D. and Ng, H. 2012, Better Evaluation for Grammatical Error Correction. *Proceedings of the 2012 Conference of the North American Chapter of the Association for Computational Linguistics: Human Language Technologies.* pp 568-572.

Dale, R. and Kilgarriff, A. 2011, Helping Our Own: The HOO 2011 Pilot Shared Task. *Proceedings of the 13th European Workshop on Natural Language Generation.* pp 242-249.

Devlin, J. et al., 2019, BERT: Pre-training of Deep Bidirectional Transformers for Language Understanding. arXiv preprint arXiv:1810.04805.

Gamon, M. et al., 2008, Using Contextual Speller Techniques and Language Modeling for ESL Error Correction. *In Proceedings of the Third International Joint Conference on Natural Language Processing.*

Granger, S. 2014, The computer learner corpus: a versatile new source of data for SLA research.

Grundkiewicz, R. et al., 2019, Neural Grammatical Error Correction Systems with Unsupervised Pre-training on Synthetic Data. arXiv preprint arXiv:1804.05945.

Grundkiewicz, R. and Junczys-Dowmunt, M. 2018, Near Human-Level Performance in Grammatical Error Correction with Hybrid Machine Translation. arXiv preprint arXiv:1804.05945.

Heafield, K. 2011, KenLM: Faster and Smaller Language Model Queries. In *Proceedings of the Sixth Workshop on Statistical Machine Translation,* Association for Computational Linguistics. WMT '11, Stroudsburg, USA.

Katsumata, S. and Komachi, M. 2019. Towards Unsupervised Grammatical Error Correction using Statistical Machine Translation with Synthetic Comparable Corpus. arXiv preprint arXiv: 1907.09724.

Kiyono, S. et al., 2019, An Empirical Study of Incorporating Pseudo Data into Grammatical Error Correction. In *EMNLP/IJCNLP*, pp1236-1242.

Lahiri, S. 2014. Complexity of Word Collocation Networks: A Preliminary Structural Analysis. *In Proceedings of the Student Research Workshop at the 14th Conference of the European Chapter of the Association for Computational Linguistics,* pp 96–105.

Mizumoto, T. et al., 2011, Mining Revision Log of Language Learning SNS for Automated Japanese Error Correction of Second Language Learners. In Proceedings of 5th International Joint Conference on Natural Language Processing.

Torfi, A. et al., 2020. Natural Language Processing Advancements By Deep Learning: A Survey. arXiv preprint arXiv:2003.01200.

Warstadt, A. et al., 2019. Neural Network Acceptability Judgments. Transactions of the Association for Computational Linguistics, Vol. 7625-641.

Zhao, W. et al., 2019, Improving Grammatical Error Correction via Pre-Training a Copy-Augmented Architecture with Unlabeled Data. *Proceedings of the 2019 Conference of the North American Chapter of the Association for Computational Linguistics: Human Language Technologies*, Volume 1, pp 156-165.

DIGITAL HEALTH AND ILLNESS: BALANCING IT

António Bandeira[1] and Henrique Martins[2]
[1]*Faculdade de Medicina da Universidade do Porto, Portugal*
[2]*ISCTE-IUL, Portugal*

ABSTRACT

Digital Illness can be conceptualized as a state of less health resulting from either "too much" or "too little" exposure to the Digital. In order to evaluate the state of health we suggest the use of the Health Index. It will allow us to measure the level of Health of each person in each moment. This Health Index is negatively affected by the under and overuse of the Digital. In order to best benefit from the Digital, we have to understand how much the right amount of Digital is, which maximizes the Health Index of the individual. To do this we have to understand the extremes of "too little" and "too much" Digital. In what concerns the use of "too much" Digital, we divide this topic in four areas, and we present evidence regarding the existence of each of those areas.

KEYWORDS

Digital Illness, Digital Obesity, Digital Sickness, Digital Addiction, Digital Overdose, Digital Accident

1. INTRODUCTION

There is no doubt that technology plays today an essential role in our daily lives. It is present in almost everyday strands of our daily lives. In order to collect the best from Digital, first we must understand that it is over, and underuse entail different but very important problems in what concerns our health. This understanding will help us to comprehend better where we can find the turning point from where more digital does not mean more health but, on the contrary, it starts to mean a reduction in our health.

In what concerns Digital Illness, it can be conceptualized as a state of less health resulting from either "too much" or "too little" expositor to digital means in today's reality. It may occur as people experience lack or excess of Digital. One could say that lack of digital leads certainly to Digital Segregation as is the case with over 21% of people in Portugal and higher percentage worldwide with no access to internet/digital means and with less access to health literacy and even digital health services such as tele-health. Excess of digital seems more evidently harbor more pathological potential as it can leads to various problems that should also receive our attention. In this paper we will reflect mainly about the problems entailed by the digital overuse. To do this we suggest the use of a new concept - the Health Index (HI).

2. BODY OF PAPER

In order to evaluate the impact of any agent that change our level of health, we must first be able to measure our level of health. In any day of a person's life is possible to be 100% healthy neither 100% sick. Accordingly, we must understand how much the percentage of our healthy and unhealthy self is in every day of our life, and how to manage that. To do this we suggest the use of the concept of HI. This variation of our HI happens not only along the day, but also along our lives, and even beyond! HI is a concept that may be applied since before birth until after death! When talking about before birth we should think about the fluctuations of our health that modifies our HI, even when we are still a fetus inside of a uterus. In what concerns the after death we may think about a possible organ donation, where "our" organs still face state variations that change HI. The "basal" health level is modified by HI, either increasing (when positive) or decreasing (when negative). It is also important to understand that HI is variable in time, changing its value each moment. Thus, HI can be a broadly applied concept.

Assuming Health status is a moving constant, we can conceptualize it to range from "total health", to total Sickness (near death situation). As such a health index (HI) could be conceived to range between 100%, meaning totally healthy, and -100% meaning totally sick. The option of using -100% is made on purpose as moving constant daily and even hourly can be assumed for "health" as a "measurable" entity. As we already stated, no one is either on the upper or lower end for, eventually, more than a few instants. In what concerns to the topic of this paper, we understand that not only the little exposition to Digital leads to a lower HI, but also too much exposition leads to an equally low HI (as an example, the over digital professional aspect of life can have a high impact). Taking this into account, it is important to understand each one of these extremes in order to accomplish the appropriate exposition to Digital that enhances our HI as close to 100% as possible. Actually there are already studies suggesting the use of "personalized Family Media Use Plans" (Reid Chassiakos et al., 2016).

As already stated, we intend to reflect about the different areas that negatively impact our HI due to Digital Overuse. According with our research the Digital Illness due to excess of digital may be divided in four main areas. Digital Overweight/Obesity, Digital Sickness, Digital Addition/Overdose and Digital Accident/Death. In the next paragraphs we will sum up existing scattered evidence for each one of these areas. To facilitate the understanding, we organized this concepts on Figure 1. On Table 1 we share some evidence about each one of this area regarding Digital illness due to Digital Excess.

2.1.1 Digital Obesity/Overweight

In what concerns to the concept of Digital Overweight/Obesity there are complaints about almost all aspects of our lives. From physical symptoms, as vision and tendinitis, neurological symptoms, as irritation, mental symptoms, as information overload, to psychiatric symptoms as Burnout. A very current example of this Digital Obesity is the one that we are living with the Covid-19 pandemic. Every day we are bombed with so many information, either true or negative, that our anxiety levels rise due, not only to the disease, but also to the enormous amount of information. (Rathore and Farooq, 2020)

2.1.2 Digital Sickness

When there is discomfort and pathology, we start to refer it as Digital Sickness. In this area we have very aspects to consider.

The concept of Digital Anorexia / Role Play refers to those who "see" themselves in a different way when compared to who they really are. This happens due to an altered perception of who they really are.

Dependency Syndrome refers to those who need approval for their ideas on social media.

Also, there are some people that have Multiple Personalities or personality dysmorphia, that changes accordingly with the fact that they are in the "real world" or on the social media.

2.1.3 Digital Addiction/Overdose

A more understandable concept is the Digital Addition and Digital overdose. Now, more than ever, we pursue the digital to every place where we go, many times, over the social norms. For example, when we ask for the Wi-Fi password even before a nice compliment to the waitress or when we keep checking our phone when we are at the dinner table or in a bar with friends or family.

2.1.4 Digital Accident/Death

Last, but not the least, there is a growing number of accidents due to the digital. Not only traffic accidents, both from distracted pedestrians being hint by cars as they surf their smartphone to more abstract yet harmful social rupture, where people are physically alive but so disconnected that they do "not live" or "are dead" to those around them. Regarding this specific area, it is important to remember that wearables also represent a risk to our health, in what concerns traffic accidents (Sacks et al., 2018).

2.2 Figures and Tables

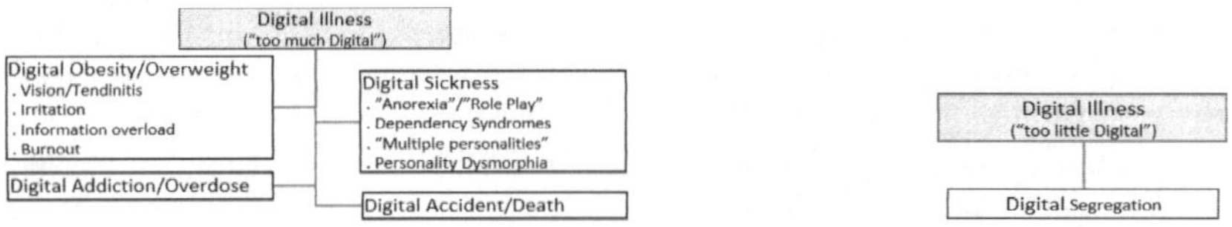

Figure 1. Digital Illness

Table 1. Exemplar papers about the Different Areas of Digital Illness due to "too much Digital"

Author	*Main Messages*	*Topic*
(Klerings et al., 2015)	''It results in a richer range of resources to support practice and learning, but also creates conflicting evidence, insecurity about the knowledge and greater demands on the professional to identify the appropriate knowledge for their problem in question.'' ''Filtering the information overload for better decisions'	Digital Obesity / Overweight
(Byyny, 2016)	"average workers spend 28% of their time managing e-mail"; "we check our phones on average 221 times a day, or about every 4.3 minutes"; "nearly one in eight Americans exhibit problematic Internet use" "average young adult moves between media platforms 27 times per hour, which can lower IQ by as much as 15 points"	Digital Obesity / Overweight
(Lee et al., 2017)	"we operationally define information overload as either a perceived or actual occurrence whereby the volume or complexity of information accessed by an individual exceeds their capacity to process the information within a given timeframe"	Digital Obesity / Overweight
(Milne, 2019)	Clinicians should not feel threatened or frustrated by informed patients; instead, we should see this as an opportunity to challenge our own perceptions and address misinformation. How do we use the information to best effect? How does health literacy of the public and co-workers impact information giving and how do our beliefs and values influence the processing of information? What is our sphere of influence? What do we need people to know to enable care?	Digital Obesity / Overweight
(Rathore and Farooq, 2020)	COVID-19. "infodemic" in which false news, conspiracy theories, magical cures and racist news are being shared at an alarming rate, with the potential to increase anxiety and stress and even lead to loss of life.	Digital Obesity / Overweight Digital Accident/Death
(Steele et al., 2020)	"social media use specifically can be associated with diminished psychological functioning in adolescents and young adults" Related with "digital stress: including availability stress, approval anxiety, fear of missing out, and communication overload"	Digital Sickness
(Mihajlov and Vejmelka, 2017)	The difficulty in finding a precise definition of Internet Addiction makes it harder to classify, measure, diagnose, treat and prevent this Addiction. There are many different types of Internet Addictions that should be faced differently. About Prevention: Universal Prevention, Selective Prevention, Indicated Prevention	Digital Addiction / Overdose
(Eichenberg et al., 2017)	There is a positive relation between Insecure attachment style (Attachment Theory). Users with Internet Addiction (report different motives for Internet use when compared with users without Internet Addiction.	Digital Addiction / Overdose
(Kuss and Griffiths, 2017)	"Social Networking Sites and Addiction: Ten Lessons Learned: (i) social networking and social media use are not the same; (ii) social networking is eclectic; (iii) social networking is a way of being; (iv) individuals can become addicted to using social networking sites; (v) Facebook addiction is only one example of SNS addiction; (vi) fear of missing out (FOMO) may be part of SNS addiction; (vii) smartphone addiction may be part of SNS addiction; (viii) nomophobia may be part of SNS addiction; (ix) there are sociodemographic differences in SNS addiction; and (x) there are methodological problems with research to date."	Digital Addiction / Overdose
(Kircaburun and Griffiths, 2018)	Relationship between personality and social networking site addiction (Instagram®)	Digital Addiction / Overdose
(Atchley and Strayer, 2017)	Using a cell phone while driving was one of the most common sources (12%) of distraction recorded in the 6 seconds before the crash. "The National Safety Council estimates that approximately one-quarter of the crashes in the United States are because of small-screen distraction" "In 1 survey,2 nearly one-third (31%) of the respondents reported texting when they were distressed (including being bored), one-quarter (24%) reported texting when it was socially inappropriate, one-fifth (20%) reported texting when it was dangerous, and nearly one-fifth (17%) reported feeling the need to increase how much they texted"	Digital Accident Digital Sickness – Dependency Syndromes
(Sacks et al., 2018)	"if drivers intuitively believe or are frequently told that Google Glass is less disruptive to driving performance than smartphones, our current data showed that frequent use and quick access to wearable devices (such as Google Glass) in actual daily driving may potentially put wearable device users at higher risks than smartphone users." "although wearable devices, voice recognition and head-mounted display, are designed in a hope to reduce visual and manual distraction and these technologies do work to some extents, however, these technologies are not distraction-free or risk-free. Drivers are discouraged to engage in distraction tasks not just in a smartphone, but also Google Glass and smartwatch, as all these devices impair driving performance"	Digital Accident / Death

(Ortiz et al., 2018)	"texting WhatsApp messages while driving worsens driving performance for all age groups, most notably among older participants." "negative effect of the use of the smartphone during driving was also reflected in the number of collisions, with a greater risk of accidents in all the groups of drivers (by 8.3% for young adults, 25.0% for adults, 80.5% for middle-aged adults, and 134.5% for older drivers)" "participants' subjective responses indicated that younger drivers (18-24 years) had a higher risk of deliberately violating safe driving practices ($p < 0.05$)."	Digital Accident / Death

3. CONCLUSION

We may define the Digital Illness as any negative impact of Digital on Health. The concept of a Health Index (HI) is presented and used to plot HI versus digital exposure, creating different clusters of problematic areas. This negative impact of digital in humans can happen either due to a lack or excess of Digital. When thinking about "too much" Digital we may divide it in four big areas: Digital Obesity/Overweight, Digital Sickness, Digital Addiction/Overdose and Digital Accident/Death. It is important to understand the impact of Digital in order to use it to make our HI as close to 100% as possible. There is evidence for the existence of these problems and that they are deserving increasing interest by researchers. We believe, however, that there is a lot more work to do in what concerns other impacts of overuse of Digital that may result on more evidence supporting any of this areas, but also evidence that require the creation of a new area. It is important that, sooner than later, we start to look to Digital Illness as a threat to our HI. This understanding of Digital will allow us to transform this threat in a way to potentiate our health to its maximum.

ACKNOWLEDGEMENT

The authors report no acknowledgment.

REFERENCES

Atchley, P. & Strayer, D. L. 2017. Small Screen Use and Driving Safety. *Pediatrics,* 140, S107-s111.

Byyny, R. L. 2016. Information and cognitive overload: How much is too much? *Pharos Alpha Omega Alpha Honor Med Soc,* 79, 2-7.

Eichenberg, C., Schott, M., Decker, O. & Sindelar, B. 2017. Attachment Style and Internet Addiction: An Online Survey. *J Med Internet Res,* 19, e170.

Kircaburun, K. & Griffiths, M. D. 2018. Instagram addiction and the Big Five of personality: The mediating role of self-liking. *J Behav Addict,* 7, 158-170.

Klerings, I., Weinhandl, A. S. & Thaler, K. J. 2015. Information overload in healthcare: too much of a good thing? *Z Evid Fortbild Qual Gesundhwes,* 109, 285-90.

Kuss, D. J. & Griffiths, M. D. 2017. Social Networking Sites and Addiction: Ten Lessons Learned. *Int J Environ Res Public Health,* 14.

Lee, K., Roehrer, E. & Cummings, E. 2017. Information overload in consumers of health-related information: a scoping review protocol. *JBI Database System Rev Implement Rep,* 15, 2457-2463.

Mihajlov, M. & Vejmelka, L. 2017. Internet Addiction: A Review of the First Twenty Years. *Psychiatr Danub,* 29, 260-272.

Milne, J. 2019. Tackling the information overload in healthcare. *Br J Nurs,* 28, S3.

Ortiz, C., Ortiz-Peregrina, S., Castro, J. J., Casares-López, M. & Salas, C. 2018. Driver distraction by smartphone use (WhatsApp) in different age groups. *Accid Anal Prev,* 117, 239-249.

Rathore, F. A. & Farooq, F. 2020. Information Overload and Infodemic in the COVID-19 Pandemic. *J Pak Med Assoc,* 70(Suppl 3), S162-s165.

Reid Chassiakos, Y. L., Radesky, J., Christakis, D., Moreno, M. A. & Cross, C. 2016. Children and Adolescents and Digital Media. *Pediatrics,* 138.

Sacks, D., Baxter, B., Campbell, B. C. V., Carpenter, J. S., Cognard, C., Dippel, D., Eesa, M., Fischer, U., Hausegger, K., Hirsch, J. A., Shazam Hussain, M., Jansen, O., Jayaraman, M. V., Khalessi, A. A., Kluck, B. W., Lavine, S., Meyers, P. M., Ramee, S., Rüfenacht, D. A., Schirmer, C. M. & Vorwerk, D. 2018. Multisociety Consensus Quality Improvement Revised Consensus Statement for Endovascular Therapy of Acute Ischemic Stroke. *Int J Stroke,* 13, 612-632.

Steele, R. G., Hall, J. A. & Christofferson, J. L. 2020. Conceptualizing Digital Stress in Adolescents and Young Adults: Toward the Development of an Empirically Based Model. *Clin Child Fam Psychol Rev,* 23, 15-26.

A NEW PERSPECTIVE ON THE ISSUE OF PRIVACY: COVID-19 PANDEMIC VS PRIVACY

Adewale Adegoroye, Marc Conrad[1] and Xiaohua Feng[1]
School of Computer Science and Technology, University of Bedfordshire
Luton, United Kingdom
[1]Dr.

ABSTRACT

The current COVID-19 experience seems to expose the need for a new approach about how we interpret and handle privacy. This paper investigates the notion of privacy whether it is old, current, or simply misunderstood. The use of technologies is limited by a shortage of data, and by too many data that cannot be accessed due to privacy rights. The authors present the limitations, constraints, and pitfalls that privacy could pose on the use of AI and emerging technology as a potential nonpharmaceutical weapon against the current and future pandemic. Addressing these restrictions would require careful balancing among data protection, economy and public health, and robust engagement between human and digital world. This paper seeks to encourage governments, decision makers and developers to rethink their perspective of user privacy.

KEYWORDS

COVID-19, Data Protection, Privacy, GDPR (General Data Protection Regulation)

1. INTRODUCTION

We often look quizzical on privacy whenever we speak of addressing crime, terrorism, even corruption issues with digital technology. As of August 28, 2020, the COVID-19 coronavirus had affected 213 countries and territories across the world, infecting more than 28.5 million people and causing more than 840,000 deaths and counting since the first case in December 2019 (Worldometers, 2020). Thus, posing an unprecedented economic and social challenge to the citizens, businesses, and government worldwide. In response to this global challenge, social distancing, contact tracing app, location tracking app, and digital surveillance are among the proposed nonpharmaceutical interventions to delay and/or reduce the spread of this virus. Thus, opening yet another critical question on how to balance the privacy challenges of these technologies with eradicating that which threatens our health and economy - the public and the government alike. How should privacy be handled during a pandemic? Which is more important, the country's economy: citizens' privacy or their safety? To date, there has not been an easy way of addressing any of these questions. The notion of using location history data, for example, to trace the COVID-19 coronavirus spread is among the new ethical and security concerns raised about privacy. This implies infectious people who might not know, either because they have not yet developed symptoms, or because their symptoms are mild will be identified, monitored, and supported where possible. With the use of this list, it would be possible to find any other smartphone (or smartphone user) that was close to the phone at that time (Fair, 2020). In the following, this paper seeks to examine the concept of privacy from a different point of view during the pandemic.

2. THE CONCEPTS OF PRIVACY AND THE COVID-19 PANDEMIC

In 1967, Alan Westin identifies privacy from two unique points of view, in basic context and the socio-environment. In basic context, he defines privacy as the right of people, associations or organisations to decide for themselves where, how and to what degree knowledge about them is transmitted to others (Westin, cited in; Margulis, 2003). With social engagement, Westin defines privacy as the voluntary and temporary isolation of an individual from the wider public by physical or psychological means, either in the state of isolation or in the intimacy of a small group or a situation of anonymity or reservation by large groups (Margulis, 2003). Altman 1975 cited in; Margulis (2003) argue that when a person regulates their social interaction, he/she gets privacy and therefore defined it as "the selective control of access to the self". Over the years, there had been several debates on the interpretations of privacy among scholars and business leaders. Several studies (e.g. Bennett, 1992; Solove, 2007; Gutwirth, 2002) argue that efforts to define the concept of privacy have proven to be famously challenging, complex and outside the reach of just about any scholar exploring it. Furthermore, Fuchs (2011) believes that privacy is valuable to firms and affluent people in the economic sense, as it conceals wealth disparity; yet it is also exploited by the very same industries who tend to manipulate employees and/or customers. Nissenbaum (2004) states that it is not the sharing of information that is a problem, but the gathering, exchange and exploitation of it outside the right mutually agreed with social boundary. However, with the rise of new digital technology and AI, a further consensus has been reached on understanding that privacy occupies several dimensions: (1) Privacy of the person; (2) Privacy of behaviour and action; (3) Privacy of communication; (4) Privacy of data and image; (5) Privacy of thoughts and feelings (6) Privacy of location and space (7) Privacy of association (Finn, Wright and Friedewald, 2013).

One of the COVID-19 pandemic's implications is working from home. Zoom, Hangout Meets, Houseparty are among the top video conferencing software adopted as an essential productivity tool during this period (Sydow, 2020); even the British Prime Minister Boris Johnson also claimed to use Zoom for his cabinet meetings (BBC, 2020). Reports suggested that while there was no evidence of Zoom selling user data to third parties of any sort, the terms of use of the company offer a lot of leeways to collect and exchange information. Its instant messages among others can be used to promote advertising campaigns (O'Flaherty, 2020). The hosts could turn on 'attention monitoring' to test whether the audience is paying attention during the call (O'Flaherty, 2020). While Zoom may meet the United State privacy standards, it is believed that it does not meet the European Union's GDPR standards (European Parliament and EU Council, 2018).

On 23 March 2020, the EU Commission called on European mobile network operators to provide anonymised and aggregated data to the Commission to track the spread of viruses and to identify priority areas for medical supplies (Mark Scott, Laurens Cerulus and Laura Kayali, 2020). Another example, all mobile service providers in Australia are expected to retain onto their network, two years of data relating to the usage of each smartphone, including location information for the customer. It complies with the Australian Telecommunications Act 1997, which requires federal, state and local governments to request access for purposes such as law enforcement, national security, and public revenue safety (Australian Government, 2020). Fair (2020) did argue against this. He explained that even though a pandemic is arguably a threat to national security, being infected with COVID-19 is not a crime. However, while it is not expressly referred to in the Australian Legislative Act, 2020, the Act requires the Federal Health Minister to take whatever action is required to prevent or monitor the "emergence, establishment or dissemination" of the declared emergency disease (Australian Legislative Act, 2020). Like several others, the Government of Australia faces a crisis that is more severe in order of magnitude. Studies suggest citizen trust in the public administration and giant tech companies may have been reduced due to events such as revealed by lawsuits against Facebook, Zoom and the disclosure of classified information or government surveillance of her people as reported by Edward Snowden in 2013 (MacAskill et al., 2013; Belot, 2018; Coyne, 2019). Nonetheless, others around the world, such as the Australians, are believed to be non-hesitant to see their private data used in this manner if it means saving lives, reduces the economic challenges, and put a stop to the spread of the virus.

So far, the latest COVID-19 surveillance metrics indicate that, relative to April and May 2020, the number of new COVID-19 cases per day in the UK has dramatically decreased at the national level as of August 2020 (Public Health England and NHSX, 2020). There is, to date, minimal or inadequate scholarly analysis and evidence to show whether these changes witnessed in the daily rate of new COVID-19 case are subject to the users' willingness to compromise their privacy with the AI and digital technology solution.

3. AI VS PRIVACY VS COVID-19: LIMITATIONS, CONSTRAINTS AND PITFALLS

Naudé (2020) examines AI as a method for monitoring and forecasting, AI as a method for diagnosis and prognosis, AI for medications and vaccination, and social regulation in the battle against the pandemic; and acknowledged limits, restrictions, and risks. The result indicates that data is vital for the effective use of AI against the pandemic, while voicing fear that public health issues may outweigh data protection issues and that mission creep may arise, with governments maintaining their citizens' excessive monitoring long after the pandemic has ended. Kapa, Halamka and Raskar (2020) indicate that further research is needed as to whether privacy-enabled measures minimise the effectiveness of contact tracing due to reliance on private consumer response rather than strict implementation by a central authority. The current study shows that with the potential of emerging epidemic control technologies, the possible advantage of combating existing pandemic threats or future outbreaks cannot be overlooked (Kapa, Halamka and Raskar, 2020). Oliver et al. (2020) conducted a COVID-19 related survey involving 156,614 general adult population (over 18) via social media posts to assess the Spanish citizens' situation and perception on their social contact behaviour during the confinement, their economic impact, their work environment situation and their health status. The study indicates that Spaniards have shown high conformity with all confinement measures, although more than a quarter of the population reports lacking the necessary means to self-isolate. The survey results revealed gender and age matter regarding social interaction behaviour, the economic and labour impact, and the ability to self-isolate. This takes us back to discussing the usage of applications such as the COVID-19 Exposure Notification System. Sakul-Ung and Smanchat (2019) 's Integrated Privacy System study revealed that the framework includes helpful components for data protection management, development and monitoring mechanisms. This may be useful in developing privacy-aware AI products and/or services. Nanni *et al.*, (2020) advocate the significant benefit of a decentralised approach where contact and location data are strictly gathered to be shared (*separately, selective and voluntarily)* only when the person tested positive while the individual has full control of his/her privacy. They recommend that:

- existing decentralized architectures be extended carefully to manage the collection of location data locally on user's device, and allow the user to share with health authorities, for instance as they deem fit and for a specific aim.
- a long-term effort to create the concept of a Personal Data Store that allows users to contribute to collective good as they wish.

4. CONCLUSION

From the 10th of April 2020, positive study figures include positive case outcomes from the swab test. But there are limited data or studies to suggest whether this is in relations to the AI and digital intervention; neither can we proof "How" nor at what rate. (Kelly, Kerr and Drennan, 2017) Findings show that while customers tend to have faith in social network sites (SNSs) to protect their private information, they are hesitant to support ads or products on such pages. Over time, the users' autonomy, connectedness and competence do change from experimenters who had little to lose to acceptors who felt their social life was more important than their privacy concerns to administrators who monitored their information strategically to reduce their exposure. Its seems evident that while the concept of privacy may not have changed, it has broadened as a result of emerging digital technologies and data consumption. It implies the notion of what constitutes 'privacy' in particular for digital service providers might need to change or at least be underpinned differently. Although the link between these non-pharmaceutical interventions and the fight against COVID-19 is lacking in evidence, there is a need for a further empirical study on the new perspective on the concept of privacy. We also recommend further study on how to measure the relationship between user privacy acceptance and AI concerning issues such as a pandemic.

REFERENCES

Australian Legislative Act (2020): *Telecommunication and Biosecurity Art*. https://www.legislation.gov.au/.

BBC (2020) *Coronavirus: Zoom under increased scrutiny as popularity soars*. https://www.bbc.co.uk/news/business-52115434 (Accessed: May 26, 2020).

Belot, h. (2018) *Security leak about spy agency referred to AFP*. https://www.abc.net.au/news/2018-04-29/labor-blames-government-for-security-leak/9708594

Bennett, C.J. (1992) *Regulating privacy: data protection and public policy in Europe and the United States.*

Coyne, H. (2019) *'The Untold Story of Edward Snowden's Impact on the GDPR'*, The Cyber Defense Review, 4(2), pp. 65-80. doi: 10.2307/26843893.

European Parliament and EU Council (2018) *General Data Protection Regulation (GDPR) – Official Legal Text*. https://gdpr-info.eu/ (Accessed: Aug 28, 2020).

Fair, P. (2020) *'Privacy vs pandemic: government tracking of mobile phones could be a potent weapon against COVID-19'*, The Conversation, Khan, Stephen

Finn, R.L., Wright, D. and Friedewald, M. (2013) *'European Data Protection: Coming of Age: Seven types of privacy'*. Springer, Dordrecht

Fuchs, C. (2011) *'Towards an alternative concept of privacy'*, Journal of Information, Communication and Ethics in Society, 9(4), pp. 220-237. doi: 10.1108/14779961111191039.

Gutwirth, S. (2002) *Privacy and the information age.* Lanham, Md [u.a.]: Rowman & Littlefield.

Kapa, S., Halamka, J. and Raskar, R. (2020) *'Contact Tracing to Manage COVID-19 Spread—Balancing Personal Privacy and Public Health'*, Mayo Clinic Proceedings, 95(7), pp. 1320-1322. DOI: 10.1016/j.mayocp.2020.04.031.

Kelly, L., Kerr, G. and Drennan, J. (2017) *'Privacy concerns on social networking sites: a longitudinal study'*, Journal of Marketing Management, 33(17-18), pp. 1465-1489. doi: 10.1080/0267257X.2017.1400994.

Lee, H., Park, H. and Kim, J. (2013) *'Why do people share their context information on Social Network Services? A qualitative study and an experimental study on users' behavior of balancing perceived benefit and risk'*, International Journal of Human-Computer Studies, 71(9), pp. 862-877. doi: 10.1016/j.ijhcs.2013.01.005.

MacAskill, E., Dance, G., Cage, F., Chen, G. and Popovich, N. (2013) *NSA files decoded: Edward Snowden's surveillance revelations explained.* http://www.theguardian.com/world/interactive/2013/nov/01/snowden-nsa-files-surveillance-revelations-decoded (Accessed: Jun 2, 2020).

Margulis, S.T. (2003) *'On the Status and Contribution of Westin's and Altman's Theories of Privacy'*, Journal of Social Issues, 59(2), pp. 411-429. doi: 10.1111/1540-4560.00071.

Mark Scott, Laurens Cerulus and Laura Kayali. (2020) *'European Commission tells carriers to hand over mobile data in coronavirus fight'*, Politico, U.S. edition.

Nanni, M., Andrienko, G., Barabàsi, A.-., Boldrini, C., Bonchi, F., Cattuto, C., Chiaromonte, F., Comandé, G., Conti, M., Coté, M., Dignum, F., Dignum, V., Domingo-Ferrer, J., Ferragina, P., Giannotti, F., Guidotti, R., Helbing, D., Kaski, K., Kertesz, J., Lehmann, S., Lepri, B., Lukowicz, P., Matwin, S., Jiménez, D., Monreale, A., Morik, K., Oliver, N., Passarella, A., Passerini, A., Pedreschi, D., Pentland, A., Pianesi, F., Pratesi, F., Rinzivillo, S., Ruggieri, S., Siebes, A., Torra, V., Trasarti, R., Van Den Hoven, J. and Vespignani, A. (2020) *'Give more data, awareness and control to individual citizens, and they will help COVID-19 containment'*, Transactions on Data Privacy, 13(1), pp. 61-66.

Naudé, W. (2020) *'Artificial intelligence vs COVID-19: limitations, constraints and pitfalls'*, AI & SOCIETY. doi: 10.1007/s00146-020-00978-0.

Nissenbaum, H. (2004) *'Privacy as contextual integrity'*, Washington Law Review, 79(1), pp. 119-157.

O'Flaherty, K. (2020) *'Zoom's A Lifeline During COVID-19: This Is Why It's Also A Privacy Risk'*

Oliver, N., Barber, X., Roomp, K. and Roomp, K. (2020) *'The Covid19Impact Survey: Assessing the Pulse of the COVID-19 Pandemic in Spain via 24 questions'*, Computers and Society.

Public Health England and NHSX (2020) 'Coronavirus (COVID-19) in the UK: Daily cases by specimen date, by nation' https://coronavirus-staging.data.gov.uk/ Last Accessed: August 28,2020.

Sakul-Ung, P. and Smanchat, S. (Dec 2019) *Towards Privacy Framework in Software Development Projects and Applications: An Integrated Framework*. IEEE, pp. 1.

Solove, Daniel J (2007) *'"I've Got Nothing to Hide" and Other Misunderstandings of Privacy'*, The San Diego law review, 44(4), pp. 745.

Sydow, L. (2020) *Video Conferencing Apps Surge from Coronavirus Impact | App Annie Blog.* Available at: https://www.appannie.com/en/insights/market-data/video-conferencing-apps-surge-coronavirus/ (Aug 28, 2020).

Worldometers *Coronavirus Update (Live):* https://www.worldometers.info/coronavirus/ (Accessed: Aug 28, 2020).

CONTINUOUS INTEGRATION OF FAAS DRIVEN BY QUALITY ATTRIBUTES

Pablo Serrano-Gutierrez
University of Málaga, Spain

ABSTRACT

The expansion of the cloud has led to the development of serverless applications in which there is no need to be concerned about infrastructure, that can be considered as a service provider in the form of functions, which is known as FaaS (Function as a Service). The development of these applications consists of implementing independent functions that will communicate with each other. This work aims to explore how to combine FaaS and the continuous integration philosophy of DevOps so that applications operators can continuously re-deploy different implementations of functions in order to meet some quality of service requirements, such as latency or energy consumption.

KEYWORDS

Serverless, FaaS, Function as a Service, DevOps, Continuous Integration, Quality of Service

1. MOTIVATION

Serverless architecture (Allen, S. et al, 2018), provides the ability to develop and run applications without the need to be concerned about managing the necessary infrastructure for it. This type of architecture represents an evolution of architectures based on microservices (Thönes, J., 2015), in which an application is built on to a set of small services that are deployed and run seamlessly independent, and implement full functionality. Serverless maintains this decomposition approach, but freeing the team from the task of preparation, configuration and maintenance of the servers that form part of the infrastructure in which each and every one of the defined functions are deployed. In this way, when creating an application, it is possible to focus solely on the development and deployment of each of these functions.

To develop a serverless application, as with any other type of application, from the point of view of software engineering, it is necessary to use a certain development methodology. The DevOps (Ebert,C. et al, 2016) philosophy, which has been implemented in the work teams of large technology companies in recent years, makes use of automation, continuous integration and monitoring tools. On the one hand, all the necessary steps to configure the components of the infrastructure are easily reproduced by the automation of the process. The use of continuous integration and continuous delivery tools makes possible to speed up the process of recompilation, testing and deployment of the products in the infrastructure while they are being modified. Finally, based on the data obtained through monitoring, it is possible to make the appropriate decisions on the development and integration process that is taking place, adapting the processes of both developers and operators, to achieve stable products in the shortest time possible. Currently, there are many companies that have decided to migrate their applications to an operating scheme based on the use of serverless functions motivated by the advantages offered by the cloud architecture. Similarly, DevOps has been established as the most common practice in work teams (Balalaie, A. et al, 2016). However, the use of generic tools does not meet the specific needs of serverless applications (Ivanov, V. and Smolander, K., 2018; Debroy, V. and Miller, S., 2020). Therefore, to apply DevOps to the development of serverless applications, more specific tools and methods are needed.

The adoption of a serverless architecture poses some challenges, since an application not only must provide a certain functionality, but it must meet other non-functional requirements, such as latency, availability or security that depends on how well the current deployed functions are behaving. One of the non-functional requirements that is more challenging in the engineering of these systems is latency, especially in applications where it can be a decisive factor, like real-time and IoT applications.

Challenges in the engineering of serverless applications are not only limited to the achievement of non-functional requirements. Other important challenge in the engineering of these applications is the testing. The ephemeral nature of functions and features of the cloud infrastructure such as the auto-scaling, make impossible the conduction of system-wide tests. Finally, the optimal configuration of the cloud infrastructure is extremely challenging due to the huge quantity of services that are involved.

2. OBJECTIVES

The DevOps philosophy is supported by a great variety of tools that facilitate the continuous development and integration of systems. These tools mainly serve two purposes, to automate the deployment and the collection of information about the running system, and the development/integration process. The objective is to use the collected information to improve the different processes involved in development and operation. This permits DevOps teams to decide on the suitability of one or another solution based on a desired quality of service. In the context of serverless applications, these decisions can be the most convenient number of replicas, or the identification of bottlenecks in the execution of the application. Despite there are many frameworks to work with serverless functions (Mohanty, S.K. et al., 2018) and monitoring tools, there is a lack of systems that support rapid decision making as it is required in DevOps environments. This kind of tools will determine, for example, the number of replicas of a specific function or when a specific function should be optimized or replaced by another implementation to guarantee a certain quality of service.

As we stated, the functionality of an application that follows the serverless architectural style is divided into different independent units called serverless functions. So, the functionality of the application is the result of the interaction between these independent functions. The decomposition of the serverless application functionality will have a huge impact on the non-functional requirements of the application (Fritzsch, J. et al., 2019), like execution time and latency. On the other hand, a functional decomposition does not have to be somewhat rigid, but it is possible to use adaptation rules that allow to alternate between different functional decompositions according to the execution context. Our objective is to study how, acting on serverless frameworks, it is possible to optimize the operation of an application according to its specific needs, and also, how an adequate functional decomposition can contribute to the fulfillment of the non-functional requirements of the system, under different execution conditions. Nevertheless, it is necessary to bear in mind that our objective is not to carry out the functional decomposition of a monolithic system to obtain a serverless system, since it is a widely discussed topic that is beyond the purposes of our research. However, it is interesting to consider how this decomposition can affect the application's quality of service requirements.

3. RESEARCH QUESTIONS

In order to achieve these objectives, it is necessary to answer several research questions:

RQ1: Is it possible to develop a system that ensures that a serverless application will meet a certain quality of service? An important consideration when creating an application is to ensure that it meets certain non-functional requirements, such as response times, resource consumption, etc. The same consideration deserves a serverless application. Therefore, it will be studied what are the mechanisms provided by serverless frameworks to address this problem and how to use them. In this way, it will be possible to find what frameworks are valid for our purposes and what are more suitable. This is essential, since we are focusing on serverless development instead of microservices in general, so our only connection with the hardware is made through these frameworks and the achievable results may be limited by them. Their degree of integration with the different tools used for DevOps procedures will also be evaluated.

RQ2: What is the optimal functional decomposition considering the conditions of use? In the case of a serverless application, how it works will depend on how the initial problem is divided into different subproblems that can be solved by executing independent functions. Hence, there may exist many possible functional decompositions that help us to solve the problem, but not all of them have to be equally adequate for each specific case. Indeed, sometimes only part of the functionality is recommendable to implement as a serverless function, and these decisions will strongly impact the quality of service of the application. Although the objective of our work is not to carry out the functional decomposition of the system, it is interesting to evaluate its behavior in terms of quality of service.

RQ3: Is it possible to design a mechanism that, automatically or semi-automatically, is able at run time, to determine the adaptation rules that are applicable to the system, based on functional decomposition? Taking into account that, in most cases, it will be possible to find several functional decompositions that solve the same problem, it would be interesting to switch between some of these implementations in real time, so that the system can be adapted to different execution conditions, like the number of users, requests, the current traffic or application load balance. These are additional measures to those taken by the framework, such as scaling. This would allow, for example, to send lower quality content or to skip non-essential steps of a certain procedure, if necessary.

4. METHODOLOGY

In order to answer the presented research questions, the development of case studies and the use of testing methodologies will have an important role. Therefore, an applied and empirical research methodology will be used. The intention is to exploit the features of FaaS platforms focusing on freely distributed ones, like OpenFaaS and OpenWhisk, two of the most popular serverless platforms. They provide mechanisms to create and encapsulate serverless functions, as well as to define their behavior in terms of replicas, scaling, etc. Other elements will be necessary to operate this platform, like containers and deployment/orchestration tools. With regard to containers, a container runtime environment will be used (i.e., Docker, the most widely used solution). These containers are managed by orchestration tools that perform actions such as the deployment of containers and the orchestration of the different nodes that constitute the application. We also plan to use free distribution platforms like Kubernetes, the most popular one.

The monitoring of the serverless applications is extremely important to answer the research questions. Therefore, it is necessary to manage monitoring applications, which will collect all the data offered by the serverless platforms (i.e., OpenWhisk or OpenFaas) and will serve to study them graphically later. A service mesh, (i.e., Istio, an extension of Kubernetes) is an application that can perform this role. It implements a dedicated infrastructure layer that allows to control the exchange of data between services. It will be used in the development of the case studies to analyze the different adaptation policies that determine the behavior of the functions.

As can be seen in Figure 1, in serverless development, applications must be designed as a composition of multiple stateless functions that can interact with each other. Such functions can be programmed independently using different languages and can be developed by different teams. The deployment of these functions in the infrastructure in which they will be executed is carried out automatically by the serverless framework. These functions are deployed in containers, thus guaranteeing that they will be able to work in the same way regardless of the physical infrastructure on which they are deployed.

Serverless frameworks are supported by an orchestrator, like Kubernetes, which controls exactly where to place each of the containers on the elements that make up the physical infrastructure. It is also responsible for replicating and maintaining the replicas of the containers, following the guidelines set by the serverless framework, so it is possible to adjust their behavior based on certain parameters of quality of service. Above all this, service mesh platforms like Istio, allow to track and monitor the services maintained by the orchestrator. All this information, which we can obtain from the execution of the application, is extremely useful for the DevOps team in charge. If one of the functions does not reach the desired quality of service, this situation will be detected and the DevOps team can reimplement the function. Figure 1 illustrates this scenario, the current QoS of the application is below the target QoS and the problematic function is f2. So, this function is re-implemented as f2' and integrated in the final application. This feedback loop will be part of the continuous integration process, since it allows the development team to obtain information about the result of their work in an automated way.

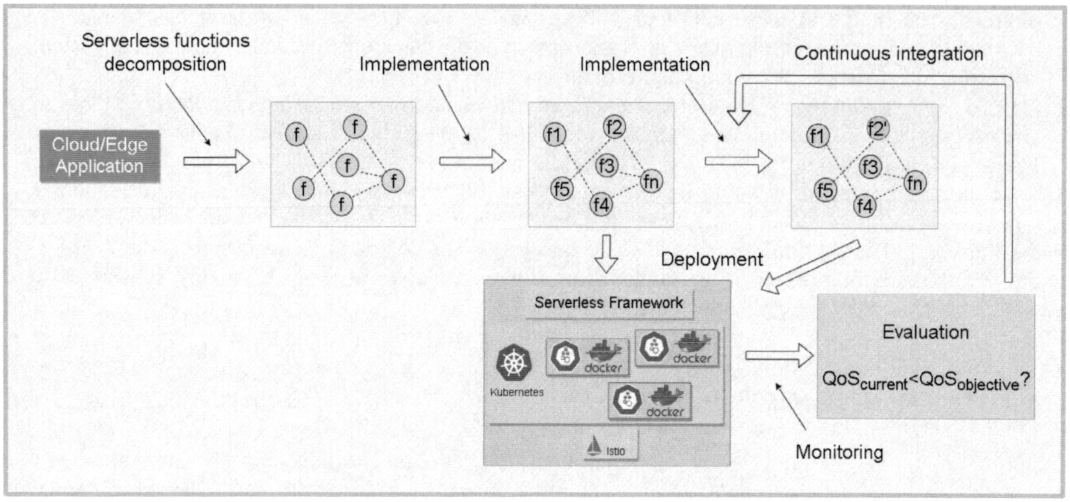

Figure 1. QoS application in serverless development

5. CURRENT AND FUTURE WORK

Our recent work is a Systematic Literature Review to know the current degree of integration between serverless development and DevOps practices, as well as existing tools and research works. The study concludes that there is the lack of development in this field and the number of research and publications is low considering the growing interest of the industry. Currently, our research work is focused on implementation tasks, specifically in the inter-operation and integration of the serverless and DevOps tools. The goal is to develop a system able to change the configuration and the deployed serverless function according to the needs of the application at a given time. As part of this work, case studies are being developed to validate this system. The expected results are strategies that can be used by DevOps teams to facilitate the development and operation of serverless-based solutions under certain QoS requirements. Finally, we are working on guidelines to facilitate the decision-making process in order to achieve the optimal decomposition of an application or service into serverless functions taking into account certain requirements.

REFERENCES

Allen, S. et al, 2018, *CNCF WG-Serverless Whitepaper v1.0*, Cloud Native Computing Foundation, San Francisco, USA

Balalaie, A. et al, 2016, Microservices Architecture Enables DevOps: An Experience Report on Migration to a Cloud-Native Architecture, *IEEE Software*,33(3), pp. 2–12.

Debroy, V. and Miller, S., 2020, Overcoming Challenges with Continuous Integration and Deployment Pipelines, *IEEE Software*,37(3), pp. 21–29.

Ebert,C. et al, 2016, Devops, *IEEE Software*, 33(3), pp. 94–100.

Fritzsch, J. et al., 2019, From Monolith to Microservices: A Classification of Refactoring Approaches, *DEVOPS 2018: Software Engineering Aspects of Continuous Development and New Paradigms of Software Production and Deployment*, pp. 128-141.

Ivanov, V. and Smolander, K., 2018, Implementation of a DevOps Pipeline for Serverless Applications, *19th International Conference PROFES 2018*, Wolfsburg, Germany, pp. 48-64.

Mohanty, S.K. et al., 2018, An Evaluation of Open Source Serverless Computing Frameworks, *IEEE International Conference on Cloud Computing Technology and Science*, Nicosia, Cyprus

Thönes, J., 2015, Microservices, *IEEE Software*, 32(1), pp. 113-116.

AUTHOR INDEX